AN INTRODUCTION
TO DATA STRUCTURES
AND ALGORITHMS
WITH JAVA

AN INTRODUCTION TO DATA STRUCTURES AND ALGORITHMS WITH JAVA

Glenn Rowe
University of Dundee

PRENTICE HALL EUROPE

LONDON   NEW YORK   TORONTO   SYDNEY   TOKYO   SINGAPORE
MADRID   MEXICO CITY   MUNICH   PARIS

First published 1998 by
Prentice Hall Europe
Campus 400, Maylands Avenue
Hemel Hempstead
Hertfordshire, HP2 7EZ
A division of
Simon & Schuster International Group

Typeset in 10pt Fenice by Wyvern 21 Ltd, Bristol

Printed and bound in Great Britain by
Arrowhead Books Ltd, Reading, Berkshire

Library of Congress Cataloging-in-Publication Data

Rowe, Glenn (Glenn W.)
    An introduction to data structures and algorithms with Java /
Glenn Rowe.
        p.   cm.
    Includes index.
    ISBN 0-13-857749-8
    1. Java (Computer program language)   2. Data structures (Computer
    science)   3. Computer algorithms.   I. Title.
    QA76.73.J38R69 1997   97-41673
    005.13'3—dc21   CIP

British Library Cataloguing in Publication Data

A catalogue record for this book is available from the British Library

ISBN 0-13-857749-8

1 2 3 4 5   02 01 00 99 98

CONTENTS

APPENDIX: JAVA SYNTAX 425

INDEX 439

PREFACE

The Java phenomenon

Over the past 2 or 3 years, the Java language has swept through the software world at a rate that is astounding, even for a field such as computing that is used to 'revolutions' every few months. World Wide Web pages are sprouting Java applets, shelves in popular bookshops are groaning under the weight of 1000-plus page tomes with multi-coloured covers and CDs in the back, and even traditional programming and software courses in universities and colleges are switching from 'academic' languages such as Pascal, Modula 2, C, and C++ to this brash newcomer.

Is Java really all that good? If so, what is so special about it?

The main appeal of Java, of course, is that it allows graphical implants inside web pages. However, if we step back from the hype and examine Java critically as a serious software development language, and as an educational language, what do we find?

Let's consider the software development angle first. Java is a fully object oriented language with a low-level syntax that is very similar to C++. That means that anyone who knows C++ and is familiar with the principles of object-oriented programming will have relatively little problem learning the basics of Java. There are a few niggling little differences between C++ and Java, but once you get used to these variants, they present little problem.

Java is touted as a 'platform-independent' language. It is meant to realize the dream of 'write once, use anywhere'. In truth, Java hasn't quite reached that standard yet, but it comes a lot closer than any other popular system. It *is* possible to write graphical Java programs on, say, an X Windows machine and run them under Windows 95/NT or on a Macintosh (or *vice versa*) with relatively little difference in appearance and behavior. No doubt, future developments in the language will iron out most of the differences that still remain.

Java's syntax, although similar to C++ in many ways, is stripped down considerably. C++ programmers, on initially moving to Java, may lament the absence of features such as operator overloading, multiple inheritance, and templates, but after a while, the elegance and simplicity of the Java way of doing things more than compensates (at least in the author's humble opinion).

The standard Java package comes with an impressive set of class libraries (called 'packages' in Java parlance) which allow many graphical interface, networking, and other utility features to be pulled off the shelf and plugged directly into the code. This was (and still is) a failing of the more standard languages such as Pascal, C, and C++. Although the low level syntax of these languages is (reasonably) standard, the available libraries depended heavily on the platform (and sometimes even the specific compiler) for which the program was being written.

On the down side, Java programs are fairly slow, compared to C or C++ code that has been optimally compiled. This is because a Java compiler translates the source code into a byte code that is interpreted by the Java system on whatever platform it is being run. Various solutions to the speed problem are being devised, including 'Just In Time' (JIT) compilers. Again, future releases of Java will no doubt improve the speed of the executable code.

What of Java as an educational language? Although no one yet has long experience in the area, it is likely that Java will prove to be a good teaching language. This is due to several factors:

- Java is fully object-oriented, so students can and should learn object-oriented principles from the outset. Some universities use C++ as an introductory language but ignore the object-oriented features until later in the course, treating them as 'advanced' features. In fact, many teachers have found that the object-oriented paradigm is actually easier to learn than the procedural one.
- The streamlined syntax of Java means that students don't have too many complicated features to master before being able to produce 'industrial strength' software.
- The availability of the standard libraries allows students to write graphical programs from the outset. One of the main drawbacks in introductory programming courses has been the difficulty of producing graphical interfaces in the more traditional languages. Students coming into university often have several years' experience in using such interfaces on a home computer or in high school, and can easily get turned off by a first year course which is entirely text based.

In summary, then, Java promises to be a versatile programming language with some features that lend themselves well to education.

Background expected of the reader

The prospective reader of this book should have some prior experience with programming in Java, such as that obtained from a first year course using Java as the main language, or from reading an introductory programming book, again using Java.

Readers are not necessarily expected to have a deep knowledge of object-oriented programming, the Java AWT (Abstract Windowing Toolkit), or any of the more 'advanced' features such as exceptions, threads, and so on. These topics are covered in this book.

Readers with programming experience in a procedural language such as C or Modula 2, or with an object-oriented language such as C++, should be able to follow the book after reading through the appendix to brush up on Java syntax.

Many books on data structures and algorithms take a more or less mathematical approach to the subject, requiring the reader to have enough knowledge of algebra to follow derivations of formulae giving the efficiencies of the various algorithms. As many courses in data structures and algorithms are trying to cater to a clientele with little or no mathematical background, this book takes a more experimental approach to algorithm analysis. Rather than deriving formulae for the efficiency of an algorithm, we devise computer experiments to count the number of steps required for a program to implement the algorithm for various sizes of data sets. The efficiency of the algorithm is then deduced from graphs of the results of these experiments.

Although such an approach is certainly not rigorous and will probably horrify many mathematicians, the author believes that it is a much clearer way of presenting the topic of efficiency to a non-mathematical audience. What is lost in rigour is recouped in understanding.

Plan of the book

Since the book contains several topics that do not strictly match the title, in that they don't deal directly with data structures or algorithms, some guidelines as to what path various readers might prefer are in order.

Chapter 1 provides a discussion object-oriented programming, assuming that the reader has had little or no exposure to this idea. Some students may have taken a first year course, even using Java as the language, in which object-oriented programming has not been covered. Therefore, Chapter 1 is essential reading for these students.

Chapter 2 contains an introduction to the Java AWT. Again, most readers who have used Java before will have done some AWT programming, if only to produce a simple applet with a text box and a button. If you feel reasonably confident in using the basic controls provided by the AWT, you can skim or skip this chapter.

Chapter 3 goes into layout managers in fair detail. If you have relied on the default `FlowLayout` manager for positioning your AWT controls within an applet, you should study this chapter, as it will provide you with several flexible methods for producing better layouts.

Chapter 4 describes exceptions – methods for catching errors or interrupts in the program before they cause the program to crash.

Chapter 5 describes Java's facilities for drawing graphics and producing animations. Again, many readers will no doubt have done some simple drawing in an introductory course, but a study of this chapter may well prove fruitful.

Chapter 6 describes how threads may be used to allow different sections of a program to operate independently of each other. The problem of synchronizing separate threads is also discussed.

Those readers who consider themselves thoroughly versed in Java, and whose main reason for reading this book is to apply their knowledge to data structures and algorithms, may start with Chapter 7. Chapters 7 through 9 cover the basic data structures: lists, stacks, queues, and sets.

The study of algorithms and methods for measuring their efficiency are introduced in Chapter 10, where we consider a few searching algorithms, introduce the technique of computer experimentation, and define the 'big-oh' notation.

Chapter 11 extends these techniques to a study of several sorting algorithms. Chapter 12 covers hashing, Chapter 13 surveys several tree structures and Chapter 14 introduces graphs and some associated algorithms.

Finally, Chapter 15 provides a large-scale Java program (an adventure game) which brings together many of the features from the rest of the book. This large case study will hopefully allow the reader to see how a larger program may be created, starting with the requirements specification, and proceeding through the object oriented design to the coding. Several of the data structures and algorithms from the earlier parts of the book are put to use in a 'real-life' setting, so that the reader can see that they are not purely abstract constructs.

In summary, the first 6 chapters provide background on the various features of Java that may be used to write professional, attractive programs. Chapters 7 through 14 provide an introduction to data structures and algorithms that should be accessible to a reader with a non-mathematical background. Chapter 15 is a large case study that integrates the material from the first 14 chapters.

Finally, it should be noted that the version of Java used in this book is version 1.0.2. Although version 1.1 has been officially released, it is not yet supported by popular Web browsers or Java development packages.

Acknowledgements

The author would like to thank all those who offered encouragement and advice throughout the writing of this book. In particular, Iain Milne and John Gregor offered helpful comments along the way, and Andy Cobley provided sterling support and conversation. Last, but by no means least, I would like to thank Jackie Harbor and the staff at Prentice Hall for their support and understanding through the sometimes difficult stages of this book's production.

CHAPTER 1

OBJECT-ORIENTED PROGRAMMING

1.1   Computer programming techniques

In order for a computer program of any size longer than a few lines to be logically and efficiently implemented, it is essential that some sort of design is specified beforehand. Novice programmers often do not see the need for the design step, preferring instead to simply jump in with the coding. Programs written this way almost always require frequent rewriting, contain a great many bugs, and are very difficult to understand and maintain.

Until the rise of C++ as a popular programming language several years ago, most programs were written using so-called *procedural languages*, in which the code was divided up into separate functions or methods. The technique of *top-down design*, in which the overall task is specified first, then split up into more and more detailed subtasks on several layers, is the preferred method of design for procedural programs. Common procedural programming languages include C, Pascal, Fortran, and some forms of BASIC.

In recent years, the technique of *object-oriented programming* has become increasingly popular. Languages, such as Smalltalk, that support object-oriented programming have been around for many years, but until the invention of C++, the object-oriented paradigm has not been widespread. The popularity of C++ is probably due mainly to the fact that its low-level syntax is identical to C, which had become an increasingly common language for many programming tasks at the time C++ arrived on the scene. C programmers could switch to C++ with relative ease, and incorporate the object-oriented features of C++ when required.

Unfortunately, the migration of procedurally oriented C programmers to the object-oriented environment provided by C++ produced mixed results. The tendency was for C++ programs to be written primarily as procedural programs with some object-oriented features bolted onto the outside. This technique produces some very badly designed object-oriented code.

Java was designed as an object-oriented language from the outset, even though its low level syntax is very similar to that of C and C++. If Java was your first programming language, you may well have been trained in the techniques of object-oriented programming at the same time. If so, you will probably find much of what is in this chapter to be familiar to you. If you have come to Java from a procedural programming background, you are urged to study this chapter carefully, in the hope that you can be cleansed of the urge to write Java programs as procedural programs within object-oriented wrappers.

Before we plunge into the specifics in this book, the reader is reminded that we assume a basic knowledge of Java syntax as might be obtained from a first programming course. The appendix to this book gives a summary of Java syntax which may be used as a refresher.

1.2   Classes and objects

In a procedural program, variables must be declared either globally (so that they are accessible to all functions in the program) or locally (so that they are accessible only to the function in which they are declared). Functions (called *methods* in Java) are all separate entities, with any function accessible to any other.

In many cases, certain variables within a program all relate to the same object, and several methods may refer only to these variables. For example, in a Formula 1 racing game, there will be many variables that describe the car driven by the game player, and many methods which operate only on the variables that relate to the car.

The main idea behind object-oriented programming is to recognize that these relationships exist, and to provide facilities in the programming language which allow the programmer to group together sets of related variables and methods in a meaningful way. The language construct that allows this grouping of variables and methods is called the *class*. A class may be thought of as a new data type, which may be used to declare variables in the program. In Java, you are no doubt familiar with the `int`, `float`, and other primitive data types that are part of the language. Each of these data types may be used to declare variables, as in the declaration statement:

```
int javaInt;
```

Here, `int` is the data type and `javaInt` is the variable, which is a particular instance of an `int`. In a similar way, when a class has been defined and named, the name of the class can be used to declare instances of that class, which may then be used as variables within the program.

It is usual in object-oriented programming for the data type to be called a *class*, and instances of a class to be called *objects*. For example, if we defined a class named `car`, we could use that definition to declare an instance of the `car` class using the statement:

```
car formula1;
```

Here, the data type (`car`) is used to declare the *object* named `formula1`, which is an instance of the `car` class.

Properties and actions   1.3

A class may contain both *properties* and *actions*. A property is a data field, which may be either a primitive data type such as `int` or `float`, or an instance of another class. An action is a method which acts on the data fields within the class. In a properly designed class, the data fields are isolated from all methods that are not part of the class, and the class methods take on the role of *interface methods*, that is, methods which provide the only access to either retrieve or change the values of any of the data fields.

Continuing with the example of the `car` class, such a class may have a data field which stores the amount of fuel in the petrol tank. This value may be retrieved by using an interface method which measures the amount of fuel in the tank and displays the result on the car's dashboard (as the pointer in the fuel gauge). The value may be altered by using other interface methods which allow the player to drive the car, or to fill the tank at a filling station. Methods not belonging to the `car` class should not have access to the data field storing the amount of fuel in the tank. If they did, it would be possible to alter this value by 'illegal' means (such as siphoning the fuel out of the tank).

The idea that data fields should be 'private' members of a class and that access to them should be allowed only through 'public' interface functions is often called *encapsulation*. As you might guess, one of the main jobs in designing an object-oriented program is that of choosing the correct classes and defining their relationships to each other.

1.4   Classes in Java

Java is a 'pure' object-oriented language, meaning that *all* data fields and methods must be members of some class. Other languages, such as C++, allow variables and methods that are not contained within a class (indeed, C++ *requires* at least one such function – the `main()` function which starts the program off).

A class is defined in Java using the following syntax:

```
class <classname>
{
private <data field name>;
// other private data fields and/or methods

public <interface method name>(arguments)
{ <method code> }

// other public interface methods
}
```

The first line contains the keyword* `class` announcing that a class definition follows. Immediately after the `class` keyword is the name of the class (items in italics in code listings are items which must be supplied by the programmer). The keyword `private` specifies that a field or method is accessible only to methods within the same class. As a general rule, all data fields should be declared in this section. Methods should be made private if they are only called by other methods within the same class, and are not meant to be used by external methods.

The `public` keyword describes methods that are accessible to other methods not contained in the current class. As a general rule, only interface methods (methods that retrieve or alter private data fields) should be made public. In Java

---

* A *keyword* is a word which has special meaning as part of the Java language. Keywords may not be used as class or variable names.

(unlike C++) the complete code for a method must be included within the class definition.

It should be mentioned that Java syntax allows public data fields – it is just not good object-oriented design to make any data fields public. The whole idea of encapsulating data fields together with interface methods is so that the methods can control all access to the data fields. Since any method, internal or external, can access a public data field, such a public field violates the very basis of object-oriented design.

Example: objects in an adventure game   1.5

As a concrete example of a class in Java, we will construct a class that might be used in an 'adventure game'. The final chapter of this book will present a large-scale Java implementation of an adventure game which illustrates many of the topics in the book, so this example should serve to get the reader into the mood for that chapter.

An adventure game (in the unlikely event that the reader has never played one) consists of an imaginary landscape (often a dungeon or castle) containing several locations. The player controls an adventurer who can move between locations, pick up and drop objects, fight monsters, collect treasure, and so on. Early adventure games consisted only of a command prompt at which the player would type an instruction. The computer would then attempt to interpret the command and perform some action, giving the player some appropriate feedback. More modern adventure games contain full multimedia environments which lend much more realism to the game.

There are obviously many candidates for classes in an adventure game – the adventurer, the various monsters, the rooms and the various items that can be carried, all have properties and actions that can be performed on these properties. A proper object-oriented design for such a game would have to list the properties and actions that are needed, group them together into classes, and define the interface functions for each class. We will illustrate the procedure in this chapter by considering a class that could be used to represent some of the items.

The process of creating classes is often more an art than a science. Usually, several attempts are necessary before the programmer can feel satisfied with the result, just as a painter often erases and repaints sections of the canvas before everything is just right. To illustrate the process, suppose we want a class that describes a sword. What properties does a sword have that might be relevant to our game?

First, a sword should have a description, so if the player asks for a list of items being carried, we can print out a text string to say that we have a sword. Next, adventurers are usually restricted in how much they can carry, so we need to give the sword a weight. Then, since a sword is a weapon and can be used to attack monsters, we need a data field stating how much damage the sword can do. Just to round things off, swords in adventure games are often magical, which means that they can do extra damage on top of the 'ordinary' damage that a non-magical sword could do, so we can add a data field that specifies how much magical damage the sword can do.

Therefore, we might start off the `sword` class as follows:

```
public class sword
{
    private String description;
    private int weight;
    private int damage;
    private int magicDamage;

    // public interface methods
}
```

We now need to consider what interface methods are needed. This must usually be done in conjunction with the other classes in the project, since we need to know what aspects of the `sword` class are required by these other classes. However, we can make a few educated guesses as to what would come in handy.

First, if a list of items being carried by the adventurer is needed, we will have to supply the description of the sword. We therefore need an interface method which will retrieve the `description` data field. Such a method might look like this:

```
public String getDescription()
{
    return description;
}
```

The method takes no arguments and returns a `String` (a built-in Java data type representing a text string). The only function of this method is to access the private `description` field.

This may seem like a lot of effort to access a single field. However, the only other way of accessing the `description` field from an external class would be to make it a `public` field of the `sword` class. As we have emphasized, that would violate the principles of object-oriented design.

In a similar vein, an interface method that allows the `description` field to be set can be written as follows:

```
public void setDescription(String newDescription)
{
    description = newDescription;
}
```

Here, the method is passed `newDescription` which is assigned to the `description` field of the `sword` class.

If your classes conform to the object-oriented paradigm, you will find yourself writing a lot of methods whose only function is to get or set a single data field. This is one of the costs of using the object-oriented method, but after doing it for a while, it becomes second nature. Similar 'get' and 'set' methods can be written to interface with the other data fields in the `sword` class. Other methods may be required to implement other actions, depending on the game play, but the technique for adding methods to a class should now be clear.

Inheritance   1.6

The example of the `sword` class in the previous section has one potential flaw. If we wish to define classes to represent many different items in an adventure game (as we probably will), a little thought will show that, if we used the same technique as in the last section for designing the class for each item, we will have an enormous amount of duplication in the data fields and interface functions.

For example, suppose we now wish to define a class that represents a water flask. As with the sword, a water flask needs a description and a weight. However, since it is not a weapon, it does not require a damage value or a magical damage value. If we design a new class, named, say, `waterFlask` to represent the water flask, we will need to duplicate the declarations of the `description` and `weight` fields, *and* copy the interface methods for getting and setting these two fields. Multiply this by all the item types you might want to put into an adventure game and you will see the extent of the problem.

It is for this reason that all object-oriented languages contain the feature of *inheritance*. In a situation where several distinct object types have some features in common, a separate class (called a *base class*) can be created which contains all these common features (and the interface functions to deal with them). Then, for each specialized object type, a new class can be defined which *inherits* the common features from the base class and adds new data fields and methods of its own. In this way, the common features need be coded only once, representing a great saving of effort and time.

In Java, one class may inherit another by using the `extends` keyword. We shall illustrate the technique by redesigning the `sword` class in the previous section. We will first define a base class named `item` which contains some features common to all items that might be carried by an adventurer. We then define a `sword` class by inheriting the `item` class and adding some fields that are required for swords but not for generic items.

The `item` class may be defined as:

```
public class item
{
   String description;
   int weight;

   public String getDescription()
   {
```

```
        return description;
    }

    public void setDescription(String newDescription)
    {
        description = newDescription;
    }
}
```

We now define the sword class:

```
public class sword extends item
{
    private int damage;
    private int magicDamage;

    public int getDamage()
    {
        return damage;
    }

    public void setDamage(String newDamage)
    {
        damage = newDamage;
    }

    // other methods
}
```

There are a few things to note about these two classes. First, we have dropped the `private` qualifier on the data fields in the `item` class. The reason for this is that `private` data fields are not accessible to *any* other class, not even classes that inherit the class containing them. Until recently, Java supported the double qualifier `private protected` for data fields, which meant that the field is accessible only to the original class and to any other class that inherits that class. However, in more recent versions of Java, the `private protected` qualifier is no longer supported. This has given rise to the rather bizarre situation that variables must be made public* in order that they be accessible to any class that inherits the base class. This is clearly a violation of the requirements of object-oriented design, and is something that will hopefully be rectified in a future release of Java.

---

* Well, almost public. A field without any qualifier is accessible to any other class in the same package, but we do not cover user-defined packages in this book. For the purposes of this book, we can assume that the fields are public. In C++, the `protected` keyword allows a field to be accessible in its own class and in any class that inherits that class, but nowhere else. The `protected` keyword exists in Java, but allows access to any other class in the same package, whether or not that class is derived from the original class.

Putting problems of accessibility aside, the `sword` class contains four data fields (the two in its own class, and the two in the `item` class), and the four methods shown (again, two in its own class, and two from `item`).

We can define as many other classes that inherit `item` as we wish. We could, for example, define a `waterFlask` class that contains a field saying how much water is in the flask, an `armour` class that has a property of reducing damage from an attack, and so on. If all these classes inherit the `item` class, they all have `description` and `weight` fields, together with their interface functions.

Java allows you to inherit at most one other class into a new class. Other languages, such as C++, allow *multiple inheritance*, in which one class may extend two or more other classes. Multiple inheritance can give rise to logical problems unless the inheritance structure is designed very carefully, so the creators of Java decided to forbid multiple inheritance in the interests of simplicity.*

Method overloading and overriding   1.7

The last main feature that any object-oriented language must support is called *polymorphism*. There are two aspects to polymorphism: *method overloading* and *method overriding*.

Let us consider method overloading first. Within the same class, two methods may have the same name provided their argument lists are different. Note that it is *not* permissible to overload a method by having the same name and argument list, but different return types, since the return value of a method need not be used when the method is called. The Java compiler must have a way of telling which of the overloaded methods is to be called, so it must rely on the argument list.

For example, we might add two methods to the `item` class above. The first method simply prints out the `description` method of the item, while the second accepts an `int` which is printed out as an index number which could be used if the item is being printed as part of a list.

```
public void printDescription()
{
   System.out.println(description);
}

public void printDescription(int index)
{
   String itemString = (new Integer(index)).toString();
   System.out.println(itemString + " " + description);
}
```

---

* A limited form of multiple inheritance can be simulated in Java using interfaces, which we consider in Chapter 9.

The two methods may be present in the same class since although they have the same name, their argument lists differ.

Method *overloading* applies within a single class, but method *overriding* applies between two classes related by inheritance. In this case, the two methods may have the same name *and* the same argument list, provided that one method is in the base class and the other is in the derived class. If the method is called on an instance of the base class, the base class version of the method is used, while if the method is called on an instance of the derived class, the version of the method defined in the derived class *overrides* the base class version and is called instead.

For example, suppose we add the following method to the sword class:

```
public void printDescription()
{
   System.out.println(description);
   System.out.println("Damage: " + damage);
   System.out.println("Magical damage: " + magicDamage);
}
```

Now suppose that in a method in another class, an object named testItem of class item and another object named testSword of class sword are declared. Then the following method calls are made.

```
testItem.printDescription();
testSword.printDescription();
```

The first line calls the printDescription() method in the item class, and the second calls the version in the sword class.

Method overriding allows each derived class to tailor the methods originally defined in the base class to its own particular needs.

1.8 Constructors

Besides the general types of methods discussed above, each class may have one or more versions of a special method called a *constructor*. A constructor has no return type (not even void), and *must* have the same name as the class in which it resides.

The main purpose of a constructor is to initialize the values of the data fields when an object is created. Thus the arguments of a constructor will typically be initial values for these data fields. As with regular methods, the constructor may be overloaded so that different combinations of data fields may be initialized.

For example, the item class may contain the following constructors.

```
item()
{
    description = "General item.";
    weight = 0;
}

item(String initDescr, int initWeight)
{
    description = initDescr;
    weight = initWeight;
}
```

The first constructor is called an *argumentless constructor*, since it has no arguments. It initializes the two data fields to default values, as shown. The second version requires two arguments, and sets the fields to values specified by the user.

Constructors are usually called in conjunction with the `new` operator, which is used to dynamically allocate space for a new object. For example, we could declare and initialize two `item` objects as follows.

```
item defaultItem = new item();
item specifyItem = new item("My new item.", 50);
```

The `defaultItem` is initialized using the argumentless constructor, so its `description` field is set to 'General item.' and its weight field is initialized to 0. The `specifyItem` object uses the second constructor which allows the user to specify the initial values for the two fields.

If an object is an instance of a derived class, the constructor of the base class can be called explicitly, provided that it is the *first* statement in the derived class's constructor. The reserved method `super()` is used for this.

For example, let us define a constructor for the `sword` class:

```
sword(String initDescr, int initWeight,
    int initDamage, int initMagicDamage)
{
    super(initDescr, initWeight);
    damage = initDamage;
    magicDamage = initMagicDamage;
}
```

Then, a `sword` object may be initialized by the statement

```
sword mySword = new sword("Excalibur", 40, 10, 15);
```

Note that if no explicit call to `super()` is made in a derived class constructor, the compiler will make an *implicit* call to the argumentless constructor of the base class as the first statement in the constructor of the derived class. If the base class has a user-defined constructor with arguments, but no argumentless constructor, a compiler error will result.

A final note to C++ programmers: Java has automatic garbage collection, which means that memory allocated with the `new` operator need not be explicitly deallocated when the object is no longer needed (in C++ parlance, no destructor is required in Java).

1.9 The `this` keyword

Once an object-oriented program grows beyond one or two classes, you will probably find that methods in one class often need to call methods in other classes in order to send them messages or adjust data values. It can be difficult trying to keep track of which object must call which other object, unless the first object has some way of storing a reference to the remote object. For this reason, Java provides the `this` keyword. The easiest way to describe how `this` works is to give an example, for which we return to our adventure game.

Suppose that we expand the game a bit by defining a `game` class, which is to be the class that oversees and co-ordinates the actions of all the other objects in the game. We also define an `adventurer` class which contains data fields and methods for running the main character in the game, and a `room` class which stores details of the rooms in the game. The `game` class will contain one instance of `adventurer` and several instances of `room`, depending on how many rooms are in the adventure. The relation between these objects might be as shown in Fig. 1.1.

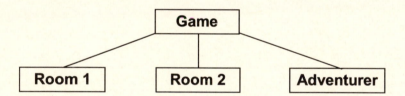

Figure 1.1

If the Adventurer enters Room 1 and enters a 'look' command, the Room 1 object must be accessed and a list of its contents retrieved. Since the Room 1 object is not one of the fields of the Adventurer object, the Adventurer object cannot call a `getContents()` method for Room 1 directly. Rather, the Adventurer must pass a message up to the Game object, which now *can* make a call to a `getContents()` method for Room 1, since Room 1 *is* one of the fields of the Game object. But the question is: how can the Adventurer pass a message back to the Game object, since the Game object lies above it in the hierarchy?

The answer lies with the `this` keyword. Suppose the `adventurer` class had a data field of type `game`, and that the constructor for the `adventurer` class looked like this:

```
class adventurer
{
   private game parent;
   // other data fields

   adventurer(game owner, /* other arguments */)
   {
      parent = owner;
      // other initializations
   }
   // other methods
}
```

Now, when the game class creates and initializes the object of type adventurer, it can pass a reference to itself via the constructor:

```
class game
{
   adventurer player = new adventurer(this,
      /* other arguments */ );

   // other code
}
```

The adventurer object player now has a reference to the game object which owns it (stored in its parent data field), and can therefore call methods in the game class. For example, suppose the game class had a method called getRoomContents(). Then the adventurer object could call this method using the statement:

```
parent.getRoomContents();
```

This technique can be used to pass messages between different layers in the hierarchy of objects. It is sometimes necessary to traverse several layers using this idea. Again, the technique takes some getting used to (especially if you are a procedural programmer), but it preserves the integrity of objects by always using interface functions to access data fields rather than simply accessing data fields directly between classes.

Object-oriented design 1.10

We have covered the main features of object-oriented design in this chapter, albeit at a somewhat hectic pace. There is much more that can be said on the subject. Indeed, object-oriented analysis and design is an academic discipline in its own right, with many weighty volumes to its credit. If this is your first foray into the area, however, you are advised to get as much practice as possible by writing small to medium-sized programs, trying to incorporate the principles in this chapter.

In summary, the main ideas behind object-oriented programming are:

- Make a list of all the properties and actions your program will require.
- Sort these properties and actions into classes.
- Examine the classes to see if there are any candidates for inheritance relationships.
- Examine the classes to see if message passing is required between hierarchical levels (using the `this` reference).
- Critically examine your class structure to be sure everything fits together logically (on the first few tries, it probably won't, so be prepared to make several attempts at the design).

Remember, time spent in getting the design right is more than repaid in the ease of coding later on. You will find that your code falls into place naturally, and is much easier to debug and maintain, than if you do little or no design and jump straight in with the coding.

1.11 Exercises

1   The following list contains attributes of a television set.

- Turn on.
- Turn off.
- Can receive teletext.
- Select channel.
- Current channel number.
- Channel is a satellite channel.
- Turn off sound (use the mute function).
- Repair television.
- Current channel's sign-off time.
- List of channels received by television.

(a) Specify which of the attributes are properties and which are actions.
(b) Group these attributes into a class or classes.
(c) Identify which attributes should be private and which public.
(d) Write a Java class or classes (declarations for the property fields and method prototypes for the action fields) to implement your class design.

2   List some properties and actions that may be included in a class designed to represent a house. Answer parts (a)–(d) of question 1 for your list.

3   Design and implement a Java program which simulates a simple *auto-teller machine* or ATM (the machines commonly found outside banks which allow you

to withdraw cash, check your account balance, and deposit cash and checks). Your simulation should define a class to represent a bank account, with properties such as 'balance', 'account number', etc., and actions such as 'getBalance()', 'depositCash()', 'withdrawCash()', etc. You should then define a second class to represent the ATM itself, which must manage several accounts. The ATM class should contain an array of 'account' objects, and other actions such as 'displayWelcomeScreen()', 'readCard()', 'checkCard()', etc.

The program should begin by declaring and initializing a single ATM object, which in turn initializes its account objects. Each account should begin with a balance of zero. After initialization, the program should display the welcome screen and ask the user to type in a card code. (The code may be taken to be the same as the account number to make things easier.) The user should then be asked to make a choice from an option list (e.g. check balance, deposit cash, withdraw cash, or quit). The appropriate action should then be carried out, followed by a return to the option list. When the user selects 'quit', the program should return to the welcome screen.

4   Extend the ATM program from question 3 by defining a couple of specialized account types. Each specialized account type should be derived from the 'account' base class using inheritance. A checking account may be defined in which any withdrawal is charged a fee of 50p. A savings account may be defined in which any withdrawal must be at least £50. Override the 'withdrawCash()' method in the 'account' base class to allow these actions in the derived classes.

5   Design and write a Java program which simulates a customer's visit to a supermarket. The program should simulate the events from the time the customer arrives at the door of the supermarket, through the various events that occur during a normal visit (collecting a trolley, selecting items from shelves, ordering something from the butcher or delicatessen, and so on) up to the checkout. Finally the customer should leave the store.

Outline an object-oriented design to implement this simulation. Begin by defining lists of properties and actions, group them into classes, and show how the various classes would communicate with each other. Make use of inheritance to group related classes together (e.g. define a 'meat' base class with derived classes representing 'beef', 'poultry', etc.).

CHAPTER 2

GRAPHICAL USER
INTERFACES

2.1   Graphical versus text user interfaces

Back in the days before the desktop computer terminal (before the mid-1970s), programming a computer required typing the code onto punched cards or paper tape and feeding the cards or tape through a special reader. The program would then be compiled and run by the computer, and the output produced, usually by means of a high-speed printer onto fan-fold paper. If there were any errors in the code, these would be printed on the output, and the programmer would have to retype the cards or tape and repeat the process. The level of frustration, to say nothing of deforestation, was high.

When the first desktop terminals appeared, users were able to type commands directly into the computer from a keyboard, and view responses directly on screen. Although interactive sessions were much more productive than the older all-paper methods, all interaction took place by means of typing and reading text.

When the graphics capabilities of desktop terminals improved, the first *graphical user interfaces*, or GUIs, appeared. In a GUI environment, a user can interact with a program primarily by using a 'point and click' device such as a mouse. Text input from a keyboard is greatly reduced or even eliminated. Virtually all home computers and many business computers now use a GUI environment, although many universities still support systems (such as UNIX) where the interaction is largely text-based.

Although most computers these days use a GUI, introductory programming courses often restrict their students to writing text-based programs. The reason for this is that, despite the popularity of the GUI environment, actually *writing* a GUI-based program is much more difficult than writing a simple, text-based program. In addition, GUI programs are notoriously non-portable, so that a program written for one platform (such as, say, Microsoft Windows) would not run on any other type of platform (such as Macintosh or UNIX/X Windows).

The Java language was designed with these problems in mind. One of its goals was to be a language in which it is easy to write GUI-based programs that are portable between all major windowing environments. Although producing a GUI program in Java still requires considerably more effort than writing a simple, text-based program, it is much easier to write such GUI programs in Java than in most other languages. Although Java programs aren't totally portable (you will find differences in appearance in the interface when it is run on different platforms), it is still possible to write Java GUI programs which look approximately the same on a wide range of platforms, without having to do any recoding. Given that Java is, as computer languages go, still quite young, we can rest assured that future versions of Java will solve many of these problems.

2.2 The Java AWT

A GUI is constructed from a set of standard components such as labels, text boxes, menus, push-buttons, radio buttons, list boxes, and so on. These components are arranged within panels using one or more of Java's *layout managers*. (We will consider layout managers in more detail in Chapter 3.)

All of the GUI components provided by Java are contained in a package called the `java.awt` package. The acronym 'AWT' has been variously expanded as *Abstract Windowing Toolkit*, or *Another Windowing Toolkit*, or *Applications Windowing Toolkit*.

Before we examine some of the GUI components provided by `java.awt`, it is worth having a look at the hierarchical structure of the package, since it provides a good example of object-oriented design. It is a good idea for the reader to browse through a Java reference manual (either in a book or on-line) to see more details of this structure.

All classes in `java.awt`, as with all classes in all Java packages, are descendents of the fundamental `Object` class. The first level descendents in `java.awt` are:

- `BorderLayout`, `CardLayout`, `FlowLayout`, `GridBagLayout`, `GridLayout`: these are all layout managers, and all implement the `LayoutManager` interface. In addition, the class `GridBagConstraints` provides some parameters used by `GridBagLayout`.
- `CheckboxGroup`: a class in which one or more `Checkbox` objects can be placed, to give them radio button behavior.
- `Color`: a class for defining a color.
- `Component`: the base class for any GUI component. Subclasses of the `Component` class include `Button`, `Canvas`, `Checkbox`, `Choice`, `Label`, `List`, and `Scrollbar`. In addition, the `Container` class is a subclass of `Component`, and it in turn contains the subclasses `Panel` and `Window`, both of which are classes which can contain other components. `Container` objects are often invisible on screen, and are used, in general, for grouping other, visible components together.
- `Dimension`: a class for representing the dimensions of an object.
- `Event`: a class that holds the values describing an *event* – an object generated by the user interacting with the interface, usually by a mouse click or a key press. Events are passed to special event handling methods which contain code that is executed whenever the event occurs.
- `Font` and `FontMetrics`: classes for specifying the font used in text.
- `Graphics`: a class that is used as a context in which graphics can be drawn on screen or into a `Canvas`.
- `Image`: a class which can hold images (loaded from external image files, for example).
- `Insets`: a class which defines the amount of space left around the edges of a component.
- `MenuComponent`: a base class containing the subclasses `MenuBar` and `MenuItem`, used for setting up menus in applications (not applets).
- `Point`, `Polygon`, and `Rectangle`: classes that provide objects that can be drawn on screen within a `Graphics` context. (Routines for other types of drawing are implemented as methods in the `Graphics` class.)

Java provides a reasonable selection of classes for designing a GUI. However, if you have used other GUI languages or packages such as the various breeds of C++ or Visual Basic for Windows, or Motif for X Windows, you will find the portfolio of classes in `java.awt` to be fairly restricted. No doubt this will be remedied in a future release of Java.

We will not attempt to provide a comprehensive tutorial on the use of all the various Java GUI features in this book. Instead, we will cover some of the main components in the toolkit and refer the reader to the documentation which should accompany any Java development environment for details on other, similar, components.

2.3 Events

If you want a Java applet or application to do anything more than just display some graphics, the user must have some way of interacting with the program. In text based programs, this is done by the user typing a command and then hitting the *Return* key to enter the command. Since the keyboard is the only device by which interaction is possible, the program needs to monitor only this one device.

In a GUI program, however, input may come from a variety of locations. Keyboard input is still possible, but other devices such as a mouse, light-pen, or even the user touching a touch-sensitive screen may provide input to the program. Even if input is restricted to a single device, such as the mouse, the type of input may depend on what part of the interface is selected by the user. Clicking on a push-button with the mouse will cause one type of response, while clicking in a scrollbar will produce another. Clicking with the left button and right button may produce different effects, as will holding down the mouse key while the mouse is moved (*dragging* the mouse).

This sort of program is called an *event-driven* program. Basically, once the program starts and the initial GUI window is constructed and displayed, the program enters a waiting loop in which it waits for the user to generate an *event*. An event can be generated by pressing a key on the keyboard, clicking the mouse, moving the mouse, or using any other input device that may be attached to the computer. If you want something to happen in response to a particular event, you must provide some code in a special method which watches for the event and then performs whatever action is required. Most of the events, however, will not require any special handling by your program, and will be handled by the default Java event handler. For example, if your program consisted of only a text box (into which users can type text from the keyboard) and a single 'OK' button, the only event you would need to program explicitly would be the press of the mouse button when the mouse cursor is over the 'OK' button. Handling keyboard input into a text box is automatic, provided that the text box is the selected control at the time.

It is important to realize, however, that even if you ignore events such as moving the mouse or pressing keys on the keyboard, these events *are* still generated and passed to your program. If you don't provide any code to handle them, they should be passed along to the default Java event handler for disposal.

The AWT and event handling – a simple example   2.4

Let us illustrate the principles of event handling in Java with a simple example. We will write an applet which contains a text box, a push-button, and a label. When the user types something into the text box and then pushes the button, a message is displayed in the label. The code is as follows:

```java
import java.awt.*;
import java.applet.Applet;

class EventDemo extends Applet
{
    private TextField userInput = new TextField("", 30);
    private Button showMessage =
        new Button("Read my message");
    private Label messageLabel =
        new Label("Please type a message in the text box
        and click the button.");

    public void init()
    {
        add(userInput);
        add(showMessage);
        add(messageLabel);
    }

    public boolean action(Event event, Object object)
    {
        if (event.target == showMessage) {
            messageLabel.setText(userInput.getText());
            return true;
        }

        return super.handleEvent(event);
    }
}
```

The first `import` statement includes the `java.awt` package, which contains all the classes needed for using the various components in the Java AWT. If your code only uses one or two components, you only need to include the specific classes needed by those components, but most applications use several components, so it is easier to just include all classes in the package using the statement shown in this example. The final asterisk is a wild card that means 'include all classes in the package `java.awt`'. The second `import` statement includes the `Applet` class necessary to define a class which is derived from `Applet`.

The `EventDemo` class contains three components from the `java.awt` package: a `TextField`; which is a one-line text box into which users can type text from the keyboard; a `Button`, which is a standard push-button control, and a `Label`, which is a one-line textual display that cannot be edited by the user. The components are created in the usual way, by calling the constructor for each. Some components have several different constructors, so you should check the documentation to see which one is most appropriate for your needs. For example, the `TextField` constructor used here takes two arguments: the first argument specifies the initial string to be displayed in the `TextField` (here, the empty string), and the second argument specifies the width (in characters) of the `TextField`. Here we have allowed for up to 30 characters.

The constructor for the `Button` gives the caption to be displayed on the `Button`, and the constructor for the `Label` gives the initial string to be displayed in the `Label`.

The `init()` method is the first method to be run when the applet starts up. In order for any component to be displayed in an applet or application, it must first be added to a layout. Java provides several *layout managers* which allow you to place the components neatly within a panel or frame, but if a particular layout manager isn't specified, Java uses a default layout manager called a `FlowLayout`. Components are added to a `FlowLayout` in rows, from left to right within each row, using the `add()` method. The appearance of an applet designed using a `FlowLayout` depends on the size of the applet as specified on the web page in which it is displayed (more on this below). In this case, the three components are added in the order `TextField`, `Button`, and `Label`. If the applet is wide enough on the web page, all three components will appear in one line. If the applet is made narrower, two or three lines may be used to display all the components.

If we stopped at this point and displayed the class as an applet in a web page, the three components would appear on screen, but any events generated by the user would not be processed by our program. Events that are automatically handled by Java *would* be processed, though, so it would be possible to type into the text box and to press the push-button with the mouse, but beyond that, nothing would happen.

In order to make something happen when the button is pushed, we need to add our own version of the `action()` method, as shown in the example. The form of the `action()` method is always the same: it must be a `public` method that returns a `boolean` value, and it must have two arguments, the first of type `Event` and the second of type `Object`.

The `Event` class stores all the information about the event that was generated by the user's action, including which control produced the event in the first place. Browsing through the documentation for the `Event` class will reveal many properties that can be tested to determine information about the event. In particular, the `target` of an `Event` is the actual control that initiated it, so we can test the `target` to see if it is the event that we are looking for. In the `action()` method here, we want to respond only to an event generated by pushing the `Button`, so we test the `target` parameter to see if it is equal to the showMessage control. If it is, we retrieve the text that the user typed into the TextField, using the getText() method, and then use the setText() method of the Label class to set the text displayed by messageLabel.

We can use the action() method to process any number of events by including a string of else if() statements, one for each event we wish to process.

The second argument of the action() method may contain extra information about the control that initiated the event. In this case, we have no need of this information, so the parameter is unused.

Finally, a word about the return value of the action() method. A true return value indicates that the action() method has successfully handled the event, and that no further action need be taken. A false value indicates that the event could not be handled, and that it should be processed further by the parent of the object of which the action() method is a member. It is a good idea either to return true, or to explicitly call the handleEvent() method of the parent, as we do here by calling the super.handleEvent() method for all events other than the pressing of the button.

To display an applet in a web page, we need to write an HTML file with (at least) some HTML tags that will load and display the applet. A skeleton file that would display the above applet is as follows:

```
<html>
<head>
<title>EventDemo</title>
</head>
<body>
<applet code=EventDemo width=500 height=700>
</applet>
</body>
</html>
```

Everything in this file is standard HTML, but the line of interest is the one containing the applet tag. The code argument of an applet tag specifies the .class file to load. Here, the file EventDemo.class would be loaded and run. The width and height parameters specify the dimensions of the applet, in pixels. Note that if you specify a different dimension for your applet within the Java code, you will only see that part of the applet that fits within the dimensions as specified in the HTML file.

Applets and applications   2.5

The EventDemo example in the previous section was run as an *applet* within a Web page. This has two implications. First, a separate HTML file must be written which calls the applet using the <applet...> tag. Secondly, a separate program (usually a web browser such as Netscape or Internet Explorer) must be run to display the web page.

Although the main use of Java at present is probably in producing applets for web pages, it must be remembered that Java is a language in its own right and is capable of producing programs that can run without the aid of an external browser. Such a stand-alone Java program is called an *application*, as opposed to an applet.

It is very easy to convert a program written as an applet into one that will run as an application. All that is needed is the addition of method called `main()` within the class that is run by the web browser when the program is run as an applet. The `main()` method carries out, for an application, the tasks that are performed by the HTML page and the web browser for an applet. It does this by creating and sizing a frame in which to display the applet, and then creating and displaying the applet itself.

A sample `main()` method which could be used to convert `EventDemo` into an application is as follows. This method is just added to the `EventDemo` class.

```
public static void main(String args[])
{
    Frame frame = new Frame("Event Demo");
    EventDemo appletEventDemo = new EventDemo();

    frame.resize(500, 200);
    frame.add("Center", appletEventDemo);
    appletEventDemo.init();
    frame.show();
}
```

Note that the `main()` method must be `public`, `static`, and `void`. It accepts an array of `String`s, which are command line arguments. That is, if the application is run by typing a command at a prompt in a text window, any arguments added after the name of the program itself will be passed to the program in the `args` array.

A `Frame` object called `frame` is created by calling the `Frame` constructor. (We will consider the `Frame` class in more detail later in this chapter.) The single `String` argument of this constructor is used for the title bar of the `frame` when it appears on screen. Next, an instance of the `EventDemo` applet itself is created. The `frame` is resized to 500 pixels wide by 200 pixels high, and the applet is added to the `frame`. The applet is started by explicitly calling its `init()` method, and finally, the `frame` is displayed using its `show()` method.

If you are running this application from a system where commands are entered in a text window, you can start the application with the command

```
java EventDemo <command line args>
```

where `<command line args>` is a list of optional command line arguments. In this case, we don't make use of any such arguments.

Standard applet methods   2.6

In the simple applet in the preceding section, we made use of two standard methods of the applet class: init() and action(). We explained the action() method, but very little was said about init(). We also neglected to mention that there are several other standard applet methods that are needed in certain cases.

Note that if EventDemo is run as an applet, no explicit call to the init() method is made, but if it is run as an application, we make an explicit call in the main() method. Since main() is mimicking what the web browser does when it loads an applet, this might give us a clue that the web browser will call an applet's init() method automatically when the applet is loaded. In fact, there are several methods that a web browser will call automatically at various times. They are:

- public void init() – a method that is called the *first* time the applet is loaded by the web browser. If the user then accesses another page and later returns to the applet page, the init() method is *not* called again (unless the page has to be reloaded from the server). Thus init() serves like a constructor for the applet, so it should contain initializations of variables, construction of GUI components and their layout within layout managers, and so on. Images and sounds (see Chapter 5) may be loaded, and threads (Chapter 6) may be created.

- public void start() – the start() method is run immediately after the init() method upon the first loading of the applet, but it is also run every time the user returns to the applet after browsing another web page. This method should be used for starting those processes that are time consuming and that need only be run when the user is actually looking at the applet. For example, graphical animation can be very resource-hungry, as it involves rapid redrawing of portions of the screen. Since there is no point in running an animation if the user isn't actually displaying the page containing the animation, the command to start it should be placed in the start() method.

- public void stop() – This is the alter-ego to the start() method – it is called whenever the user leaves the page containing the applet and goes off to browse another web page. The stop() method should, therefore, switch off any costly operations such as animation. The purpose of the stop() method is more one of suspending operations rather than permanently stopping them.

- public void destroy() – The destroy() method is the alter-ego to the init() method – it is called when the applet is removed from memory. This can happen either when the user shuts down the browser, or when the page is removed from the browser's cache to make room for more recently loaded pages. The destroy() method is used to permanently free up resources associated with the applet. Since Java has automatic garbage collection, there is no need to free up the memory associated with objects created using the new operator, so the sort of thing that is usually done in the destroy() method is to kill off any threads (Chapter 6) that have been created.

All four of these methods have default versions in the `applet` class, but these default versions do nothing. Therefore, you need to provide overridden versions of these methods in your own applet class, if you want the methods to have any effect. In the `EventDemo` example given above, we have included only the `init()` method, since that simple applet has no continuously running component that needs to be stopped and started when the user leaves and rejoins the web page on which it is displayed.

2.7   Mouse events

In the simple applet given above, the user had to use the mouse to interact with both the text box (to select the box before typing into it) and the push-button. In using the mouse, the user had to first move the mouse so that the mouse pointer was at the correct location, and then press one of the mouse buttons (assuming your mouse has more than one button). Both of these activities generate *mouse events* which are passed to the Java program and which may be used to trigger some actions within the program.

For many of the GUI components in the Java toolkit, mouse events are handled automatically, as with the text box and push-button that we used in the simple applet above. If a mouse button is clicked while the pointer is over one of these components, a separate event is generated that is specific to the component that was activated. In the example above, the push-button generated an event that was used to update the text displayed in the `Label` component. We did not need to make specific reference to the mouse event that activated the button.

However, sometimes we would like to be able to act on mouse events that are generated when the mouse pointer is at some arbitrary place inside the applet – not necessarily over a control. Java provides ways of doing this.

There are six main mouse events that can be handled explicitly by a Java program. They are:

- Mouse down – generated when the user presses a mouse button.
- Mouse up – generated when the user releases a mouse button. Note that a single press-and-release operation (as when a push-button is clicked) generates *two* mouse events: a mouse down and a mouse up.
- Mouse move – generated whenever the user moves the mouse without pressing any buttons. The usual action of a mouse move event is to move the mouse pointer across the screen, but you can add code to do other things as well.
- Mouse drag – generated whenever the user moves the mouse *while holding down one of the buttons*. You may be used to using the dragging operation in the drag-and-drop technique common to many windowing systems. Here you must first position the mouse pointer over the item you want to drag, click and hold the mouse button, drag the mouse to where you want to drop the item, and then release the mouse button. Note that a sequence of mouse move, mouse down, mouse drag, and mouse up events is required to execute a drag-and-drop.

- Mouse enter – a special event that is generated when the mouse pointer enters the applet's boundary.
- Mouse exit – generated when the mouse pointers leaves the applet's boundary.

The easiest way to handle a specific mouse event in Java is to override one of the mouse event methods provided in the `applet` class. There is a separate method for each of the six events, and they all have the same form. For example, the method for the mouse down event is:

```
public boolean mouseDown(Event event, int x, int y)
```

This method (or its overridden version) is called automatically whenever a mouse down event occurs. The arguments of the method are the `event` itself (see the Java documentation to view a list of the various methods and properties of the `Event` class – there are quite a few), and the `x` and `y` coordinates (in pixels, with (0,0) in the top-left corner of the applet) of the pixel at which the mouse pointer was located when the event was generated. The method should return `true` if the event was handled successfully and `false` otherwise.

It is important to remember that if the mouse is moved very fast, the coordinates that are passed to an event handling method may not correspond exactly to where the event occurred. This is because the program only checks for events at discrete times (every few milliseconds).

A simple program which shows how these methods may be used is as follows.

```
import java.awt.*;
import java.applet.Applet;

class MouseDemo extends Applet
{
   private Label mouseUpLabel =
      new Label("This label shows when a mouse button is
         released.");
   private Label mouseDownLabel =
      new Label("This label shows when a mouse button is
         pressed.");
   private Label mouseEnterLabel =
      new Label("This label shows when the mouse enters
         the applet.");
   private Label mouseExitLabel =
      new Label("This label shows when the mouse exits
         the applet.");
   private Label mouseDragLabel =
      new Label("This label shows the most recent
         position to which the mouse was dragged.");
   private Label mouseMoveLabel =
      new Label("This label shows the most recent
         position to which the mouse was moved.");
```

```java
public void init()
{
    add(mouseDownLabel);
    add(mouseUpLabel);
    add(mouseEnterLabel);
    add(mouseExitLabel);
    add(mouseDragLabel);
    add(mouseMoveLabel);
}

public boolean mouseDown(Event event, int x, int y)
{
    if ((event.modifiers & Event.META_MASK) != 0)
        mouseDownLabel.setText("Right mouse button down at
            " + x + "," + y);
    else
        mouseDownLabel.setText("Left mouse button down at "
            + x + "," + y);
    return true;
}

public boolean mouseUp(Event event, int x, int y)
{
    mouseUpLabel.setText("Mouse button up at " + x +
        "," + y);
    return true;
}

public boolean mouseEnter(Event event, int x, int y)
{
    mouseEnterLabel.setText("Mouse entered applet at "
        + x + "," + y);
    return true;
}

public boolean mouseExit(Event event, int x, int y)
{
    mouseExitLabel.setText("Mouse exited applet at " +
        x + "," + y);
    return true;
}

public boolean mouseDrag(Event event, int x, int y)
{
    mouseDragLabel.setText("Mouse dragged to " + x +
        "," + y);
    return true;
}
```

```
public boolean mouseMove(Event event, int x, int y)
{
    mouseMoveLabel.setText("Mouse moved to " + x + ","
        + y);
    return true;
}
}
```

The program produces an applet containing only six Labels, each of which provides some information on each of the six possible mouse events. For example, when the mouse pointer enters the applet area, a mouse enter event is generated, and the mouseEnter() method is called. The mouseEnterLabel's text is then set to say that a mouse enter event occurred, and show the coordinates of the mouse pointer when the event was generated.

All six methods work the same way, but the code for the mouseDown() event needs a bit of extra comment. You may have been wondering, if you use a mouse with more than one button, how to tell whether an event that involves a mouse button refers to the left button, the right button, or (if you have one) the middle button. The answer is that the current version of Java does not allow for more than one mouse button in most of its methods. However, for the mouseDown() event, it is possible to distinguish between either the right or middle button and the normal, left button.

The (rather non-intuitive) method for testing for a right button press is to examine the modifiers field of the event that is passed as an argument to the mouseDown() method. For a mouse down event, one of the bits in the modifiers field (which is an int) will be set if the right button was pressed. This bit can be masked using the static parameter META_MASK, which is a member of the Event class. The mask is performed using a bit-wise AND operator (a single ampersand (&)) to combine the modifiers field and the META_MASK parameter. If this mask produces a non-zero result, the bit is set, and the right mouse button was pressed.

A middle mouse button can be detected using the Event.ALT_MASK parameter. This masking procedure only appears to work properly with the mouse down event. Attempting to detect a mouse up event for the right mouse button using the same technique does not work (at least on the computer on which this program was run, which uses a two-button mouse). Perhaps in a future version of Java, more consideration will be given to mice with more than one button.

Lists, choices and checkboxes   2.8

Java provides several components in the AWT to implement the common GUI features of drop-down list boxes, scrollable lists, checkboxes and radio buttons. In this section, we will give an overview of the components and in the next section we will present an example using the components.

The reader should keep in mind that, as with the components described in the previous sections, all components in this section are derived from the `Component` class, and therefore have access to all methods in that class.

2.8.1 THE List CLASS

Java's `List` class provides a list of `Strings` that may be selected with the mouse. Various instances of the `List` class allow single or multiple selections, and lists where all items or only some items are visible at a time (with a scrollbar allowing access to the other items in the latter case). There are two forms of the `List` constructor. The argumentless version creates a `List` with no (initially) visible rows and in which only single selections are allowed. The second constructor accepts two arguments: the first is an `int` specifying the number of visible rows; the second is a `boolean` specifying if multiple selections are allowed. A `List` with five visible rows is shown if Fig. 2.1. Note the scrollbar on the right which allows access to the rows that are not displayed in the box.

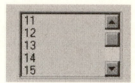

Figure 2.1.

There are many methods provided in the AWT for manipulating `Lists`, so the user is referred to the Java documentation for a complete description. In most cases, all you will need to know is how to add items to the `List` in the first place, and how to detect which item the user has selected.

To add an item to a `List`, use one of the two `addItem()` methods. The first `addItem()` method takes a single `String` as its argument and adds the item to the end of the list (that is, at the bottom of the list). The other version of `addItem()` has a second `int` argument which allows you to specify the index position in the list where the new item is to be added. The list index number begins at zero, just as an array index does: an index of 0 will place the new item at the beginning of the list – any index greater than the last index of an item already in the list will add the item at the end.

There are two methods that retrieve the currently selected item in the list. The `getSelectedItem()` method returns a `String` containing the actual label that has been selected, while the `getSelectedIndex()` method returns the index number (an `int`) of the selected item. There are corresponding methods called `getSelectedItems()` and `getSelectedIndexes()`, returning an array of `Strings` and an array of `ints`, respectively, which allow you to retrieve multiple selections from `Lists` that allow them.

2.8.2 THE Choice CLASS

The Choice class is Java's implementation of a drop-down list box – that is, a list box which, when selected with the mouse, 'drops down' the list of items it contains, allowing the user to select one of them. The Choice class is essentially a List class which allows only single selections and shows only the selected item. A Choice object containing two items is shown in Fig. 2.2. The image on the left shows what is visible when the Choice box is not selected; the image on the right shows the drop down list that appears when the box is selected with the mouse.

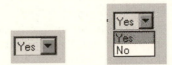

Figure 2.2.

The Choice class contains an addItem() method that accepts a String argument. The item is always added to the end of the list. As with the List class, the two methods getSelectedItem() and getSelectedIndex() respectively return a String and an int giving the selected label and its index.

2.8.3 THE Checkbox CLASS

Checkboxes and radio buttons are standard GUI features which allow the user to select an option by clicking the mouse on an empty box beside the description of the option. The usual distinction between a *checkbox* and a *radio button* is that mutiple selections are allowed from a group of checkboxes, while only one radio button of a group may be selected at any one time. In Java, both checkboxes and radio buttons are implemented using the Checkbox class. A group of Checkboxes can be made into a group of radio buttons by assigning them to a CheckboxGroup object, as we will see in a minute.

An ordinary Checkbox (that is, one that is not to be used as a radio button) may be created using either an argumentless constructor (which simply creates the box without a label) or a constructor which takes a single String argument which is used as the box's label. Once created, the label of a Checkbox may be retrieved with the getLabel() method (which returns a String). The *state* of a Checkbox (whether it is selected or not) may be obtained with the getState() method, which returns a boolean (true if selected, false if not). There are also two corresponding methods, setLabel() and setState(), which can be used to change the label and state of the box, respectively, after it has been created.

To use a group of Checkboxes as a set of radio buttons, you must associate them with a CheckboxGroup object. This is done by using the third form of the Checkbox constructor:

```
CheckboxGroup radioGroup = new CheckboxGroup();
Checkbox radio1 = new Checkbox("One", radioGroup,
    true);
Checkbox radio2 = new Checkbox("Two", radioGroup,
    false);
Checkbox radio3 = new Checkbox("Three", radioGroup,
    false);
```

The `radioGroup` object is used to associate the three `Checkboxes` together into a single set of radio buttons. When the three buttons are displayed on screen, the user will only be able to select one of them at a time. Each radio button is created using the constructor where the first argument is a `String` giving the button's label, the second argument is the `CheckboxGroup` to which the button is assigned, and the third argument is a `boolean` value stating whether the button should be created in the selected (`true`) state or the unselected (`false`) state. A set of radio buttons, with the first button selected, is shown in Fig. 2.3.

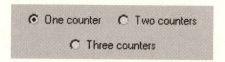

Figure 2.3.

The `CheckboxGroup` class does contain a method which retrieves which of its `Checkboxes` is selected. However, this method returns the actual `Checkbox` object, and *not* the label or the index of the `Checkbox`.

2.9   An AWT example – the game of nim

As a more complete example of some of the AWT components, we will present a Java version of the simple game of *nim*. The rules for nim are as follows.

Nim is a game for two players. At the start of the game, a certain number of counters (for example, pennies or matchsticks) are placed on the table between the players. At each turn, a player may remove one, two, or three counters from the pile. Play alternates between players, but the player who removes the last counter loses the game. The objective of the game is therefore to leave your opponent with only a single counter at the end of the game.

We will write a Java applet which will play nim against a human opponent. To add a bit of interest to the game, we will provide two modes in which the computer may play: randomly or intelligently. There is actually a very simple strategy which can be used to win virtually every game of nim, provided your opponent is unaware of the strategy. Since the object is to leave your opponent with a single counter, you can do this if there are two, three or four counters remaining when it is your turn, since you will then remove one, two or three counters respectively. At your penultimate turn, therefore, your objective should be to leave your opponent with five counters, since the opponent has no option but to leave you with two, three, or four counters after playing. Extending the argument, it is fairly easy to see that a winning strategy is always to leave your opponent with a number of counters that is one greater than a multiple of four. Once you have succeeded in doing this, you are guaranteed to win the game if you continue to use the same strategy.

Since the game is fairly simple, we will write all the code in a single class. The declarations for the class are as follows.

```
import java.applet.Applet;
import java.awt.*;

class Nim extends Applet
{
    private int startCounters;
    private int numLeft;
    private boolean humanFirst;
    private boolean computerRandom;
    private Button startGameButton;
    private Choice randomPlayChoice;
    private Choice playFirstChoice;
    private Checkbox[] chooseNumberBox;
    private List startCountersList;
    private Label numberLeftLabel;
    private Label computerMoveLabel;
    private Label gameOverLabel;
    // class methods
}
```

The parameters have the following uses:

- startCounters – the initial number of counters at the start of the game.
- numLeft – the number of counters left during the game.
- humanFirst – does the human want to play first?
- computerRandom – will the computer play randomly or use the winning strategy?
- startGameButton – push this button to start a new game.
- randomPlayChoice – select the computer's mode of play.
- playFirstChoice – decide if the human plays first.
- chooseNumberBox – an array of three Checkboxes allowing the user to specify how many counters to remove.
- startCountersList – a List giving some possible values for the initial number of counters.
- various Labels – informs the user of how many counters are left, what the computer's move is, and who won when the game finished.

The init() method creates and initializes all the controls:

```
public void init()
{
    startGameButton = new Button("Start game");

    playFirstChoice = new Choice();
    playFirstChoice.addItem("Yes");
    playFirstChoice.addItem("No");
    playFirstChoice.select(0);

    randomPlayChoice = new Choice();
    randomPlayChoice.addItem("Randomly");
    randomPlayChoice.addItem("Intelligently");
    randomPlayChoice.select(0);

    CheckboxGroup chooseNumberGroup =
        new CheckboxGroup();
    chooseNumberBox = new Checkbox[3];
    chooseNumberBox[0] = new Checkbox("One counter",
        chooseNumberGroup, false);
    chooseNumberBox[1] = new Checkbox("Two counters",
        chooseNumberGroup, false);
    chooseNumberBox[2] = new Checkbox("Three counters",
        chooseNumberGroup, false);

    startCountersList = new List(5, false);
    startCountersList.addItem("10");
    startCountersList.addItem("11");
    startCountersList.addItem("12");
    startCountersList.addItem("13");
    startCountersList.addItem("14");
    startCountersList.addItem("15");
    startCountersList.addItem("16");
    startCountersList.addItem("17");
    startCountersList.addItem("18");
    startCountersList.addItem("19");
    startCountersList.addItem("20");
    startCountersList.select(0);

    numberLeftLabel =
        new Label("                                    ");
    computerMoveLabel =
        new Label("                                    ");
    gameOverLabel =
        new Label("                                    ");

    add(new Label("How do you want the computer to
        play?"));
    add(randomPlayChoice);
    add(new Label("How many counters to start with?"));
```

```
    add(startCountersList);
    add(new Label("Do you want to play first?"));
    add(playFirstChoice);
    add(startGameButton);
    add(new Label("Select the number of counters to
        take:"));
    for (int boxNum = 0; boxNum < 3; ++boxNum) {
        add(chooseNumberBox[boxNum]);
        chooseNumberBox[boxNum].disable();
    }
    add(computerMoveLabel);
    add(numberLeftLabel);
    add(gameOverLabel);
}
```

Most of this code should be self-explanatory. The two `Choice` objects have their items added to them, and in both cases, the first item (index 0) is selected using the `select()` method.

The three radio buttons are inserted into a `CheckboxGroup` as described in the previous section. The `List` is created to display five items, and not allow multiple selections, then a range of initial counter numbers from 10 to 20 is added to the `List`. The three `Label`s are initialized to contain a long string of blanks. Note that the length of a `Label` is determined by the first `String` it displays, so if you want an initially blank `Label`, you have to make sure that you allow for the longest `String` that will subsequently be displayed in it.

Finally, we add all the components to the applet using the `add()` method. Since we haven't yet studied layout managers, we can't arrange the components in any fancy layout yet. Rather, we are relying on the size of the applet as specified in the HTML file to line up the components neatly.

Note that we disable the three radio buttons (using the `disable()` method) after we add them to the applet. This will cause them to appear greyed out when the applet first appears, and they will not respond to mouse clicks. We do this since the user should not be able to start playing the game until all the options are chosen and the 'Start game' button is pushed. The initial appearance of the game is as shown in Fig. 2.4.

Once the user makes the startup choices and presses the 'Start game' button, the action for this event is executed. We therefore examine the `action()` method:

```
public boolean action(Event event, Object object)
{
    if (event.target == startGameButton)
        startGame();
    else if (event.target == chooseNumberBox[2]) {
        numLeft -= 3;
        computerMove();
    } else if (event.target == chooseNumberBox[1]) {
        numLeft -= 2;
```

```
        computerMove();
    } else if (event.target == chooseNumberBox[0]) {
        numLeft -= 1;
        computerMove();
    }
    return true;
}
```

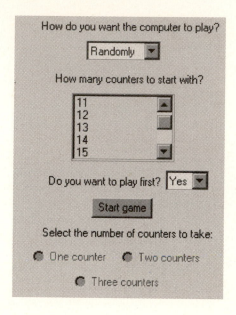

Figure 2.4.

When the `startGameButton` is pressed, the `startGame()` method is called. This looks as follows.

```
private void startGame()
{
    startCounters = Integer.parseInt
        (startCountersList.getSelectedItem());
    numLeft = startCounters;
    humanFirst = playFirstChoice.getSelectedItem() ==
        "Yes";
    computerRandom = randomPlayChoice.getSelectedItem()
        == "Randomly";
    for (int boxNum = 0; boxNum < 3; ++boxNum) {
        chooseNumberBox[boxNum].enable();
        chooseNumberBox[boxNum].setState(false);
    }
    numberLeftLabel.setText("There are " + numLeft +
```

```
          " counters left.");
      gameOverLabel.setText("                                ");
      if (humanFirst)
        computerMoveLabel.setText("The computer is
            waiting for your move.");
      else
        computerMove();
  }
```

The various parameters are initialized by reading their values from the applet's components. The three radio buttons are enabled, and their state is set to `false`. Finally, the three `Label`s are initialized with messages. If the human has elected to go first, the computer displays a waiting message, otherwise, the computer makes its move by calling the `computerMove()` method, which we now examine:

```
  private void computerMove()
  {
     int numTake, maxTake;

     if (numLeft == 0) {
        numberLeftLabel.setText("There are 0 counters
            left.");
        gameOverLabel.setText("Game over. You lose!");
        return;
     }

     if (!computerRandom && (numLeft - 1) % 4 != 0)
        numTake = numLeft % 4 == 0 ? 3 : numLeft %
            4 - 1;
     else {
        maxTake = numLeft >= 3 ? 3 : numLeft;
        numTake = (int)(maxTake * Math.random() + 1);
     }
     numLeft -= numTake;
     computerMoveLabel.setText("The computer takes " +
        numTake + " counter(s).");
     numberLeftLabel.setText("There are " + numLeft + "
        counter(s) left.");
     if (numLeft < 3)
        chooseNumberBox[2].disable();
     if (numLeft < 2)
        chooseNumberBox[1].disable();
     if (numLeft == 0) {
        gameOverLabel.setText("Game over. You win!");
        chooseNumberBox[0].disable();
     }
  }
```

The computer first checks to see if all the counters have been removed (`numLeft == 0`). If so, then the human just took the last counter and has lost the game, so a message to that effect is printed and the method returns immediately.

If there are counters remaining, the computer must decide how many to take. We first check the `computerRandom` flag to see if the computer is supposed to be playing randomly. If not, we must then check to see if the number of counters left is *not* equal to one greater than a multiple of four. If it *is* (that is, there are five or nine or 13 or ... counters left), we cannot use the winning strategy described above, since we would need to take four counters to leave the right number of counters for the strategy to work. The easiest thing to do in this case is to play randomly and hope that the human opponent doesn't know the strategy so we can catch them out next time round.

If it is possible to use the winning strategy, we take the appropriate number of counters (the reader should work through the code to be convinced that the number is right). Otherwise, or if the computer is meant to be playing randomly anyway, we use the `Math` class's `random()` method to generate a random number between 0.0 and 1.0, and scale it to the right range. Note that we must first work out the maximum number of counters that we can take: if there are at least three counters remaining, we can take one, two or three, but if there are fewer than three counters, our choices are restricted. We work out the maximum number and store it in the variable `maxTake`.

The remainder of the `computerMove()` method updates the `Labels` and, if the number of counters is less than three after the computer's move, we also disable the appropriate number of radio buttons to restrict the user's choice. If the computer took the last counter, we admit defeat and disable all the radio buttons. The user can begin a new game at any time by selecting the parameters and pushing the 'Start game' button.

Note that the human's moves are handled directly in the `action()` method by trapping the events generated when the user clicks one of the radio buttons. The required number of counters is subtracted from `numLeft`, and the `computerMove()` method is called to give the computer its turn.

2.10 Frames and dialogs

We have already used a `Frame` object in our discussion of a Java application in Section 2.5 above. A `Frame` can also be used in an applet to create a window that is independent of the browser page containing the applet. Once a `Frame` has been created, it can contain any component that an applet can contain, and respond to events in the same way as an applet. In addition, a `Frame` can have a `Menu` (see next section) attached to it, something that is not possible in an applet.

A `Dialog` is intended to be similar to a `Frame`. However, it is not normal for a `Dialog` to be the main window of an applet or application – rather a `Dialog` is intended as a subsidiary window designed to request data from the user, or to inform the user of some condition in the program.

Dialogs may be either *modal* or *non-modal*. A modal Dialog will not permit any other part of the program to be accessed until it is closed, while a non-modal dialog box does allow such access. You have probably seen modal dialog boxes in other, window-based applications (not necessarily written in Java). A common modal dialog box will ask you whether you want to save changes to a document before a word processor is shut down, for example. If such a dialog box appears, you cannot interact with any other part of the word processor until you have answered the question in the dialog box.

Unfortunately, in the first version of Java (version 1.0.x), modal Dialogs do not work – all Dialogs are non-modal. Since a Dialog is essentially the same thing as a Frame in all other respects, we will consider only Frames in this book.

To illustrate how a Frame may be used in an applet, we present a program which displays a Frame containing three Buttons and a Label. The applet itself contains only a single Button, which, when pressed causes the Frame to appear. The Frame looks as shown in Fig. 2.5 (on a PC running Microsoft Windows 95 – on other platforms, the title bar will be different).

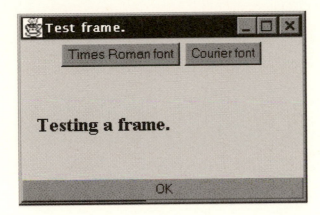

Figure 2.5.

Pressing one of the Buttons at the top of the Frame changes the font in which the Label is printed. Pressing the 'OK' button at the bottom hides the Frame from view.

The code is as follows.

```
import java.applet.Applet;
import java.awt.*;

public class Frames extends Applet {
    private TestFrame testFrame;
    private Button showTestFrame;

    public void init()
```

```
        {
            showTestFrame = new Button("Test the frame.");
            add(showTestFrame);
            testFrame = new TestFrame("Test frame.");
            testFrame.resize(300, 200);
        }

        public boolean handleEvent(Event event)
        {
            if (event.target == showTestFrame) {
            testFrame.show();
            }
            return true;
        }
}

class TestFrame extends Frame {
    private Font testFrameFont;
    private Label testFrameLabel;
    private Button timesRomanFont, courierFont,
        okButton;

    TestFrame(String testFrameTitle)
    {
        super(testFrameTitle);
        testFrameFont = new Font("TimesRoman", Font.BOLD,
            20);
        testFrameLabel = new Label("Testing a frame.");
        testFrameLabel.setFont(testFrameFont);
        add("Center", testFrameLabel);
        Panel buttonPanel = new Panel();
        timesRomanFont = new Button("Times Roman font");
        courierFont = new Button("Courier font");
        buttonPanel.add(timesRomanFont);
        buttonPanel.add(courierFont);
        add("North", buttonPanel);
        okButton = new Button("OK");
        add("South", okButton);
    }

    public boolean handleEvent(Event event)
    {
        if (event.target == okButton) {
            hide();
            return true;
        } else if (event.target == timesRomanFont) {
            testFrameFont = new Font("TimesRoman", Font.BOLD,
                20);
            testFrameLabel.setFont(testFrameFont);
```

```
            return true;
      } else if (event.target == courierFont) {
         testFrameFont = new Font("Courier", Font.BOLD,
            20);
         testFrameLabel.setFont(testFrameFont);
         return true;
      }
      return super.handleEvent(event);
   }
}
```

Let us consider the class `TestFrame` first (its code appears at the end of the listing above). The `TestFrame` class extends the `Frame` class, since the bare bones `Frame` class will display only an empty window with a title bar. In order to add components to a `Frame`, you need to derive your own class from it.

In the `TestFrame` constructor, we first call the `Frame` constructor by using the `super()` method. The `Frame` constructor takes a single argument, which is the `String` to be displayed in the title bar.

The remainder of the constructor is concerned with adding the components to the `Frame`. This is done the same way as in an ordinary applet, except that the layout manager is different for a `Frame`. We will consider layout managers in more detail in Chapter 3, but for reference, the default layout manager used in a `Frame` is the `BorderLayout` manager. This manager allows up to five components to be placed in a `Frame`, one on each edge (where edges are referred to by compass directions: North, South, East and West), and one in the center. The `add()` method calls in the `TestFrame` constructor shows how components are added to a `Frame` using the `BorderLayout` manager.

The constructor also illustrates how fonts may be set in Java. We will consider fonts in more detail in Chapter 5, but for now, we can set a font by declaring a data field of class `Font`, and initialize it using the three argument constructor. The first argument gives the typeface, the second specifies any special type for the font (here we use BOLD), and the last argument gives the font size in points.

The `handleEvent()` method handles the button presses for the `Frame`. Pressing either of the top two buttons changes the font in which the `Label` is displayed. If the 'OK' button is pressed, the `Frame`'s `hide()` method is called, which makes the `Frame` invisible, but does not remove it from memory. The `Frame` can be redisplayed by calling the `show()` method.

In the `Frames` class, we define a data field of class `TestFrame`, and a `Button` which will be displayed in the applet, and will display the `Frame` when it is pressed.

In the `init()` method, `testFrame` is created by calling the `TestFrame` constructor. Note that the `add()` method is *not* called for the `Frame` since it will not be displayed within the applet's display area – it is a separate window which will appear elsewhere on screen. However, a size must be specified for the `Frame` before it is displayed, since by default, a `Frame` has no size. If the `resize()` method is not called, all that is visible of the `Frame` is its title bar.

It is also important to note that the `Frame` will not appear on screen until its `show()` method is called. Thus the initial view of this applet will show only the `showTestFrame` button. When this button is pressed, the `handleEvent()` method of the `Frames` class is called, and the `show()` method of the `testFrame` object is called to display the `Frame`.

Apart from setting up the `Frame` in the first place, adding and managing components is done in the same way as with an applet.

2.11 Menus

A menu in Java can be attached only to a `Frame`. Thus, stand-alone applications, which are based on `Frames`, can have menus attached to them. Although it is *not* possible to attach a menu directly to an applet (that is, you can't display a menu on a web page), a `Frame` created from an applet (for example, by pushing a `Button` on the applet, as in the last section) can have an attached menu.

Creating a menu in Java is a three-step process. First, a `MenuBar` must be created. The `MenuBar` class merely defines the bar at the top of the `Frame` where the menu will be placed – it does not add any menu items to the bar.

Secondly, a `Menu` object must be created and attached to the `MenuBar`. The `Menu` object contains a title which is displayed in the `MenuBar`. Finally, one or more `MenuItems` must be created and attached to the `Menu` object.

Selecting a `MenuItem` with the mouse generates an event, just like clicking on a `Button`, so that menu events can be processed in the `Frame`'s `handleEvent()` method.

The following program alters the example in the previous section by replacing the buttons with menu items. The interface produced by this program is as shown in Fig. 2.6. The first menu is titled 'File' and contains a single `MenuItem` labelled 'Exit' – this choice will perform the `hide()` operation.

Figure 2.6.

The second menu illustrates that Java supports nested menus. The 'Font' sub-menu contains the two options from the last section – selecting one of them will set the font of the Label displayed in the main part of the Frame. The other item ('Title') changes the text that appears in the title bar. Note that these two items are separated by a horizontal line called a *separator*.

We now examine the code for this Frame.

```java
import java.applet.Applet;
import java.awt.*;

public class MenuFrame extends Applet {
   private TestMenuFrame testFrame;
   private Button showTestFrame;

   public void init()
   {
      showTestFrame = new Button("Test the frame.");
      add(showTestFrame);
      testFrame = new TestMenuFrame("Test frame.");
      testFrame.resize(300, 200);
   }

   public boolean handleEvent(Event event)
   {
      if (event.target == showTestFrame) {
         testFrame.show();
      }
      return true;
   }
}

class TestMenuFrame extends Frame {
   private Font timesRomanFont, courierFont;
   private Label testFrameLabel;
   private MenuBar testMenuBar;
   private Menu fileMenu, labelMenu, fontSubMenu,
      colorSubMenu;

   TestMenuFrame(String testFrameTitle)
   {
      super(testFrameTitle);
      timesRomanFont = new Font("TimesRoman", Font.BOLD,
         20);
      courierFont = new Font("Courier", Font.BOLD, 20);
      testFrameLabel = new Label("Testing a menu.");
      testFrameLabel.setFont(timesRomanFont);
      add("Center", testFrameLabel);
```

```
        testMenuBar = new MenuBar();
        fileMenu = new Menu("File");
        fileMenu.add(new MenuItem("Exit"));

        labelMenu = new Menu("Label");
        fontSubMenu = new Menu("Font");
        fontSubMenu.add("Times Roman");
        fontSubMenu.add("Courier");
        colorSubMenu = new Menu("Title");
        colorSubMenu.add("Java");
        colorSubMenu.add("C++");
        colorSubMenu.add("Pascal");
        labelMenu.add(fontSubMenu);
        labelMenu.addSeparator();
        labelMenu.add(colorSubMenu);

        testMenuBar.add(fileMenu);
        testMenuBar.add(labelMenu);
        setMenuBar(testMenuBar);
    }

    public boolean handleEvent(Event event)
    {
        if (event.target instanceof MenuItem) {
            if (event.arg.equals("Exit")) {
                hide();
            } else if (event.arg.equals("Java")) {
                setTitle("Java");
            } else if (event.arg.equals("C++")) {
                setTitle("C++");
            } else if (event.arg.equals("Pascal")) {
                setTitle("Pascal");
            } else if (event.arg.equals("Times Roman")) {
                testFrameLabel.setFont(timesRomanFont);
            } else if (event.arg.equals("Courier")) {
                testFrameLabel.setFont(courierFont);
            }
            return true;
        }
        return super.handleEvent(event);
    }
}
```

The `MenuFrame` class is the same as the `Frames` class from the previous section, except that it loads up a `TestMenuFrame` object. The `TestMenuFrame` class extends the `Frame` class, as before. Within this class, we declare a `MenuBar` and four `Menus`.

The constructor initializes all the various components of the menu. The

`MenuBar` is constructed first. Then the 'File' `Menu` is created, and the 'Exit' `MenuItem` is created and added to it.

The 'Label' `Menu` is then constructed, and its two sub-menus, titled 'Font' and 'Title'. The `MenuItems` are added to these sub-menus in the same way as for a top-level `Menu`. Once the two sub-menus have been created, they are added to `labelMenu`, just like `MenuItems`. The `addSeparator()` method inserts the separator between the two items.

Finally, the two top-level `Menus` are added to the `MenuBar`, and the `MenuBar` is attached to the `Frame` using the `setMenuBar()` method.

To process an event generated by selecting one of the menu options, we use the code in the `Frame`'s `handleEvent()` method. We use Java's `instanceof` keyword to see if the event is a selected `MenuItem`. If so, we examine the `arg` field of the event to see which item was selected. The `arg` field for a `MenuItem` contains the text that appears on the `MenuItem` on screen, so `event.arg` is a `String`, and we can use the `equals()` method of the `String` class to compare this `String` with various possibilities.

Java allows one other type of menu item to be added to a `Menu`: the `CheckboxMenuItem`. When a `CheckboxMenuItem` is selected, its *state* toggles between the boolean values `true` and `false`, in addition to the normal `MenuItem` event being generated. Also, a small check mark appears beside the `CheckboxMenuItem` title on screen when its state is `true`. The state of a `CheckboxMenuItem` can be read with the `getState()` method, and set with the `setState()` method.

Exercises   2.12

When answering the exercises for this chapter, try to get into the habit of checking in the Java documentation (either on-line or in a reference book) to see if there are any methods attached to the component you are using that may be useful. The majority of Java AWT methods are easy to understand and use.

1   Write a Java applet which could be used as part of a trivia quiz (or an on-line examination). The applet should consist of a `Label` containing the question (such as 'What is the largest planet in our solar system?'). Next, add a `TextField` into which the user should type the answer ('Jupiter' in this case). Then, add a `Button` with the caption 'Check answer', which the user should push to see if the answer is correct. Finally, another `Label` should say whether the answer is correct or not after the `Button` has been pushed. This second `Label` should be blank when the applet first appears.

Compare the `String` entered by the user in the `TextField` with another `String` containing the correct answer by using the `equals()` method of the `String` class. Note that the `==` operator *cannot* be used to check if two different `Strings` contain the same value – it will only return `true` if the two `Strings` it compares occupy the same location in memory (that is, they are the same `String`).

2   Add a `main()` method to the applet in question 1 so that the program can be run as an application.

3   Write an applet which asks a multiple choice trivia question. As in question 1, ask the question in a `Label` (e.g. 'Which planet in the solar system comes closest to the Earth?'). Then, add three radio buttons, each with a possible answer (e.g. 'Mercury', 'Venus', 'Mars'). This time, however, do *not* add a `Button` for the user to press to check the answer. Catch the event generated by the user selecting one of the three radio buttons directly, and print a message in a second `Label` to indicate if the choice is correct or not. (The correct answer here is 'Venus'.)

4   Write an applet which asks another kind of multiple choice trivia question. As before, ask the question in a `Label` (e.g. 'How many moons does Mars have?'). Add a `Choice` object containing at least 5 options (e.g. '0', '1', '2', '3', '4'), and catch the event generated by the user selecting one of these choices with the mouse. Then use a second `Label` to indicate if the choice is correct or not. (The correct answer is '2'.)

5   Write an applet which contains no components, but which changes its background color in response to various mouse events. When the applet first appears, its color should be white. When the mouse pointer enters the applet from outside, the color should be set to green; when the left mouse button is pressed, the color should turn to red; when the right mouse button is pressed, the color should be set to blue; and when the mouse leaves the applet, the color should return to white.

Apart from the mouse methods mentioned in this chapter, you will also need the `setBackground()` method in the `Applet` class. This method takes a single argument, an object of the built-in `Color` class, and sets the applet's background color. For a full description of the `Color` class, see Section 5.4. However, for now, you may simply use the `static Color` objects `Color.white`, `Color.red`, and so on. For example, the statement

```
setBackground(Color.red);
```

sets the applet's background color to red.

Depending on your computer platform, you may also need to call the `repaint()` method after resetting the background color. The `repaint()` method is described in Section 5.2, but for now, just call it after any change to the applet's color.

6   Enhance the applet in question 5 by adding a `Frame` which displays the current date and time whenever the mouse is clicked within the applet. To do this, investigate the `Date` class in the package `java.util` (see Java documentation for details). You should find the documentation self-explanatory – use the argumentless constructor to create a `Date` object, then use the other methods to extract the information you want. Note that you will need to include the line

```
import java.util.Date;
```

at the beginning of your code in order to use the `Date` class.

The `Frame` should be invisible when the applet first appears and become visible when the mouse is clicked within the applet. The date and time should be displayed as a `Label`, and a `Button` labelled 'Close' should hide the `Frame` when pressed.

7 Add a menu to the `Frame` in question 6. The `MenuBar` should contain one `Menu`. The `Menu` should be labelled 'Get Date Info', and contain the `MenuItems` 'Day of Month' (an integer between 1 and 31), 'Month' (an integer between 0 = January and 11 = December), and 'Day of Week' (an integer between 0 = Sunday and 6 = Saturday). Using methods from the `Date` class, each `MenuItem` should retrieve the corresponding information and display it as a `Label` within the `Frame`.

8 Add a second `Menu`, labelled 'Set Date Info', to the `MenuBar` in question 7. This `Menu` should contain `MenuItems` with the same labels as in the first menu. When a `MenuItem` is selected, another `Frame` should appear, requesting the value to which the corresponding `Date` field should be set. The information should be entered by using an appropriate component, so that the user is not able to enter invalid data. For example, the 'Month' value must be an integer between 0 and 11, so a `Choice` object with options from 0 to 11 is appropriate.

In order to convert a `String` (returned by the `Choice` object) to an `int` (required by the `setMonth()` method in the `Date` class), use the `parseInt()` method of the `Integer` class. For example, to convert the `String` '42' to the `int` 42, use the statement:

```
int number = Integer.parseInt("42");
```

After reading the information from the component within the second `Frame`, the corresponding `Date` field should be set, and the second `Frame` should be hidden. You can then check that the value was correctly set by accessing the information from the 'Get Date Info' `Menu`.

CHAPTER 3

LAYOUT MANAGERS

3.1 Arranging the screen

The simple Java applets and applications we have seen in the first two chapters have placed their components on the screen using the built-in `add()` method. Components appear within the applet starting at the upper-left-hand corner and progress from left to right. If more components are added than will fit on a single row, a new row is started, just as text is arranged on the page of a book.

In many applets, however, you will want somewhat more control over where the various buttons, text boxes and so on appear. In some GUI languages, the only way to position controls is to specify the actual coordinates for each control relative to some fixed point in the window. Although it is possible to do this in Java as well, it is usually more convenient to use one of Java's predefined *layout managers* to position the controls within an applet.

Apart from the convenience of using a layout manager, there is a more practical reason for not specifying each control with exact pixel coordinates. One of the goals of Java is platform independence – the ability to develop an applet on one type of computer and be able to rely on that applet running in the same form on all other types of computer. You will quickly discover, however, that although Java comes closer to this ideal than most other languages, it is still some distance from being totally portable. It is still the responsibility of the Java programmer to write code that is as portable as possible. One of the areas where portability is still difficult to achieve is in the exact placement of controls on the screen. The fact that Java's layout managers use *relative* positioning of the controls, both to each other and to the boundaries of the applet, means that there is a much higher chance that an applet designed using a layout manager will be portable between systems than one that relies on exact coordinates.

At the time of writing (1997), there are several commercial Java development packages available. Most of these packages contain a feature which allows placement of controls within an applet using a graphical editor. In the author's experience, the code produced by these editors is often not as portable as it could be. Some editors, such as Symantec's Café, produce code that creates exact pixel coordinates for the positioning of the controls that have been edited within the graphical editor. Other editors, such as Microsoft's Visual J++, construct their own layout manager that reproduces the design within the editor. Although the second method is usually more robust than the first, both are often inferior to simply using one of Java's predefined layout managers and writing the code without the aid of a graphical editor.

It should be remembered that writing GUI programs in Java is, in one sense, a more demanding task than writing GUI programs for specific window environments, such as Microsoft Windows or the Motif window system on an X Windows terminal. Specific window environments can rely on finding specific libraries of GUI routines, while a Java applet must reproduce its graphics in all of these different environments.

In this chapter, we will survey the main layout managers provided by a standard Java installation. We will conclude the chapter with a case study illustrating how the layout managers are used in practice.

Panels and layouts   3.2

Before we begin our study of the individual layout managers, there is one important principle in layout design that must be emphasized. For all but the very simplest layouts, it is usually easier to break the overall design up into smaller sections, within each of which a simple layout can be defined. Each of these sections is placed with a Java `Panel`. The collection of `Panels` can then be treated as individual components and arranged within another layout at a higher level.

We will see examples of this technique throughout this chapter, but to give the reader a thread to follow as we wade through the various layout managers, let us set as the goal of this chapter the creation of a simple four-function calculator. A possible layout for the calculator might be as shown in Fig. 3.1.

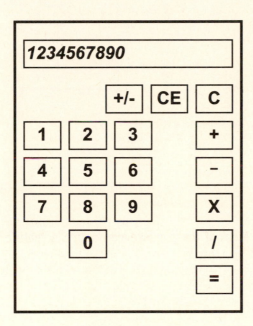

Figure 3.1.

The buttons should all be familiar to any user of pocket calculators. The number buttons are for entering digits (we have omitted the decimal point button to keep things simple). There are four buttons for performing arithmetic, and an = button for generating the answer. The +/– button changes the sign of the number in the display. The CE button clears the current entry without affecting whatever is stored in the memory, while the C button clears the entire memory of the calculator.

The display consists of a single text area at the top and 18 buttons arranged in various patterns underneath. Trying to position all these buttons within a single layout manager would be fairly difficult. It is much easier (and better interface design) to break the layout up into several separate panels, as shown in Fig. 3.2.

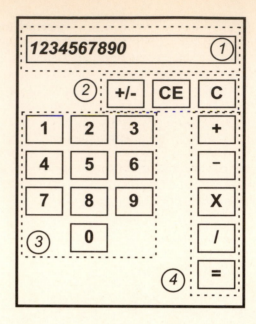

Figure 3.2.

Here, we have broken the design up into four panels. (The numbers inside circles in Fig 3.2 are there as labels only and are not part of the design.) The text area comprises a panel all by itself. The +/– key and the two clear keys together comprise panel 2; the ten digit keys make up panel 3, and the arithmetic operations comprise panel 4.

It can be seen that the layouts within each of the panels are all much simpler than the overall layout of the entire calculator. Therefore, we can construct each of the panels, and then combine the four panels in another layout to complete the construction of the calculator.

3.3 Flow layouts

The simplest layout manager is called the *flow layout*. This is, in fact, the layout that we have been using all along, although it was never mentioned either in the text or in the Java code. This was possible because the flow layout is Java's default layout manager.

As you would expect, the flow layout places all its components in the left-to-right, top-to-bottom order that we have seen in the examples so far. The appearance of an applet constructed using a flow layout depends not only on the controls which have been placed in the applet, but also on the size of the applet within the HTML page (or the size of the window for an application). Since controls are added left-to-right, and a new line is started only when the current line is full, changing the width of the applet in the HTML page will change the number of controls that appear on each line.

To see this, consider the following code which attempts to construct the digit panel (10 buttons numbered 1 – 9, with a 0 at the end) in the calculator above.

```java
// FlowNumberPanel.java
import java.applet.Applet;
import java.awt.*;

public class FlowNumberPanel extends Applet {
    private Button button1, button2, button3,
        button4, button5;
    private Button button6, button7, button8,
        button9, button0;

    public void init()
    {
        // Create the 10 buttons
        button1 = new Button("1");
        button2 = new Button("2");
        button3 = new Button("3");
        button4 = new Button("4");
        button5 = new Button("5");
        button6 = new Button("6");
        button7 = new Button("7");
        button8 = new Button("8");
        button9 = new Button("9");
        button0 = new Button("0");

        // and add them to the FlowLayout
        add(button1);
        add(button2);
        add(button3);
        add(button4);
        add(button5);
        add(button6);
        add(button7);
        add(button8);
        add(button9);
        add(button0);
    }
}
```

This program merely creates 10 buttons and adds them to a `FlowLayout`. If this applet is viewed in an HTML page with the command:

```
<applet code="FlowNumberPanel.class"
    width=90 height=120>
```

the buttons appear arranged exactly as shown in panel 3 of Fig. 3.2. above.*

---

* At least, they do on the computer on which I am writing this. Because of inconsistencies in various window environments, the panel may appear differently on your computer.

However, if you change the `width` to 200, you will find buttons 1 – 8 appearing on one row, with buttons 9 and 0 displayed, centered, in a second row underneath them. Increasing the `width` still more, of course, will result eventually in all 10 buttons appearing on one row. All these changes come about without changing anything in the Java code above – all you have to do is change the size of the applet in the HTML page. Had we written this applet as an application, the same result could be obtained by resizing the window in which the buttons are displayed.

To ensure that the set of 10 buttons always appears in the configuration shown in the panel above, we will need to use a different layout manager. However, before we do that, it is worth having a look at some of the other properties of the `FlowLayout` manager.

One thing we can do even without using a fancier manager is ensure that the grouping of the buttons shown in the panel is maintained. That is, we can ensure that buttons 1, 2, 3 always appear on the same line, and similarly with the groups 4, 5, 6 and 7, 8, 9. We can do this by making use of `Panel`s. Consider the following code:

```java
// FlowNumberPanels.java
import java.applet.Applet;
import java.awt.*;

public class FlowNumberPanels extends Applet {
    private Button button1, button2, button3,
        button4, button5;
    private Button button6, button7, button8,
        button9, button0;
    Panel panel123, panel456, panel789, panel0;

    public void init()
    {
        // Create the 10 buttons
        button1 = new Button("1");
        button2 = new Button("2");
        button3 = new Button("3");
        button4 = new Button("4");
        button5 = new Button("5");
        button6 = new Button("6");
        button7 = new Button("7");
        button8 = new Button("8");
        button9 = new Button("9");
        button0 = new Button("0");

        // Create panels
        panel123 = new Panel();
        panel456 = new Panel();
        panel789 = new Panel();
        panel0 = new Panel();
```

```
// Create FlowLayouts for each panel
panel123.setLayout(new
    FlowLayout(FlowLayout.LEFT, 5, 5));
panel456.setLayout(new
    FlowLayout(FlowLayout.LEFT, 5, 5));
panel789.setLayout(new
    FlowLayout(FlowLayout.LEFT, 5, 5));
panel0.setLayout(new
    FlowLayout(FlowLayout.CENTER, 5, 5));

// Add buttons to panels
panel123.add(button1);
panel123.add(button2);
panel123.add(button3);
panel456.add(button4);
panel456.add(button5);
panel456.add(button6);
panel789.add(button7);
panel789.add(button8);
panel789.add(button9);
panel0.add(button0);

panel123.setBackground(Color.orange);
panel456.setBackground(Color.yellow);
panel789.setBackground(Color.red);
panel0.setBackground(Color.green);

add(panel123);
add(panel456);
add(panel789);
add(panel0);
    }
}
```

The idea here is that the buttons from 1–9 are arranged in groups of three, with each group being assigned to a single `Panel`. We have introduced a separate `FlowLayout` for each `Panel` by using the `setLayout()` method of the `Panel` class. We haven't used this method up to now, since the `FlowLayout` is the default layout manager and will be invoked whether or not we explicitly say so. However, the `FlowLayout` manager has several properties that can be set when it is created and, unless we wish to accept the default values of these properties, we must explicitly create and assign the layout to obtain them.

We can specify the orientation of controls within the space allocated to the `Panel` by the first argument to the `FlowLayout` constructor. The `FlowLayout` class contains three `static` constants called LEFT, RIGHT, and CENTER.* These

---

* Readers outside the USA are cautioned that the American spelling is used for all names in Java. Don't make the mistake of referring to `FlowLayout.CENTRE`, for example, or of referring to a `Colour` class!

values determine how the controls are placed relative to the boundary of their container. The second and third arguments to the constructor specify that some padding space is to be left horizontally (second argument) and/or vertically (third argument) around the enclosing container. In this case, we have left five pixels on all sides. The default for the orientation is CENTER, and the defaults for the padding space are to set both values to 0.

After defining the `Panels`, we add each button to its correct `Panel`. Then we set the background color of each `Panel`. Besides making the result more interesting to look at (if a bit garish), this allows you to see where the boundaries of the various `Panels` are. Note that there is actually a bit more space between `Panels` than what is specified by the padding values. Even if we set the padding values to 0, the `FlowLayout` will still allow a bit of space between columns and rows.

If we display this applet with a `width` of 90 and a `height` of 150, we will see the correct layout for the digit panel of the calculator. We need a bit more height than in our first attempt to allow for the extra space between rows. If we increase the `width`, the first thing we will notice is that the lone 0 button gets tacked onto the end of the row containing `panel789`. If we make the `width` large enough, of course, we can eventually get all the buttons on one row again.

However, if we try decreasing the `width` from 90, we will see that the buttons do *not* eventually form one long column from 1–0. Each `Panel` is now a unit, and if the display space allocated to the applet in the HTML page is too narrow for the `Panel`, the ends of the `Panel` are chopped off.

Although the `FlowLayout` manager is adequate for many simple applets, we really need something a bit more sophisticated if we want a more attractive interface.

3.4   Grid layouts

The `GridLayout` manager is similar to the `FlowLayout` manager in that it also adds controls in a left-to-right, top-to-bottom manner. However, a `GridLayout` allows you to specify the number of rows and columns into which the components are placed. Unlike `FlowLayout`, `GridLayout` makes all components the same size.

To see a `GridLayout` in action, we rewrite the code in the previous section so that the digit buttons from 1–9 are positioned using a `GridLayout`.

```
// GridNumber.java
import java.applet.Applet;
import java.awt.*;

public class GridNumber extends Applet {
    private Button button1, button2, button3,
        button4, button5;
    private Button button6, button7, button8,
```

```
      button9, button0;
    private Panel panel1_9;

    public void init()
    {
        // Create the 10 buttons
        button1 = new Button("1");
        button2 = new Button("2");
        button3 = new Button("3");
        button4 = new Button("4");
        button5 = new Button("5");
        button6 = new Button("6");
        button7 = new Button("7");
        button8 = new Button("8");
        button9 = new Button("9");
        button0 = new Button("0");

        // Create panel
        panel1_9 = new Panel();

        // Create GridLayout with 3 rows, 3 cols,
        // 5 pixels spacing
        panel1_9.setLayout(new GridLayout(3, 3, 5, 5));

        // Add buttons to panel
        panel1_9.add(button1);
        panel1_9.add(button2);
        panel1_9.add(button3);
        panel1_9.add(button4);
        panel1_9.add(button5);
        panel1_9.add(button6);
        panel1_9.add(button7);
        panel1_9.add(button8);
        panel1_9.add(button9);

        add(panel1_9);
        add(button0);
    }
}
```

This program is very similar to the `FlowLayout` programs in the last section. Ten buttons are created and initialized.

The `GridLayout` constructor requires at least two arguments, and can optionally take another two. The two forms of the constructor are:

```
public GridLayout(int rows, int cols);
public GridLayout(int rows, int cols,
    int hgap, int vgap);
```

The arguments `rows` and `cols` specify the number of rows and columns, respectively, in the grid. The optional arguments `hgap` and `vgap` specify the horizontal and vertical gap, in pixels, between adjacent components, just as with `FlowLayout`.

A `Panel` is created and initialized to contain a `GridLayout` with three rows and three columns and a spacing of five pixels in both horizontal and vertical directions. The first nine buttons are then added to the `Panel`. Finally, the `Panel` and the last button are added to the default `FlowLayout` used by the overall applet. If the applet is displayed with a `width` of 90 (again, this value may vary on different computers), the button layout given in panel 3 in Fig. 3.2 is obtained.

If we make the applet any wider, however, the final '0' button is placed just to the right of the block of nine buttons, rather than below it. This is because we are using a `FlowLayout` for the overall applet, even though we are using a `GridLayout` for the block of nine buttons. The buttons from 1 – 9 will always appear in a three-by-three block no matter what the dimensions of the applet are, but the final button will move around depending on the size of the surrounding container.

You might think that one way around this would be to assign a `GridLayout` to the overall applet, rather than a `FlowLayout`. If we specify the master `GridLayout` to have two rows and one column, and place the panel containing buttons 1 – 9 in the top row and button 0 in the bottom row, we will guarantee the arrangement we want.

This would work, except that all components in a `GridLayout` must have the same size. Therefore, we find that button 0 has the same size as all of buttons 1 through 9 put together. Another solution is obviously needed.

3.5 Border layouts

The `BorderLayout` allows up to five components to be placed in fixed relative positions. This may sound much more restrictive than either the `FlowLayout` or the `GridLayout`, both of which allow arbitrarily many components to be added to an applet. However, if components are first grouped into `Panels` using other layout managers, the `BorderLayout` can be very useful for arranging the `Panels` on screen.

The five locations supported by `BorderLayout` are named 'North', 'West', 'Center', 'East', and 'South'. Their locations within a container are as shown in Fig. 3.3.

The relative sizes of the five components can vary, depending on the sizes of the controls being stored in each location. If a component is omitted, one or more of its neighbors expands to fill in the gap. For example, if the 'North' component is omitted, the 'West', 'Center', and 'East' components would stretch upwards to fill in the space. If any of the three components in the central band are omitted, the other central components stretch horizontally to fill up the gap. If all three central components are missing, 'North' and 'South' stretch to fill in the central section.

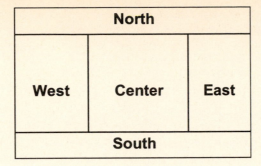

Figure 3.3

Components can be added to a `BorderLayout` in any order, since the location tag must be included in the call to the `add()` method, as we will see in the example below.

Let us see how we might construct our number keypad using a `BorderLayout`.

```java
// BorderNumber.java
import java.applet.Applet;
import java.awt.*;

public class BorderNumber extends Applet {
    private Button button1, button2, button3,
        button4, button5;
    private Button button6, button7, button8,
        button9, button0;
    private Panel allnumbers, panel1_9, panel0;

    public void init()
    {

        // Create the 10 buttons
        button1 = new Button("1");
        button2 = new Button("2");
        button3 = new Button("3");
        button4 = new Button("4");
        button5 = new Button("5");
        button6 = new Button("6");
        button7 = new Button("7");
        button8 = new Button("8");
        button9 = new Button("9");
        button0 = new Button("0");

        // Create panels
        panel1_9 = new Panel();
        panel0 = new Panel();
```

```
        allnumbers = new Panel();
        allnumbers.setLayout(new BorderLayout());

        // Create GridLayout with 3 rows, 3 cols,
        // 5 pixels spacing
        panel1_9.setLayout(new GridLayout(3, 3, 5, 5));

        // Add buttons to panel
        panel1_9.add(button1);
        panel1_9.add(button2);
        panel1_9.add(button3);
        panel1_9.add(button4);
        panel1_9.add(button5);
        panel1_9.add(button6);
        panel1_9.add(button7);
        panel1_9.add(button8);
        panel1_9.add(button9);

        panel0.add(button0);

        allnumbers.add("North", panel1_9);
        allnumbers.add("South", panel0);

        add(allnumbers);
    }
}
```

We make use of three `Panels`: `panel1_9`, as before, stores the number buttons 1–9. The 0 button is stored in a separate `Panel` named `panel0`. Finally, the `Panel allnumbers` is a container into which `panel1_9` and `panel0` are placed. The reason for all these `Panels` will become apparent as we discuss the code.

After the `Buttons` are created, we create the three `Panels` and assign a `BorderLayout` to the `Panel` `allnumbers`. The constructor for a `BorderLayout` takes either no arguments, as here, or two arguments for setting the horizontal and vertical spacing between components, as with the other layout managers we have discussed so far.

We use a `GridLayout` as before to place the buttons 1–9 in `panel1_9`. Next, we add `button0` to `panel0`. Then, we add `panel1_9` as the "North" (top) component in the `BorderLayout` in the `allnumbers` `Panel`. The `Panel` containing `button0` is added as the "South" (bottom) component.

Note that the `add()` method requires the position of the component as its first argument, in contrast to the `add()` method in other layout managers, where only the component itself needs to be passed as a parameter. It is also worth noting that for some reason, the position parameter must be passed as a character string, rather than a constant such as `BorderLayout.NORTH`, which would seem more consistent with other layout managers. This appears to be a flaw in the design of the `BorderLayout` class.

Finally, the `allnumbers` `Panel` is added to the overall applet.

If you run this applet, you will find that it displays the number keypad exactly as we want it, no matter what size the applet is (providing it is large enough for the entire keypad to be seen, of course). It is worthwhile fiddling with this code to see what happens if you change a few things.

The most obvious question is: why do we need separate `Panel`s to store `button0` and for holding `panel1_9` and `panel0`? Since `panel0` contains only a single `Button`, why couldn't we just add the `Button` itself to the applet instead of enclosing it within a `Panel` first? Similarly, why do we need a `Panel` at the top level? Why not just define a `BorderLayout` for the applet as a whole and add `panel1_9` and `panel0` to it?

The easiest way to see the answers to these questions is to try it and see what happens. First, let's try just adding `button0` to the `allnumbers` `Panel` without enclosing it in `panel0` first. We can do this by replacing the line

```
allnumbers.add("South", panel0);
```

by

```
allnumbers.add("South", button0);
```

We now find that `button0` stretches across the entire bottom of the applet, rather than appearing as a small button centered below the 8 button. The reason for this is that the `BorderLayout` manager allocates space for its five components in a definite order: 'North' and 'South' are done first, and always stretch horizontally so that they reach the left and right borders of the bounding container. If the component that is placed in either of these locations is resizeable, as a `Button` is, then the component will get stretched as well. By first enclosing the `Button` within a `Panel`, the `Panel` sizes itself to fit its contents and will not automatically change its size afterwards. Thus when a `Panel` is added as a "South" component in a `BorderLayout`, it won't change its size.

The reason for using the overall `Panel` allnumbers is the same. If we set the layout manager for the overall applet to be `BorderLayout` and add `panel1_9` and `panel0` directly to the applet, rather than to a `Panel`, `panel1_9` and `panel0` would position and size themselves independently, so we couldn't ensure that the `Button` sizes and positions would be uniform. By enclosing both `panel1_9` and `panel0` inside a larger `Panel`, and then adding *that* `Panel` to the applet, we make the appearance of the `Button`s independent of the size of the applet.

By now you are probably beginning to realize that Java's layout managers are more powerful than they first appear. By combining components into `Panel`s using one type of layout manager, and then arranging the `Panel`s using different layout managers we can create quite a variety of layouts in the finished applet.

GridBag layouts   3.6

The three layout managers we have seen so far offer a fair degree of flexibility, but once your ambition grows to the point where you want more impressive interfaces to your applets, you really need something more general. The `GridBagLayout` manager provides such an interface.

The `GridBagLayout` is, however, considerably more complicated than its predecessors. The complexity can be greatly reduced by writing a little class that inherits `GridBagLayout` and provides a few utility routines. More on this a bit later.

The main purpose of a `GridBagLayout` is to generalize the `GridLayout` by allowing each component to be placed at a specific location in the grid, rather than following the left-to-right, top-to-bottom order of the `GridLayout`. Components are also allowed to occupy more than one cell in the grid. Beyond this, the `GridBagLayout` offers a fair bit more control over the sizing and orientation of each component than the simpler layout managers we have considered so far.

Let us begin with the essentials of placing components at specific locations in a grid. The easiest way to see how this is done is to examine some code which defines, once again, our numeric keypad for the calculator.

```java
// OldGridBagNumbers.java
import java.applet.Applet;
import java.awt.*;

public class OldGridBagNumbers extends Applet {
    private Button button1, button2, button3,
        button4, button5;
    private Button button6, button7, button8,
        button9, button0;
    private Panel allnumbers = new Panel();
    GridBagLayout layout = new GridBagLayout();
    GridBagConstraints constraints =
        new GridBagConstraints();

    public void init()
    {
        // Create the 10 buttons
        button1 = new Button("1");
        button2 = new Button("2");
        button3 = new Button("3");
        button4 = new Button("4");
        button5 = new Button("5");
        button6 = new Button("6");
        button7 = new Button("7");
        button8 = new Button("8");
        button9 = new Button("9");
        button0 = new Button("0");

        allnumbers.setLayout(layout);
        constraints.anchor = GridBagConstraints.CENTER;
```

```
    constraints.fill = GridBagConstraints.BOTH;
    constraints.insets = new Insets(5,5,5,5);
    constraints.ipadx = 0;
    constraints.ipady = 0;
    constraints.weightx = 1;
    constraints.weighty = 1;
    constraints.gridwidth = 1;
    constraints.gridheight = 1;

    constraints.gridx = 0;
    constraints.gridy = 0;
    layout.setConstraints(button1, constraints);
    allnumbers.add(button1);
    constraints.gridx = 1;
    layout.setConstraints(button2, constraints);
    allnumbers.add(button2);
    constraints.gridx = 2;
    layout.setConstraints(button3, constraints);
    allnumbers.add(button3);
    constraints.gridx = 0;
    constraints.gridy = 1;
    layout.setConstraints(button4, constraints);
    allnumbers.add(button4);
    constraints.gridx = 1;
    layout.setConstraints(button5, constraints);
    allnumbers.add(button5);
    constraints.gridx = 2;
    layout.setConstraints(button6, constraints);
    allnumbers.add(button6);
    constraints.gridx = 0;
    constraints.gridy = 2;
    layout.setConstraints(button7, constraints);
    allnumbers.add(button7);
    constraints.gridx = 1;
    layout.setConstraints(button8, constraints);
    allnumbers.add(button8);
    constraints.gridx = 2;
    layout.setConstraints(button9, constraints);
    allnumbers.add(button9);
    constraints.gridx = 1;
    constraints.gridy = 3;
    layout.setConstraints(button0, constraints);
    allnumbers.add(button0);

    add(allnumbers);
  }
}
```

Our plan is the same as before: define a `Panel` at the top level into which we write all the components, and then add that `Panel` to the applet. We therefore define the `Panel allnumbers` for this purpose.

After this, we define a `GridBagLayout` object called `layout`. Next is a curious declaration of an object of class `GridBagConstraints`. Every `GridBagLayout` object must have a 'partner' object of class `GridBagConstraints`. This partner keeps track of all the settings for positioning and sizing the next component to be added to the layout. The procedure for adding a component to the layout is:

1   Set all the constraints that apply to the component by setting the corresponding fields in the `GridBagConstraints` object.

2   Attach the constraints to the component.

3   Add the component.

The constraints that can be set are:

- `anchor` – the `anchor` field specifies how the component is to be arranged within its cell. The possible values are all `static` constants defined in the `GridBagConstraints` class, so all constants should be prefixed by 'GridBagConstraints'. The values are CENTER, NORTH, NORTHEAST, NORTHWEST, EAST, SOUTH, SOUTHWEST, SOUTHEAST, and WEST. The default is CENTER.
- `fill` – the component can be made to stretch to fill its cell in either the horizontal or vertical direction, or both, or neither. The acceptable values are again `static` fields in `GridBagConstraints`, and are NONE, BOTH, HORIZONTAL, and VERTICAL. The default is NONE.
- `insets` – padding can be introduced independently on all four sides of a component by defining an object of type `Insets`. This can be done by calling the `Insets` constructor, which takes four `int` arguments, giving the number of pixels' padding on the top, left, bottom, and right, in that order. The default is to have a zero inset on all sides.
- `ipadx` and `ipady` – these parameters only have an effect if the `fill` parameter is switched off in the corresponding direction. An `ipadx` value increases the size of the component by that many pixels *on each side* in the horizontal direction; `ipady` has a similar effect in the vertical direction. The default value for both parameters is 0.
- `gridx` and `gridy` – these give the column and row number, respectively, of the upper-left corner of the component. As with arrays in Java, numbering for columns and rows begins at 0.
- `gridwidth` and `gridheight` – these give the number of columns and rows, respectively, spanned by the component. The default value in both cases is 1.
- `weightx` and `weighty` – these values only have an effect if the container to which the layout applies is resized. Consider `weightx` as an example. If the applet is increased in width, then each row in the layout must decide how to respond. Suppose we have a layout with three rows and four columns. The

`weightx` values in row 0 are (0, 1, 3, 5) and in row 1 are (0, 2, 1, 4). In row 2, all `weightx` values are 0. To see what effect these values have, we locate the *maximum* weight in each column (in our example, this gives the values 0, 2, 3, and 5), and then add them up, obtaining 10 in our example. The fraction of the extra width allocated to each column is then obtained by dividing that column's maximum `weightx` value by this sum. In the example here, column 0 doesn't change in width at all, since its maximum `weightx` value is 0. Column 1 increases in width by 20% of the total size increase of the applet, column 2 increases in width by 30%, and column 3 by 50%. Changes in height for each row are worked out by considering `weighty` values in a similar way.

Values for any of these constraints are set by assigning values directly to the corresponding field(s) of the `GridBagConstraints` object. (This violates proper object-oriented programming principles, but we will fix that in a moment.)

In the example program here, we have explicitly given values to all the constraints, even though many of them are the default values. It is useful to have one reference program where this is done so we can see what format is used to set the constraints.

Once the constraints have been set, we must associate the constraint values with the component that is to be added to the layout. This is done using the method `setConstraints()`. It takes two arguments: the first is the component to be added to the layout, and the second is the `GridBagConstraints` object containing the constraint values.

Finally, we add the component to the layout in the usual way, using the `add()` method.

The code above places all 10 buttons at the correct place in the grid. Note that once a constraint value is set, it remains in effect until it is explicitly changed. That is, you need to specify only those constraints that change from one component to the next.

Although this program works properly, and the code involved is not significantly longer than that required for the other layout managers we have considered, it is possible to streamline the use of the `GridBagLayout` considerably. We can also correct the violation of object-oriented programming principles in the process.

To this end, we define a new class that is derived from `GridBagLayout`:

```java
// NewGridBagLayout.java
import java.awt.*;

public class NewGridBagLayout extends GridBagLayout
{
    private GridBagConstraints constraints;

    NewGridBagLayout()
    {
        super();
```

```
        constraints = new GridBagConstraints();
    }


    void setRareConstraints(int anchor, int fill,
        Insets insets, int ipadx, int ipady,
        double weightx, double weighty)
    {
        constraints.anchor = anchor;
        constraints.fill = fill;
        constraints.insets = insets;
        constraints.ipadx = ipadx;
        constraints.ipady = ipady;
        constraints.weightx = weightx;
        constraints.weighty = weighty;
    }


    void setPositionSizeAdd(Component control,
        Container parent,
        int gridx, int gridy,
        int gridwidth, int gridheight)
    {
        constraints.gridx = gridx;
        constraints.gridy = gridy;
        constraints.gridwidth = gridwidth;
        constraints.gridheight = gridheight;
        setConstraints(control, constraints);
        parent.add(control);
    }
}
```

The `NewGridBagLayout` class encapsulates all that is required for a `GridBagLayout` object by containing its own `GridBagConstraints` object, and providing interface methods to set the constraint values. The constructor calls the `GridBagLayout` constructor using the `super()` method, and then initializes the `GridBagConstraints()` object.

The `setRareConstraints()` method provides an interface for setting the less-often used constraints. In many cases, this method need only be called once after the layout manager has been defined, since the same settings are used for all components.

The `setPositionSizeAdd()` method is called each time a new component is to be added to the layout. The method allows the grid location and cell size constraints to be set. Besides passing values for these parameters, the `setPositionSizeAdd()` method also requires the component which is to be added, and the `Container` object to which the layout manager belongs. This method may be used with `Panels` and `Applets`, since both these classes are derived from the `Container` class.

Using the `NewGridBagLayout` manager, we can rewrite the code for producing the calculator numeric keypad as follows:

```java
// GridBagNumbers.java
import java.applet.Applet;
import java.awt.*;
import NewGridBagLayout;

public class GridBagNumbers extends Applet {
   private Button button1, button2, button3,
      button4, button5;
   private Button button6, button7, button8,
      button9, button0;
   private Panel allnumbers = new Panel();
   NewGridBagLayout layout = new NewGridBagLayout();

   public void init()
   {
      // Create the 10 buttons
      button1 = new Button("1");
      button2 = new Button("2");
      button3 = new Button("3");
      button4 = new Button("4");
      button5 = new Button("5");
      button6 = new Button("6");
      button7 = new Button("7");
      button8 = new Button("8");
      button9 = new Button("9");
      button0 = new Button("0");

      allnumbers.setLayout(layout);
      layout.setRareConstraints(
         GridBagConstraints.CENTER,
         GridBagConstraints.BOTH,
         new Insets(5,5,5,5), 0, 0, 1, 1);

      layout.setPositionSizeAdd(button1, allnumbers,
         0, 0, 1, 1);
      layout.setPositionSizeAdd(button2, allnumbers,
         1, 0, 1, 1);
      layout.setPositionSizeAdd(button3, allnumbers,
         2, 0, 1, 1);
      layout.setPositionSizeAdd(button4, allnumbers,
         0, 1, 1, 1);
      layout.setPositionSizeAdd(button5, allnumbers,
         1, 1, 1, 1);
      layout.setPositionSizeAdd(button6, allnumbers,
         2, 1, 1, 1);
```

```
        layout.setPositionSizeAdd(button7, allnumbers,
            0, 2, 1, 1);
        layout.setPositionSizeAdd(button8, allnumbers,
            1, 2, 1, 1);
        layout.setPositionSizeAdd(button9, allnumbers,
            2, 2, 1, 1);
        layout.setPositionSizeAdd(button0, allnumbers,
            1, 3, 1, 1);

        add(allnumbers);
    }
}
```

After creating the `NewGridBagLayout` object `layout`, we construct the `Button`s and call the `setRareConstraints()` method with values that will be used for all components. After this, we simply call the `setPositionSizeAdd()` for each `Button` we wish to add to the layout. The `Panel` `allnumbers` is passed as the `Container` argument. The coordinates of each `Button` are passed to allow the method to place the `Button` at the correct location on the grid.

The code has been simplified greatly by using the `NewGridBagLayout` class, and proper object-oriented techniques have been introduced. The `NewGridBagLayout` class can be used in any program where a `GridBagLayout` manager is required.

3.7 Case study – a four-function calculator

To illustrate the use of the various layout managers in constructing a complete interface, we will now present a complete program for a simple four-function calculator. The calculator will have the interface shown in Fig. 3.1, and will allow arithmetic calculations with integers only.

Coding the interface Before we consider the functionality of the calculator, let us see how the complete interface can be constructed by using separate layout managers for each of the sections shown in Fig. 3.2, and then combining these sections using an overall layout manager.

We have already considered several implementations of the number keypad, and the most straightforward one would seem to be that based on the `NewGridBagLayout` manager. The layouts for the sections containing the sign change and clear keys and the arithmetic operations are simple grids, so we can use a `GridLayout` for them. Finally, the text box in which the numbers are displayed is a single component, so it can be added on its own to the master `Panel`.

Let us have a look at the definitions of the components we will use:

```
// Calculator.java
import java.applet.Applet;
```

```
import java.awt.*;
import NewGridBagLayout;

public class Calculator extends Applet {
    private long operand1, operand2, answer;
    private String operation;
    private boolean newNumber;

    // Number buttons
    private Button button1 = new Button("1");
    private Button button2 = new Button("2");
    private Button button3 = new Button("3");
    private Button button4 = new Button("4");
    private Button button5 = new Button("5");
    private Button button6 = new Button("6");
    private Button button7 = new Button("7");
    private Button button8 = new Button("8");
    private Button button9 = new Button("9");
    private Button button0 = new Button("0");

    // Textbox for numerical display
    private TextField numberBox = new TextField("0",12);

    // Sign change and clear buttons
    private Button plusMinusButton = new Button("+/-");
    private Button CEButton = new Button("CE");
    private Button CButton = new Button("C");

    // Arithmetic operations
    private Button plusButton = new Button("+");
    private Button minusButton = new Button("-");
    private Button timesButton = new Button("X");
    private Button divideButton = new Button("/");
    private Button equalsButton = new Button("=");
```

The variables operand1, operand2, answer, operation, and newNumber are required for handling the calculations, and will be considered later.

The 10 Buttons are declared and initialized, followed by the TextField. We initialize numberBox to display the string "0", and allow strings up to 12 characters in length.

The remaining components are all Buttons whose meanings should be clear from their names.

Next, we examine the init() method in which the layouts are constructed.

```
public void init()
{
    // Panels
        // Number keypad
```

```
Panel numberPanel = new Panel();

   // Sign change and clear buttons
Panel signClearPanel = new Panel();
   // Arithmetic operators
Panel arithmeticPanel = new Panel();
   // Overall panel
Panel masterPanel = new Panel();


// Layouts
NewGridBagLayout numberLayout =
   new NewGridBagLayout();
   // Keypad
NewGridBagLayout masterLayout =
   new NewGridBagLayout();
   // Overall layout

operand1 = operand2 = answer = 0;
operation = "+";

setFont(new Font("Helvetica", Font.BOLD, 14));

signClearPanel.setLayout(new GridLayout(1,3,2,2));
signClearPanel.add(plusMinusButton);
signClearPanel.add(CEButton);
signClearPanel.add(CButton);

numberPanel.setLayout(numberLayout);
numberLayout.setRareConstraints(
   GridBagConstraints.CENTER,
   GridBagConstraints.BOTH,
   new Insets(2,2,2,2), 0, 0, 1, 1);
numberLayout.setPositionSizeAdd(button1,
   numberPanel, 0, 0, 1, 1);
numberLayout.setPositionSizeAdd(button2,
   numberPanel, 1, 0, 1, 1);
numberLayout.setPositionSizeAdd(button3,
   numberPanel, 2, 0, 1, 1);
numberLayout.setPositionSizeAdd(button4,
   numberPanel, 0, 1, 1, 1);
numberLayout.setPositionSizeAdd(button5,
   numberPanel, 1, 1, 1, 1);
numberLayout.setPositionSizeAdd(button6,
   numberPanel, 2, 1, 1, 1);
numberLayout.setPositionSizeAdd(button7,
   numberPanel, 0, 2, 1, 1);
numberLayout.setPositionSizeAdd(button8,
   numberPanel, 1, 2, 1, 1);
```

```
numberLayout.setPositionSizeAdd(button9,
    numberPanel, 2, 2, 1, 1);
numberLayout.setPositionSizeAdd(button0,
    numberPanel, 1, 3, 1, 1);

arithmeticPanel.setLayout(new GridLayout(5,1,2,2));
arithmeticPanel.add(plusButton);
arithmeticPanel.add(minusButton);
arithmeticPanel.add(timesButton);
arithmeticPanel.add(divideButton);
arithmeticPanel.add(equalsButton);

masterLayout.setRareConstraints(
    GridBagConstraints.NORTHEAST,
    GridBagConstraints.NONE,
    new Insets(2,2,2,2), 0, 0, 1, 1);
masterPanel.setLayout(masterLayout);
masterLayout.setPositionSizeAdd(numberBox,
    masterPanel, 0, 0, 2, 1);
masterLayout.setPositionSizeAdd(signClearPanel,
    masterPanel, 0, 1, 2, 1);
masterLayout.setPositionSizeAdd(numberPanel,
    masterPanel, 0, 2, 1, 1);
masterLayout.setPositionSizeAdd(arithmeticPanel,
    masterPanel, 1, 2, 1, 1);

add(masterPanel);
}
```

First, we define the `Panels` that will be used for the layouts. Note that all `Panels` are local to the `init()` method, since they are required only for laying out the components, and play no part in the actual use of the calculator.

Next, we define the two `NewGridBagLayouts` that are needed for the number keypad and the overall layout. The other layouts are defined later, where they are used, since there is no need for an explicit reference to them.

After the variables used in the calculations are initialized, we set the font for the calculator to be 14-point Helvetica bold, since the default font used for applets on most computers is often hard to read.

The sign change and clear `Buttons` are laid out in the `signClearPanel` using a `GridLayout` with one row and three columns, and an inter-component spacing of two pixels. The `Buttons` are added to the `Panel`. Following this, the number keypad is laid out using the code from the last section. Finally, the `arithmeticPanel` is defined using another `GridLayout`, and the arithmetic operator `Buttons` are added to it.

The final section of the `init()` method combines all these `Panels` to create the overall interface for the calculator. We define another `NewGridBagLayout`, this time orienting all components to the `NORTHEAST`, and turning off any filling.

It is a good idea when planning a compound layout to examine a sketch on paper first, in order to see what grid coordinates to use for each component. From Fig. 3.2, we see that Panels 1 and 2 each occupy the entire width of the applet, while Panels 3 and 4 must share the last row. Therefore, we need a layout with three rows and two columns.

The numberBox is placed at grid coordinates (0,0), and given a width of two columns and a height of one row. The signClearPanel is placed at coordinates (0,1) (remember that the gridx coordinate is given first, so the first number specifies the *column* and not the row) and given a width of 2 and a height of 1.

The numberPanel is placed at the beginning of row 2 (coordinates (0,2)), with a width and height of 1. Finally, the arithmeticPanel is placed at coordinates (1,2), also with a height and width of 1. If the code to this point is run as an applet, we obtain the display shown in Fig. 3.4.

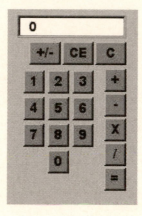

Figure 3.4.

Functionality of the calculator   Having decided upon the layout, we must now specify exactly what effect each button has when pressed. This is actually a bit more complicated than you might expect. If you have used a calculator a lot, you probably take its functionality for granted, and you might not realize that pressing a particular button doesn't always have the same effect.

We therefore need to spell out in some detail the effects of pressing the various buttons.

- *Number keys* – if a number key is pressed to enter the first digit of a new number (such as pressing '2' to enter the first digit of the number 241), the corresponding digit should appear in the display. If a number key is pressed immediately after another number key, the display should be modified according to the rules that follow. If the number in the display is *positive*, the number currently being displayed should be multiplied by 10 and added to the new digit, with the result being displayed. If the number in the display is *negative*, the number currently being displayed should be multiplied by 10 and added to the *negative* of the new digit. Finally, assuming that we are allowing a maximum number of digits to be displayed (10 digits is typical for many calculators), we must not allow numbers greater than 9,999,999,999 or less than –9,999,999,999 to be entered.

- *Operator keys* – if one of the operator keys (+, –, ×, /) is pressed we need to check several things. First, if a previous operation is waiting to be performed, we must do it and display the result. (For example, in the calculation 1 + 3 – 2, when the – is entered, the previous calculation of 1 + 3 must be done.) Secondly, we must set the next operation to be performed to correspond with the key that was pressed. (When the – is pressed, the calculator must remember that a subtraction is to be done after the next number is entered.) Finally, pressing an operator key tells the calculator that the entry of one number is complete, and the next time a digit key is pressed, a new number should be started. (Pressing the – key in the calculation 1 + 3 – 2 means that the 3 and the 2 are separate numbers, and should not be combined to make 32.) Note that we are *not* including any operator precedence in the calculator – operations are performed strictly in the order in which they are entered. For example, if you are used to doing multiplications and divisions before additions and subtractions, the calculation 1 + 3 × 5 = would give you 16, whereas our calculator will give you 20.
- *Equals key* – pressing the equals (=) key must, of course, complete the current calculation and display the result in the display window. However, sometimes we decide that, after pressing the = key, we would like to use the result in another calculation, so we should remember the answer and treat it as if it had been entered by hand as the first number in a calculation. For example, if we pressed the keys 1 + 2 = × 4 =, the answer 3 would be displayed in the window after the first press of the = key. The 3 is remembered at this point so that pressing the next three keys (× 4 =) results in the answer 12.
- *CE (clear entry) key* – this key should clear the display to 0 and delete from memory *only* the number currently being entered. Any other previously entered information, such as the first number in a calculation or a function key, should be retained. For example, pressing the keys 1 2 × 3 CE 4 should have the same effect as pressing 1 2 × 4, and give the answer (after pressing another function key or the = key) 48.
- *C (clear all) key* – this key should erase all information previously entered into the calculator, restoring it to the state it was in when it was first switched on.
- *+/– key* – the number currently displayed in the window should have its sign reversed from positive to negative or *vice versa*. The corresponding number in memory must also be updated. (Remember that the sequence of symbols displayed in the window is a Java `string`, while the actual number used in calculations is an `int` or a `long`.)

Designing the functionality   As described in Chapter 2, all graphical user interface (GUI) programs are *event-driven*. This means we must provide the code to be run whenever some event occurs as a result of a user action (such as a button being pushed). Recall from Chapter 2 that this is done in Java by providing either a `handleEvent()` method or an `action()` method (or both). These functions are automatically sent events by Java as they occur, but it is up to the programmer to sort out the events and provide actions for those that require special treatment.

In this case, the only events that we need to process are button pushes, so we must catch any button-press events and provide the code to handle them. In doing so, we can follow the requirements set out in the previous section.

- *Number keys* – the requirements for pressing a number key will be handled by a method `addDigitToDisplay()`. After checking a flag variable to see if this digit is the first digit of a new number, this method implements the updating of the display by first extracting the text from the `TextField` and converting it to a `long` (ordinary `int`s cannot handle all integers of 10 digits). The new digit is added, and the `TextField` updated.

- *Operator keys* – the event generated by pressing an operator key (one of +, −, ×, or /) is handled by a method `doOperation()`. A operator key specifies an operator for the next calculation, and also performs the previous calculation, if any. For example, in the expression 3 × 4 + 9, pressing the × (multiply) key sets the operator for the next calculation to be ×, but does not perform any calculation since it is the first operator in the expression. Pressing the + key, however, must first perform the calculation 3 × 4, then set the operator to + for the next calculation.

   These two cases can be combined into one if we initialize the calculator so that both operands are 0 and initialize the operator to +. Then, in the expression 3 × 4 + 9, for example, when the × key is pressed, the calculator 'thinks' the expression that has been entered so far is 0 + 3 ×, so the effect of pressing the × key is to do the previous calculation (0 + 3), then set the next operation to be ×. Doing things this way means that we don't need to write special code to handle the first operator in an expression.

   Once the previous calculation is done, the answer must be displayed in the `TextField` and saved as the first operand for the next calculation. The flag indicating that a new number is to be entered is also set. Finally, the operation for the next calculation is set to the key that was just pressed.

- *Equals key* – the equals key is handled by the method `doEquals()`. This method is similar to the `doOperation()` method for handling an arithmetic operation, but we wish to leave the calculator in the state identical to the 'just switched on' state, except that the answer that has just been displayed should be treated as though it had just been keyed in by the user. Therefore, after completing and displaying the calculation, the `doEquals()` method sets both operands and the answer variable to 0, and the operation to +. The new number flag is switched off, since the answer from the previous calculation now becomes the newly input number. For example, the key sequence 3 × 4 = + 9 = will display 12 after the first = is entered, and at this point, the 12 will behave as though it had just been typed into the calculator immediately after the calculator had been switched on. After entering the second =, the answer 21 will be displayed.

- *+/– key* – this key is handled by the `changeSign()` method, which toggles the sign of the number displayed in the `TextField`, by converting the string in the `TextField` to a `long`, changing the sign, and converting the result back to a `String`.
- *CE and C keys* – the CE key is handled by the method `clearDisplay()`, which simply sets the display to 0 without affecting any other variables. The C key is handled by the method `clearAll()`, which resets the calculator to the state it was in when it was switched on.

All events are handled by the `action()` method. Since all events are `Button` presses, we first check the `target` of `event` to single these out. We then determine which `Button` was pressed by examining its `label`, obtained from the `arg` passed to the `action()` method. Once we discover which `Button` was pressed, we call the corresponding method to process the event.

```
public boolean action(Event event, Object arg) {
    if (event.target instanceof Button) {
        String label = (String) arg;
        if (label.equalsIgnoreCase("1")) {
            addDigitToDisplay(1);
        } else if (label.equalsIgnoreCase("2")) {
            addDigitToDisplay(2);
        } else if (label.equalsIgnoreCase("3")) {
            addDigitToDisplay(3);
        } else if (label.equalsIgnoreCase("4")) {
            addDigitToDisplay(4);
        } else if (label.equalsIgnoreCase("5")) {
            addDigitToDisplay(5);
        } else if (label.equalsIgnoreCase("6")) {
            addDigitToDisplay(6);
        } else if (label.equalsIgnoreCase("7")) {
            addDigitToDisplay(7);
        } else if (label.equalsIgnoreCase("8")) {
            addDigitToDisplay(8);
        } else if (label.equalsIgnoreCase("9")) {
            addDigitToDisplay(9);
        } else if (label.equalsIgnoreCase("0")) {
            addDigitToDisplay(0);
        } else if (label.equalsIgnoreCase("CE")) {
        clearDisplay();
        } else if (label.equalsIgnoreCase("+/-")) {
            changeSign();
        } else if (label.equalsIgnoreCase("C")) {
        clearAll();
        } else if (label.equalsIgnoreCase("=")) {
```

```
        doEquals();
        } else if (label.equalsIgnoreCase("+")) {
        doOperation("+");
        } else if (label.equalsIgnoreCase("-")) {
        doOperation("-");
        } else if (label.equalsIgnoreCase("X")) {
        doOperation("X");
        } else if (label.equalsIgnoreCase("/")) {
        doOperation("/");
        }
        return true;
    }
    return super.action(event, arg);
}
```

The remaining methods merely implement the design that we described in the preceding sections.

The `addDigitToDisplay()` method adds the number to the `TextBox` whenever a number `Button` is pressed.

```
private void addDigitToDisplay(int newDigit) {
    if (newNumber) {
       numberBox.setText("0");
       newNumber = false;
    }
    long displayValue =
       Long.parseLong(numberBox.getText());
    if (displayValue >= 0 && displayValue
       <= 999999999)
    displayValue = displayValue * 10 + newDigit;
    else if (displayValue < 0 &&
                displayValue >= -999999999)
    displayValue = displayValue * 10 - newDigit;
    numberBox.setText(Long.toString(displayValue));
}
```

The `changeSign()` method toggles the sign of the number displayed in the `TextBox`:

```
private void changeSign() {
    long display =
       Long.parseLong(numberBox.getText());
    display = -display;
    numberBox.setText(Long.toString(display));
}
```

The two clear methods handle the CE and C `Buttons`:

```
    private void clearDisplay() {
       numberBox.setText("0");
    }

    private void clearAll() {
       operand1 = operand2 = answer = 0;
       operation = "+";
       newNumber = true;
       numberBox.setText("0");
    }
```

When the = key is pressed, nothing is done if `newNumber` is `true`, since that means that the calculator is expecting a number to be entered. Otherwise, the second operand is extracted from the `TextBox`, the operation is carried out, and the answer is displayed in the `TextBox`. Finally, the state of the calculator is set so that the answer can be used as the first operand in a new calculation.

```
    private void doEquals() {
       if (newNumber)
          return;
       operand2 = Long.parseLong(numberBox.getText());
       if (operation == "+")
          answer = operand1 + operand2;
       else if (operation == "-")
          answer = operand1 - operand2;
       else if (operation == "X")
          answer = operand1 * operand2;
       else if (operation == "/")
          answer = operand1 / operand2;
       numberBox.setText(Long.toString(answer));
       operand1 = operand2 = answer = 0;
       operation = "+";
    }
```

When an operator key is pressed, nothing is done if the calculator is expecting a number to be entered. Otherwise, the second operand is extracted from the `TextBox` in the same way as in the `doEquals()` method, the previous operation is carried out, and the answer displayed. Then the answer is set to be the first operand for the next operation, and `operation` variable is set to the operation selected by the user. Finally, the `newNumber` flag is set to `true` to indicate that the calculator is now expecting another number to be keyed in.

```
    private void doOperation(String newOperation) {
       if (newNumber)
          return;
       operand2 = Long.parseLong(numberBox.getText());
       if (operation == "+")
```

```
        answer = operand1 + operand2;
    else if (operation == "-")
        answer = operand1 - operand2;
    else if (operation == "X")
        answer = operand1 * operand2;
    else if (operation == "/")
        answer = operand1 / operand2;

    numberBox.setText(Long.toString(answer));
    operand1 = answer;
    operand2 = answer = 0;
    operation = newOperation;
    newNumber = true;
}
```

3.8   Exercises

1   Write a Java applet (or application) which will display a fragment of English text (one or two sentences). The text should be displayed with word wrap – that is, if the applet isn't wide enough to accommodate the entire text on one line, the remainder of the text should be displayed on additional lines. The text should be broken at the end of a line *only* between words.

The idea here is to split the text into individual words and create a separate `Label` for each word. The `Label`s should then be displayed within the applet using a `FlowLayout`.

You will find the `StringTokenizer` class (part of the `java.util` package – see the Java documentation for details) useful in splitting the `String` up into separate tokens. Create a `StringTokenizer` object by passing the `String` to its constructor. Then use a loop to split off tokens using the `nextToken()` method, continuing until the `hasMoreTokens()` method returns `false`. Remember to include the line

```
import java.util.*;
```

at the beginning of your code.

When writing this program, experiment with the different forms of the `FlowLayout` constructor. Note that the argumentless constructor creates a layout which centers each line of text within the applet, and produces large spaces between words and lines. Try to left-justify the text on each line, and reduce the spacing between words and lines. (Hint: try using negative spacing in the constructor.)

2   Extend the program from question 1 by allowing the user to input their own text, which is then formatted. The main applet should now contain a `Label` giving a title (such as "Text formatting experiment."). Below this, a `TextArea` component with, say, five rows and 40 columns should be added. Finally, at

the bottom, add a `Button` which, when pressed, brings up a `Frame` containing the formatted version of the text typed into the `TextArea`.

As before, use a `FlowLayout` within the `Frame` to format the text. Within the main applet, however, use a `BorderLayout` to arrange the `Label`, `TextArea`, and `Button`. Each time the user enters new text in the `TextArea` and presses the `Button` to see the formatted text, hide the previous `Frame` and create a new `Frame` to view the new text. Note that the `Labels` within the `Frame` are repositioned automatically if the `Frame` is resized by the user.

3   Modify the program from question 2 by making use of the `CardLayout` manager. The `CardLayout` class allows several components to be defined within the same area on the screen. These components then form a stack of 'cards' sitting on top of the applet or panel, rather like a pack of playing cards sitting on a table. Once all the components have been added to a `CardLayout`, one (and only one) component is specified as the visible component. Various methods are provided within `CardLayout` to change which card is visible in response to other events.

To use a `CardLayout`, create a new `CardLayout` object and set the applet's layout to this object in the usual way, using the `setLayout()` method. Then prepare the components you wish to add to the applet. Add each component using the `add()` method, except this time, you must provide a name (by which the component can be identified later) for each component you add. Then call the `show()` method to display whichever component you want to appear. For example:

```
CardLayout appletLayout = new CardLayout();
setLayout(appletLayout);
add("DataEntry", dataEntryPanel);
add("FormatText", formatTextPanel);
appletLayout.show(this, " DataEntry");
```

Note that the `show()` method requires as its first argument the container which owns the `CardLayout`. In this case, the applet itself owns the layout, so we pass the `this` pointer as the first argument. In other cases, a `Panel` within the applet may have a `CardLayout` defined as its layout manager, so we would then pass the `Panel` object to `show()`.

To make things easier, place the `Label`, `TextArea`, and `Button` within a `Panel` (referred to as `dataEntryPanel` in the sample code above), and the formatted text in another `Panel` (`formatTextPanel`), then add these two `Panels` to the `CardLayout`. You can, of course, use nested `Panels` if you think it will facilitate the layout of your components.

When the applet starts, the `dataEntryPanel` should be visible. The user then types some text into the `TextArea` and presses the `Button`. Within the `handleEvent()` method for the applet, the `Panel` within the `CardLayout` should be switched to the `formatTextPanel`. A `Button` should be provided on this `Panel` to allow the user to switch back to the `dataEntryPanel`.

Note that, since it is not possible to alter the layout of a component after it has been initialized and displayed, you will need to create a new instance of the `formatTextPanel` for each entered text. Since this is contained within the `CardLayout`, you will need to create a new instance of the `CardLayout` as well. For small displays such as this, this will not cause a noticeable delay. However, a more efficient method for displaying text involves using the `paint()` method to draw text as a graphics object directly onto an applet or canvas. We will cover these techniques in Chapter 5.

4   Write an applet which allows two (human) players to play a game of tic-tac-toe (otherwise known as noughts and crosses, or X's and O's). The layout should consist of a three-by-three grid of `Buttons`, a `Label` giving a title (initially) and feedback during and after the game, and a 'reset' `Button` which clears the applet and starts a new game.

The grid of nine `Buttons` should be contained within a `Panel` using a `GridLayout`. The `Buttons` should start with blank captions. Assume that the 'X' player always plays first, and begins by pushing one of the `Buttons` in the grid. The applet should respond by setting the `Button`'s caption to 'X' and disabling the button (that is, graying it out so that it is still visible but does not respond to mouse clicks). The second player then presses another button, whose caption is set to 'O' and the `Button` disabled.

The computer should check the grid of `Buttons` after each move to see if the last move won the game (remember that a player wins by having a row, column, or diagonal all marked with the same symbol). If so, the `Label` should announce that the game has been won, and *all* remaining `Buttons` should be disabled. If all nine `Buttons` are pressed without a win, the `Label` should announce that the game is drawn. The reset `Button` should reset the applet by setting all `Button` captions to blank, and enabling all the `Buttons` in the grid. (If you like, have a `Frame` with the caption "Do you really want to start a new game?", and "Yes" and "No" `Buttons`, appear after the reset `Button` is pressed, but remember that `Frames` cannot be made modal in the current version of Java, so the user is free to ignore the question.)

Use a `BorderLayout` to arrange the `Label`, central `Panel` of nine buttons, and the reset `Button`.

5   (Larger project.) Video recorders are notorious for their poor user interfaces – one customer survey revealed that more than half the video recorders in private homes still show a flashing '12:00', indicating that the owners have never even set the time. Try to design a better interface for a video recorder in Java, making use of the various layout managers and GUI components.

The main applet should show the layout of buttons, either on the video recorder itself, or on the remote control. Assume that the video recorder can use the television to which it is attached to display a `Frame` when some of the controls are pressed.

The main applet should contain controls to do the following:

- Rewind, play, fast forward, pause, stop.
- Record.
- Choose TV channel.
- Show date and time.
- Set date and time.
- Enter program mode (to allow the video recorder to be programmed to automatically tape a TV program later).
- View entered programs.
- Edit/cancel a program.

Choosing 'show date and time' should bring up a `Frame` showing the current date and time. Choosing 'set date and time' should bring up a `Frame` allowing the user to enter the current date and time.

Entering the program mode should bring up a `Frame` which allows users to enter the details for a TV program which they wish to record later. This usually requires data such as the channel number, start and finish times, the date, and (optionally) whether this program is to be recorded every day or every week at the same time.

The 'view entered programs' option allows the user to see what TV programmes will be taped automatically. The 'edit/cancel' option allows users to change data in, or cancel, programs to be taped.

Other options may be included according to your preference. Plan out the interface carefully, considering what would be most convenient and easiest to understand for the user. Disable or hide any controls that shouldn't be useable in a given context. Don't put too many controls on the screen at once.

Make judicious use of the various layout managers (especially the `GridBagLayout`) and other methods in the Java AWT.

C H A P T E R 4

EXCEPTIONS

4.1 Handling unexpected data

Most introductory programming courses emphasize that, when designing and writing a program, it is good practice to allow for unexpected or incorrect data entered by users. To do this, you should try to anticipate what errors a user may make when entering data into your program and insert extra code which checks for this data and gives informative error messages. Failure to insert these checks can often result in the program 'crashing' or 'hanging' with no indication as to what has gone wrong, beyond a cryptic system message such as 'General protection fault at location 0x3443FEA7'.

Oddly enough, it is only relatively recently that designers of programming languages have included features which allow error handling in a natural way. Languages such as Pascal, C, and Fortran and early versions of C++, contain no special features allowing the handling of so-called *exceptional conditions*. Recent versions of C++, and now Java, have included such features.

Before plunging into the syntax of exception handling in Java, it is worth considering when such exceptions should be generated. Like any other language feature, it is easy to overuse or abuse exceptions if their purpose is not fully understood.

An *exception* should be generated by a method if that method is asked to do something that is either impossible or that would violate the system integrity in some way. Java has many built-in exceptions that will be generated, or *thrown*, to use the accepted terminology, if your program attempts an illegal operation.

For example, the following Java method divides two `ints`:

```java
int Divide2Ints(int a, int b)
{
   return a / b;
}
```

If you insert this method into a Java applet or application and then call it with the call `int answer = Divide2Ints(4, 0);` Java will throw an `ArithmeticException`. An `ArithmeticException` is thrown whenever an illegal arithmetic operation (in this case, division by zero) is performed. The exception will produce some information (that can be accessed by methods we will consider later) that tells you the origin of the problem.

Although the method given above, as it is written, will still cause the program to crash if it is called with the argument b set to zero, the important point is that Java provides you with a way of *catching* an exception and possibly doing something to correct the problem without having the program crash. Languages that do not support exception handling do not have this luxury. We will consider the syntax for catching exceptions in the next section.

It is important to realize that an exception should not be treated simply as an alternative `if` statement. In one sense, what the method above is doing is saying: "if parameter b is zero, then throw an `ArithmeticException`, otherwise, perform the division a/b as requested and return the result". Since it is possible to generate information on the cause of an exception when it is thrown, it is easy to fall into the habit of using exceptions as a quick and dirty way of generating system messages within methods.

We could, for example, write our own exception for integer division which generated messages not only when we attempted division by zero, but also when either a or b is negative, or when b is not a factor of a, or for any other condition we wanted. However, these other conditions are not illegal operations or exceptional conditions, so they should be detected by more conventional means, such as the if statement.

Trying and catching 4.2

There are two main aspects to exception handling in Java: generating or throwing exceptions, and handling or *catching* exceptions that have been thrown. Since Java has a lot of built-in exceptions, it is possible to write a Java program which only catches some of these built-in exceptions. We will consider how this is done first, and then describe how you can throw your own exceptions in the next section.

Catching an exception means providing some code that identifies a particular type (or set of types) of exception, and then processes the exception in some way that allows execution of the program to continue. To catch an exception, you must first identify a number of lines of code in which the exception may occur. This code must be made the body of a try block, where try is a Java keyword that means to try out the code contained within the block and check for any exceptions that might be thrown. If an exception *is* thrown within a try block, the code immediately following the try block is examined to see if there is a catch statement that is watching for the kind of exception that was thrown. One try block can have any number of catch statements following it, each of which can test for a particular type of exception.

As an example, let us modify the method in the preceding section so that an ArithmeticException is caught.

```java
int Divide2Ints(int a, int b)
{
   int quotient = 0;

   try {
      quotient = a / b;
   } catch (ArithmeticException exception) {
      System.out.println("Error: division by zero.");
   }

   return quotient;
}
```

In this case, there is only one statement in which an `ArithmeticException` can be thrown, so that statement forms the body of the `try` block. Unlike the `if`, `for`, and `while` statements, if the body of the statement contains only a single statement, braces *are* required (in all but the earliest versions of Java).

Following the `try` block, there is a single `catch` statement which will catch an `ArithmeticException`. The body of the `catch` statement prints an error message to the standard output, although a `catch` statement can, in general, be much more involved.

It is important to realize that as soon as an exception is thrown by one of the statements within a `try` block, the entire block becomes invalid and control is passed to the first statement following the `try` block (which must be a `catch` statement). Thus, if there are any statements within the `try` block following the one which threw the exception, they will not be executed.

Note the differences between this version of `Divide2Ints()` and the previous version. First, we have declared a local variable, `quotient`, which is used to store the quotient of `a` and `b`. The reason for this is that the `Divide2Ints()` method is declared as returning an `int`, and so an `int` must be returned, or else a compilation error will result. Suppose we had tried to introduce exception handling into the method by writing:

```
int Divide2Ints(int a, int b)
{
  try {
    return a / b;
  } catch (ArithmeticException exception) {
    System.out.println("Error: division by zero.");
  }
}
```

We would be OK provided no exception was thrown. However, if `b = 0`, the division operation would throw an exception, and execution of all code within the `try` block would stop at that point. Control is transferred to the appropriate `catch` statement following the `try` block, or, if no `catch` is provided that handles the type of exception being generated, to the first line of code following the `catch` statement(s). In this case, that means that the `return` statement would never be executed.

The second difference between the two versions illustrates the whole point of exception handling. In the first version, if an exception occurs, the program will crash (if it is text-based) or ignore the event which caused the exception (if it is GUI-based). Introducing exception handling allows the exception to be caught, an error message printed, and execution of the program to continue.

Let us have a look at a slightly more involved example. We will expand on the simple `Divide2Ints()` method above by constructing an applet in which the user can type in the two `int`s to be used in the quotient. In addition, we will store each quotient in an array, and allow the user to search the array for a given number. As we will see, adding these features provides several opportunities for Java exceptions to be thrown.

The definition of the applet and its fields is as follows.

```
import java.applet.Applet;
import java.awt.*;

public class ArrayZero extends Applet {
   static final int ARRAYSIZE = 10;
   Button addButton =
      new Button("Add quotient to array");
   Button searchButton =
      new Button("Search for number");
   TextField num1Field = new TextField(5);
   TextField num2Field = new TextField(5);
   TextField searchField = new TextField(5);
   Panel displayPanel = new Panel();
   int[] numArray = new int[ARRAYSIZE];
   int numStored = 0;

   public void init()
   {
      displayPanel.setLayout(new GridLayout(2,3));
      displayPanel.add(num1Field);
      displayPanel.add(num2Field);
      displayPanel.add(addButton);
      displayPanel.add(searchField);
      displayPanel.add(searchButton);
      add(displayPanel);
   }
```

The first two `TextFields` allow the user to enter the two numbers to be used in the quotient, with the numerator in the first box and the denominator in the second. Pressing `addButton` will extract the two numbers from these `TextFields`, take their quotient, and store the quotient in `numArray` at the next available location.

The `searchField` box allows the user to enter a single number. Pressing `searchButton` will search `numArray` to see if the number entered in `searchField` is present in the array.

All messages will be printed in the status bar of the browser (the bar at the bottom of the browser window).

The remaining methods for this applet are as follows.

```
public boolean action(Event event, Object object)
{
   if (event.target == addButton) {
      try {
         int num1 =
            Integer.parseInt(num1Field.getText());
```

```
                    int num2 =
                        Integer.parseInt(num2Field.getText());
                    int quotient = num1 / num2;
                    showStatus(num1 + "/" + num2 + " = " +
                        quotient);
                    addToArray(quotient);
                } catch (ArithmeticException exception) {
                    showStatus("Division by zero.");
                } catch (NumberFormatException exception) {
                    showStatus("Enter integers only.");
                } catch (ArrayIndexOutOfBoundsException
                    exception) {
                    showStatus
                        ("Array is full. Cannot add quotient.");
                }
            } else if (event.target == searchButton) {
                try {
                    int searchNum =
                        Integer.parseInt(searchField.getText());
                    showStatus(searchArray(searchNum) ? "Found." :
                        "Not found.");
                }
                catch (NumberFormatException exception) {
                    showStatus("Enter an integer in search box.");
                }
            }
            return true;
        }

        private void addToArray(int number)
        {
            numArray[numStored] = number;
            ++numStored;
        }

        private boolean searchArray(int number)
        {
            for (int index = 0; index < numStored; ++index)
                if (numArray[index] == number)
                    return true;
            return false;
        }
    }
```

The `action()` method processes the two `Button` presses, and includes exception handlers for several exceptions that could be thrown in the process. When `addButton` is pressed, the values entered by the user must be extracted from the two `TextFields`. Since a `TextField` allows the user to type in any ASCII text, not just numbers, it is possible that the user has entered a string that cannot be converted to an `int`. The `parseInt()` method of the `Integer` class will throw a `NumberFormatException` if this has happened, so we provide a `catch` clause which prints an error message.

If the numbers are successfully extracted from the `TextFields`, we take the quotient as before, and catch an `ArithmeticException` if the user has entered a zero in `num2Field`. Finally, when we call the `addToArray()` method to add the quotient to the array, we must allow for the possibility that the array is full. If we try to add an element beyond the end of an array, an `ArrayIndexOutOfBoundsException` is thrown, so we catch that and print an error message.

In the case of `searchButton`, the only exception that can be thrown occurs if the user enters an incorrect string for an `int`, so we catch that as before. The remaining methods are straightforward.

Some things to note about this applet are:

- The `try` block for processing an `addButton` event contains four statements. If any of those statements throws an exception, all following statements within the same `try` block will not be executed. For example, if the user enters an incorrect string into `num2Field`, the last three statements (from calculating `quotient` to the call to `addToArray()`) will be skipped.
- If we had not included a `catch` clause for one of the possible exceptions, the action for that event would be terminated and the applet would return to its 'waiting for input' state if that exception is thrown. For example, if we omitted the `catch` clause for the `NumberFormatException`, then execution of the action for the `addButton` event would stop if the user entered an incorrect string for an `int`. However, no error message would be printed (except in the Java console, if you are using the Netscape browser) so the user would be unaware that anything had gone wrong.
- Exceptions are passed upwards in a chain of called methods. For example, when we call the `addToArray()` method, an `ArrayIndexOutOfBounds-Exception` is thrown inside the method if `numStored` contains a value that is larger than the last array index. This exception is passed back to the method that called `addToArray()` (in this case, the `action()` method), and can be caught at that point.
- It is not appropriate to use an exception to indicate that the `searchArray()` method failed to find a number in the array. It is perfectly acceptable for the user to enter a number which is not in the array and perform a search to verify this. For this reason, we rely on the return value of the method (a `boolean`) to determine the result of the search. Exceptions should be used only to indicate that something has gone wrong during the running of the program.

4.3 Throwing exceptions

4.3.1 THROWING BUILT-IN EXCEPTIONS

Up to now we have considered how to handle exceptions that are thrown automatically by built-in features of Java. One of the main benefits of the exception handling feature of Java, however, is that it allows you to throw your own exceptions, and even to define new types of exceptions which are tailored to specific purposes.

An instance of an exception in Java is simply an object which is an instance of Java's `Exception` class, or of a class derived from it. To throw an exception, we need to create a new instance of the type of exception we wish to throw, and then throw it using the Java keyword `throw`. Usually, both steps are accomplished in one statement, such as:

```
throw new ArithmeticException();
```

or

```
throw new ArrayIndexOutOfBoundsException
    ("Integer array index out of bounds.");
```

These two examples show that all built-in Java exceptions have two constructors: one without arguments and one that accepts a `String`. The `String` contained within an exception can be displayed by a `catch` statement:

```
catch(ArrayIndexOutOfBoundsException exception) {
    showStatus(exception.toString());
}
```

Here, if an `ArrayIndexOutOfBoundsException` thrown by the second example above is caught, the message "Integer array index out of bounds." will be displayed in the browser's status bar.

Although it is fairly easy to throw built-in exceptions using this technique, there are not many places where you would wish to do so, since most of the situations where it is appropriate for such exceptions to be thrown have already been built into the Java language. It is more common for a programmer to define some new type of exception by deriving a class from one of the existing exception classes, and then to throw exceptions of this type in some critical section of the code being written.

To give some examples of how this can be done, we will add a few embellishments to our simple applet above.

We already check the text typed into the various `TextFields` to ensure that the user has entered a valid integer. However, one thing we have not checked is that the number is within the range allowed for an `int`. Since a Java `int` uses 32 bits, the range of `ints` is −2147483648 to 2147483647. Numbers outside this

range are still accepted by the `Integer.parseInt()` method, but when converted to `int`s they will be incorrect.* Since Java provides no way of testing the
range of an `int`, it would be nice if we could provide one that throws an exception if an attempt is made to enter an `int` that is out of bounds.

4.3.2 RUNTIME AND NON-RUNTIME EXCEPTIONS

First, we show how to define a new type of exception. In Java, there are two main
types of exception: runtime exceptions, and non-runtime exceptions. All the exceptions we have dealt with so far are derived from the `RuntimeException` class.
A runtime exception is one that arises from some invalid data being produced while
the program is running. The invalid data may be produced by a logic error in the
program itself (for example, an array index may go out of bounds if a loop over
that array index doesn't stop soon enough), or by the user entering invalid data
(as with the user typing in some non-numerical text into the applet above).

A `RuntimeException` object (or one derived from the `RuntimeException`
class) need not be explicitly caught in a Java program. If such an exception is not
caught, it will cause a text-based application to exit, and a GUI-based program to
ignore the event that caused the exception. It is good programming practice, however, to catch `RuntimeExceptions` in those areas where they are likely to occur,
such as in testing user input. Catching exceptions and producing error messages
is much more helpful to the user than just letting a program die or a button press
be ignored. However, it obviously isn't practical to enclose within a `try` block
every bit of code that could give rise to any type of `RuntimeException`. If we
did this, we would, for example, have to catch an `ArithmeticException` every
time we used the division operator, and an `ArrayIndexOutOfBounds-`
`Exception` every time we referenced an array element.

Statements that could give rise to non-runtime exceptions, however, *must* be
enclosed in a `try` block with a `catch` clause that checks for that type of exception. Such exceptions usually arise in situations where some external process has
an effect on a running program. We will see an example of a non-runtime exception when we consider threading in Chapter 6.

4.3.3 DEFINING A NEW EXCEPTION CLASS

For most new exception classes, all that is required is a class definition which
inherits one of the built-in Java exception classes, together with one or two
constructor definitions.

For example, we may define an `IntegerOverflowException` class to handle
the case where a user enters a string that is too large to be converted to an `int`.
We will derive the class from the `RuntimeException` class.

---

* If you understand two's complement binary notation, you will know the reason for this. If not,
just accept the fact that a positive number that is larger than the maximum value allowed for
an `int` may turn out to be negative when an attempt is made to store it as an `int`, and *vice
versa*.

```
import java.lang.RuntimeException;

class IntegerOverflowException extends
  RuntimeException
{
  IntegerOverflowException(String message)
  {
    super(message);
  }

  IntegerOverflowException()
  {
    super();
  }
}
```

This definition really does nothing more than define a class that is identical to the `RuntimeException` class. The advantage of doing this is that we now have a new type of exception that can be thrown precisely when an integer overflow is about to occur, rather than having to use a `RuntimeException` and then trying to figure out exactly what exceptional condition caused it to be thrown.

We can now add a method to the applet above that accepts a `String` and converts the `String` to an `int` while checking that no integer overflow occurs. The method is as follows.

```
private int stringToInt(String numString)
{
  String testString;
  String refString;

  // Do a parseInt first to test number format
  int number = Integer.parseInt(numString);

  // Now check for overflow
  if (numString.charAt(0) == '-') {
    testString = numString.substring(1);
    refString = new String("2147483648");
  } else {
    testString = numString;
    refString = new String("2147483647");
  }

  if (testString.length() > 10 ||
    (testString.length() == 10 &&
    testString.compareTo(refString) > 0)) {
    throw new IntegerOverflowException
      ("Integers must be in the range -2147483648 to
        2147483647.");
```

```
        }
        return number;
    }
```

The method calls the `Integer.parseInt()` method first. If the `String` contains any invalid characters, a `NumberFormatException` will be thrown at this point and the rest of the method will be skipped. Remember that exceptions are passed back to whatever code called this method, so the exception can be caught at that point.

If `numString` does contain a valid integer format, we must now test it to see if it lies in the correct range for an `int`. We check the first character to see if it is a minus sign, if so it is removed by copying the substring of `numString` from position 1 onwards into the local `String` variable `testString`. The largest negative `int` is defined as `refString`. If `numString` represents a positive integer, it can be used directly.

The final `if` statement tests for overflow. If `testString` contains more than 10 digits, or if it contains exactly 10 digits but is a number larger than that stored in `refString`, overflow has occurred, and we throw an `IntegerOverflow-Exception`. Note that we have used the `String` method `compareTo()` to do the comparison. This method returns 0 if the two `Strings` are the same, a negative number if `testString` is lexicographically less than `refString`, and a positive number for the opposite relationship. 'Lexicographical order' means essentially alphabetical order, except that `Strings` are arranged using the entire ASCII character set as the alphabet. Since the ASCII codes for the digits 0–9 occur in ascending order, a lexicographical comparison of two digit strings of the same length is the same as a numerical comparison.

4.3.4 CATCHING BASE AND DERIVED EXCEPTIONS

If there is more than one `catch` clause following a `try` block, each `catch` clause is tried, in order, until either a clause that catches the type of thrown exception is found, or there are no more `catch` clauses. This behavior can be combined with another property of the `catch` statement to provide 'catchall' `catch` statements.

A `catch` statement that is defined to watch for a particular exception class, will also catch all exceptions of classes derived from that class. Suppose, for example, that we defined several specialist exceptions, all of which are derived from `RuntimeException`, as `IntegerOverflowException` was above. We can include a `catch` clause for each of these specialist exceptions, and after all of the specialist `catches`, we can include a `catch` that catches any `Runtime-Exception`. Any exception that is an instance of either `RuntimeException` itself, or any class derived from `RuntimeException` that wasn't caught by one of the specialist `catch` clauses, will be picked up by this final `catch` statement.

Note that it is a syntax error to place a `catch` statement for a more general class of exceptions *before* a `catch` statement for an exception derived from that general class. This is because the second `catch` statement would never be executed.

As an example, let us define a specialist exception that is thrown specifically for division by zero. Such a class is a special case of the `ArithmeticException` class, so we derive our new exception from that:

```
import java.lang.ArithmeticException;

class DivideByZeroException extends
    ArithmeticException
{
    DivideByZeroException(String message)
    {
        super(message);
    }

    DivideByZeroException()
    {
        super();
    }
}
```

Again, this new exception is identical to an `ArithmeticException`, but provides more flexibility in the interpretation of exceptions. If we now have a `try` block that contains some code that may throw either a `DivideByZero-Exception` or some other, more general, type of `ArithmeticException`, we could include the following two `catch` clauses after the `try` block.

```
catch (DivideByZeroException exception) {
    showStatus(exception.toString());
} catch (ArithmeticException exception) {
    showStatus(exception.toString()
        + "Miscellaneous exception.");
}
```

The first `catch` statement will catch divisions by zero, and the second will catch all other `ArithmeticExceptions`. Reversing the order of the two `catch` statements would produce a syntax error, since catching `Arithmetic-Exceptions` before `DivideByZeroExceptions` would catch the `DivideBy-ZeroExceptions` in the first `catch`, leaving nothing for the second `catch` to do.

4.3.5 MORE GENERAL EXCEPTION CLASSES

The new exception classes that we have derived so far have been direct copies of their superclasses; all we did was inherit the superclass, and provide a couple of constructors that did nothing more than call the `super()` method to invoke the base class constructor.

However, a new exception class can contain as much functionality as any other class. In particular, it provides a mechanism for passing as much information as necessary about the nature of the exception back to the `catch` statement that handles the exception.

As an example, let us expand the `ArrayIndexOutOfBoundsException` so that it tells us not only that an exception occurred, but also what value of the array index caused the exception. The new exception class is as follows.

```java
import java.lang.ArrayIndexOutOfBoundsException;

class ArrayIndexException
   extends ArrayIndexOutOfBoundsException
{

   private int errorIndex;

   ArrayIndexException(int index)
   {
      super();
      errorIndex = index;
   }

   ArrayIndexException(int index, String message)
   {
      super(message);
      errorIndex = index;
   }

   public int getErrorIndex()
   {
      return errorIndex;
   }
}
```

The `ArrayIndexException` class contains a `private` field for storing the value of the array index that caused the exception. The two constructors both require this value to be supplied; other than that, they are the same as the usual constructors for an exception class in that they call the two forms of the super-class constructor. Finally, there is a method `getErrorIndex()` which returns the value of the array index.

Rather than relying on Java to throw an `ArrayIndexOutOfBounds-Exception` on its own, we can provide a special method which tests an array index to see if it is within the bounds for a particular array. If not, we can throw an `ArrayIndexException`, which includes the offending array index. For example, assuming we have defined an array called `numArray` earlier in the code, the following method tests the parameter `number` to see if it is a valid array index.

```java
   private void checkArrayIndex(int number)
```

```
    {
      if (number < 0 || number >= numArray.length)
        throw new ArrayIndexException(number);
    }
```

Note that we have used the built-in array parameter `length` which gives the number of elements in an array.

A `catch` statement which catches an `ArrayIndexException` can make use of this extra class method to display the array index as part of the error message. For example:

```
    catch (ArrayIndexException exception) {
      showStatus("The array index " +
        exception.getErrorIndex() +
        " is too large.");
    }
```

If the array contained 10 elements, and an attempt was made to access element 10 (remember the elements are numbered 0–9), the `catch` statement would display the message "The array index 10 is too large." in the status bar.

4.3.6 AN EXPANDED EXAMPLE

To see how all the variations on the exception theme are used in a complete applet, we present an expanded version of the applet from the last section. The components and layout of the applet are the same as before, so we present only the `action()` method and other auxiliary methods.

```
    public boolean action(Event event, Object object)
    {
      if (event.target == addButton) {
        try {
          int num1 = stringToInt(num1Field.getText());
          int num2 = stringToInt(num2Field.getText());
          if (num2 == 0)
            throw new DivideByZeroException
              ("Denominator is zero.");
          int quotient = num1 / num2;
          showStatus(num1 + "/" + num2 + " = "
            + quotient);
          addToArray(quotient);
        }
        catch (IntegerOverflowException exception) {
          showStatus(exception.toString());
        } catch (DivideByZeroException exception) {
          showStatus(exception.toString());
        } catch (ArithmeticException exception) {
          showStatus(exception.toString() +
```

```
                  "Miscellaneous exception.");
            } catch (NumberFormatException exception) {
               showStatus("Enter integers only.");
            } catch (ArrayIndexException exception) {
               showStatus("The array index " +
                  exception.getErrorIndex() +
                  " is too large.");
            }
      } else if (event.target == searchButton) {
         try {
            int searchNum =
               stringToInt(searchField.getText());
            showStatus(searchArray(searchNum) ? "Found." :
               "Not found.");
         }
         catch (IntegerOverflowException exception) {
            showStatus(exception.toString());
         } catch (NumberFormatException exception) {
            showStatus("Enter an integer in search box.");
         }
      }
   }
   return true;
}


private void addToArray(int number)
{
   if (numStored < 0 || numStored >= numArray.length)
      throw new ArrayIndexException(numStored);
   numArray[numStored] = number;
   ++numStored;
}


private boolean searchArray(int number)
{
   for (int index = 0; index < numStored; ++index)
      if (numArray[index] == number)
         return true;
   return false;
}


private int stringToInt(String numString)
{
   String testString;
   String refString;

   int number = Integer.parseInt(numString);
   if (numString.charAt(0) == '-') {
      testString = numString.substring(1);
      refString = new String("2147483648");
```

```
        } else {
          testString = numString;
          refString = new String("2147483647");
        }
        if (testString.length() > 10 ||
          (testString.length() == 10 &&
          testString.compareTo(refString) > 0)) {
            throw new IntegerOverflowException
              ("Integers must be in the range -2147483648
                to 2147483647.");
        }

      return number;
    }
```

We have replaced the direct calls to `Integer.parseInt()` by calls to the method `stringToInt()`, which we discussed above. This method may throw two exceptions: a `NumberFormatException` (one of the Java built-in exceptions) and the user-defined `IntegerOverflowException`.

If both numbers are in the correct format and range, we then test to see if num2 is zero. If so, we throw a `DivideByZeroException` directly inside the `try` block. If num2 is not zero, we calculate the quotient and display the result in the status bar.

Finally, we attempt to store the quotient in the array. The new version of the `addToArray()` method (discussed below) may throw our new user-defined `ArrayIndexException`.

Following the `try` block, we include a list of `catch` statements that check for all the types of exception that are likely to happen in that block. The `try` block and associated `catch` statements for the `searchButton` action are modified in a similar way.

The new version of the `addToArray()` method shows how an `Array-IndexException` can be thrown, including the array index that caused the problem. A test is made to see if the next available storage location `numStored` is within the bounds of the array. If not, a new `ArrayIndexException` is thrown and the current value of `numStored` is passed to the constructor for this exception. From there, it makes its way back to the `catch` statement in the `action()` method and gets displayed in the status bar.

The `searchArray()` method is the same as before, and the `stringToInt()` method was discussed earlier.

4.4 Exercises

1   Write a Java applet or application which acts as a simple calculator. The applet should contain a `TextField` into which the first number is typed, a `Choice` containing the four arithmetic operators (+, −, *, /), a second `TextField`

into which the second number is entered, a `Button` which, when pressed, calculates the answer, and a `Label` which displays the answer.

The `handleEvent()` method for this applet should extract the `Strings` from the two `TextFields` and convert them floats, then examine the `Choice` object to see which operator has been chosen and calculate the result. Enclose all this code in a `try` block, and `catch` only the most general `Exception` class. (Because of the way Java handles inheritance in a `catch`, this will catch *all* exceptions.) Use either the `showStatus()` method or the `toString()` method of the `Exception` class to display the message produced by the caught `Exception` (as a message in the status bar, or as another `Label` within the applet, respectively).

Test your applet by entering various erroneous `Strings` in the two `TextFields`. Try various incorrectly formatted `Strings` and division by zero. Take note of the information provided by the default exception handler you are using.

2   Enhance the program from question 1 by taking note of the different types of `Exception` that your program can generate. Provide a separate `catch` clause for each type of `Exception`, and print out a more informative message which better describes the specific `Exception` being handled.

3   Although the program from question 2 provides a better user interface, it could be improved by, for example, stating which of the two `TextFields` is causing the `Exception`, and reproducing the offending `String` in the error message. Write your own exception class (or classes), derived from the appropriate built-in exception class, which contain data fields for the number of the `TextField` (1 or 2) causing the problem, and for the `String` which caused the exception to be thrown. Modify the set of `catch` clauses so that it catches your new exceptions, and provide a 'catch-all' `catch` clause at the end to pick up any exceptions you haven't explicitly allowed for.

4   Add two more operations to the `Choice` object in the applet: a 'square root' and a 'logarithm'. Use the library methods in the `Math` class to implement these operations by calculating the square root or logarithm of the number in the *first* `TextField`. (If you haven't used logarithms before, see Section 10.6 for a description of them.) From the documentation for the `Math` class, you will see that both the `log()` method and the `sqrt()` method may throw an `ArithmeticException`. The `sqrt()` method will throw this exception if its argument is strictly negative (that is, less than but *not* equal to zero); the `log()` method will throw an exception if its argument is either negative or zero.

Define two specialized exception classes, both derived from `Arithmetic-Exception`, called `LogException` and `SqrtException`. The first exception should be thrown when the user attempts to calculate the logarithm of a number that is either zero or negative; the second when the user attempts to calculate the square root of a strictly negative number. Both exception classes should be capable of identifying the exact cause of the error, and of providing an informative error message that includes the number that caused the problem. Add tests for these conditions to your applet, and add `catch` clauses which produce user-friendly error messages. Note that these exceptions should be caught *after* any other exceptions that are thrown due to a `String` containing an invalid number format.

CHAPTER 5

GRAPHICS AND ANIMATION

5.1 The graphics context

Up to now, all the graphics that we have used in writing Java applets have been obtained from the `java.awt` package, and have consisted of pre-defined objects such as push-buttons, text boxes, and so on. The procedure for using these graphical objects has been fairly simple: `import` the `java.awt` classes needed to define the objects, declare and create them, add them to the layout manager, and, if necessary, provide some code to handle any events that they generate.

The components in the `java.awt` package are, of course, just pre-written objects using more primitive graphics commands, such as drawing lines and polygons, drawing text strings, changing colors, and so on. Most GUI programming packages provide the programmer with tools for drawing more primitive graphics objects, and Java is no exception. The rules for using primitive graphics commands in Java are a bit different, however, from those for using the GUI components in the `java.awt` package.

Once you have defined the applet size (by giving its dimensions in the HTML file) or the application size (by giving the size of its enclosing `Frame`), it is possible to draw directly onto the background of the applet or application. It is also possible to use a special `java.awt` component called a *canvas* on which graphics may be drawn. A canvas may be added to a layout manager, just like any other GUI component, so that the drawing area may be restricted to a part of the applet.

Wherever you wish to draw the graphics in an applet, the technique for doing so requires at least a nodding acquaintance with the ideas of the *graphics context* and the `Graphics` class.

A graphics context is an abstract term meaning 'a facility by which drawing may be done on the screen'. All languages that allow graphics to be drawn have a graphics context, although some languages (such as Visual Basic) hide this from the programmer more than others (such as Java). An analogy may be drawn between the graphics context for drawing graphics and the layout manager for positioning GUI components. In Java, all GUI components must be added (using the `add()` method) to a layout manager before they can be displayed on the screen. Similarly, all graphics actions (such as drawing lines or polygons) must be 'added' to the graphics context before they can be seen on the screen.

The main difference between adding components to a layout manager and adding graphics objects to a graphics context, is that GUI components are instances of Java classes from the `java.awt` package, while graphics objects, such as lines, text strings, and so on, are *not* instances of a class. Drawing a line, for example, requires calling a method which draws the line, not creating a `Line` object and adding it to the graphics context.

The interface between the programmer and the graphics context is provided by an abstract Java class called `Graphics`. An *abstract class* in Java is a class that provides declarations of data fields and methods, but not definitions for the methods. Abstract classes may only be used as base classes for other classes derived from them, and these derived classes must provide definitions for all methods that are declared in the abstract base class.

The `Graphics` class provides declarations for all the methods that allow drawing of graphics objects. The fact that the `Graphics` class is abstract may worry you somewhat – does this mean that you have to provide your own method definitions for doing all the drawing operations? The answer, fortunately, is 'no' – the `Graphics` class works in a special way.

To see why the `Graphics` class is implemented in this seemingly perverse way, we need to remember that one of the goals of the designers of Java was to write a language which is truly portable across different computer platforms. This means that a Java program, including all its graphics, may be written on any type of machine (for example, a Windows-based PC, a UNIX workstation, or a Macintosh) and, *without any further modification*, be runnable on any other type of computer which supports Java.

If you have ever done any graphics programming in languages other than Java, you will know just how challenging this goal is. For example, a program written in, say, C or C++ that runs on a Microsoft Windows machine will not run on any other type of machine. Converting Windows programs to run on, say, UNIX/X Windows machines (or *vice versa*) is a very time-consuming task, and often a fully compatible port is never achieved.

The portability of Java is achieved by providing built-in conversions for all graphics, so that a command to draw a line is executed at run time by reading the byte code in the `.class` file produced by the Java compiler and interpreting the byte commands in that file in terms of whatever graphics system is supported by the machine on which the program is running. That is, the work in creating the graphics is done by the platform-specific Java implementation.

All of this explains why the `Graphics` class is implemented as an abstract class. Each different computer system on which the Java applet will run provides its own, platform-dependent version of the `Graphics` class, which is derived from the abstract class, and provides all the platform-specific definitions of all the methods. (So you don't need to write your own versions of all the methods!)

Having said all that, you must be warned that the 'total portability' feature of Java isn't quite all it's cracked up to be. You will probably find that an applet written on one computer doesn't look quite the same on another, or even with two different browsers on the same computer. Fonts and colors often do not port very well between machines. If you are planning on writing an applet which is to be used on a wide variety of platforms (for example, an applet that will be placed on a web page that is available around the world), it is a good idea to be fairly conservative in your use of exotic fonts or non-standard colors.

The `paint()`, `update()`, and `repaint()` methods   5.2

Java's `applet` class contains three methods that are common in programs using graphics.

The `paint()` method, as its name implies, paints the applet with whatever graphics commands it contains. It is called whenever an applet starts up, in order to paint the graphics into the applet for its first appearance on screen. The default version of `paint()`, of course, doesn't draw anything, so if you want graphics to appear in your applet, you need to provide an overridden version of `paint()`. More on this a bit later.

The default version of the `update()` method clears the applet and then calls the `paint()` method. By 'clears the applet', we mean that it paints the applet with its own background color, wiping out any graphics that had been drawn on it. Thus the `update()` method provides a way of changing the graphics in an applet after the applet has started running.

The default version of the `repaint()` method just calls the `update()` method. An obvious question, therefore, is why do we have two methods which both essentially just update the applet? The answer is that the `update()` method requires the graphics context (in the form of a `Graphics` object) as an argument, while the `repaint()` method requires no arguments. Therefore, calling `repaint()` is the easier of the two ways to update the applet, and is the preferred method in practice.

In summary, if we want any graphics to appear in an applet, we *must* override the `paint()` method, since that is ultimately where all the drawing is done. The default versions of `update()` and `repaint()` are adequate for most purposes, and it is more usual to update the graphics in an applet by calling `repaint()`.

5.3 The `Graphics` class – a simple example

As mentioned earlier, the interface between the programmer and the graphics context is provided by the `Graphics` class. We will present a simple example of an applet which uses the `Graphics` class to draw a few objects on the screen.

The code is as follows:

```
import java.applet.Applet;
import java.awt.Graphics;

public class SimpleGraphics extends Applet
{
  public void paint(Graphics g)
  {
    g.drawString("This is a simple example.",
      20, 100);
    g.drawLine(20, 110, 300, 110);
    g.drawRect(15, 80, 300, 50);
  }
}
```

This produces an underlined text string surrounded by a box (Fig 5.1).

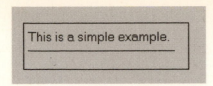

This is a simple example.

Figure 5.1

Note that if you run this applet on your own computer, you may find that the length of the text string relative to the line and the box varies – this is one of the portability problems referred to earlier.

Now for a closer look at the code which produces this applet. First, note that we must import the `java.awt.Graphics` class (or just import `java.awt.*`), since the `Graphics` class is part of the `java.awt` package. The applet itself has only the `paint()` method – there is no initialization to perform apart from drawing the graphics, so we don't need an `init()` method.

The `paint()` method given in this applet is an overridden version of the default `paint()` method in the `Applet` class, which as we mentioned before, does nothing. The `paint()` method takes a single `Graphics` object as its argument. Since `paint()` is called automatically by Java whenever the applet is initialized, we don't need to worry about obtaining this `Graphics` object – it is provided by the system and passed to the `paint()` method for us.

The three statements inside the `paint()` method illustrate how the `Graphics` object is used to draw onto an applet. You should consult the Java documentation to see a full list of the methods in the `Graphics` class. We first draw a text string using the `drawString()` method. Its three arguments are the `String` to be drawn, and the *x* and *y* coordinates (in pixels) at which the `String` should start. Note that all *x* coordinates are measured from the left edge of the applet towards the right, and all *y* coordinates are measured from the top edge of the applet towards the bottom. Thus, the coordinates *x* = 10 and *y* = 100 mean to start 10 pixels from the left border and 100 pixels from the top border.

The `drawLine()` method draws a one-pixel wide line. The first two arguments are the *x* and *y* coordinates of the start point, and the last two arguments are the *x* and *y* coordinates of the end point of the line.

The `drawRect()` method draws a rectangle with a one-pixel wide outline. Here, the first two arguments are the *x* and *y* coordinates of the upper-left corner of the rectangle, and the last two arguments are the width and height of the rectangle.

The `Graphics` class supports many other methods, the use of which is fairly obvious from consulting the Java documentation. There are methods for drawing ovals, 'round' rectangles (rectangles with rounded corners), 3D rectangles (rectangles with raised edges), polygons, and arcs. There are also methods for drawing filled versions of all these objects, where the interior of the object is filled with the current color.

Although the `Graphics` class contains most of the basic drawing methods you need to create graphics, if you are used to other graphics packages you may be a bit disappointed by the absence of some more advanced features. For example, there is no method in the `Graphics` class to draw thick lines, dashed or dotted lines, or lines with arrows on the end. If you want to draw such lines, you need to write your own methods that do this. For example, to draw a line two pixels wide, you must draw two one-pixel wide lines beside each other. Most likely, future versions of Java will include these more advanced features.

5.4 Colors

Java offers a simple way to control the color of a feature drawn using a `Graphics` object. The `Color` class is provided for handling of colors.* There are two ways to specify colors in Java – one of the `static` predefined colors provided in the `Color` class may be used, or a color may be specified using its RGB (red–green–blue) value.

If you are unfamiliar with the RGB theory of color, have a close look at the picture tube on your television set (assuming, of course, that it is a color TV!) or computer screen. If you use a magnifying glass, you will see that the screen is covered with small dots arranged in triplets, where each triplet contains a red, green and blue dot. All colors that you see on a TV or computer screen are composed by mixing these three so-called *primary* colors in varying intensities.† Depending on the resolution of your TV or computer screen, anything from around 16 up to millions of different colors may be produced by using varying intensities of the red, green and blue pixels. The Java `Color` class allows 256 different intensities (ranging from 0 to 255) for each of the R, G and B pixels, for a total of 256^3 = 16,777,216 different colors.

First, let us consider the pre-defined `static` colors provided in the `Color` class (Table 5.1). Non-American readers are again cautioned that the American spelling of 'gray' (not the British 'grey') must be used.

The RGB values for these basic colors should give you a good starting point for creating your own shades, by varying the color that is closest to the one you want.

Let us modify the simple applet in the last section by painting each of its three objects in a different color.

```
import java.applet.Applet;
import java.awt.*;
```

* Readers outside the USA are cautioned that the American spelling of 'color' must be used – trying to refer to a `Colour` class will cause compiler errors.

† If you are an artist, you may know that the three primary colors used in painting are red, yellow (not green), and blue. When a color is created by reflection of light (as in a painting) the RYB system is used; when by projection of light (as in a TV) the RGB system is used.

TABLE 5.1.

Color constant	RGB value
white	255, 255, 255
black	0, 0, 0
red	255, 0, 0
green	0, 255, 0
blue	0, 0, 255
yellow	255, 255, 0
magenta (purple)	255, 0, 255
cyan (light blue)	0, 255, 255
gray	128, 128, 128
lightGray	192, 192, 192
darkGray	64, 64, 64
orange	255, 200, 0
pink	255, 175, 175

```
public class SimpleGraphics extends Applet
{
   public void paint(Graphics g)
   {
      g.setColor(Color.red);
      g.drawString("This is a simple example.",
         20, 100);
      g.setColor(new Color(243, 10, 145));
      g.drawLine(20, 110, 175, 110);
      g.setColor(new Color((float)0.0, (float)1.0,
         (float)0.7));
      g.drawRect(15, 80, 175, 50);
   }
}
```

We use the setColor() method of the Graphics class to set the color for all drawing operations that follow it, up until the next setColor() operation. The setColor() method requires a Color object as its argument, but there are three ways this Color can be specified.

The first call to setColor() uses one of the static colors provided in the Color class to set the color to 'red', so that the text string is drawn in red. The second call to setColor() creates a new Color object using one of the Color constructors. This constructor expects three int arguments, each of which must be in the range from 0 to 255. The RGB values specified here (243, 10, 145) produce a dull purple color.

The final call to setColor() takes three float arguments. In this case, each float must lie in the range from 0.0 to 1.0. A value of 0.0 means that that color component should be absent, while a value of 1.0 means that that component should be present to its maximum extent (a value of 255 if we were using an int to specify the color). Using `floats` to construct a color is often more convenient, since you can specify each of the red, green and blue components as a fraction of its maximum intensity. The values given in the example (0.0, 1.0, 0.7) indicate an absence of red, full intensity for green, and 70% intensity for blue, which produces a turquoise color. Note that, if you specify a color using `float` constants, as we have here, you must explicitly cast the constants to be `floats`, since a bare constant such as 0.7 is interpreted by the Java compiler as a `double`.

There are other color-related methods in both the `Color` class and the `Graphics` class, so the user is, as usual, advised to consult the Java documentation for more details.

5.5 Fonts

5.5.1 SPECIFYING FONTS

As with colors, Java makes it quite simple to specify the font in which text will be drawn to the screen. Fonts are specified using the `Font` class.

If you have used a word processor or desktop publishing system, you will no doubt be familiar with many different fonts. In principle, a Java applet is capable of displaying any font available on your computer, but when you are designing applets, you should keep in mind that many computers will not have as many fonts installed as you may have. Therefore, it is a good idea to restrict the fonts you use to those that are guaranteed to be present in all Java installations. These are:

- `TimesRoman` – originally the font used to publish London's *Times* newspaper, it is now one of the most common proportional spacing (meaning that the horizontal space allocated to each letter varies), serifed (a *serif* is a small line attached to the end of a stroke in a character – the main font used to write this book is a serifed font) fonts.
- `Courier` – a constant spacing font (one where each character takes up the same horizontal space) which resembles many typewriter fonts. `This sentence is written in Courier.`
- `Helvetica` – a proportional-spacing, sans-serif font This sentence is written in Helvetica. (Sometimes known as `Arial`).
- `Dialog` and `DialogInput` – the font used in dialog boxes.

In addition to these basic font styles, each font can also be drawn in plain or **bold**, and normal, *italic*, or ***bold italic*** style. Fonts may also be drawn in a wide variety of sizes, or *points*, to use the technical term for the size of a font.

In order to set the font for a text string, an object of the `Font` class must be declared and passed to the `setFont()` method of the `Graphics` class. The `Font` constructor requires three arguments: a `String` containing the name of the font, an `int` specifying the font's style (plain, bold, etc.) and a final `int` giving the font's point size.

A simple applet demonstrating the use of the `Font` class is as follows.

```
import java.applet.Applet;
import java.awt.*;

public class FontDemo extends Applet
{
   public void paint(Graphics g)
   {
      g.setFont(new Font("TimesRoman", Font.BOLD, 14));
      g.drawString("This is TimesRoman, BOLD, 14 pt.",
         20, 100);
      g.setFont(new Font("Helvetica", Font.ITALIC, 14));
      g.drawString("This is Helvetica, ITALIC, 14 pt.",
         20, 150);
      g.setFont(new Font("Courier", Font.PLAIN, 14));
      g.drawString("This is Courier, PLAIN, 14 pt.", 20,
         200);
      g.setFont(new Font("Dialog", Font.BOLD, 14));
      g.drawString("This is Dialog, BOLD, 14 pt.", 20,
         250);
      g.setFont(new Font("DialogInput", Font.BOLD, 36));
      g.drawString("DialogInput, BOLD, 36 pt.", 20, 300);
      g.setFont(new Font("TimesRoman", Font.BOLD +
         Font.ITALIC, 20));
      g.drawString("This is TimesRoman, BOLD + ITALIC, 20
         pt.", 20, 350);
   }
}
```

This applet produces the output shown in Fig. 5.2.

Note that the font style is specified by using one of the `static` values from the `Font` class. For example, to specify a bold style, the second argument of the `Font` constructor is `Font.BOLD`. Combining two or three styles is possible by simply adding together the corresponding values. For example, the last line drawn by the applet combines the bold and italic styles for a Times Roman font.

The font size is specified, in points, by the third argument to the `Font` constructor. As a rough guide to point sizes, most books and newspapers are printed in 10 or 12 point type. Anything smaller than 10 point is usually hard to read and should not be used excessively, although small text has its place for things like superscripts, subscripts, and other labels. It is also important to remember that specifying a particular point size for a font does *not* guarantee that the text will appear the same size on all computer screens. Even on machines running on the same platform, screens with different resolutions will display applets at different sizes. Viewing an applet on two different platforms (for example, a Windows-based PC and a UNIX workstation) may produce quite different text sizes for the same font size, even relative to other graphics objects (such as lines and rectangles) within the same applet.

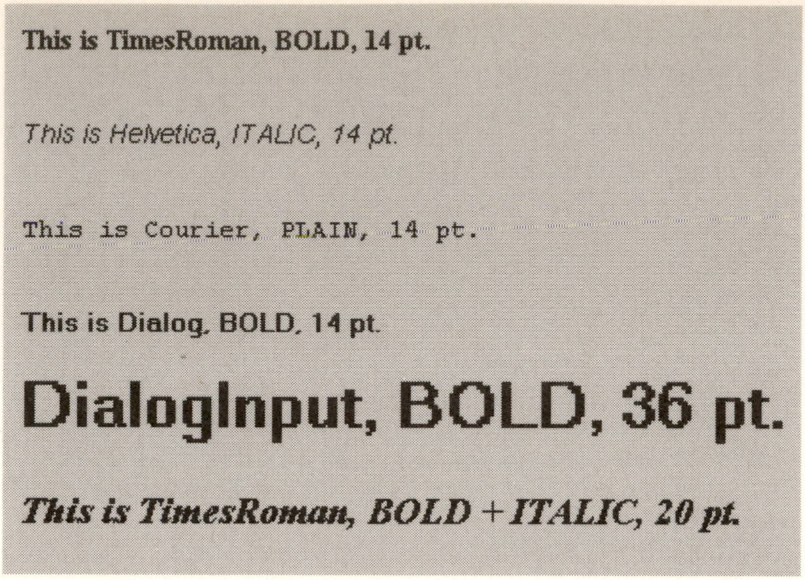

This is TimesRoman, BOLD, 14 pt.
This is Helvetica, ITALIC, 14 pt.
This is Courier, PLAIN, 14 pt.
This is Dialog, BOLD, 14 pt.
DialogInput, BOLD, 36 pt.
This is TimesRoman, BOLD + ITALIC, 20 pt.

Figure 5.2.

5.5.2 FONT METRICS

When drawing text on an applet, it is often necessary to position the text relative to other graphics objects fairly precisely. Java offers a reasonable degree of control over the positioning of text with the methods in the `FontMetrics` class. In order to understand these methods, we need to learn a bit of printing terminology (see Fig. 5.3).

ascent
descent
baseline
abg
fyi
leading
height

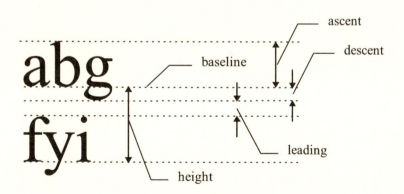

Figure 5.3.

Fig. 5.3 shows two lines of text. Recall that the *x* and *y* coordinates required in the `drawString()` method of the `Graphics` class specify the starting point for the *baseline* of the text string to be drawn. If you cast your mind back to primary school when you were learning how to print the letters of the alphabet, you probably practiced your printing using a lined notebook. You were taught that most letters 'sat on the line', but some letters (such as 'g', 'p', 'y', and so on) had parts that extended below the line. From Fig. 5.3, we see that the baseline is the horizontal line which marks the bottom of most of the letters in the Roman alphabet (except for those which drop below the baseline, such as g, p, etc.).

The distance between two adjacent baselines on a page of text is called the *height* of the font. Note that the height includes not only the actual height of the characters themselves, but also a small gap between the lines where no printing occurs. This gap is called the *leading* (pronounced 'ledding', not 'leeding', since it refers to the thin strip of lead that printers inserted between lines of type to create the gap).

The final two measurements are the *ascent* and *descent* of the font. The ascent is the vertical distance from the baseline to the top of the tallest character. In the Roman alphabet, all upper case letters and some lower case letters, such as b, d, f, and so on, have a vertical size equal to the ascent. Other lower case letters, such as a, c, e, and so on, have a vertical size that is smaller than the ascent, but no special name is attached to this size.

The descent of a font is the vertical distance from the baseline to the bottom of the characters that extend below the baseline, such as g, j, p, q, and y.

Java's `FontMetrics` class allows the height, leading, ascent, and descent to be found for a `Font` object. This information is useful when graphics objects must be placed precisely relative to some text. For example, if we want to underline some text, we might wish the underline to appear exactly at the location of the descent of the font.

The following applet shows an example of the use of the `FontMetrics` class, together with a few other useful methods dealing with fonts.

```
import java.applet.Applet;
import java.awt.*;

public class FontMetricsDemo extends Applet
{
   public void paint(Graphics g)
   {
      g.setFont(new Font("TimesRoman", Font.BOLD, 14));
      Font currentFont = g.getFont();
      FontMetrics currentFontMetrics =
         g.getFontMetrics(currentFont);
      int ascent = currentFontMetrics.getAscent();
      int descent = currentFontMetrics.getDescent();
      int leading = currentFontMetrics.getLeading();
      int height = currentFontMetrics.getHeight();
```

```
String fonts[] =
   Toolkit.getDefaultToolkit().getFontList();

g.drawString("Font loaded:", 10, 25);
g.drawRect(5, 25 - ascent - leading,
   currentFontMetrics.stringWidth("Fonts loaded:") +
   10, height);
g.drawString(currentFont.toString(), 10, 50);
g.drawString("Ascent: " + ascent, 10, 75);
g.drawString("Descent: " + descent, 10, 100);
g.drawString("Leading: " + leading, 10, 125);
g.drawString("Height: " + height, 10, 150);

g.drawString("Fonts available:", 10, 175);
g.drawRect(5, 175 - ascent - leading,
   currentFontMetrics.stringWidth("Fonts
   available:") + 10, height);

for (int fontNum = 0; fontNum < fonts.length;
   ++fontNum)
   g.drawString(fonts[fontNum], 10, 200 +
   fontNum*25);
   }
}
```

This applet produces the result shown in Fig. 5.4. Some information on the font being used is drawn to the screen, and this information is used to draw a neat box around two of the labels.

After setting the font to be Times Roman, bold, and 14 point, we use the `getFont()` method of the `Graphics` class to obtain a `Font` object containing this font. We could, of course, have achieved the same result by saving the result of the call to the `Font` constructor in the `Font` object `currentFont`, but we wanted to show the use of the `getFont()` method.

Next, a `FontMetrics` object is created and initialized to the properties of `currentFont` by using the `getFontMetrics()` method of the `Graphics` class. The `currentFontMetrics` object is then used to obtain the ascent, descent, leading, and height of the font, using the corresponding methods from the `FontMetrics` class.

The next line uses a class we haven't mentioned so far: the `Toolkit` class. In most cases, you will not use the `Toolkit` class directly, since it is the abstract base class of the Java AWT, and most of its functions are implemented automatically for you by the Java installation on your machine. In this way, it works in much the same way as the `Graphics` class. However, in this case, we use the `getFontList()` method of the `Toolkit` class to obtain a list of the available fonts in the current Java installation. This may be useful, for example, if you use an exotic font in your applet and want to check to see if that font is available on another system. If it is, you can proceed to use it, otherwise you may wish to load

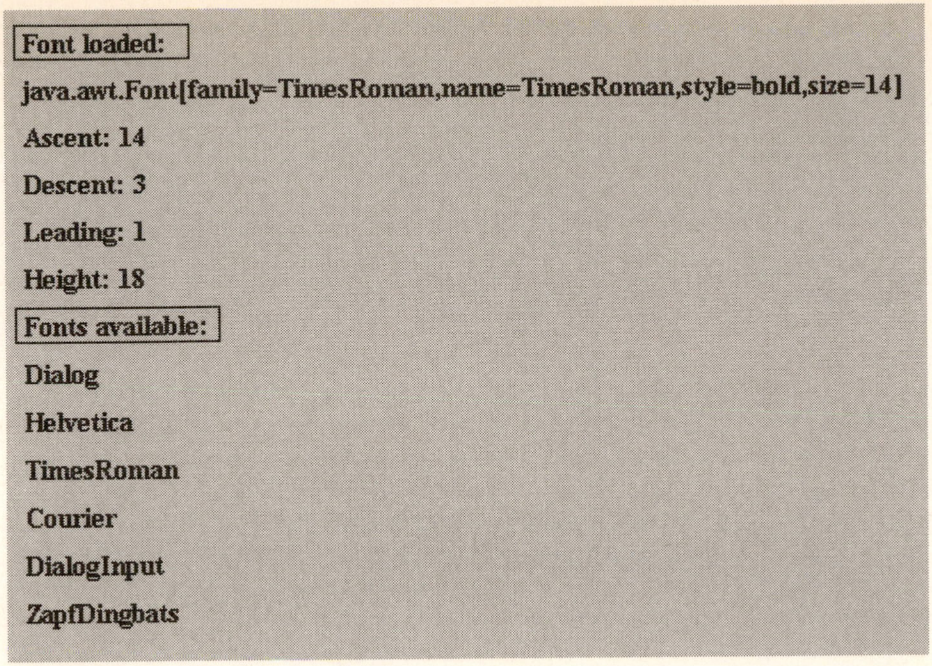

Font loaded:

java.awt.Font[family=TimesRoman,name=TimesRoman,style=bold,size=14]

Ascent: 14

Descent: 3

Leading: 1

Height: 18

Fonts available:

Dialog

Helvetica

TimesRoman

Courier

DialogInput

ZapfDingbats

Figure 5.4.

one of the ordinary fonts. The `getFontList()` method returns an array of `Strings` that contains a list of the font names.

After obtaining all the information, we proceed to draw it to the screen. The first string to be drawn is the label 'Font loaded:'. To highlight this label, we wish to draw a box around it. Rather than trying to guess what coordinates to use for the enclosing rectangle, we can calculate them directly by using the information from `currentFontMetrics`. The upper-left corner of the rectangle will be five pixels to the left of the starting point, and at the top of the leading strip above the string. Since the string was drawn starting at a *y* coordinate of 25, this is the level of the baseline. To find the correct place for the top edge of the rectangle, we need to move upwards from the baseline by a number of pixels equal to the ascent plus the leading. Since the *y* coordinate is measured from top to bottom, this means that we must *subtract* that amount from the *y* coordinate for the baseline.

To calculate the width of the rectangle, we can make use of the `stringWidth()` method of the `FontMetrics` class. This method requires a `String` argument, and returns the width, in pixels, of that `String` when it is drawn in the current font. We add 10 pixels to this value to give the box a border of five pixels at each side. Finally, the height of the rectangle is just the height of the font, since that will draw the lower edge of the rectangle at a *y* coordinate of baseline + descent.

The current font is written out using the `toString()` method. This method is provided in the `Object` class, which is the base class for *all* Java classes. Therefore, any Java object has a `String` representation which may be drawn to the screen.

The remainder of the applet uses the same techniques to write out the rest of the information. As usual, the reader is referred to the Java documentation to find out more information on other methods available in the `FontMetrics` class.

5.6 Canvases

The `Canvas` class is a member of the Java AWT which we have not yet considered. A `Canvas` is essentially what its name implies: a blank surface which can be used for drawing. The advantages of using a `Canvas` over just drawing directly onto the background of an applet are twofold. First, a `Canvas` is a GUI component and can be positioned within an applet by using a layout manager. Therefore, two or more `Canvases` can be used within a single applet.

Secondly, all components drawn onto a `Canvas` are automatically clipped at the boundaries of the `Canvas`. It is therefore easy to guarantee that drawings will not overlap other GUI components within an applet.

Each `Canvas` has its own graphics context, which is independent of the graphics context for the applet as a whole. It is therefore still possible to draw onto the applet's background even if the applet contains a `Canvas`. A `Canvas` has its own `paint()` method which, just as with the `paint()` method for an applet, does nothing in its default form. In order for a `Canvas` to actually show anything, therefore, it must be inherited by a user-defined class.

The following applet illustrates the principles of using a `Canvas`.

```
import java.applet.Applet;
import java.awt.*;

public class CanvasDemo extends Applet
{
   MyCanvas drawingArea = new MyCanvas();

   public void init()
   {
      drawingArea.resize(200, 200);
      add(drawingArea);
   }

   public void paint(Graphics g)
   {
      g.drawLine(0, 100, 500, 100);
   }
}
```

```
class MyCanvas extends Canvas
{
  MyCanvas()
  {
    super();
    setBackground(Color.white);
  }

  public void paint(Graphics canvasG)
  {
    canvasG.drawLine(0, 50, 500, 50);
  }
}
```

First, note the class `MyCanvas`, which extends the `Canvas` class. As mentioned above, attempting to use a `Canvas` on its own is pointless, since its `paint()` method does nothing, so it will be invisible on screen.

The `MyCanvas` class contains a constructor which calls the `Canvas` class constructor first (via the call to the `super()` method). Then, the background color of `MyCanvas` is set to white. The `paint()` method draws a horizontal line 50 pixels down from the top border.

The `CanvasDemo` class defines the applet which tests a `MyCanvas` object. The `init()` method resizes the canvas to be a 200 by 200 pixel square, and then adds it to the default layout. The `paint()` method of the `CanvasDemo` class draws a horizontal line 100 pixels down from the applet's top edge.

The result of running this applet is shown in Fig 5.5.

Figure 5.5.

Although the result looks rather boring, it illustrates some important points. First, as claimed above, the graphics contexts of `MyCanvas` and its parent applet are independent. The line drawn on the canvas is clipped at the edges of the canvas so it does not extend onto the background applet. Secondly, the line drawn on the applet passes 'underneath' the canvas.

Although a `Canvas` can be used to display non-interactive graphics within an applet, it is probably more useful as a mini-window in which graphics can be displayed in response to input from the user. The possibilities are, of course, limited only by the programmer's imagination, but to illustrate the point, we will modify the applet above by adding a push-button to the main applet. When the user presses the button, another line is drawn inside the canvas. The code follows.

```java
import java.applet.Applet;
import java.awt.*;

public class ButtonCanvas extends Applet
{
    MyCanvas drawingArea = new MyCanvas();
    Button addLineButton =
        new Button("Add a vertical line");

    public void init()
    {
        drawingArea.resize(200, 200);
        add(drawingArea);
        add(addLineButton);
    }

    public void paint(Graphics g)
    {
        g.drawLine(0, 100, 500, 100);
    }

    public boolean action(Event event, Object object)
    {
        if (event.target == addLineButton)
            drawingArea.addLine();
        return true;
    }
}

class MyCanvas extends Canvas
{
    boolean verticalLine;

    MyCanvas()
    {
        super();
        setBackground(Color.white);
        verticalLine = false;
```

```
      }

      public void paint(Graphics canvasG)
      {
         canvasG.drawLine(0, 50, 500, 50);
         if (verticalLine)
            canvasG.drawLine(50, 0, 50, 500);
      }

      public void addLine()
      {
         verticalLine = true;
         repaint();
      }
   }
```

The push-button is added to the applet and an `action()` method is added to the `ButtonCanvas` class. When the button is pushed, the `addLine()` method of the `MyCanvas` class is called.

Within the `MyCanvas` class, a boolean variable called `verticalLine` has been added. Inside the `paint()` method, the same horizontal line as in the previous applet is drawn, but the vertical line is drawn only if `verticalLine` is true. The `addLine()` method, which is called when the user presses the push-button, sets `verticalLine` to `true`, and then calls the `repaint()` method. Remember that `repaint()` first calls the `update()` method, which clears the canvas of all graphics, and then calls the `paint()` method. Since `verticalLine` is now `true`, both the horizontal and vertical lines are drawn.

Note that if we had written the `paint()` method as:

```
      public void paint(Graphics canvasG)
      {
         if (verticalLine)
            canvasG.drawLine(50, 0, 50, 500);
         else
            canvasG.drawLine(0, 50, 500, 50);
      }
```

then pushing the button would *erase the horizontal line* and then draw only the vertical line, due to the fact that the `update()` method erases all the graphics before calling the `paint()` method.

Apart from the differences between applets and canvases mentioned in this section, all graphical operations that can be applied to applets can also be applied to canvases.

5.7 Scrollbars

A `Scrollbar` is another GUI component that is part of the Java AWT. The standard scrollbar found in most window environments consists of three parts: the bar itself, a slider or movable button that slides along the bar, and two buttons, one at either end of the bar. Clicking on either end button usually moves the slider slowly towards the button that was clicked. Clicking within the bar, but not on either the slider or an end button, usually moves the slider towards the end of the bar that was clicked, but at a faster rate than by clicking an end button. (This action is sometimes called *paging*.) Finally, clicking and dragging the slider allows it to be positioned wherever the user desires.

A `Scrollbar` in Java acts in a similar way to any other AWT component. Its constructor allows the `Scrollbar`'s properties to be initialized. Clicking on various parts of the `Scrollbar` generates `Events`, which can be caught and acted on in the `handleEvent()` method, just as with any other component.

There are five parameters that can be specified when a `Scrollbar` is constructed. They are:

- `orientation` – this must be one of the constants `Scrollbar.VERTICAL` or `Scrollbar.HORIZONTAL`.
- `value` – this `int` specifies the initial value of the slider when the `Scrollbar` first appears on screen.
- `visible` – this `int` is the number of pixels occupied by the slider button. The value of `visible` depends on the application to which the scrollbar is being applied. If the scrollbar is controlling a document or an image, the size of the slider should indicate what fraction of the document or image is actually visible. If the scrollbar is used simply to select a single value from a range, the value of `visible` may be set to 0, in which case a default slider will be drawn. (Note that the `visible` parameter does *not* determine whether or not the `Scrollbar` is visible on screen, nor does it control the amount by which the slider moves when the scrollbar is paged.)
- `minimum` and `maximum` – these two `ints` specify the minimum and maximum values represented by the `Scrollbar`. The minimum value is represented when the slider is farthest up (in a vertical scrollbar) or farthest left (in a horizontal scrollbar).

Whether or not a `Scrollbar` is associated with another AWT component within the applet, a `Scrollbar` component is always treated as a separate entity in Java. Some built-in AWT components, such as multiple-line text boxes, have scrollbars attached to them automatically, but these are not `Scrollbar` components – they are an integral part of the component in which they appear, and no code need be written by the user to handle them. When a `Scrollbar` component is used, its association with any other AWT component must be explicitly programmed by the user.

To illustrate how `Scrollbars` are used, we present a Java version of a 'color chooser'. A color chooser is a GUI component that allows users to select a color by viewing a palette of available colors and selecting one with the mouse. Most GUI environments have some form of color chooser built in. The interface presented by the sample program is shown in Fig. 5.6.

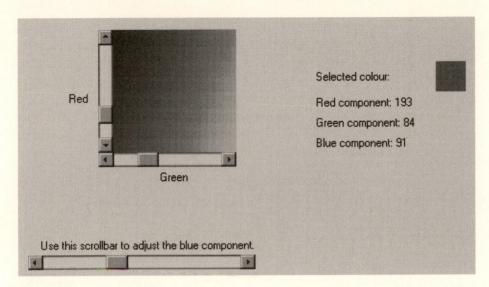

Figure 5.6.

Since a `Color` object is constructed from three parameters (red, green and blue), we need some way of representing these three parameters on a two-dimensional screen. We have chosen to do this by showing a square in which the red and green values are varied, for a fixed blue value. The blue value can be changed by a separate scrollbar.

Java allows each of the three color parameters to vary over a range from 0 to 255. We could represent the entire possible range of red and green values by displaying them in a square that is 256 pixels on each side, but to illustrate how scrollbars may be used to view a portion of a larger image, we have elected to display only a 128 × 128 pixel square. Using a horizontal scrollbar, we can vary the portion of the green range that is visible, and using a vertical scrollbar, we can do the same for the red range. A third horizontal scrollbar below the image allows the blue value to be set for the entire image.

When the user obtains that portion of the image that contains the desired color, the color may be selected by clicking on it with the mouse. The selected color is displayed in a 32 × 32 pixel square on the right side of the applet. The red, green, and blue parameter values comprising this color are displayed in `Labels`.

We now consider the code for this applet. First, we will have a look at the class derived from the `Canvas` class that is used to display the color map:

```
class ScrollCanvas extends Canvas
{
   private int startRed, startGreen, blue;
   private int selRed, selGreen;
   private ColorChooser parent;

   ScrollCanvas(ColorChooser owner)
   {
      super();
      parent = owner;
      startRed = startGreen = blue = 0;
      selRed = selGreen = 0;
   }

   public void setWindow(int offsetRed, int offsetGreen)
   {
      startRed = offsetRed;
      startGreen = offsetGreen;
      repaint();
   }

   public void setBlue(int offsetBlue)
   {
      blue = offsetBlue;
      repaint();
   }

   public int getRed()
   {
      return selRed;
   }

   public int getGreen()
   {
      return selGreen;
   }

   public int getBlue()
   {
      return blue;
   }

   public boolean mouseDown(Event event, int x, int y)
   {
      selRed = y + startRed;
      selGreen = x + startGreen;
      parent.updateSelectedColor(selRed, selGreen,
         blue);
      return true;
```

```
    }

    public void paint(Graphics canvasG)
    {
        for (int redPixel = 0; redPixel < 128; ++redPixel)
            for (int greenPixel = 0; greenPixel < 128;
                ++greenPixel) {
                canvasG.setColor(new Color(redPixel + startRed,
                    greenPixel + startGreen, blue));
                canvasG.drawRect(greenPixel, redPixel, 1, 1);
            }
    }
}
```

Since a `ScrollCanvas` object will only display a portion of the total 256 × 256 color map, we need to know which portion to display. The parameters `startRed` and `startGreen` contain the color levels for the red and green components of the pixel in the upper-left corner of the canvas. The `blue` parameter contains the blue level that is used for all pixels in the display.

The parameters `selRed` and `selGreen` store the red and green components of the pixel selected by the mouse. Finally, `parent` is a reference to the `ColorChooser` applet which contains this canvas, and is used for communication with other components in the same applet.

The `setWindow()` method is called in response to an event in either of the scrollbars controlling the red and green ranges to be displayed (that is, the two scrollbars attached to the image). It sets the values of `startRed` and `startGreen` and repaints the image to display the correct portion of the overall color map. Similarly, the `setBlue()` method is called in response to an event generated by the separate scrollbar used to set the blue level.

The three methods that follow are used by the parent applet to retrieve the red, green, and blue values for display.

The standard `mouseDown()` method determines the red and green levels for the selected pixel, and calls the `updateSelectedColor()` method in the parent applet to update the display and labels on the right side of the applet. We will consider this updating later on.

The `paint()` method for `ScrollCanvas` draws a filled rectangle that is only one pixel wide and one pixel deep for each color that is to be displayed. This isn't a terribly efficient way of displaying a color map, and in fact, the applet does run quite slowly. However, the applet serves its purpose of illustrating the use of scrollbars.

Next, we examine a simple class for representing the small square on the right side of the applet.

```
class ColorCanvas extends Canvas
{
    ColorCanvas()
    {
```

```
            super();
            setBackground(Color.black);
        }
    }
```

Since the only purpose of `ColorCanvas` is to display a square of uniform color, it has no other methods than its constructor. The `setBackground()` method will be used later to change the color displayed.

The main class will now be considered. The variables to be used are as follows.

```
import java.applet.Applet;
import java.awt.*;

public class ColorChooser extends Applet
{
    private ScrollCanvas redGreenCanvas = new
        ScrollCanvas(this);
    private ColorCanvas chosenColorCanvas = new
        ColorCanvas();
    private Scrollbar redScroll, greenScroll, blueScroll;
    private Label redLabel, greenLabel, blueLabel;
    private NewGridBagLayout layout;
    // class methods
}
```

One of each type of canvas is declared, along with three `Scrollbars`. Although more than three `Labels` are used in the applet, we only declare three of them as class variables, since they must be updated when the user selects a color. All other `Labels` display static messages, and are defined where they are needed.

Finally, we use the `NewGridBagLayout` defined in Chapter 3 as the layout manager for the applet and some of its `Panels`. All the initialization is done in the `init()` method:

```
public void init()
{
    layout = new NewGridBagLayout();
    setLayout(layout);
    layout.setRareConstraints(
        GridBagConstraints.CENTER,
        GridBagConstraints.NONE, new Insets(0,0,0,0), 0,
        0, 1, 1);
    redScroll = new Scrollbar(Scrollbar.VERTICAL, 0,
        128, 0, 128);
    greenScroll = new Scrollbar(Scrollbar.HORIZONTAL,
        0, 128, 0, 128);
    blueScroll = new Scrollbar(Scrollbar.HORIZONTAL, 0,
        0, 0, 255);
    redGreenCanvas.resize(128, 128);
```

```
// Red-green canvas panel
Panel redGreenPanel = new Panel();
redGreenPanel.setLayout(new BorderLayout());
redGreenPanel.add("West", redScroll);
redGreenPanel.add("South", greenScroll);
redGreenPanel.add("Center", redGreenCanvas);
Panel redGreenFrame = new Panel();
NewGridBagLayout redGreenFrameLayout = new
   NewGridBagLayout();
redGreenFrame.setLayout(redGreenFrameLayout);
redGreenFrameLayout.setRareConstraints(
   GridBagConstraints.CENTER,
   GridBagConstraints.NONE, new Insets(0,10,0,0), 0,
   0, 1, 1);
Label redScrollLabel = new Label("Red");
Label greenScrollLabel = new Label("Green");
redGreenFrameLayout.setPositionSizeAdd(
   redScrollLabel, redGreenFrame, 0, 0, 1, 1);
redGreenFrameLayout.setPositionSizeAdd(
   redGreenPanel, redGreenFrame, 1, 0, 1, 1);
redGreenFrameLayout.setPositionSizeAdd(
   greenScrollLabel, redGreenFrame, 1, 1, 1, 1);
layout.setPositionSizeAdd(redGreenFrame, this, 0,
   0, 1, 1);

// Blue scrollbar
Panel bluePanel = new Panel();
NewGridBagLayout bluePanelLayout = new
NewGridBagLayout();
bluePanel.setLayout(bluePanelLayout);
bluePanelLayout.setRareConstraints(
   GridBagConstraints.CENTER,
   GridBagConstraints.HORIZONTAL,
   new Insets(0,0,0,0), 0, 0, 1, 1);
Label blueScrollLabel = new Label("Use this

   scrollbar to adjust the blue component.");
bluePanelLayout.setPositionSizeAdd(
   blueScrollLabel, bluePanel, 0, 0, 1, 1);
bluePanelLayout.setPositionSizeAdd(blueScroll,
   bluePanel, 0, 1, 1, 1);
layout.setPositionSizeAdd(bluePanel, this, 0, 1, 1,
   1);

   // Selected color
Panel selectedColorPanel = new Panel();
NewGridBagLayout selectedColorPanelLayout = new
   NewGridBagLayout();
selectedColorPanel.setLayout(
```

```
        selectedColorPanelLayout);
   selectedColorPanelLayout.setRareConstraints(
      GridBagConstraints.WEST,
      GridBagConstraints.NONE, new Insets(0,10,0,0),
      0, 0, 1, 1);
   Label selectedColorLabel = new Label(
      "Selected color:");
   selectedColorPanelLayout.setPositionSizeAdd(
      selectedColorLabel, selectedColorPanel,
      0, 0, 1, 1);
   chosenColorCanvas.resize(32,32);
   selectedColorPanelLayout.setPositionSizeAdd(
      chosenColorCanvas, selectedColorPanel,
      1, 0, 1, 1);
   redLabel = new Label("Red component: " +
      redGreenCanvas.getRed() + "          ");
   greenLabel = new Label("Green component: " +
      redGreenCanvas.getGreen() + "          ");
   blueLabel = new Label("Blue component: " +
      redGreenCanvas.getBlue() + "          ");
   selectedColorPanelLayout.setPositionSizeAdd(
      redLabel,   selectedColorPanel, 0, 1, 1, 1);
   selectedColorPanelLayout.setPositionSizeAdd(
      greenLabel, selectedColorPanel, 0, 2, 1, 1);
   selectedColorPanelLayout.setPositionSizeAdd(
      blueLabel, selectedColorPanel, 0, 3, 1, 1);

   layout.setPositionSizeAdd(selectedColorPanel,
      this, 1, 0, 1, 1);
}
```

Most of this code should be familiar from examples in earlier chapters. To review the `NewGridBagLayout`, see Chapter 3.

The three `Scrollbar`s are constructed using the five argument `Scrollbar` constructor. The first argument specifies the orientation, and the second, the initial value of the `Scrollbar`, which is 0 in all cases here. The third argument is the `visible` parameter. The scrollbars that control the red and green parameters in the image have a `visible` parameter of 128, since there are 128 pixels visible in the canvas. Note that the slider button takes up half the bar length, which indicates that the visible portion of the total color map is half the total map in both directions.

We have specified a `visible` value of 0 for the blue scrollbar, since that scrollbar just controls the blue parameter value, and does not indicate a range of a document or an image that is visible on screen. As you can see, the default slider is displayed when the `visible` argument is 0.

The last two arguments specify the minimum and maximum values for the `Scrollbar`. Since the starting color value for both red and green can vary from

0 to 128 (so that the maximum displayed value for red or green varies between 128 and 255), the red and green scrollbars have a maximum value of 128. The blue scrollbar, however, must vary over the full range of blue values, so has a maximum value of 255.

The easiest way of attaching scrollbars to an image or canvas is to enclose the `Canvas` and its associated `Scrollbars` in a `Panel` that uses the `BorderLayout`. We place the red scrollbar on the left, and the green scrollbar on the bottom, with the canvas in the center. In this case, we would like labels for the scrollbars, so we define another `Panel` (the `Panel` called `redGreenFrame`, which uses a `NewGridBagLayout`) to hold these labels, together with the `redGreenPanel` containing the canvas and its scrollbars.

The remainder of the applet's layout should be fairly obvious from the code.

Any events generated by clicking on any of the three `Scrollbars` are processed in the `handleEvent()` method:

```
public boolean handleEvent(Event event)
{
    if (event.target == redScroll ||
        event.target == greenScroll) {
        redGreenCanvas.setWindow(redScroll.getValue(),
            greenScroll.getValue());
        return true;
    }
    else if (event.target == blueScroll) {
        redGreenCanvas.setBlue(blueScroll.getValue());
        return true;
    }
    return super.handleEvent(event);
}
```

If either of the `Scrollbars` attached to the canvas are adjusted, we call the `setWindow()` method of the `ScrollCanvas` class, passing it the new values of the two `Scrollbars`. If the blue `Scrollbar` is adjusted, we call the `setBlue()` method. Note that we do not worry about what part of the `Scrollbar` was clicked – it could have been one of the end buttons, or the slider could have been dragged, or the mouse could have been clicked somewhere within the bar itself to cause the `Scrollbar` to page forward or backward.

A `Scrollbar` does, however, generate different `Events` if its various parts are clicked, and you can tailor your code to respond differently depending on how the user interacts with the `Scrollbar`. The specific events are:

- `Event.SCROLL_ABSOLUTE` – slider button has been moved. Note that this event behaves much like a mouse dragging event, in that if the slider button is dragged, `SCROLL_ABSOLUTE` events are continuously generated until the mouse button is released. This can be a problem if you redraw a complex image each time this event is received.

- Event.SCROLL_LINE_DOWN – line down button (the button with the small arrow in it that is either on the bottom or the right side of the scrollbar) was pressed.
- Event.SCROLL_LINE_UP – line up button was pressed.
- Event.SCROLL_PAGE_DOWN – page down section (empty portion of the scrollbar between the slider and the line down button) was clicked.
- Event.SCROLL_PAGE_UP – page up section was clicked.

To test these events, compare the event.id field in the handleEvent() method with one of these constants.

Finally, we consider the method that updates the display about the color selected by the user. The updateSelectedColor() method is called by the ScrollCanvas class in response to a mouse click on the image:

```
public void updateSelectedColor(int selRed, int
   selGreen, int selBlue)
{
   chosenColorCanvas.setBackground(new Color(selRed,
      selGreen, selBlue));
   chosenColorCanvas.repaint();
   redLabel.setText("Red component: " + selRed);
   greenLabel.setText("Green component: " + selGreen);
   blueLabel.setText("Blue component: " + selBlue);
}
```

This method simply updates the background color of the small canvas, and updates the Labels to display the selected color levels.

As a final note on scrollbars, we should note that they still have a few bugs. For example, there is a method in the Scrollbar class called setPage-Increment(), which is supposed to change the amount by which the slider button moves when the scrollbar is paged. The method did not appear to have any effect when the author tried it, in both a PC/Windows environment and in a UNIX/X Windows environment. Several other features of scrollbars have different effects in different environments. For example, dragging the slider produces SCROLL_ABSOLUTE events at different rates on different systems. With Internet Explorer, dragging the slider seems to produce no effect until the mouse button is released, while in Netscape, events are produced more continuously.

5.8 Animation

5.8.1 THE IDEA BEHIND AN ANIMATION

Graphical animation is the technique of making images move. Creating animations in Java is similar in spirit to creating TV cartoons – a series of still images is drawn and displayed on screen with an appropriate time lag between each pair of images. If the images are designed to fit smoothly together, and the time lag between each pair of images is set to a reasonable interval, even quite simple animations can appear very realistic. As with most good things, though, there are pitfalls.

Producing an animation in Java involves two main steps: first, a set of images must be generated, and secondly, these images must be drawn onto the screen using the `repaint()` method. Depending on the complexity and size of the images, either or both of these steps can take a fair bit of time. Since a smooth animation requires that each image be ready when it is needed, and that it appear on screen with no apparent jerkiness or flicker, any animation that deals with large, complex images will not work very well, especially on a slow or time-sharing computer. Thus, in addition to the problems caused by some of the graphical components not being truly portable between computers, animations suffer from the additional problem that they may appear smooth and flicker-free on a high-powered, stand-alone computer, but look atrocious when they are run on slow, networked machines.

There are a few methods that can be used to improve the appearance of an animation on a slower machine, but, even when these methods are applied, there is a limit to the performance that can be squeezed out of a weak computer.

Before we examine a simple animation, there is one further warning that must be made. If an animation is run without creating a separate *thread* (see Chapter 6) in which it can run, the animation will lock up the web page (and possibly the browser) in which it runs. This means that the user can do nothing with the web page until the animation finishes. Obviously, if your animation is designed to run continuously (as with, for example, an animated logo on a company's home page), you are in big trouble. Therefore, we will ensure that all the animations we write in this chapter are *finite* (and, in fact, fairly short).

5.8.2 A FIRST TRY AT ANIMATION

We will now show a simple animation to get an idea of the principles involved. The applet will display a filled circle which gradually expands and changes color. The code is as follows.

```
import java.applet.Applet;
import java.awt.*;

public class Animation extends Applet
{
   int circleX, circleY, circleDiameter;
   int red, green, blue;
   boolean redOn, greenOn, blueOn;
   Color circleColor;

   public void start()
   {
```

```
        circleX = 248;
        circleY = 248;
        circleDiameter = 4;
        redOn = true; greenOn = false; blueOn = false;
        red = 255; green = blue = 0;
    }

    private void animateCircle()
    {
        circleDiameter += 2;
        circleX--; circleY--;

        if (redOn && !greenOn && !blueOn) {
          green++;
          if (green == 255)
            greenOn = true;
        }
        else if (redOn && greenOn && !blueOn) {
          red--;
          if (red == 0)
            redOn = false;
        }
        else if (!redOn && greenOn && !blueOn) {
          blue++;
          if (blue == 255)
            blueOn = true;
        }
        else {
          green--;
          if (green == 0)
            greenOn = false;
        }
    }

    public void paint(Graphics g)
    {
        circleColor = new Color(red, green, blue);
        g.setColor(circleColor);
        g.fillOval(circleX, circleY, circleDiameter,
          circleDiameter);
        try
          Thread.sleep(10);
        catch (InterruptedException e)
          showStatus(e.toString());
        if(!(red <= 0 && green <= 0 && blue >= 255)) {
          animateCircle();
          repaint();
        }
    }
}
```

Note that we include a `start()` method instead of an `init()` method, since we want the animation to restart every time the applet is loaded, so we must reset all the parameters each time.

We will use the `fillOval()` method of the `Graphics` class to draw the filled circle. This method takes the same arguments as the `drawRect()` method (which draws a rectangle), but instead of drawing a rectangle, it draws an oval which fits exactly inside the rectangle, and fills it with the current `Color` value. In order to draw a circle, therefore, the surrounding rectangle must be a square.

We will display the applet in a 500 by 500 pixel area inside the browser, so we will center the circle, and start if off with a diameter of four pixels. The parameters `circleX` and `circleY` specify the upper-left corner of the enclosing square, and `circleDiameter` specifies the side length of the square (which is, of course, also the diameter of the circle).

The algorithm we will use to change the color of the circle is as follows. We start with a pure red `Color` (RGB = (255, 0, 0)). Then, we increase the green component until it reaches maximum, at which point the `Color` will be RGB = (255, 255, 0), giving bright yellow. Then, we decrease the red component until it reaches 0, giving pure green. Then we increase the blue component to give RGB = (0, 255, 255), giving cyan (light turquoise blue). Finally, we decrease the green component to zero, ending with a pure blue. The three `boolean` parameters `redOn`, `greenOn`, and `blueOn` are flags indicating whether the corresponding color has reached its maximum value (255) yet. The values of the flags determine which colors should be changed at each step, and in what direction. The final initialization step in the `start()` method sets the initial `Color` to RGB = (255, 0, 0).

The animation is done inside the `paint()` method (with calls to the `private` method `animateCircle()`). The `Color` is specified in the `circleColor` parameter and the circle is drawn. Next, we call the `Thread.sleep()` method. The `sleep()` method pauses execution of the thread (see Chapter 6 for more information on threads) which calls it. Its argument is an `int` which specifies the number of milliseconds (thousandths of a second) to pause. In this case, we pause for 10 milliseconds (one-hundredth of a second).

Note that we enclose the call to `Thread.sleep()` inside a `try...catch` block. This is because the `sleep()` method throws an `Interrupted-Exception`, which is *not* a runtime exception, and therefore *must* be explicitly caught at some point in the program (see Chapter 4). An `Interrupted-Exception` is thrown when some factor external to the program interrupts the `sleep()`. In this program, all we do if such an exception is caught is display the exception's message in the brower's status bar.

The remainder of the `paint()` method is fairly straightforward. The `animateCircle()` method is called to circle's diameter is increased by two pixels, and move the coordinates of its bounding square one pixel back in both the *x* and *y* directions to keep the circle centered within the applet. The chain of `if...else` statements makes the correct color change. Finally, if we have not yet reached the final state (a pure blue circle), the `repaint()` method is called.

Note that, although the `paint()` method may call other methods (such as `animateCircle()` here), the call to the `repaint()` method *must* come inside the `paint()` method. If we had attempted to do the animation by calling `repaint()` from inside the `animateCircle()` method, for example, we would find that, when the applet is run, nothing would appear to happen for a few seconds, and then a large, blue circle would appear.

The reasons for this are fairly technical, having to do with the threads that Java runs automatically. However, even if you do call `repaint()` from within the applet's `paint()` method, the animation has a major design flaw. Because an applet that contains an animation continues to run after the initial web page is loaded and the `init()`, and `start()` methods have been executed, if the user switches to a different web page, the animation will still be running in the background. Recall that the applet's `stop()` method is called automatically when a page is unloaded (no longer in view in the browser), so it is a good idea to stop any animations in the `stop()` method. We need to understand threads in order to do this properly, so we must defer discussion of this until Chapter 6.

There is, however, another problem with the animation example shown here. If you run the animation yourself, you will no doubt notice that it flickers as the circle grows. Flickering is due primarily to the inability of the computer's hardware to keep up with the rate of transfer of video data. In general, the faster your computer, the less flickering you will see. However, there are some techniques that can be programmed into a Java applet that will reduce flickering.

Before we examine these techniques, it is worth emphasizing that they are not guaranteed to 'eliminate' flickering, as some other books claim. They will only reduce it.

5.9 Overriding the `update()` method

One very simple method that can often reduce flickering is a simple override of the `update()` method. Recall that the default `update()` method clears the drawing area (by drawing a filled rectangle with the background color) and then calls the `paint()` method. If each frame in an animation completely overwrites the previous one, there is obviously no point in clearing the drawing area between each pair of frames. For example, in the animation in the previous section, where each frame draws a circle that is larger than the preceding one, the previous frame is overwritten each time. Therefore, we can reduce the flicker by writing an overridden version of `update()` that skips the clearing operation and just calls `paint()`. The overridden version of `update()` looks like this:

```
public void update()
{
   paint(getGraphics());
}
```

Since `paint()` requires a `Graphics` object as its argument, we use the `getGraphics()` method of the `Applet` class to obtain the graphics context for the applet.

Clipping 5.10

Whenever the `paint()` method is called, it redraws the entire graphics area, even if it hasn't changed. This obviously takes more time than just drawing those areas that need to be refreshed. The `Graphics` class provides a method that allows the programmer to restrict the area that is updated to any rectangle within the overall graphics area. This technique is called *clipping*.

To apply clipping, use the `clipRect()` method of the `Graphics` class. This method takes the same arguments as the `drawRect()` method: the coordinates of the upper-left corner of the rectangle, and the width and height of the rectangle. For example, to clip the drawing area in the applet above so that only the rectangle containing the circle is drawn, we could change the beginning of the `paint()` method to the following.

```
public void paint(Graphics g)
{
    circleColor = new Color(red, green, blue);
    g.setColor(circleColor);
    g.clipRect(circleX, circleY, circleDiameter,
        circleDiameter);
    g.fillOval(circleX, circleY, circleDiameter,
        circleDiameter);
```

Unfortunately, in this case, applying clipping would make no difference to the efficiency of the animation, since nothing is drawn outside the circle's bounding rectangle anyway. However, in a more complex applet, where the animation only took place on one corner while other, static graphics were displayed elsewhere, restricting the drawing area to the animation would prevent the static graphics from being redrawn every time the animation was updated, thus saving processor time.

There is a `Rectangle` class (part of the `java.awt` package) which can be very useful for determining clipping regions, and doing other operations with rectangles. The `Rectangle` class has several constructors, one of which allows a `Rectangle` object to be constructed from the four parameters we have been using all along: the *x* and *y* coordinates of the upper-left corner, and the width and height. Once a `Rectangle` has been created, many common graphical operations such as resizing, moving, and comparisons can be done. There are also methods for calculating the intersection and union of two `Rectangles`. The intersection is that `Rectangle` that comprises the overlap of two other `Rectangles`, while the union of two `Rectangles` is a single `Rectangle` that encloses the other two.

The union method, in particular, can be very useful in animation. A common operation in animation is moving an object smoothly across the screen, without changing the object's shape. For example, an object might be drawn at a certain location, then the `sleep()` method called to wait for 10 milliseconds, then the object redrawn five pixels to the right of its previous position. If this operation is repeated many times, the object appears to drift to the right across the screen.

In such animations, often only a rectangle surrounding the two locations of the object (before and after the move) need be redrawn. The `union()` method of the `Rectangle` class may be used to calculate this bounding area, which may then be used to clip the drawing area.

Paradoxically, although the `Rectangle` class is part of the standard `java.awt` package, no other methods accept `Rectangle` arguments, even those that do such things as draw rectangles. If you use `Rectangle` objects to determine a clipping area, you will need to convert the result back to the standard four-parameter form before using it in methods such as `clipRect()`. Probably because of this, the data fields `x`, `y`, `width`, and `height` are `public` rather than the more usual `private`. Therefore, you can access these fields directly, without having to use interface functions such as `getWidth()`. See the exercises for some examples of the use of the `Rectangle` class.

5.11 Double buffering

The final method that can be used to reduce flickering in animation is a technique called *double buffering*. In the animation above, all drawing was done directly to the screen in the `paint()` method. Drawing to the screen often uses more hardware than writing data into memory, and can be more time-consuming, resulting in slower, flickering graphics. With double buffering, a frame in an animation is constructed by drawing to an off-screen graphics buffer, and then the buffer is copied all at once from memory to the screen.

Although double buffering often results in smoother, reduced-flicker animations, it obviously makes greater demands on the memory of your computer, since two copies of each frame must be created – first in memory, and then on the screen. However, memory is becoming more plentiful in recent computers, so often this is a small consideration.

An off-screen buffer is very similar to a `Canvas`, in that it is a drawing area with its own graphics context, which will accept all the drawing commands in the `Graphics` class. The only new techniques that need to be mastered are the creation of the buffer, and the copying of the buffer to the screen.

The off-screen buffer is an object of the abstract class `Image`. Since `Image` is an abstract class, like `Graphics`, it is not possible to create `Image` objects directly using the `new` operator. For the same reasons as with the `Graphics` class, each implementation of Java on each platform has its own methods for creating `Image` objects, so the programmer doesn't have to worry about this.

The main steps to be followed in using an off-screen buffer are as follows:

- Declare a data field (in the applet) of type `Image`.
- In the applet's `init()` method, use the `createImage()` method to create the `Image` object. The `createImage()` method will provide the platform independence that allows the `Image` to be created under any Java implementation.
- Use the `getGraphics()` method to obtain a `Graphics` object representing the graphics context of the `Image`.
- Draw graphics to the `Image`'s graphics context in the same way as you would to a `Canvas` or an applet background.
- When the drawing is ready for transfer to the screen, use the `drawImage()` method of the `Graphics` class to copy the `Image` to the screen.

We now illustrate these steps by converting the circle-drawing applet so that it uses an off-screen buffer. The code is as follows.

```
import java.applet.Applet;
import java.awt.*;

public class DoubleBuffer extends Applet
{
   private int circleX, circleY, circleDiameter;
   private int red, green, blue;
   private boolean redOn, greenOn, blueOn;
   private Color circleColor;
   private Image offScreen;
   private Graphics offScreenG;

   public void init()
   {
      offScreen = createImage(500, 500);
      offScreenG = offScreen.getGraphics();
   }

   public void start()
   {
      circleX = 248;
      circleY = 248;
      circleDiameter = 4;
      redOn = true; greenOn = false; blueOn = false;
      red = 255; green = blue = 0;
   }

   public void update()
   {
      paint(getGraphics());
   }

   private void animateCircle()
```

```
    {
        circleDiameter += 2;
        circleX--; circleY--;

        if (redOn && !greenOn && !blueOn) {
            green++;
            if (green == 255)
                greenOn = true;
        }
        else if (redOn && greenOn && !blueOn) {
            red--;
            if (red == 0)
                redOn = false;
        }
        else if (!redOn && greenOn && !blueOn) {
            blue++;
            if (blue == 255)
                blueOn = true;
        }
        else {
            green--;
            if (green == 0)
                greenOn = false;
        }
    }

    public void paint(Graphics g)
    {
        circleColor = new Color(red, green, blue);
        offScreenG.setColor(circleColor);
        offScreenG.fillOval(circleX, circleY,
            circleDiameter, circleDiameter);
        g.drawImage(offScreen, 0, 0, this);
        try
            Thread.sleep(10);
        catch (InterruptedException e)
            showStatus(e.toString());
        if(!(red <= 0 && green <= 0 && blue >= 255)) {
            animateCircle();
            repaint();
        }
    }
}
```

Here, we have added two fields (`offScreen` and `offScreenG`) which represent the `Image` and its graphics context. We have also added an `init()` method, since the creation of the `Image` and acquiring its graphics context need only be done the first time the applet is loaded – they do not need to be reinitialized each time the animation is started.

There are no changes to the `start()`, `update()`, or `animateCircle()` methods. In the `paint()` method, we do all the drawing to `offScreenG`, rather than directly to the screen's graphics context. When the drawing is finished (which requires only the two statements to set the color and draw the filled circle), we insert a statement that copies the off screen image `offScreen` to the screen. The statement

```
g.drawImage(offScreen, 0, 0, this);
```

accomplishes this. The first argument of `drawImage()` is the `Image` to be copied. The second and third arguments are the *x* and *y* coordinates within the screen's graphics context where the `Image` is to be loaded. In our case, the `Image` and the applet should coincide, so we copy the `Image` to the origin (with coordinates (0,0)) of the applet. The final argument is an `ImageObserver` object. In practice, if the off-screen image is complete before it is copied, you need not worry about this parameter – you can just pass the `this` object and then forget about it. Java will pass notifications about the construction of the `Image` back to an `ImageObserver`.

In summary, note that all drawing is done to the off-screen graphics context `offScreenG`, but that the `drawImage()` method is called by the on-screen graphics context g.

Animation – final comments   5.12

If you have been faithfully running all the variants of the growing-circle applet in this chapter, you may have noticed that even in the final version, where we override the `update()` method and use double buffering, the animation *still* flickers. This example was chosen on purpose to illustrate that there are some animations that will flicker no matter how many programming tricks you try. There is only so much you can do to overcome the limitations of the hardware you are using. (We will see some examples in the exercises of animations where these techniques *do* make a difference!)

It would be worth trying these applets on several different computer systems, if you have access to them. If possible, try UNIX workstations, PCs, stand-alone machines, networked machines, and so on. You may be surprised at how much variation there is between different systems.

If you are developing applets for use on the World Wide Web, it is even more important that you test them on as many different systems as possible. Applets, especially ones using animation, may run smoothly on the high-powered, stand-alone PC you have on your desk, but flicker more than a 1920s silent film when run on a heavily-loaded network.

5.13 Exercises

1 Produce a graphical form of the noughts and crosses game that was first studied in the exercises in Chapter 3 (see Exercise 4 in that chapter).

(a) Use a class derived from the `Canvas` class for the display of the main playing area. At the start of a game, draw a suitable title (for example, 'Welcome to Noughts and Crosses') in red, in a large font centered at the top of the `Canvas`. (To center the text, you will need to know the width of the `Canvas`, and use methods from the `FontMetrics` class to determine the width of the text.) Draw the empty playing area as two vertical lines and two horizontal lines to provide the three-by-three grid.

(b) Allow users to play the game by clicking with the mouse over the desired square in the playing area. The 'X' player plays first, and play alternates between 'X' and 'O' after the first move. Use the `mouseDown()` method (inside the `Canvas`) to detect the coordinates of the mouse click, and calculate the location on the `Canvas` relative to the squares in the playing area. If the click occurs within an unoccupied square in the playing area, draw either an 'X' or an 'O' (use either text or a `Graphics` drawing method to do this), depending on whose turn it is, in the corresponding box. If the click occurs over an occupied square in the playing area, print a message stating that the move is illegal. If the click occurs outside the playing area, but within the `Canvas`, ignore it.

(c) Check after each move to see if the player has won the game. Provide a 'New Game' `Button` (outside the `Canvas`) which clears the `Canvas` and redraws it in its starting state.

2 Provide a graphical version of the 'word wrap' applet first studied in Chapter 3 (see exercises 1, 2, and 3 in that Chapter). Write an applet with two main `Panels`: one on the left containing a `TextArea` and a `Button`, and one on the right containing a `Canvas`. The user should be able to type text into the `TextArea` in the left `Panel`, then push the `Button`. The entered text should then appear, left-justified and neatly formatted, in the `Canvas` on the right. Breaks in the text at the end of each line should occur only between words. Each time the user pushes the `Button`, the `Canvas` should be cleared and redrawn with whatever text is in the `TextArea`.

   In order to do this, you will need to know the width of the `Canvas`, and use the methods from the `FontMetrics` class to keep track of the width of a line of text as you add each word to it. (Use a `StringTokenizer` as in Chapter 3 to read a single word at a time from the `String` in the `TextArea` and add it to the line being displayed in the `Canvas`.) Use an array of `Strings` to store the lines of text to be displayed. When the addition of the next word would extend beyond the edge of the `Canvas`, start a new line of text. Use methods from `FontMetrics` to determine the line spacing.

3 Modify the program in question 2 by adding several `Lists` or `Choices` in the left `Panel` which allow the user to specify the characteristics of the `Font`

used in the `Canvas` to draw the text. The user should be able to specify the
font type (by choosing from a list of available fonts – see Section 5.5), font
size, font style (normal, italic, bold, and so on), and the color (provide a list
of a few standard colors). When the `Button` is pushed, all this information,
along with the text itself, should be passed to the `Canvas` and used to display
the text.

4   Modify the program in question 2 (or extend the program in question 3) by
adding a vertical `Scrollbar` to the `Canvas`. If the amount of text to be displayed is more than can be displayed within the `Canvas`, the `Scrollbar`
should allow the `Canvas` to be scrolled up or down to view all the text. Set
the `Scrollbar` up so that a single click on one of the end buttons scrolls the
`Canvas` by a single line of text. A single click within the bar itself (on either
side of the slider button) should scroll the `Canvas` by a number of lines that
is one less than the maximum number of lines that can be displayed within the
`Canvas`. When the slider button is at the top, the first line of text should be
displayed at the top of the `Canvas`; when the slider button is at the bottom,
the *last* line of text should be displayed at the top of the `Canvas`.

To implement the scrolling, you will find it helpful to define an additional
data field in the class derived from `Canvas` which contains the index of the
first line of text to be displayed. Whenever an event from the `Scrollbar` is
generated, modify this variable and redraw the `Canvas` starting from the first
line to be displayed. For example, if the `Canvas` can hold a maximum of 10
lines of text, and 15 lines are to be displayed, then when the slider button is
at the top of the `Scrollbar`, the 'first displayed line' index should be 1, and
the last line visible within the `Canvas` is line 10. Clicking the bottom end button on the `Scrollbar` should increment the 'first displayed line' index to 2,
the first line displayed is line 2, and the last line displayed is line 11.

5   Write an applet which allows two human players to play a game of draughts
(or checkers in North America). Do this in stages as follows:
(a) Draw the checkerboard in a `Canvas`. (A checkerboard is a playing board
consisting of an 8-by-8 array of squares, alternately colored black and white
(or any two contrasting colors). See Fig. 5.7.) Used filled rectangles for the
squares, and choose two colors that are easily distinguishable, but will still
allow filled circles of black and white (the playing pieces) to be visible on
top of them. Dark and light grey will do, but you may prefer something a
bit more colorful.
(b) Set up the board for a new game by placing the black and white pieces on
their initial squares. Each player starts with 12 pieces which are placed
only on the dark squares. Place the black pieces on the bottom three rows
of squares, and the white pieces on the top three rows (so the middle two
rows of squares should be empty). See Fig. 5.7.
(c) To begin a game, black always moves first. A piece may move one square
diagonally forward (that is, away from the corresponding player, so that black
pieces move up and white pieces move down). To implement a move, the

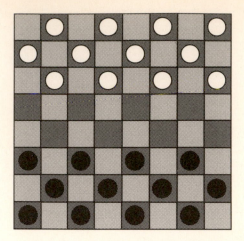

Figure 5.7.

player should click the mouse on the piece that is to be moved, then click the square to which the piece should be moved. After the piece is moved, redraw the `Canvas` to show the new position. (Don't bother including a check that each move is legal unless you feel ambitious – the main purpose of the question is to give you experience in writing a graphical applet.)

(d) (This and the next part of this question are not necessary in order for you to continue with Exercise 6 below, but in order for the applet to be fully useable as an on-line checkers game, you may like to do them.) A player may capture an enemy piece by jumping over it. In order for a capture to be possible, the square on the far side of the enemy piece must be empty. If another capture is possible starting from the square to which the friendly piece has just jumped, it may be made in the same turn, so that one piece may capture several enemy pieces in a chain of jumps. For example, in Fig. 5.8, assuming it is black's turn, the black piece may capture two white pieces by jumping to the two squares marked with an 'X'. Captures, like ordinary moves, may only be made in a 'forward' direction. Captured pieces are removed from the board.

Add the ability to capture a piece to the applet. Check each move to see if the rule for a capture has been satisfied, and if so, removed the captured piece from the board, move the capturing piece to its new location, and redraw the `Canvas`. A chain of captures will require individual mouse clicks and redrawings for each capture in the series.

(e) The final rule in checkers is that when a piece reaches the opposite end of the board, it becomes a 'king'. A king moves in the same way as an ordinary piece (diagonally only) except that it may move (and capture) backwards as well as forwards. For example, after the black piece has captured the two white pieces in Fig. 5.8, it will have reached the opposite end of the board and will become a king.

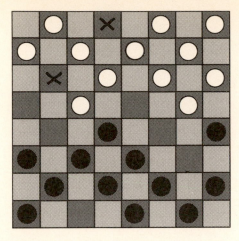

Figure 5.8.

Implement kings in the applet by (i) checking for a piece reaching the opposite end of the board; (ii) designing a new symbol for a king to distinguish it from an ordinary piece of the same color. (For example, adding a small red circle to the center of the main circle.)

6   Add some animation to the applet from question 5. In order to do this, you need not have completed question 5, but you must have written at least parts (a), (b), and (c). When a player has selected a piece to move and the square to which it is to be moved, animate the motion by redrawing the piece at intervals along its path. Experiment with the number of pixels to move the piece in each step, and with the time interval between each move. Try to get the piece to appear to move smoothly, without any jerkiness. For this question, redraw the entire checkerboard after each step in the animation (this will probably cause the animation to flicker quite noticeably, unless you have a very fast computer).

7   Try to reduce the flickering in the animation by using double buffering, but still redraw the entire checkerboard after each step in the animation. Does this help much? (Why would overriding the `update()` method not be worth trying here?)

8   Instead of (or in addition to) double buffering, try using clipping to reduce the flickering. Since the only parts of the checkerboard that change during one animation step are those occupied by the moving piece before and after the move step, the clipping area should be the union of the rectangles enclosing the piece before and after the move. Use methods from the `Rectangle` class to determine the clipping area.

CHAPTER 6

THREADS

6.1 Multitasking and multithreading

When you run a program on your computer, it is allocated memory in the system's RAM (and possibly some swap space on the hard drive, if the program is large enough), and it is allocated time on the machine's processor. Depending on the operating system being used by the computer, you may be able to run more than one program on the machine at a time. Since most desktop computers contain only a single processor, only one program can actually be active at any one time, however. The illusion of several programs running at once can be produced by rapidly swapping between the programs that have been loaded, allocating a few milliseconds to each program in rotation. This technique is known as *multitasking*.

Whether or not a computer supports multitasking depends on the operating system it is running. Many operating systems, including UNIX and recent versions of Microsoft Windows, support multitasking to varying degrees. The technique of *multithreading*, however, depends more on the language in which the program is written. The idea behind multithreading is that, within a single program, there are often separate sections which are more or less independent of each other, and could be run as separate sub-processes, or *threads*, within the overall program.

Older computer languages, such as C, usually do not support multi-threading. However, since the trend in software is more towards packages that run in a GUI environment, multithreading is becoming increasingly desirable. Often each control on a GUI interface starts a process that can run independently of processes started by other controls, so it makes more sense to run each process as a separate thread.

Java is an implicitly threaded language – several threads are started automatically every time you run a Java applet or application. For example, one thread in Java watches for events generated when the user interacts with the applet, while another thread performs 'garbage collection' (watching for previously allocated memory that is no longer used by the program, and freeing it up). Java also allows programmers to create their own threads for running sections of the program independently.

Probably the most common use of user-defined threads in Java is in running animations. If we run an animation as we did in Chapter 5, by placing the commands directly in the applet's `paint()` method, we cannot use the `paint()` method to do any other graphics while the animation is running. We also have no way of stopping the animation if the user chooses to leave the page containing the animation and browse a different page.

By placing the animation within a separate thread, however, we can obtain much more control over its operation. A thread can run independently of the automatic Java threads, and of any other user-defined threads, so it can draw its own graphics. Threads can also be stopped and started independently, so an animation can be stopped when the user leaves the page in which it is running by including code in the applet's `stop()` method to do this.

Threads and animation   6.2

We will begin our study of threads in Java by examining an applet containing two separate animations, each within its own thread. The applet appears as shown in Fig. 6.1.

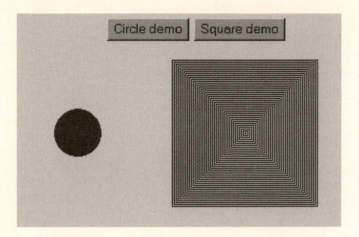

Figure 6.1.

When the user pushes the 'Circle demo' button, a red filled circle appears on the left. The color of the circle gradually changes through yellow, green, cyan and blue, in the same way as with the animation example in Chapter 5. Here, however, the circle remains the same size. Once the color of the circle becomes pure blue, the animation stops. Pushing the 'Circle demo' button again, before the animation has finished, will stop the animation. Pushing the button again will restart the demo from the beginning, with a red circle.

Pushing the 'Square demo' button starts an animation which draws a series of concentric, black squares which appear to grow out from a central point. When the set of squares reaches the edge of the applet, the right half of the applet is cleared, and the animation starts again. The square demo will continue cycling indefinitely until the 'Square demo' button is pressed again.

The two animations should run independently, and the applet should respond to button presses whether or not either animation is running at the time. Therefore, we will create a separate thread for each animation.

There are two main ways that threads can be used in Java. As with the `Canvas` class, we can derive a user-defined class from the `Thread` class and add our own methods to give the thread some functionality. If a `Thread` is defined in this way, the derived class *must* contain an overridden `run()` method, since it is this method that is called when the `Thread` is started.

It is more usual, however, for a thread to be required as part of a user-defined class which is derived from another class, such as the `Applet` class.

Unlike some other object-oriented languages, such as C++, Java does not support the technique of *multiple inheritance*. What this means is that a class may extend at most one other class. Therefore, if we would like a user-defined class, derived from the `Applet` class, to implement threads, we cannot inherit both the `Applet` and `Thread` classes to achieve the functionality of both.

To get around this problem, Java provides the `interface`. We will consider interfaces in more detail in Chapter 9, where we need some more of their properties. All that need be understood at this point is that an `interface` is a special type of *abstract class*, in which methods are declared by giving their prototype (name, return type, and argument list), but not defined (no code is given for them).

Although a class may extend at most one other class, it may *implement* any number of interfaces, provided that the class provides definitions for *all* methods declared in *all* interfaces that it implements.

To define an applet containing threads, we may extend the `Applet` class, and implement the `Runnable` interface. The `Runnable` interface contains only a single abstract method called `run()`, which is the method called by a thread to run its commands. Therefore, the user-defined class must provide a `run()` method of its own.

To use a `Thread` in an applet, the following steps must be followed:

- Define the main class so that it `extends Applet` and `implements Runnable`.
- Declare a `Thread` variable inside the main class.
- At the appropriate point in the applet, create the `Thread` using one of the `Thread` constructors that takes as one of its arguments a `Runnable` object. This registers the main class with the `Thread` so that the `Thread` will execute the `run()` method in the main class.
- Start the `Thread` using the `start()` method from the `Thread` class.
- Use other `Thread` methods (such as `suspend()`, `resume()`, and `stop()`) to manage the thread at the appropriate points.

We will now examine the code for the circle/square applet above to see how all these steps work in practice. We begin with the variable declarations and initialization methods for the applet:

```
import java.applet.Applet;
import java.awt.*;

public class TwoAnimations extends Applet
   implements Runnable
{
   private int circleX, circleY, circleDiameter;
   private int squareX, squareY, squareSide;
   private int red, green, blue;
   private boolean redOn, greenOn, blueOn;
   private boolean circleOn, squareOn;
```

```java
    private Color circleColor;
    private Button circleButton, squareButton;
    private Thread circleThread, squareThread;
    static final int maxSquareSide = 200;
    static final int squareCentreX = 300;
    static final int squareCentreY = 125;

    public void init()
    {
        circleButton = new Button("Circle demo");
        squareButton = new Button("Square demo");
        add(circleButton);
        add(squareButton);
        circleOn = squareOn = false;
    }

    public void start()
    {
        startCircle();
        startSquare();
    }

    public void startCircle()
    {
        circleX = 100;
        circleY = 100;
        circleDiameter = 50;
        redOn = true; greenOn = false; blueOn = false;
        red = 255; green = blue = 0;
    }

    public void startSquare()
    {
        squareX = squareCentreX;
        squareY = squareCentreY;
        squareSide = 1;
    }
    // other methods
}
```

The class `TwoAnimations` extends the `Applet` class as usual, and implements the `Runnable` interface. Most of the data fields are used to define the parameters needed to display the circle and square animations. However, we define two `Button`s, one to start each of the animations, and two `Thread`s, one for each animation.

The `init()` method (which is run once only, the first time the applet is loaded into the browser) creates the two `Button`s and adds them to the applet. The boolean variables `circleOn` and `squareOn` indicate whether the corresponding animation is running or not. Initially, the animations will not be running, so these variables are set to `false`.

The `start()` method (which is run each time the applet is redisplayed in the browser) sets up the initial values for drawing the circle and square.

Nothing will happen in this applet until one of the buttons is pushed, so we next examine the `action()` method:

```
public boolean action(Event event, Object object)
{
    if (event.target == circleButton) {
        if (!circleOn) {
            startCircle();
            circleThread =
                new Thread(this, "Circle thread");
            circleThread.start();
            circleOn = true;
        } else {
            circleThread.suspend();
            circleOn = false;
        }
    } else if (event.target == squareButton) {
        if (!squareOn) {
            startSquare();
            squareThread =
                new Thread(this, "Square thread");
            squareThread.start();
            squareOn = true;
        } else {
            squareThread.suspend();
            squareOn = false;
        }
    }
    return true;
}
```

If `circleButton` is pressed, and the circle animation is not currently running (so that `circleOn` is `false`), `startCircle()` is called to reset the graphics parameters for the circle. Then `circleThread` is created by calling the `Thread` constructor with two arguments. The first argument is a `Runnable` object; the second is a `String` which serves as a name for the `Thread`. We pass `this` as the `Runnable` object, which means that when the `Thread` is started, the `run()` method (to be considered below) for the `TwoAnimations` class will be run by `circleThread`.

After `circleThread` is created, it is started by calling the `start()` method, and `circleOn` is set to `true` to indicate that the circle animation is running.

If the circle animation is running when the button is pressed, the `circleOn` flag will be `true`. In this case, `circleThread` is suspended by calling the suspend() method, which halts the execution of the Thread, but retains the state of the Thread. A suspended Thread can be restarted at the point where it was suspended by calling the resume() method. In this case, though, pressing the button after a Thread has been suspended simply starts a new Thread so the animation starts again from the beginning.

The code which handles squareButton works the same way.

The run() method is as follows:

```
public void run()
{
    Graphics g = getGraphics();
    String executingThread =
        Thread.currentThread().getName();

    if (executingThread.equals("Circle thread")) {
        updateCircle(g);
    }
    else if (executingThread.equals("Square thread")) {
        updateSquare(g);
    }
}
```

We retrieve the graphics context for the applet and store it in the Graphics object g. Since we have two Threads running in the same applet, and both of them use the same run() method, we need to distinguish between the code that is to be run by each Thread. We do this by determining the name of the currently executing Thread. The currentThread() method of the Thread class returns a Thread object, and the getName() method of the Thread class returns a String containing the name of the Thread.

Depending on which Thread is running at the time, we call either updateCircle() or updateSquare(). The updateCircle() method handles the color changes in the circle animation:

```
private void updateCircle(Graphics g)
{
    do {
        circleColor = new Color(red, green, blue);
        g.setColor(circleColor);
        g.fillOval(circleX, circleY,
            circleDiameter, circleDiameter);
        try
            Thread.sleep(10);
        catch (InterruptedException e)
            showStatus(e.toString());
        animateCircle();
    } while (!(red <= 0 && green <= 0 && blue >= 255));
    circleOn = false;
```

```
         circleThread = null;
    }

    private void animateCircle()
    {
        if (redOn && !greenOn && !blueOn) {
            green++;
            if (green == 255)
                greenOn = true;
        }
        else if (redOn && greenOn && !blueOn) {
            red--;
            if (red == 0)
                redOn = false;
        }
        else if (!redOn && greenOn && !blueOn) {
            blue++;
            if (blue == 255)
                blueOn = true;
        }
        else {
            green--;
            if (green == 0)
                greenOn = false;
        }
    }
```

The code for running the circle animation is similar to that in the animation in Chapter 5. However, note that after the animation has finished, we set `circleOn` to `false`, and `circleThread` to `null`, to indicate the thread is no longer required.

The code for the square animation is:

```
    private void updateSquare(Graphics g)
    {
        do {
            if (squareSide == 1) {
                g.setColor(getBackground());
                g.fillRect(squareCenterX - maxSquareSide/2,
                    squareCenterY - maxSquareSide/2,
                    maxSquareSide, maxSquareSide);
            }
            g.setColor(Color.black);
            g.drawRect(squareX, squareY, squareSide,
                squareSide);
            try
                Thread.sleep(10);
            catch (InterruptedException e)
```

```
            showStatus(e.toString());
        animateSquare();
    } while (true);
}

private void animateSquare()
{
    squareX -= 2; squareY -= 2;
    squareSide += 4;
    if (squareSide >= maxSquareSide) {
        squareSide = 1;
        squareX = squareCenterX;
        squareY = squareCenterY;
    }
}
```

Each cycle of the square animation starts with a single point (when `squareSide = 1`). We clear the drawing area at this time by drawing a filled rectangle with the applet's background color. We then draw a series of concentric squares by drawing the square and calling `animateSquare()` to change the size of the square. The `animateSquare()` method also resets the size of the square to 1 after the square reaches its maximum size.

Finally, we insert a `stop()` method in this applet:

```
public void stop()
{
    if (circleThread != null)
        circleThread.stop();
    if (squareThread != null)
        squareThread.stop();
}
```

Recall that the `stop()` method is called when the user leaves the page containing the applet and browses a different page. The `stop()` method stops execution of the `Thread` and does not retain the state of the `Thread`. It is important to do this, especially with animations that run indefinitely, in order to avoid a drain on the processor from animations that are not being viewed at the time.

Synchronization 6.3

6.3.1 THREADS THAT DEPEND ON EACH OTHER

The example of a threaded program in the last section assumes implicitly that the commands being executed in each thread are independent of each other. The rate at which the color of the filled circle changes doesn't depend on how fast the concentric squares are drawn, and *vice versa*. In some applications, however, the processes that are being run as separate threads do depend on each other.

In this case, one thread may require some data that are being calculated by another thread. If the thread requiring the data, often called the *consumer*, requests the data before the other thread, called the *producer*, has managed to provide it, the consumer must wait until the producer has finished producing the data. In other words, the threads must be *synchronized*.

Synchronization is a common problem in writing truly parallel programs, where the code is run on a computer with two or more processors. Most desktop computers (and even mainframes) are, at the time of writing, still single-processor machines, however, so the illusion of multithreading is created by sharing out the time on the single processor. However, the logic is much the same, since whether or not the computer has more than one processor, it is still possible for that part of a program running in one thread to 'get ahead' of the other threads.

Java provides a mechanism by which code running in separate threads can be synchronized. Before we describe this aspect of Java syntax, however, we will present a program which attempts to make several threads cooperate without using synchronization. As we will see, the attempt is less than successful.

6.3.2 AN UNSYNCHRONIZED APPLET

We will attempt to write a 'bucket brigade' program in which we have three buckets in a line. To get things started, the bucket on the far left must be filled with red paint. Then this bucket is poured into the middle bucket, where the color of the paint changes magically (or chemically, if you don't believe in magic) from red to green. The middle bucket is, in turn, poured into the third bucket, where the color changes from green to blue. Finally, the bucket of blue paint is emptied into some other receptacle which doesn't concern us here.

We could implement the process in real life by hiring four people to do the pouring operations. Person 1 is in charge of filling the first bucket with red paint, person 2 empties the first bucket into the second, person 3 empties the second bucket into the third, and person 4 empties the third bucket. The idea in converting this to a threaded program is to use four threads to play the roles of the four people. Thread 1 fills the red bucket, thread 2 pours the red bucket into the green bucket, and so on.

The catch with this operation, of course, is that the four threads must be synchronized. If thread 1 attempts to fill the red bucket before thread 2 empties it into the green bucket, the red bucket will overflow. If the thread in charge of emptying the green bucket into the blue bucket attempts to do this when either the green bucket is empty or the blue bucket is full, disaster results. We therefore must ensure that, when a particular thread gets its chance to do something, the conditions are correct for that thread's job to proceed. We can summarize the requirements as follows:

Thread	Thread's job	Conditions for thread to do its job
1	Fill the red bucket	Empty red bucket
2	Pour red bucket into green bucket	Full red bucket and empty green bucket
3	Pour green bucket into blue bucket	Full green bucket and empty blue bucket
4	Empty the blue bucket	Full blue bucket

We can write an applet which attempts to perform the bucket brigade using four threads. We now consider the code for this applet. First, the data declarations and initialization methods:

```java
import java.applet.Applet;
import java.awt.*;

public class BucketBrigade extends Applet implements
   Runnable
{
   static final int BOXWIDTH = 50;
   static final int BOXHEIGHT = 50;

   private Thread redThread, greenThread, blueThread,
      emptyBlueThread;
   private boolean redFull, greenFull, blueFull;
   private String redError, greenError, blueError,
      emptyBlueError;
   private Label redLabel, greenLabel, blueLabel,
      emptyBlueLabel;

   public void init()
   {
      redThread = new Thread(this, "Red");
      greenThread = new Thread(this, "Green");
      blueThread = new Thread(this, "Blue");
      emptyBlueThread = new Thread(this, "EmptyBlue");
      redError = new String();
      greenError = new String();
      blueError = new String();
      emptyBlueError = new String();
      redLabel = new Label("                              ");
      greenLabel = new Label("                            ");
      blueLabel = new Label("                             ");
      emptyBlueLabel = new Label("                       ");
```

```
        add(redLabel);
        add(greenLabel);
        add(blueLabel);
        add(emptyBlueLabel);
    }

    public void start()
    {
        redFull = greenFull = blueFull = false;
        redThread.start();
        greenThread.start();
        blueThread.start();
        emptyBlueThread.start();
    }

    public void stop()
    {
        if (redThread != null)
            redThread.stop();
        if (greenThread != null)
            greenThread.stop();
        if (blueThread != null)
            blueThread.stop();
        if (emptyBlueThread != null)
            emptyBlueThread.stop();
    }
    // other methods
}
```

Since the applet will be using threads, it implements the `Runnable` interface. We define the four threads, and then define three `boolean` variables (`redFull`, `greenFull`, `blueFull`) which specify the states of the three buckets. The `Strings` and `Labels` are used to display messages within the applet.

The `init()` method initializes the variables in the usual way, and adds the four `Labels` to the applet's layout. The `start()` method starts up the four threads, and the `stop()` method stops them.

The `paint()` method draws the three buckets onto the applet's background:

```
    public void paint(Graphics g)
    {
        g.setColor(Color.red);
        if (redFull)
            g.fillRect(50, 150, BOXWIDTH, BOXHEIGHT);
        g.setColor(Color.green);
        if (greenFull)
            g.fillRect(150, 150, BOXWIDTH, BOXHEIGHT);
        g.setColor(Color.blue);
        if (blueFull)
```

```
      g.fillRect(250, 150, BOXWIDTH, BOXHEIGHT);
   g.setColor(Color.black);
   g.drawLine(50, 150, 50, 200);
   g.drawLine(50, 200, 100, 200);
   g.drawLine(100, 200, 100, 150);
   g.drawLine(150, 150, 150, 200);
   g.drawLine(150, 200, 200, 200);
   g.drawLine(200, 200, 200, 150);
   g.drawLine(250, 150, 250, 200);
   g.drawLine(250, 200, 300, 200);
   g.drawLine(300, 200, 300, 150);
}
```

The buckets are drawn as open-topped squares, and filled with the correct color if they are full. The applet appears as shown in Fig. 6.2.

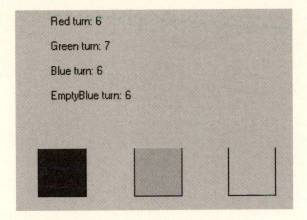

Figure 6.2.

The run() method sorts out the code for each of the four threads:

```
public void run()
{
   String executingThread =
      Thread.currentThread().getName();

   if (executingThread.equals("Red"))
      for (int redTurn = 0; redTurn < 50; ++redTurn)
         updateRedBox(redTurn);
   if (executingThread.equals("Green"))
      for (int greenTurn = 0; greenTurn < 50;
         ++greenTurn)
         updateGreenBox(greenTurn);
   if (executingThread.equals("Blue"))
```

```
            for (int blueTurn = 0; blueTurn < 50; ++blueTurn)
                updateBlueBox(blueTurn);
        if (executingThread.equals("EmptyBlue"))
            for (int emptyBlueTurn = 0; emptyBlueTurn < 50;
                ++emptyBlueTurn)
                updateEmptyBlueBox(emptyBlueTurn);
    }
```

Each of the threads calls its corresponding update method 50 times. Each update method tests to see if the states of the various buckets are correct for that thread to do its job, and, if so, updates the states of the buckets and repaints the applet on screen. The code for the four update methods is as follows.

```
private void updateRedBox(int turn)
{
    if (!redFull)
        redFull = true;
    redLabel.setText("Red turn: " + turn);
    repaint();
    try
        Thread.sleep((int)(Math.random()*3000));
    catch (InterruptedException e);
}

private void updateGreenBox(int turn)
{
    if (redFull && !greenFull) {
        greenFull = true;
        redFull = false;
    }
    greenLabel.setText("Green turn: " + turn);
    repaint();
    try
        Thread.sleep((int)(Math.random()*3000));
    catch (InterruptedException e);
}

private void updateBlueBox(int turn)
{
    if (greenFull && !blueFull) {
        blueFull = true;
        greenFull = false;
    }
    blueLabel.setText("Blue turn: " + turn);
    repaint();
    try
        Thread.sleep((int)(Math.random()*3000));
    catch (InterruptedException e);
```

```
   }

   private void updateEmptyBlueBox(int turn)
   {
      if (blueFull)
         blueFull = false;
      emptyBlueLabel.setText("EmptyBlue turn: " + turn);
      repaint();
      try
         Thread.sleep((int)(Math.random()*3000));
      catch (InterruptedException e);
   }
```

In `updateRedBox()`, a test is made to ensure the red bucket is empty. If so, it is filled by setting the `boolean` parameter `redFull` to `true`. The `redLabel` is set to display the iteration number for the red thread, the screen is repainted, and the thread sleeps for up to 3 seconds (3000 milliseconds).

The other three update methods work in a similar way, with each method testing for the correct condition for that thread.

When the applet is run, it is instructive to watch the turn numbers as shown in Fig. 6.2 in conjunction with the display of the states of the three buckets. You will notice that on many of the turns, there is no change in the display of the buckets. In these cases, when a thread was given its time slice, the conditions of the buckets were not correct for that thread to do its job, so the turn for that thread was passed by, with only the `Label` being updated on screen to show the new turn number. As the simulation proceeds, you may notice that some threads are running through their iterations much faster than other threads, so that the difference between the smallest and largest turn numbers in the display gets quite large. The actual number of buckets of blue paint that are emptied into the external receptacle will probably be quite a bit less than the total number of turns.

Obviously, things would go much more smoothly if we could ensure that, when a thread is given its time slice and conditions are not correct for it to do its job, that thread would wait until conditions *become* correct. We can do that by the use of synchronized methods, as we now demonstrate.

6.3.3 A SYNCHRONIZED APPLET

A Java class can implement synchronization by defining one or more of its methods to be `synchronized`. The effect of this is best described with an example.

Suppose we have a Java class that contains two methods that are defined to be `synchronized` (we will see how to do this in a minute). Then, if a threaded Java program contains two or more threads that both operate on an instance of this class, at most one of the `synchronized` methods is allowed to be running at a time. In a sense, the object containing the `synchronized` methods is *locked* once one of the `synchronized` methods is started. The lock remains in effect until that method finishes, at which time another `synchronized` method may be started, either by the same thread that just finished the first method, or by a different thread. (Any non-synchronized methods may run concurrently, in other threads, with the single `synchronized` method.)

This locking mechanism allows the programmer to write, say, two methods, the second of which requires data from the first. If the two methods are to be run in different threads, it is possible to ensure that the first method finishes before the second method starts if both methods are defined as `synchronized`.

It is probably easier to understand how synchronization works if we now show how the applet from the previous section can be altered to ensure that the bucket brigade works in the correct fashion. The synchronized version will guarantee that, if each thread is given 50 iterations, 50 buckets of blue paint will be emptied from the last bucket in the chain.

The code for all variable declarations, and all methods except the update methods, is identical to that given in the previous section, so we will not repeat it here. The new `synchronized` versions of the update functions are as follows.

```
private synchronized void updateRedBox(int turn)
{
   while (redFull) {
      try {
         wait();
      }
      catch (InterruptedException e);
   }

   redFull = true;
   redLabel.setText("Red turn: " + turn);
   repaint();
   notify();
   try
      Thread.sleep((int)(Math.random()*3000));
   catch (InterruptedException e);
}

private synchronized void updateGreenBox(int turn)
{
   while (!redFull || greenFull) {
      try {
         wait();
      }
      catch (InterruptedException e);
   }
   greenFull = true;
   redFull = false;
   greenLabel.setText("Green turn: " + turn);
   repaint();
   notify();
```

```
        try
            Thread.sleep((int)(Math.random()*3000));
        catch (InterruptedException e);
    }

    private synchronized void updateBlueBox(int turn)
    {
        while (!greenFull || blueFull) {
            try {
                wait();
            }
            catch (InterruptedException e);
        }
        blueFull = true;
        greenFull = false;
        blueLabel.setText("Blue turn: " + turn);
        repaint();
        notify();
        try
            Thread.sleep((int)(Math.random()*3000));
        catch (InterruptedException e);
    }

    private synchronized void
        updateEmptyBlueBox(int turn)
    {
        while (!blueFull) {
            try {
                wait();
            }
            catch (InterruptedException e);
        }
        blueFull = false;
        emptyBlueLabel.setText("EmptyBlue turn: " + turn);
        repaint();
        notify();
        try
            Thread.sleep((int)(Math.random()*3000));
        catch (InterruptedException e);
    }
```

First, note that we have added the Java keyword `synchronized` to the method's definition line (between `private` and `void`). This labels the method as a `synchronized` method, and will engage a lock on any object of this class whenever this method is being executed.

The first thing we should do inside a `synchronized` method is test to see if conditions are right for that method to be run at all. In the case of `updateRedBox()`, we cannot fill the red bucket if it is already full, so we test this condition at the start of the method. Rather than using an `if` statement, though, we use a `while`. This is because we don't want this method to be run until `redFull` is `false`.

What happens if `redFull` is `true`? In this case, a method called `wait()` is executed. The `wait()` method is one of the methods in the fundamental `Object` class, and so is available to all classes. Its effect is to suspend the thread that called the method, and place that thread in a 'wait set' (a set of threads waiting for access to one of the synchronized methods in that object). The lock originally held by this thread is also released, so that another thread may attempt to run a `synchronized` method from this object. The suspended thread will remain in the wait set until it is notified (by a method we will consider in a second) that it is now allowed to try again.

The `wait()` method *must* be enclosed within a `try...catch` block for the same reason as the `Thread.sleep()` method: the `InterruptedException` thrown by the `wait()` method is not a runtime exception and so must be explicitly caught.

If `redFull` is `false`, the `while` loop is bypassed and the remainder of the method may be executed. It performs the same functions as the old `update-RedBox()` method from the unsynchronized applet, but notice that there is a call to a method called `notify()` just after the `repaint()` command.

The `notify()` method is another method of the `Object` class. It sends a signal to the wait set for the object from which it was called. If any threads are waiting for access to a synchronized method within this object (that is, the wait set contains at least one thread), one of the threads is chosen (at random) and can try again to run the method that resulted in it being told to wait.

For example, suppose that `redThread` was told to wait when it tried to run the `updateRedBox()` method, because `redFull` was `true`. It would then be placed in the wait set. If `greenThread` was then successful in running the `updateGreenBox()` method, the `notify()` command within that method would send a signal to the waiting `redThread` that it is now permissible to try running `updateRedBox()` again. Since `greenThread`'s action was to empty the red bucket, `redFull` would now be `false`, so `redThread` would be able to successfully run the `updateRedBox()` command.

If you run this applet (its interface is identical to that shown in Fig. 6.2), you should notice two main differences from the unsynchronized applet in the previous section. First, there is an orderly progression of events from red, through green to blue. The iteration numbers displayed in the four labels change in an steady fashion, and the difference between the largest and smallest iteration numbers never exceeds two. (It is possible for the red bucket to be refilled before the blue bucket from the previous cycle has been emptied, so the EmptyBlue turn could be two cycles behind the Red turn.)

The second difference is that the simulation runs more slowly, despite the fact that the sleep times are still restricted to a maximum of 3 seconds each. This is because a thread will wait until it is permissible for it to perform its job, rather than simply observe that conditions are not right and then give up. The waiting time for a thread is in addition to the sleeping time, so it could be longer than 3 seconds between iterations for each thread.

6.3.4 DEADLOCK

Clearly, synchronization allows threads to cooperate with each other to produce efficient, multithreaded programs. However, one of the potential problems with synchronized threads is that, if the synchronization conditions are not properly thought out, two or more of the threads could result in a *deadlock*. A deadlock is a situation where none of the threads can execute because they are all waiting for another thread to finish and release the lock on a synchronized object.* If the arrangement of synchronized methods in a class allows a deadlock, it is possible for the program to seize up under certain conditions.

For example, in our bucket brigade, suppose that instead of emptying the final blue bucket into an external receptacle, we required that it be poured back into the red bucket at the start of the chain. In such a case, a deadlock would occur if all buckets were full at the same time.

A deadlock is a logical flaw in the design of a program, and therefore can only be prevented in the same way as any other fault in the logic of a program – you must be certain that you think through the design of your algorithm thoroughly before you commit it to code.

Thread miscellany 6.4

We present in this section a few thread-related topics that are often useful.

6.4.1 THREAD GROUPS

In some programs, several related threads are created and used in very similar ways. In these cases, it may be convenient to combine the threads into a `ThreadGroup`, in which a set of threads may be given the same command. The procedure for using a `ThreadGroup` and associating some threads with it goes as follows.

A `ThreadGroup` object is declared and created in the usual way. Whichever threads are to be included in the `ThreadGroup` must be associated with the `ThreadGroup` when they are constructed – you can't create a `Thread` and associate it with a `ThreadGroup` later.

Once a `ThreadGroup` and its associated `Threads` are constructed, any of the methods in the `ThreadGroup` class may be applied. A simple example will show how this works. In the bucket brigade applet given in the last section, we may associate all four threads with a `ThreadGroup`, and then use the `stop()` method

---

* I was once told of a law that was rumored to exist in the state of Kansas in the USA that when two trains approached a junction, both trains must stop and neither train can move until the other one is gone. That is a rather silly example of a deadlock.

of the `ThreadGroup` class to stop all four threads using a single command in the applet's `stop()` method.

The definition of the `ThreadGroup` and its associated `Threads` is done using the following code:

```
private ThreadGroup bucketThreadGroup;
private Thread redThread, greenThread, blueThread,
    emptyBlueThread;

public void init()
{
    bucketThreadGroup = new ThreadGroup("BucketGroup");
    redThread = new Thread(bucketThreadGroup, this,
        "Red");
    greenThread = new Thread(bucketThreadGroup, this,
        "Green");
    blueThread = new Thread(bucketThreadGroup, this,
        "Blue");
    emptyBlueThread = new Thread(bucketThreadGroup,
        this, "EmptyBlue");
    // other commands....
}
```

Having done the initialization, we can replace the applet's `stop()` method with the following:

```
public void stop()
{
    bucketThreadGroup.stop();
}
```

The single command in this method stops all `Threads` in `bucketThread-Group` with a single command.

There are several other methods defined in the `ThreadGroup` class which are fully described in the Java documentation.

6.4.2 THE `suspend()`, `resume()`, AND `yield()` METHODS

We have already met the `sleep()`, `wait()`, and `notify()` methods. There are three other methods that control the execution of `Threads` which should be mentioned.

The `suspend()` and `resume()` methods form a pair. When a `Thread` is suspended, it ceases execution at the point where the `suspend()` method is called, and remains suspended until the `resume()` method is called. Calling `resume()` will cause the `Thread` to resume execution at the point where it left off.

The functions of the `wait()`-`notify()`and of the `suspend()`-`resume()` pairs of methods may seem very similar, in that they both cause a `Thread` to suspend execution and resume at a later time. However, recall that the `wait()` and `notify()` methods are members of the `Object` class, not the `Thread` class, and should be used only in managing access to a method containing synchronized methods. These two methods manage the set of `Thread`s waiting for access to a `synchronized` object, as described above.

The `suspend()` and `resume()` methods are members of the `Thread` class, and may be called by a `Thread` at any point in a program. A `Thread` whose execution is suspended is *not* placed in the wait set – it is simply suspended until a `resume()` call restores the `Thread` to active duty.

Programmers should be cautioned that some browsers, such as Netscape (versions 3.0 and higher), do not support the `suspend()` method in all cases. The reason given for this lack of support is that the `suspend()` method can lead to a deadlock in some cases (though it would seem to make more sense to leave support for `suspend()` in the browser and rely on the programmer to ensure that deadlock does not occur). The `suspend()` and `resume()` methods also exist for the `ThreadGroup` class.

The final `Thread` method is `yield()`. As its name implies, calling the `yield()` method on a `Thread` causes it to suspend execution, allowing other `Thread`s to run. The difference between `yield()` and `suspend()` is that a `Thread` that has yielded to another `Thread` will automatically resume execution when the other `Thread` finishes execution (or when the other `Thread` calls its own `yield()` method), while a suspended `Thread` must make an explicit call to `resume()` to resume execution.

The `yield()` method is used primarily on operating systems that do not allow 'time-slicing' for the various `Thread`s in a Java program. In a non-time-sliced operating system, a `Thread` will run to completion before another `Thread` gets any time at all, so in order to allow two or more `Thread`s to appear to run concurrently, periodic calls to `yield()` may be made in each `Thread`.

In an operating system where time slicing is supported, two `Thread`s will automatically appear to run concurrently even without any calls to `yield()`, since each `Thread` is given a small time slice, then forced to yield to the other `Thread` for its time slice, and so on. Therefore, it is usually only sensible to call `yield()` if you expect your program to be run on systems that do not support time slicing. Most popular operating systems in use today do support time slicing.

6.4.3 THREAD PRIORITIES

We have discussed `Thread`s so far under the assumption that they are all treated equally by the operating system. That is, on a time sliced system, all `Thread`s are assumed to be given time slices in a round robin fashion until they all complete execution.

This is, in fact, true for all user-defined `Thread`s, unless the *priority* of one or more of the `Thread`s is explicitly changed. A `Thread` with a higher priority than another `Thread` will *always* run to completion before the lower-priority `Thread` gets any time at all.

The priority of a `Thread` is an `int` property, with a minimum value of `Thread.MIN_PRIORITY` (a constant of 1) and a maximum value of `Thread.MAX_PRIORITY` (a constant of 10). The priority can be set using the `setPriority()` method of the `Thread` class, and retrieved with the `getPriority()` method.

Only `Threads` sharing the highest priority value of all running `Threads` will run at any one time. Other, lower priority, `Threads` must wait until the higher priority `Threads` complete execution (or yield or are suspended). For example, in a program containing two `Threads` with priority 10, one with priority 8, and three with priority 5, the two priority 10 `Threads` will be time sliced alternately until they are both finished, at which point the priority 8 `Thread` will get all the processor time until it finishes. Then the three priority 5 `Threads` share the processor time until they finish.

Note that if a new `Thread` with a higher priority than any `Threads` currently running is started, all the currently running `Threads` are forced to yield – no explicit call to the `yield()` method is required. User-created `Threads` are given a default priority of `Thread.NORM_ PRIORITY` (a constant of 5).

All Java applets and applications actually run several `Threads` even if none is created by the programmer. For example, garbage collection (the freeing up of dynamically allocated memory that is no longer used by the program) runs in a separate `Thread` with a lower priority than the program itself, so that whenever the program isn't doing anything, the garbage collector can run.

6.5 Exercises

1   Write an applet that displays a 'company logo' for a web page. The applet should consist of a `Canvas` (with a colored background) that displays the name of the company (choose some name that is less than 10 characters) centered in the `Canvas`. The logo should be animated so that the name starts out in a small font (say, 5 point), and grows to a large font (say, 36 point) by being displayed at various intermediate sizes with a suitable time delay between each pair of displays.

The applet should also contain a `Button` which will start the animation if it has stopped, and stop it if it is running. Run the animation from the beginning (with the smallest font) whenever the `Button` is pushed to start it. Run the animation in a separate thread so that the `Button`'s events will be effective whether or not the animation is running.

2   Add a `Panel` to the applet in question 1 containing a `Canvas` which shows a bar chart of the profit and loss for your 'company' over the four quarters for last year. Invent four profit and loss figures (but make sure that some quarters have profits and some have losses), and draw these on the chart as filled rectangles. The vertical axis should be labelled to show its maximum and minimum values. Profits should be drawn as black rectangles starting at the

midpoint and extending upwards; losses as red rectangles extending downwards (see Fig. 6.3).

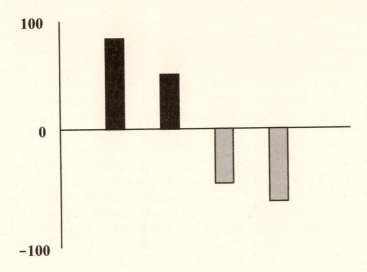

Figure 6.3.

Animate the display of the bar chart so that each bar grows up or down from the center line, with the bars being displayed one at a time, starting from the left. Provide a `Button` which clears the chart and starts the animation from the beginning. Write the chart in a separate thread from the animated logo, and use clipping (see Chapter 5) to reduce flickering.

3   Add another `Button` to the bar chart `Panel` in question 2 which must be pressed after each bar is displayed in order to proceed to the next bar. (This 'pause' feature could be used to allow additional information, such as an explanation of the profit or loss for the quarter just shown, to be displayed after each bar is drawn, for example.) Implement this feature by using the `suspend()` and `resume()` methods of the `Thread` class. (If you find that your browser will not support the `suspend()` method, implement the pause by defining a `boolean` variable called `paused` which is set to `true` after a bar is fully drawn. When `paused` is true, use a `while` loop (containing a `sleep()` method call which causes the thread to sleep for a short time such as 100 milliseconds) which loops until the `Button` is pushed, causing `paused` to be set to `false`.)

4   To gain experience in using synchronization, write another applet similar to that in question 2. This time, however, each bar in the bar chart should show the *total* profit (or loss) for a single year, and the chart should show results for five consecutive years.

To introduce synchronization, split the task into two threads. The first thread will generate (randomly, in the range −100 to +100) the four profit/loss figures for the four quarters within a single year. In order to force this operation to take a noticeable time, have the thread sleep for a time interval between 0 and 1000 milliseconds (generated randomly) after generating the profit or loss figure for each quarter. When all four figures for a given year have been produced, they should be displayed as a `Label` within the applet.

The second thread will take the four figures for a single year produced by the first thread, add them up to get the total profit or loss for that year, and then draw, using animation as in question 2, the bar for that year on the chart. The total procedure should be repeated five times, to show the profit or loss for five years on the chart. The vertical scale on the bar chart will, therefore, range between −400 and +400.

Clearly, the second thread cannot draw the bar until the first thread has finished producing the data for that year, so the two threads must be synchronized. Use techniques similar to those in the bucket brigade example in this chapter to ensure that the second thread waits for the first thread to finish, and that the second thread finishes drawing the bar for the current year before the calculations for the next year are started.

CHAPTER 7

LISTS

7.1 Arrays and lists

There are two basic methods by which collections of related data can be stored: as *arrays* or *lists*. An array is a data structure where all elements are stored in contiguous memory; the defining parameters of an array are the memory address of its first element (called the *base address*), the size of each element (e.g. 4 bytes for an integer, 1 byte for a char, etc.), and the number of elements. Arrays allow *random access* to their elements, which means that, given the index of the element required, its location can be calculated by adding an offset to the base address. This calculation involves the same number of steps for all elements of the array, so the access time for any array element is constant. Arrays also require only as much space as is needed to store the data itself; no extra space for pointers or other markers is needed.

The main disadvantage of an array is that its size is fixed, either at compilation or when space is allocated dynamically (by using the Java `new` operator). Sufficient space must be allocated for the largest number of elements that will ever be used in the program, which can result in a lot of wasted space if most applications only require a fraction of that space. Also, certain algorithms are less efficient if used on data stored in arrays.*

The main alternative to the array is the *linked list*. A list is a data structure in which the first element is stored on its own, but is provided with a pointer† to the location of the second object, which may be stored in a different area of memory. The second object in turn has a pointer to the third, and so on, until the last object has a null pointer associated with it to indicate that it is the end of the list.

The main advantage of a linked list over an array is that the size of the list need not be determined in advance, since extra space can be allocated as needed. Disadvantages are that extra space is needed to store the pointer associated with each element, and that access to internal list elements may take more time than with an array, since finding an internal list element requires starting at the first element and following the chain of pointers until the required element is located.

---

* Some languages support arrays that will dynamically change their size. In such languages, you are required to specify an initial size and an increment for the array. The initial instance of the array will be of the initial size. If the array ever exceeds the initial size, an extra block of elements given by the increment size is allocated to the array. This can be inefficient, since the program must locate a new block in memory that is large enough to store the new, larger array, and in most cases will have to shift all the data from the original array into the new location.

† Java purists would have us believe that Java does not allow the programmer to deal with pointers. Although it is true that you cannot handle pointers in the carefree nature of C or C++, it is actually clearer in many cases to think of certain Java actions in terms of pointers. If the 'p-word' bothers you in connection with Java, think of a pointer in its ordinary English sense – as something which points to something else.

Lists in Java **7.2**

Although it is possible to implement a linked list using arrays, it is inefficient to do so, so we will concentrate on the pointer form in this chapter. Before we get into this, we need to examine the structure of a list in a bit more detail.

In Java, we will define two classes to represent a linked list. The first class will define the data type for an individual list *node*, that is, one of the links in the list. The second class will define the overall list, which is a chain of individual nodes.

A list node consists of two main parts. The first part contains the actual information that is stored in the node. This could be something as simple as an `int`, or something as complex as a complete dossier of information on some employee in a company. The other part of a list node is the pointer to the next node in the list.

The overall list contains only a single pointer which points to the beginning of the list. We will find that many of the list algorithms are easier to implement if we *always* begin a list with a dummy node called the *head node*. The head node is not used to store any of the actual data present in the list, although it could be used to store information pertaining to the list as a whole, such as the number of nodes. Note that the pointer in the head node points to a value of `null` at this stage. The list pointer plus the head node thus constitutes an empty list (see Fig. 7.1).

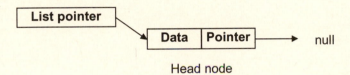

Head node

Figure 7.1.

The head node contains a pointer to the first data node in the list (or a null pointer if the list is empty). The space for this first data node, however, is not allocated until the data to be inserted in the node are actually provided to the program. Thus the class method for inserting a new node into a linked list must handle this process.

In Fig. 7.2, a list containing one data node after the head node is to have a new node inserted between the head node and the first data node. The new node must first be allocated space in memory (using the `new` operator). Then its pointer is directed to point to the data node which is to follow it in the list. Finally the pointer from the head node is redirected to point to the new node.

Similarly, when a node is removed from the list, another class method will handle the deallocation of this node.

We now examine the class `ListNode` which defines a data type which stores an `int` as the data field in a list node:

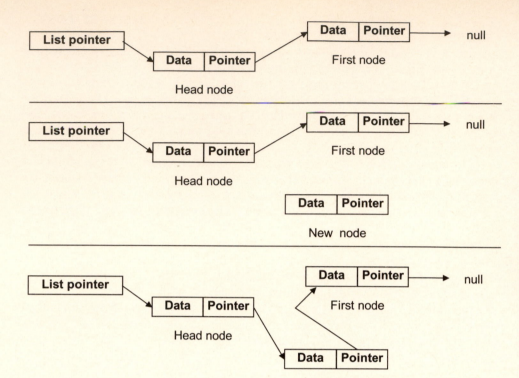

Figure 7.2.

```
public class ListNode
{
   int Element;
   ListNode Next;

   ListNode(int NewElement, ListNode Node)
   {
      Element = NewElement;
      Next = Node;
   }
}
```

Note that the ListNode class contains a field named Next which is of type ListNode, that is, of the same data type as the class within which it appears. This may look a bit dodgy – after all, how can we include a ListNode field before we have completed the definition of ListNode itself? To understand how this works, remember that defining a variable in Java is a two-stage process: first you need to declare the variable (as we have done here with Next), then you need to allocate the space for it. The declaration of Next really does nothing more than tell the compiler that a variable called Next will form part of the ListNode class, and that this variable will have type `ListNode`. Since no actual space needs to be allocated to `Next` just yet, we don't need to know how much space is needed. In other words, we don't need to know the full definition of the `ListNode` class in order to declare a variable of type `ListNode`.*

The constructor for `ListNode` is quite a clever piece of code. Remember that, when a `ListNode` object is inserted into a list, its `Next` field should point to the node which is to follow it in the list. The constructor expects two arguments: the first is the data portion of the node (the actual information that is to be stored in the new node), and the second is the node which is to follow the new node. The constructor thus assigns both these quantities to their correct location within the new node. In the process it performs one of the linking operations required to insert the new node into the list. (The second link – that from the preceding node to the new node – is done by the method which calls this constructor. We'll worry about that below.)

Now we can consider the main class to represent the list itself. Its code is as follows.

```
public class IntList
{
   ListNode Head;

   IntList()
   {
      Head = new ListNode(0, null);
   }

   void InsertEnd(int NewElement)
   {
      ListNode Marker;
      for (Marker = Head; Marker.Next != null;
         Marker = Marker.Next);
      Marker.Next =
         new ListNode(NewElement, Marker.Next);
   }
   // other methods
}
```

The class `IntList` contains only one data field – a `ListNode` called `Head`. The constructor initializes the list by allocating space for the head node. The data value stored in `Head` is given as 0, though since this particular data value is never used, it could be anything. The `Next` field of `Head` is set to `null` to indicate that `Head` is the last node in the list. Therefore, an empty list is created.

We have included two common list methods in the `IntList` class. The `InsertEnd()` method inserts a new node at the *end* of the list (that is, the end

* If you're not averse to thinking about pointers, what we are *really* doing is declaring a *pointer* to a `ListNode` object, and allocating space for the pointer to point to later on.

farthest from the head node). To find the end of the list, you must start at the head node and step through the list one node at a time until you encounter the `null` pointer which indicates the end of the list. This is done by the one-line `for` loop. A local `ListNode` variable named `Marker` is declared as used to mark the position within the list. `Marker` is initialized to point to `Head`. The termination condition in the `for` loop is `Marker.Next != null`, which tests the current node to see if it is the last node in the loop. If it is, the loop stops; if there are still more nodes to traverse, `Marker` is moved one link along in the list by setting it to its own `Next` field. (You will find it very helpful to draw a list on paper and trace the action of this method.)

Once the end of the list has been reached, the new node is to be attached. When the `for` loop finishes, `Marker` will be pointing to the last node in the list, and its `Next` field will be `null`. The new node should be attached so that `Marker.Next` points to it, and the `Next` field of the new node should point to whatever formerly followed `Marker`, that is, to `Marker.Next`. The final statement in `InsertEnd()` accomplishes all these tasks. A new node is created by calling the `ListNode` constructor. The constructor is passed the data value (`NewElement`) to be stored in the new node, and the node to follow the new node (`Marker.Next`). Finally, the end of the list is made to point to the new node by setting `Marker.Next` to the result of the `new ListNode()` operation.

This statement is actually a little more general than it needs to be in this particular method. Since `Marker.Next` is always `null` when the `for` loop finishes, we could equally well have used the statement

```
Marker.Next = new ListNode(NewElement, null);
```

instead of what appears in the method. However, if we wish to insert the new node in the *middle* of the list, then we would need to use the more general form. In that case, assuming `Marker` points to the node immediately preceding the location at which the new node is to be added, `Marker.Next` will *not* be `null`, but will point to the node in the list that must follow the new node.

The other method we will consider is one for deleting an element from the list:

```
void Delete(int DelElement) throws ListException
{
   ListNode Marker;
   for (Marker = Head;
      Marker.Next != null &&
         Marker.Next.Element != DelElement;
      Marker = Marker.Next);

   if (Marker.Next != null &&
         Marker.Next.Element == DelElement)
      Marker.Next = Marker.Next.Next;
   else
      throw new ListException("Cannot delete:
```

```
                    element not in list.");
    }
```

The `Delete()` method accepts an `int` argument and, if a node containing this argument is found in the list, it is deleted. To delete a node, we must redirect the pointer immediately prior to the node so that it skips over the node to be deleted and points to the node just after. Therefore, we need to scan the list until we find the node just *before* the node to be deleted. The `for` loop does this by setting `Marker` to point to `Head`, then testing (i) that we are not at the end of the list (`Marker.Next != null`) and (ii) that the *next* node doesn't contain the data we are looking for (`Marker.Next.Element != DelElement`). Note that we must do the test for the end of the list *before* the test for the value of `Element` in the next node, since if we did it the other way round, we might attempt to examine the next node at the end of the list. This would result in one of Java's built-in exceptions* being thrown.

Once the `for` loop finishes, we test that we have actually found the required element (the loop could have finished because we reached the end of the list without finding a node containing `DelElement`). If so, we redirect the `Next` field of the node just before this node to point to the node just after it (`Marker.Next = Marker.Next.Next`). Otherwise, we throw a new exception called `ListException` stating the element isn't in the list.

Recall from Chapter 4 that an exception is thrown by a method whenever that method is asked to do something for which it was not designed. It is a clean way of handling incorrect operations in a program, much better than just allowing the program to crash or hang.

The exception defined here is just an instance of the standard `Exception` type described in Chapter 4:

```
import java.lang.Exception;

class ListException  extends Exception
{
    public ListException() { super(); }
    public ListException(String s) { super(s); }
}
```

There are many other operations that can be performed on lists, but they all use essentially the same techniques as those we have illustrated here.

List iterators   7.3

Before we discuss the applet which will test the list we have developed, we need to consider the problem of how to access the list elements from an external class.

---

* The exception that is thrown is called a `NullPointerException`, which makes it fairly obvious that the designers of Java, at least, do think in terms of pointers.

We might provide a utility method such as `getElement(int index)`, which would accept an index as an argument and return the corresponding list element. We could then iterate through the elements in the list by calling `getElement()` with successive `index` values.

However, retrieving elements this way can be inefficient in some cases. For example, suppose we wish to step through the list and print out all its data values. If we used code such as:

```
for (index = 0; index < ListSize; ++index)
  value = List.getElement(index);
```

to retrieve the elements in the list, where `ListSize` is the (externally determined) number of elements in `List`, the `getElement()` method would need to start at the head node and step through the list for *every* element that it retrieved. This is because of the way a list is stored in memory: to find the sixth element, say, we must start at the beginning and follow the chain of pointers until we reach element number six. Clearly it would be more efficient if we could remember the position we were at in the list so that the next access could just pick up where we left off.

Another possible solution is to access the `ListNode` fields directly, but this violates the principles of object-oriented programming.

Yet another solution to this problem might be to add some methods to the linked list class which allow an external class to step through the list one item at a time. For example, we might define a method `Start()` which returns the first item in the list, a method `Next()` which returns the next item in the list, and a `boolean` method `End()` which returns `true` if we are at the end of the list. The list class would also need a marker field so that it could keep track of where it was in the list. We could then use code like the following to loop through a list:

```
for (Node = List.Start(); !List.End();
  Node = List.Next())
  value = Node.Data;
```

This solution works well enough, provided that we don't try nesting two or more loops. Since there is only one marker field defined in the list class, if we try writing a nested loop where both the outer and inner loops cover the *same* list, the marker will get confused between the two layers of the loop. For example, if we wanted to write a database which searched the list to see if any two entries contained the same address, we need to write a nested loop where the outer loop steps through the list one item at a time and the inner loop traverses the *same* list, comparing the address of each item with the current item from the outer loop. If we are using the special list methods to step through the loop, we would need two different markers to keep track of where we were in the two layers of the nested loop.

We could, of course, add another marker field to the list class, but then someone no doubt would want to try a triply-nested loop over list, and so *ad infinitum*.

The generally accepted solution to this problem is to provide what is called an *iterator* class for the linked list. The iterator class contains methods such as `Next()`, `End()`, and so on, as well as a marker to keep track of the location in the list. A *separate* iterator object is defined for each iteration over the list. In the nested loop example, we would define one iterator for the outer loop, and a different iterator for the inner loop. Since we are using separate iterator objects for the two levels of the loop, two separate markers are used for keeping track of the locations in each loop, so there is no confusion. Also, the technique works no matter how many layers of nesting are required, since for each layer we simply declare a new iterator for the list.

A suitable iterator for the `IntList` class is:

```
public class IntListIterator
{
   ListNode CurrentNode;

   IntListIterator(IntList List)
   {
      CurrentNode = List.Head;
   }

   int Next() throws ListException
   {
      if (!End())
         CurrentNode = CurrentNode.Next;
      if (!End())
         return CurrentNode.Element;
      else
         throw new ListException("Attempt to access
            beyond end of list.");
   }

   boolean End()
   {
      return CurrentNode == null;
   }
}
```

The iterator class `IntListIterator` has a single data field which serves as the marker. The constructor initializes the marker to the head node of the list over which this class will iterate, so there is no need for a special `Start()` method. The `Next()` method advances `CurrentNode` by one link if we have not reached the end of the list. After `CurrentNode` has been advanced, another test is made to see if the end of the list has been reached (if `CurrentNode` had been at the end of the list when `Next()` was called, advancing it by one link would set it to the `null` value at the end of the list). If we are still inside the list, the value stored at `CurrentNode` is returned; otherwise an exception is thrown.

The End() method merely checks if CurrentNode is null.

An example of the use of this iterator will be seen in the next section where we consider the applet which tests the code developed in this chapter.

7.4 An applet for a linked list

We will write a simple applet to test our linked list classes. The applet looks as shown in Fig. 7.3.

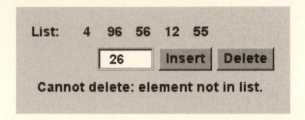

Figure 7.3.

The user types a number into the text box and presses 'Insert' to add the number to the end of the list, or 'Delete' to search for and delete the item. In the figure, the user has tried to delete a number not in the list, so an error message is printed.

The panel layouts and event handling are all very similar to those used in other applets we have considered, so we will not go through the details of the code for setting up the controls. The elements of the list are displayed as an array of Labels, and an additional Label at the bottom of the applet displays messages resulting from error conditions. When the 'Insert' button is pressed, the action() method calls a method in the main applet class which in turn calls the InsertEnd() method in the IntList class. Similarly, when the 'Delete' button is pressed, the Delete() method of the IntList class is called in an attempt to delete the element containing the number in the text box. After each operation on the list, a method called Update() is called to update the display. The Update() method for the panel is as shown:

```
void Update(IntList List)
{
    IntListIterator Source = new IntListIterator(List);
    int index = 1;

    while(index < NUMELEMENTS && !Source.End())
    {
        try
            ListLabel[index++].
                setText(Integer.toString(Source.Next()));
        catch (ListException e)
```

```
        { }
            --index;
    }

    while(index < NUMELEMENTS)
        ListLabel[index++].setText("");
}
```

The `Update()` method accepts an `IntList` as its argument. It must then step through this list and print each value inside the applet. An iterator called `Source` is declared and initialized by calling the `IntListIterator` constructor with `List` as its argument. At this point, the `CurrentNode` field of `Source` is initialized to point to the head node of `List`. The `index` parameter is used to step through the array of `Labels` in which the list elements are displayed on screen. There is a maximum of `NUMELEMENTS` `Labels` available.

The `while` loop uses the iterator to step through the list. The termination condition for the `while` loop first checks that we haven't used up all the `Labels` (`index < NUMELEMENTS`), and then that we haven't reached the end of the list (`!Source.End()`).

If everything is OK at this point, the body of the `while` loop uses the iterator to get the next node in the list (`Source.Next()`), converts the returned `int` to a `String`, and sets the text in the corresponding `Label`. We `catch` a possible `ListException` since the last node in the list will *always* throw one (trace through the iterator code for the `Next()` method to see why). We don't need to do anything with this exception, since it isn't an error.

Finally, the second `while` loop sets all unused `Labels` to be blank.

Exercises 7.5

1   Using inheritance, define a new linked list class with the following new methods:
   (a) An insertion routine which keeps the list in ascending order by using the *insertion sort* algorithm to insert each new element. Insertion sort is discussed more fully in Chapter 11, but for now, you may implement it by stepping through the list until either the end of the list is reached (in which case you insert the new element at the end of the list) or until the *next* element is larger than the new element (in which case you insert the new element immediately before the first element that is larger than it). Allow duplicate elements to be inserted.
   (b) A method which deletes duplicates of all elements from the list, so that after running this function, each list element occurs only once.
   (c) A method which counts the number of elements in the list.

2   Design a class to implement a *bi-directional* or *symmetric* linked list. Each element in a bi-directional list has two associated pointers: one pointing to the previous element in the list and the other to the following element. Design

methods which allow insertion and deletion of elements from such a list, and provide appropriate constructor(s).

3   One application of a bi-directional list allows a computer to deal with integers of arbitrarily large size. Write a program which uses your bi-directional list template to allow addition of two integers of any size. To do this, remind yourself of how addition of two numbers is done with pencil and paper. To add two numbers such as 176 + 892, for example, you start with the units column, add the two numbers (6 + 2 = 8), write down the answer and proceed to the tens column. Adding 7 + 9 gives 16, so we write down the 6 and carry 1 to the hundreds place. The sum here is the carried digit (1) plus 1 + 8, giving 10. The 0 is written down, the 1 carried to the left, but since we are done, we can just write down the final carried 1 to give the answer: 1068. Use the same technique to add together two very large numbers, except that instead of storing only a single digit as a list node, store a larger block (say numbers from 0 to 999,999) at each node. Then a large number can be read into the list from left to right (in the conventional way), and two numbers can be added by traversing the list from right to left (in the conventional way for addition).

4   Rewrite the 'text display' program from exercise 4 in Chapter 5 so that each line of text is stored as a node in a linked list, rather than in an array. This has the advantage that no upper limit need be imposed on the number of lines that can be displayed.

In order to do this, you will need to rewrite the list classes (including the iterator) defined in this Chapter so that they store a `String` in each node. You should also use an iterator object to step through the list as required when printing it to the `Canvas`.

CHAPTER 8

STACKS AND QUEUES

8.1   Stacks

8.1.1   THE STACK DATA STRUCTURE

To get a feel for what a stack is, and why it might be useful, suppose you wanted to design an algorithm for reversing a string of characters. If the characters are stored in an array, the simplest way to reverse them might be to locate the end of the string and just list the characters from that point back to the beginning of the array, using a simple `for` loop. However, suppose you don't know in advance how many characters there are in the string. This might be the case if you are reading the characters in, one at a time, from the keyboard or a file. One particularly simple method of reversing such a string might be the following:

1   Read in a character.

2   Place the character 'on top' of any previously read characters.

3   Repeat steps 1 and 2 until no more characters are presented for reading.

4   Remove the top character from the pile you created in the first part of the algorithm.

5   Print the character to the right of any previously printed characters.

6   Repeat steps 4 and 5 until all the characters have been printed out.

If you try this algorithm for a string of your own devising, you will see that it produces as its output the original string in reverse order. The pile of characters that you created by repeated application of steps 1 and 2 is an example of a *stack*. The main features of a stack are:

- Access is allowed at one end (the *top* of the stack) only. Data are added and removed at this end.
- The action of adding a data element to a stack is called *pushing*.
- The action of removing a data element from a stack is called *popping*.
- Stacks handle data in a *last-in-first-out*, or *LIFO*, fashion: the last item pushed onto the stack is always the first item popped off the stack.

8.1.2   IMPLEMENTING A STACK

There are two main ways of implementing a stack in Java: arrays and linked lists. We will consider the linked list version in the exercises. For the purposes of this chapter, we will concentrate on arrays.

If we wanted to implement stacks directly from their definition, we might try the following implementation in terms of arrays. First, we reserve some specific data value (such as ASCII 0, if we are storing characters on a stack) which we know will never form part of the valid data that are to be stored on the stack. We fill the array with this value to indicate an empty stack.

To push an item onto an empty stack, we insert it at array location 0 (since all Java arrays start at 0). To push the next item onto the stack, we must first move the item at location 0 over to location 1 to make room for the new item, which is placed at location 0. We can continue pushing items onto the stack in this fashion: first move all previously added items over one location to make room for the new item, then store the new item at location 0.

Popping data from the stack works just like pushing in reverse. We remove (or read) the item at location 0, test to see if it is the special character indicating an empty stack and, if not, move over all the other items in the stack to fill in the gap left by removing the top element. We can continue popping data from the stack until we encounter the special character indicating that all the data have been removed from the stack.

While this method of doing things follows the definition of a stack very closely, it is also highly inefficient. Every time we push data onto or pop data from the stack, we must move all the other elements in the stack to compensate. If the type of data we are storing is complex, or if there are a lot of data on the stack (or both), this can be very costly in terms of computing time. It turns out that there is a much more efficient way of doing things.

Rather than defining the top of the stack to be at location 0 in the array, we will define the *bottom* of the stack at that location. The stack will then grow into the array, so that the location of its top (in terms of the array index) depends on the amount of data in the stack. The first item added to an empty stack is, therefore, added at location 0, the next at location 1, the next at location 2, and so on.

Doing things this way obviously requires that we keep track of where the top of the stack is after each push and pop. This is easily done by defining an auxiliary integer variable known as the *stack pointer*, which stores the array index currently being used as the top of the stack. Therefore, we have algorithms for pushing and popping data:

Push:

1   If stack is not full then:

2   add 1 to the stack pointer,

3   store item at stack pointer location.

Pop:

1   If stack is not empty then:

2   read item at stack pointer location,

3   subtract 1 from the stack pointer.

In an array with STACKSIZE elements, the array locations are indexed from

0 to `STACKSIZE` - 1. A full stack will therefore have its stack pointer pointing to location `STACKSIZE` - 1, and an empty stack will have a stack pointer of -1.

8.1.3 A STACK IN JAVA

To begin, let us write a simple Java class to implement a stack that stores `int`s. To make the class as flexible as possible, we would like to be able to specify the size of the stack when we declare it, so we will include the variable `StackSize` as one of the class fields.

The definition of `IntStack` is given below. Following the definition, we will discuss the methods it contains.

```java
public class IntStack
{
    private int StackSize;
    private int StackPointer;
    private int[] Element;

    IntStack(int stacksize)
    {
       StackSize = stacksize;
       Element = new int[StackSize];
       StackPointer = -1;
    }

    public boolean Empty()
    {
       return StackPointer == -1;
    }

    public boolean Full()
    {
       return StackPointer == StackSize - 1;
    }

    public int Pop() throws StackException
    {
       if (Empty())
          throw new StackException("Stack is empty.");
       else
          return Element[StackPointer--];
    }

    public void Push(int newElement)
      throws StackException
    {
       if (Full())
```

```
          throw new StackException("Stack is full.");
      else
          Element[++StackPointer] = newElement;
   }

   public int getElement(int index)
   {
      return Element[index];
   }

   public int getStackPointer()
   {
      return StackPointer;
   }
}
```

There are three data fields. We have already mentioned `StackSize`. `StackPointer` is the stack pointer referred to in the last section – its value is the index of the array element containing the top of the stack, or –1 if the stack is empty. The `int` array `Element` will contain the actual values stored in the stack.

The constructor contains a single parameter which allows the user to specify the size of the stack. The constructor sets this size, allocates space for the array, and initializes `StackPointer` to –1. This defines an empty stack with all the array elements set to 0 (remember that Java automatically sets all `int`s to zero when they are declared).

The next two methods, `Empty()` and `Full()`, implement the tests described in the previous section for an empty and full stack, respectively.

The next two methods implement the pop and push operations. The `StackException` used here is just an instance of the standard `Exception` type described in Chapter 4, and is defined in the same way as the `ListException` in Chapter 7.

The `Pop()` method can throw an exception if it is called on an empty stack, since if there are no data on the stack, nothing can be popped. Similarly, the `Push()` method throws an exception if it is called on a full stack. Thus these two methods first perform a test to see if the stack is in an acceptable state for that method. If not, an exception is thrown and the method terminates.

For the `Pop()` method, if the stack contains data, the value stored at index `StackPointer` is returned, and then `StackPointer` is decremented by 1. (Recall that the `--` operator placed *after* its operand is only applied after the value of that operand has been used. Thus in this case the value of `StackPointer` is used as an index in the `Element` array *before* it is decremented.)

Note that the array is not altered in a pop operation – only the stack pointer is moved. There is no need to clear the array element, since the stack pointer keeps a record of where the top of the stack is. If another `int` is subsequently pushed onto the stack, it will simply overwrite the value left there by a previous pop operation.

Similarly, for the `Push()` method, `StackPointer` is incremented first (the ++ operator is used as a prefix operator), and then `newElement` is stored at the top of the stack.

The last two methods are simply interface methods which allow values of an `IntStack` object to be retrieved. Remember that it is not correct object-oriented design to allow direct access to the data fields of a class, so whenever the value of one of these fields is required, an interface method should be provided.

8.1.4 TESTING THE `IntStack` CLASS

In order to test the `IntStack` class and demonstrate how the exceptions can be handled, we will design a simple GUI which allows the user to enter `int`s and push them onto the stack, pop elements from the stack, and see the state of the `Element` array and `StackPointer` at each step. The applet should look like Fig. 8.1.

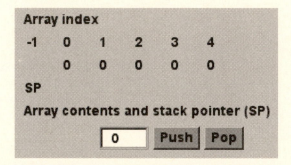

Figure 8.1

The stack array is shown in its initial state, with all array elements set to 0, and the stack pointer (SP) at location −1. The user types an `int` into the text box at the bottom and presses the 'Push' button. The array is modified, and the stack pointer moves to position 0 (so that the letters 'SP' appear under array location 0). When the 'Pop' button is pressed, the stack pointer moves one location to the left, but the contents of the array are not altered, as described above.

Tests should be included to detect the empty and full stack conditions, and display an appropriate message when these conditions are encountered.

As with the applet in Chapter 7 for testing the linked list classes, the techniques used here in laying out the components and handling events should all be familiar from earlier chapters. Three arrays of `Labels` are used in this applet. One array of `Labels` is used to display the index numbers of the `Element` array in the `IntStack` class (the top row of numbers in the applet), a second array of `Labels` is used to display the contents of the stack (the row of zeroes in Fig. 8.1), and the third array is used to print the 'SP' label at the correct location. The text will be blank at all locations but one in the third array.

When the user types a number in the text box and pushes the 'Push' button, the number is read as a `String`, converted to an `int`, and pushed onto the stack by calling its `Push()` method. Similarly, when the 'Pop' button is pressed, the stack's `Pop()` method is called. If either method results in an error (due to a full or empty stack), an error message is printed in the bottom `Label`. The `action()` method that implements all this is as shown:

```
public boolean action(Event event, Object arg)
{
    if(event.target == PushButton) {
        try
            Parent.PushStack(Integer.
                parseInt(PushNumber.getText()));
        catch (NumberFormatException e)
            Parent.SetComment("Please enter an integer
                between 1 and 99");
        return true;
    }
    else if(event.target == PopButton) {
        Parent.PopStack();
        return true;
    }
    return super.action(event,arg);
}
```

As with the linked list applet, an `Update()` method updates the display:

```
void Update(IntStack Stack)
{
    int index;
    for (index = 0; index < NUMELEMENTS - 1; ++index) {
        StackValue[index + 1].setText
            (Integer.toString(Stack.getElement(index)));
        if (index == Stack.getStackPointer()) {
            StackPointer[index + 1].setText("SP");
            StackPointer[0].setText("");
        }
        else
            StackPointer[index + 1].setText("");
    }
    if (Stack.getStackPointer() == -1)
        StackPointer[0].setText("SP");
}
```

The `getElement()` method in the `IntStack` class is used to retrieve the values in that class's `Element` array. Since these values are `int`s, the `toString()` method of the built-in Java `Integer` class is used to convert each value to a `String`, which is then assigned to the correct `Label`.

The location of the stack pointer is determined by using the `getStackPointer()` method from the `IntStack` class. The 'SP' label is set at that location, and all other `Labels` in the `StackPointer` array are cleared. Finally, if the stack is empty, the 'SP' `Label` is set at location −1.

8.2 Postfix notation

8.2.1 COMPUTER ARITHMETIC

Most humans are used to doing simple arithmetic using what is known as *infix* notation. An addition problem, such as the sum of 5 and 4, is written using the + operator as 5 + 4. The + operator is a *binary* operator, as it requires two *operands* (here, the 5 and the 4 are the operands) on which to operate. In infix notation, a binary operator is placed between its operands.

Doing things this way, however, has its problems. For example, given the problem 5 + 4 * 8 (where the * operator represents multiplication), is the answer found by doing the sum or the product first? If we do the sum first, we get 9 * 8 = 72, while if we do the product first, we get 5 + 32 = 37. You have probably been trained always to do multiplications and divisions before additions and subtractions, but there is no particular reason why this must be the case. If you want to give multiplication a higher precedence than addition, you must state this as an extra rule in your system of arithmetic. Furthermore, if you ever want to perform an addition before a multiplication, you have to introduce extra notation in the form of brackets to indicate this. For example, if you really did want to add the 5 and 4 before doing the multiplication in the problem 5 + 4 * 8, you would have to put brackets around the 5 + 4: (5 + 4) * 8.

Therefore, using infix notation requires us to introduce two extra concepts into arithmetic: precedence of operators, and brackets to override this precedence if necessary.

It turns out that there is a simpler way of writing arithmetic expressions which eliminates the need for both operator precedence and brackets. This notation, known as *postfix* notation (or *reverse Polish notation* (RPN)), is used to store arithmetic instructions in a compiled computer program. That is, although in a Java program you would write arithmetic expressions in the standard infix notation, the Java compiler translates your infix expressions into postfix expressions before the program is executed. The reason for this is that postfix expressions are easier and faster to run than their infix counterparts.

8.2.2 EVALUATING A POSTFIX EXPRESSION

Postfix notation, as its name implies, puts the operator *after* its operands, rather than between them as with infix notation. For example, the infix sum 5 + 4 would be written 5 4 + in postfix.

It is probably not obvious how this simple change can result in a system of arithmetic which eliminates the need for operator precedences and brackets. In order to see how this can be done, we need to introduce the algorithm for evaluating a postfix expression. The algorithm makes use of a stack. The input is assumed to consist of individual *tokens*, which can be either operators (such as +, *, etc.) or operands (numbers). The algorithm works as follows:

- Initialize an empty stack.
- While tokens remain in the input stream:
  - read next token;
  - if token is a number, push it onto the stack;
  - else, if token is an operator, pop top two tokens off the stack, apply the operator, and push the answer back onto the stack.
- Pop the answer off the stack.

For example, consider how we would evaluate the expression 5 4 + 8 *. In Fig. 8.2, the state of the stack is shown at each stage of the algorithm. The first token (5) is read and pushed onto the stack. The next token (4) is read and pushed onto the stack. The third token (+) is an operator, so the top two tokens (4 and 5) are popped off the stack, the operator is applied to them producing the sum (9), which is pushed back onto the stack. The next token (8) is a number, so it is pushed onto the stack. The last token (*) is an operator, so the top two tokens are popped, the operator applied to generate the product of 9 and 8, and the answer pushed back onto the stack. The final step of the algorithm pops the answer (72) from the stack, leaving an empty stack.

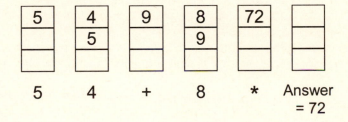

Figure 8.2.

Notice that we were able to do the infix problem (5 + 4) * 8 without the use of operator precedence or brackets. If we wished to do the infix problem 5 + (4 * 8), we could write this in postfix as 5 4 8 * + (try it and see), again without precedence rules or brackets.

The algorithm we have given above assumes that the postfix expression on which it operates is a legal one. It makes no allowances for what to do if we should input, say, an expression such as 5 4 8 + (where there are too few operators) or 5 + 4 8 * (where the + operator has only a single operand on which to operate). Error checks are quite easy to build into the algorithm, however.

In the first case (as you can verify by going through the algorithm yourself), if we have too few operators for the number of operands, we will always have an extra number on the stack after the answer is popped off at the end. Therefore, we must check the state of the stack at the end of the algorithm to ensure that it is empty.

In the second case, where we have too few operands for an operator, we will attempt to pop an operand from an empty stack. Thus we must insert a check in the part of the algorithm where an operator is applied to its operands to ensure that at least two operands are present on the stack.

In either of these cases, an error message should be printed and the algorithm should stop.

8.2.3 A POSTFIX CALCULATOR IN JAVA

We will now implement the postfix algorithm in Java by producing an applet which allows the user to input integers and operators and view the state of the stack at each point. The layout for this applet is virtually the same as that for the stack earlier in this chapter. The applet looks as shown in Fig. 8.3.

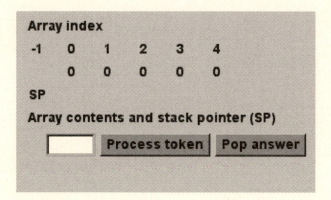

Figure 8.3.

The user enters a number or an operator in the text box and presses the 'Process token' button. If an number is entered, it is pushed onto the stack and the stack pointer (SP) moves along by one space. Tokens are entered until the end of the postfix expression, at which point the user presses the 'Pop answer' button to retrieve the answer. If no errors have occurred, the answer appears as text below the button panel; otherwise an error message is printed.

Since we will allow only integers in our applet, we can make use of the `IntStack` class defined in the previous section. The extra methods required to perform the postfix arithmetic can be added to the main applet class, which we will call `Postfix`. The methods added to the `Postfix` class to perform the calculations are as follows:

```
public void PushStack(int newNumber)
{
```

```
      SetComment("");
      try {
         RPNStack.Push(newNumber);
      }
      catch (StackException e) {
         SetComment(e.getMessage());
      }
      IndexPanel.Update(RPNStack);
}

public void PopAnswer()
{
   int Answer;

   SetComment("");
   try {
      Answer = RPNStack.Pop();
   }
   catch (StackException e) {
      SetComment(e.getMessage());
      return;
   }
   IndexPanel.Update(RPNStack);

   if (!RPNStack.Empty())
      SetComment("Too many operands");
   else
      SetComment("Answer: " +
         Integer.toString(Answer));

}

private boolean TestOperator(String operator)
{
   if (operator.equals("*") || operator.equals("/") ||
      operator.equals("+") || operator.equals("-") )
      return true;
   return false;
}

public void ApplyOperator(String operator)
   throws RPNException
{
   int operand1, operand2;

   if (!TestOperator(operator))
      throw new RPNException("Invalid operator");

   try {
```

```
      operand1 = RPNStack.Pop();
      operand2 = RPNStack.Pop();
   }
   catch (StackException e) {
      SetComment("Too few operands");
      IndexPanel.Update(RPNStack);
      return;
   }

   try {
      if (operator.equals("*"))
         RPNStack.Push(operand2 * operand1);
      else if (operator.equals("/"))
         RPNStack.Push(operand2 / operand1);
      else if (operator.equals("+"))
         RPNStack.Push(operand2 + operand1);
      else if (operator.equals("-"))
         RPNStack.Push(operand2 - operand1);
   } catch (StackException e);
   IndexPanel.Update(RPNStack);

}
```

The stack used to store the integers is called `RPNStack`, and is an instance of the `IntStack` class defined earlier in this chapter.

The `PushStack()` method is used to push an integer onto the stack and is identical to the equivalent method in the `Stacks` class used in the previous demo.

As described earlier, when the postfix expression has been completely entered into the calculator, the answer should be the sole remaining entry in the stack. The `PopAnswer()` method is used to retrieve the answer from the stack, and check that the stack is empty afterwards. If the stack is not empty, a message stating that there are too many operands is printed; otherwise the answer is printed as a Java `Label`.

Consider next the `ApplyOperator()` method. It accepts a `String` which should contain the operator to be applied. If the user has made a mistake and entered some character which is not one of the accepted operators (`*`, `/`, `+`, `-`), this must be detected before an attempt is made to apply the operator. The method `TestOperator()` is called to do this. This method simply tests the string to make sure it contains a legal operator, and returns a `boolean` result. If the string is not a legal operator, the `ApplyOperator()` method throws a new type of exception: `RPNException`.

If the operator is legal, the next step is to attempt to retrieve two operands off the stack. The stack is popped twice, with the popped numbers being stored in `operand1` and `operand2`. If a `StackException` is thrown by the `Pop()` method in the `IntStack` class, this means that the stack is empty and there are too few operands available, so an error message is printed and the `ApplyOperator()` method finishes. Otherwise, the operator is applied to the two operands, and the result pushed back onto the stack.

The whole process is set in motion by the user entering tokens and pushing the 'Process token' button, so the only other method we need to examine is the `action()` method from the button panel. It is as follows.

```
public boolean action(Event event, Object arg)
{
   if(event.target == PushButton) {
      try
         Parent.ApplyOperator(PushNumber.getText());
      catch (RPNException e2)                                    {
         try
            Parent.PushStack(Integer.parseInt
               (PushNumber.getText()));
         catch (NumberFormatException e1)
            Parent.SetComment("Enter either an integer or
               an operator");
      }
      return true;
   }
   else if(event.target == PopButton) {
      Parent.PopAnswer();
      return true;
   }
   return super.action(event,arg);
}
```

When the 'Process token' button (represented by the `Button` object `PushButton`) is pushed, the contents of the `TextField PushNumber` are passed to the `ApplyOperator` method. If an exception is thrown by this method, the `action()` method knows that the text box does not contain an operator. However, the input could still be legal if it is an integer, so inside the `catch` clause, an attempt is made to extract an integer (using `Integer.parseInt()`) from the text box. If this succeeds (no `NumberformatException` is thrown), the `PushStack()` method of the parent is called to push the number onto the stack. If the contents of the text box are neither operator nor number, an error message is printed.

Finally, if the 'Pop answer' button is pressed, the `PopAnswer()` method in the parent is called.

Queues 8.3

8.3.1 THE QUEUE DATA STRUCTURE

A queue is used in computing in much the same way as it is used in everyday life: to allow a sequence of items to be processed on a first-come-first-served basis. In most computer installations, for example, one printer is connected to several different machines, so that more than one user can submit printing jobs to the same printer. Since printing a job takes much longer than the process of actually transmitting the data from the computer to the printer, a queue of jobs is formed so that the jobs print out in the same order in which they were received by the printer. This has the irritating consequence that if your job consists of printing only a single page while the job in front of you is printing an entire 200-page thesis, you must still wait for the large job to finish before you can get your page.*

From the point of view of data structures, a queue is similar to a stack, in that data are stored in a linear fashion, and access to the data is allowed only at the ends of the queue. The actions allowed on a queue are:

- Creating an empty queue.
- Testing if a queue is empty.
- Adding data to the tail of the queue.
- Removing data from the head of the queue.

These operations are similar to those for a stack, except that pushing has been replaced by adding an item to the tail of the queue, and popping has been replaced by removing an item from the head of the queue. Because queues process data in the same order in which they are received, a queue is said to be a *first-in-first-out* or *FIFO* data structure.

8.3.2 IMPLEMENTING A QUEUE

Just as with stacks, queues can be implemented using arrays or lists. For the present, we will consider the implementation using arrays. If we attempt to follow the algorithm for adding and removing data from a queue directly, we might try to implement a queue using an array as follows.

Define a class containing an array for storing the queue elements, and two markers: one pointing to the location of the head of the queue, and the other to the first empty space following the tail. When an item is to be added to the queue, a test to see if the tail marker points to a valid location is made, then the item is added to the queue and the tail marker is incremented by 1. When an item is to be removed from the queue, a test is made to see if the queue is empty and, if not, the item at the location pointed to by the head marker is retrieved and the head marker is incremented by 1.

This procedure works well until the first time when the tail marker reaches the end of the array. If some removals have occurred during this time, there will be empty space at the beginning of the array. However, because the tail marker points to the end of the array, the queue is thought to be 'full' and no more data can be added. We could shift the data so that the head of the queue returns to the beginning of the

---

* All of which illustrates that Murphy's law applies equally well to the computer world as to the 'real' world, where, when you wish to buy one bottle of ketchup in a supermarket, you are stuck behind someone with a trolley containing enough to stock the average house for a month.

array each time this happens, but shifting data is costly in terms of computer time, especially if the data being stored in the array consist of large data objects.

A more efficient way of storing a queue in an array is to 'wrap around' the end of the array so that it joins the front of the array. Such a *circular array* allows the entire array (well, almost, as we'll see in a bit) to be used for storing queue elements without ever requiring any data to be shifted. A circular array with `QSIZE` elements (numbered from 0 to `QSIZE` − 1, as usual for Java arrays) may be visualized as shown in Fig. 8.4.

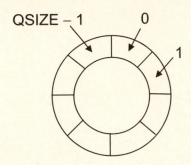

Figure 8.4.

The array is, of course, stored in the normal way in memory, as a linear block of `QSIZE` elements. The circular diagram is just a convenient way of representing the data structure.

We will need `Head` and `Tail` markers to indicate the location of the head and the location just after the tail where the next item should be added to the queue, respectively. An empty queue is denoted by the condition `Head == Tail`, as shown in Fig. 8.5.

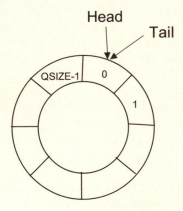

Figure 8.5.

At this point, the first item of data would be added at the location indicated by the `Tail` marker, that is, at array index 0. Adding this element gives us the situation shown in Fig. 8.6.

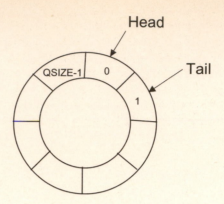

Figure 8.6.

Let us use the queue until the `Tail` marker reaches `QSIZE` – 1. We will assume that some items have been removed from the queue, so that `Head` has moved along as well (Fig. 8.7).

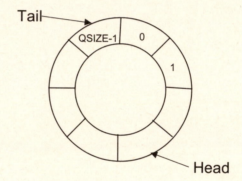

Figure 8.7.

Now we add another element to the queue at the location marked by `Tail`, that is, at array index `QSIZE` – 1. The `Tail` marker now advances one step, which positions it at array index 0. The `Tail` marker has wrapped around the array and come back to its starting point. Since the `Head` marker has moved along, those elements at the beginning of the array from index 0 up to index `Head` – 1 are available for storage. Using a circular array means that we can make use of these elements without having to shift any data.

In a similar way, if we keep removing items from the queue, eventually `Head` will point to array index `QSIZE` – 1. If we remove another element, `Head` will advance another step and wrap around the array, returning to index 0.

We have seen that the condition for an empty queue is that `Head == Tail`. What is the condition for a full queue? If we try to make use of all the array elements, then in a full queue, the tail of the queue must be the element immediately prior to the head. Since we are using the `Tail` marker to point to the array element immediately *following* the tail element in the queue, `Tail` would have to point to the same location as Head for a full queue. But we have just seen that the condition Head == Tail is the condition for an *empty* queue. Therefore, if we try to make use of all the array elements, the conditions for full and empty queues become identical. We therefore impose the rule that we must always keep at least one free space in the array, and that a queue becomes full when the Tail marker points to the location immediately prior to Head.

We may now formalize the algorithms for dealing with queues in a circular array.

- Creating an empty queue: set Head = Tail = 0.
- Testing if a queue is empty: is Head == Tail?
- Testing if a queue is full: is (Tail + 1) % QSIZE == Head?
- Adding an item to a queue: if queue is not full, add item at location Tail and set Tail = (Tail + 1) % QSIZE.
- Removing an item from a queue: if queue is not empty, remove item from location Head and set Head = (Head + 1) % QSIZE.

Recall that the % operator is the modulus operator in Java. This ensures that Head and Tail wrap around the end of the array properly. For example, suppose that Tail is QSIZE - 1 and we wish to add an item to the queue. We add the item at location Tail (assuming that the queue is not full) and then set Tail = (QSIZE - 1) + 1 % QSIZE = QSIZE % QSIZE = 0.

8.3.3 A QUEUE IN JAVA

We can now define a Java class that implements the queue operations. As before, we will embed this class in a small applet that illustrates the operation of a queue. The applet is very similar to that for the stack demo earlier in the chapter, so the layout and event handlers will be left as an exercise. The applet should look as shown in Fig. 8.8.

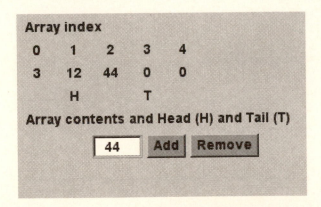

Figure 8.8.

The contents of the array are shown as usual, with the locations of the `Head` and `Tail` markers shown using the letters H and T. The 'Add' and 'Remove' buttons perform their respective actions, or else display error messages if the queue is full or empty.

A Java class that handles `ints` stored in a queue is as follows:

```java
public class IntQueue
{
    static final int QSIZE = 5;
    int Head, Tail;
    int[] Element = new int[QSIZE];

    IntQueue()
    {
        Head = Tail = 0;
    }

    public boolean Empty()
    {
        return Head == Tail;
    }

    public boolean Full()
    {
        return (Tail + 1) % QSIZE == Head;
    }

    public int Remove() throws QueueException
    {
        int HeadElement;

        if (Empty())
            throw new QueueException("Queue is empty.");
        else {
            HeadElement = Element[Head];
            Head = (Head + 1) % QSIZE;
            return HeadElement;
        }
    }

    public void Add(int newElement)
        throws QueueException
    {
        if (Full())
            throw new QueueException("Queue is full.");
        else {
            Element[Tail] = newElement;
            Tail = (Tail + 1) % QSIZE;
```

```
        }
    }

    public int getElement(int index)
    {
        return Element[index];
    }

    public int getHead()
    {
        return Head;
    }

    public int getTail()
    {
        return Tail;
    }
}
```

The operation of the various methods follows the algorithms given above precisely and so should be self-evident.

Generic classes   8.4

One point that may have occurred to you during the course of this chapter is that all the stacks and queues that we defined and used stored only one type of data, in this case `ints`. What do we do if we want a stack or queue that stores a different type of data, such as `chars`, `floats`, or even objects of some more complex class?

At first, we might think that we would need to rewrite all the code for the stack or queue, replacing `int` by the other data type wherever necessary. Obviously, this would rapidly become very tedious.

It is possible in Java to define so-called *generic classes* to get around this problem.* To understand what a generic class is and why it is useful, recall from Chapter 2 that, with the exception of Java's primitive data types, all classes in Java are derived ultimately from the `Object` class. Remember also that any variable declared to be of one data type can also handle any other data type that is descended from the original type. Therefore, if we define a stack class, say, in which the elements stored in the stack are of type `Object`, such a stack could also be used to store data of *any* type. In fact, we could even store mixed data types in the same stack.

This technique appears attactive at first sight, but there is one rather severe drawback. If the generic class is written to handle data of the `Object` type, it can

---

* If you are familiar with C++, you will know that C++ contains the `template` facility which allows you to define a prototype for a class and then declare instances of that class using other data types. There is no explicit template facility built in to Java, but the ability to define generic classes serves many of the same purposes.

use only those methods available in the `Object` class, and not any methods that might be defined in classes derived from the `Object` class. The repertoire of methods provided by the `Object` class is pretty sparse, consisting of an `equals()` method for testing if two data are equal, a `toString()` method which converts the data fields of the `Object` to `Strings`, a `hashCode()` method which produces an `int` code allowing data to be stored in hash tables (see Chapter 12), and a `clone()` method which allows an `Object` to be copied.

Fortunately, stacks require no more than what is provided by the `Object` class, so we can construct a generic stack using this technique. We will see in Chapter 9 that there is another technique, using interfaces, which allows more sophisticated generic classes to be constructed.

It is necessary to use a bit of caution when dealing with generic classes, however. We mentioned above that all Java classes are descended from the `Object` class. However, the primitive data types such as `ints` and `chars` are not included in this family tree, so we can't use a generic class directly to hold any primitive data types. To get around this problem, the java.lang library has defined so-called *wrapper* classes for all the primitive data types so that they can be converted into 'real' Java classes which *are* descendents of the `Object` class.

To illustrate the procedure for defining a generic class, we will consider a stack in which the elements stored are all `Objects`. The code follows.

```java
public class Stack
{
    static final int STACKSIZE = 5;
    int StackPointer;
    Object[] Element = new Object[STACKSIZE];

    Stack(Object initValue)
    {
        int index;
        StackPointer = -1;
        for (index = 0; index < STACKSIZE; ++index)
            Element[index] = initValue;
    }

    private boolean Empty()
    {
        return StackPointer == -1;
    }

    private boolean Full()
    {
        return StackPointer == STACKSIZE - 1;
    }

    public Object Pop() throws StackException
    {
```

```
      if (Empty())
         throw new StackException("Stack is empty.");
      else
         return Element[StackPointer—];
   }

   public void Push(Object newElement)
      throws StackException
   {
      if (Full())
         throw new StackException("Stack is full.");
      else
         Element[++StackPointer] = newElement;
   }

   public Object getElement(int index)
   {
      return Element[index];
   }

   public int getStackPointer()
   {
      return StackPointer;
   }
}
```

The code is very similar to that for `IntStack` given earlier in this chapter, but there are a few important differences. The `Element` array is declared as an array of `Objects`, but note that it is also necessary to initialize the individual elements of the array in the constructor. It was not necessary to do this in `IntStack`, since there we were dealing with primitive data types. Here, we have chosen to require the user of this generic stack to pass an initial value to the constructor, but we could equally well have used the `new` operator to create a new `Object` for each array element. A second, argumentless constructor could be provided for this purpose if desired, to give the user the choice of which initialization to use.

The only other differences are that the `Pop()` and `getElement()` methods return an `Object`, and that the `Push()` method requires an `Object` as an argument.

To construct the simple stack applet that we used in section 8.1 using this generic stack, we need to alter the `action()` method in the button panel, and the `PushStack()` method in the `Stacks` class so that they deal with the wrapper `Integer` class, rather than with the primitive `int` data type, since the generic stack can only store descendents of the `Object` class. The `action()` method becomes:

```
   public boolean action(Event event, Object arg)
   {
```

```
if(event.target == PushButton) {
   try
      Parent.PushStack(new
         Integer(PushNumber.getText()));
   catch (NumberFormatException e)
      Parent.SetComment("Please enter an integer
         between 1 and 99");
   return true;
}
else if(event.target == PopButton) {
   Parent.PopStack();
   return true;
}
return super.action(event,arg);
}
```

The `Integer()` constructor is used to attempt to create a new `Integer` from the `String` in the text box. If the user has entered text that cannot be interpreted as an `Integer`, the constructor throws a `NumberFormatException`, which is caught and results in an error message, just as before. Otherwise, the new `Integer` object is passed back to the parent's `PushStack()` method, which is shown below:

```
public void PushStack(Integer newNumber)
{
   SetComment("");
   try {
      stack.Push(newNumber);
   }
   catch (StackException e) {
      SetComment(e.getMessage());
   }
   IndexPanel.Update(stack);
}
```

This method is identical to that used in the original `IntStack` class, except that its argument is an `Integer` instead of an `int`. The `Integer newNumber` is passed to the `Push()` method in the generic `Stack` class. Since `Integer` is a descendent of `Object`, this is perfectly legal. If you had tried to pass an `int` to the generic `Stack` class's `Push()` method, however, you would get an error.

One final note on using generic classes. When we retrieve an item of data from a generic class, we must cast it back to the derived data type we are dealing with in the parent class. For example, although the `PopStack()` method in the stacks demo doesn't make any use of the value popped off the stack, we would usually wish to save this value in a variable and use it for something later. If we alter the code in `PopStack()` to save the popped value from a generic stack, we obtain the following:

```
public void PopStack()
{
   Integer popped;

   SetComment("");
   try {
      popped = (Integer)stack.Pop();
   }
   catch (StackException e) {
      SetComment(e.getMessage());
   }
   IndexPanel.Update(stack);
}
```

Here we have declared an `Integer` variable called `popped`. When the `Pop()` method is called, we must cast its return value to the data type we wish, in this case, `Integer`. This is done by putting the data type, enclosed in parentheses, in front of the call to the `Pop()` method. If we try writing simply:

```
popped = stack.Pop();
```

we get a compile-time error that an `Object` cannot be implicitly converted to an `Integer`. An explicit cast is always required.

The remainder of the code is identical to that in the demo with `IntStack` shown in section 8.1. The advantage of using a generic stack, though, is that the same class can be used without any modification to store *any* data type, which obviously saves a lot of effort and prevents many potential coding errors.

Exercises 8.5

---

1   Given an initially empty stack which accepts single characters, the following operations are performed:

> Push T
> Push E
> Push X
> Pop
> Push R
> Push V
> Pop
> Push Y
> Pop
> Pop

(a) Write out the composition of the stack after these operations.
(b) What sequence of letters was popped off the stack?

2 The string MOUSE is subjected to the following sequence of stack operations, beginning with M and working left to right:

> push push pop push push pop pop pop push pop

What string is produced by the output from the pops off the stack?

3 The string SMOKESTACK is to be rearranged to give the string MSOSEKCATK. Give a sequence of stack operations (push or pop) that would give the desired reordering, assuming that the string SMOKESTACK is to be processed left to right, i.e. beginning with the first S and ending with the last K.

4 An algorithm for converting a decimal (base 10) number into binary (base 2) is:

- Let the decimal number be D.
- While $D > 0$:
  - Let $R = D$ mod 2 (that is, R is the remainder when D is divided by 2, so that $R = 1$ if D is odd, and 0 if D is even). Write R to the left of any previous values of R.
  - Let $D = D/2$.
- The binary number is the number constructed by writing down the values of R.

Try this algorithm on paper for several small numbers, like 2, 5, and 10. Note that what you are doing is saving the series of remainders and writing them down in reverse order.

Use the `IntStack` class in this chapter to write a Java program which will read in a decimal number and produce the equivalent number in binary.

5 Modify (use inheritance if appropriate) the postfix evaluation program in this chapter so that it can handle non-negative numbers with more than one digit. To do this, you will need a subsidiary routine that can read in a string of ASCII characters representing the digits 0 to 9, and convert this string into an `int` variable. Various methods exist, but in the spirit of this chapter, use this algorithm:

- Initialize empty stack.
- While character is a number
  - push number onto a stack.
- Initialize N to 0; initialize P to 1.
- While stack is not empty
  - pop number off stack and multiply it by P,
  - add number to N,
  - multiply P by 10.

Your revised program will now have two stacks in it: one for evaluating individual operands, and the other for carrying out the postfix calculation.

6 Further modify your postfix calculator so that it can handle negative integers. In order to do this you will need to distinguish between the binary form of the − operator (signifying subtraction) and the unary form (signifying negation). You will find it easier to do this if you require that all binary operators are separated by blanks from their operands and other operators, while the minus sign must *not* have a blank between it and the number to which it applies. For example, the expression:

76 −34 −

in postfix is equivalent to 76 − (−34) = 110 in infix.

7 Use inheritance to define a new class called `PriorityQueue` which is a queue in which each item is inserted into the queue at a location determined by its *priority*. To keep things simple, assume that the elements in the queue are simple `int`s. When a new `int` is added to the queue, it moves in front of all other elements in the queue whose values are greater than it. For example, if the number 3 is to be added to the queue:

1 1 2 4 5 5 7 9

where the head of the queue is on the left, it would be inserted between the 2 and the 4. Note that the only difference between a priority queue and an ordinary queue is in the insertion method, so all other methods may be inherited directly from the queue class given in the text.

8 Modify the priority queue from the previous question so that the data structure being stored in the queue is a user-defined class containing at least two data fields. One field should be an `int` field giving the priority of that element. The other field may be anything you like (for example, a `String` giving a person's name). Modify the class methods so that they can handle this user-defined class.

9 Write the code that will produce the applets shown in Fig. 8.1 and Fig. 8.8 for testing the stack and queue classes.

10 Using the technique in section 8.5, write a generic queue class which can be used to define a queue in which the elements are any data type.

CHAPTER 9

SETS

9.1 The mathematical set

A *set* in mathematics is an unordered collection of objects of any type. To keep things simple in our introductory examples, we'll consider only sets of integers.

We can denote a set by the notation $A = \{1,2,3,4,5\}$ where A is the name of the set, and the elements of the set are the integers 1 through 5, enclosed in braces (curly brackets). A set can exist on its own, but it is also possible to define a *universal set*, which is a set that contains all elements from which other sets in the problem you are considering can be taken. For example, we might define a universal set such as $U = \{1,2,3,4,5,6,7,8,9,10\}$ which is the set of all integers from 1 through 10. In this case, any other set would have to contain only integers chosen from the universal set.

The basic operations defined for sets are:

- *Union* – the union of two sets A and B is the set containing all elements in A and B. The union is written $A \cup B$. Elements common to both A and B are *not* duplicated in the union. For example, if $A = \{1,2,3,4,5\}$ and $B = \{3,4,5,6,7\}$, the union is $A \cup B = \{1,2,3,4,5,6,7\}$. The elements 3, 4, and 5, which are common to both sets, are not duplicated in the union.
- *Intersection* – the intersection of two sets A and B, written $A \cap B$, is the set containing elements common to both A and B. For example, with A and B defined as above, the intersection is $A \cap B = \{3,4,5\}$.
- *Difference* – the difference of two sets A and B, written $A - B$, is the set of all elements of set A that are not in set B. Using A and B from the previous example, we have $A - B = \{1,2\}$.
- *Complement* – a complement of a set can only be defined if a universal set U exists. The complement of a set A, written $\bar{A}$, is defined as $U - A$. For example, with U defined as above (the set of all integers from 1 through 10), we have $\bar{A} = \{6,7,8,9,10\}$.

There is a bit more notation that is necessary to understand set terminology:

- *Membership* – an object x (which is *not* a set, merely an object) is a *member* of a set A if A contains x. This is written as $x \in A$. If an object x is not a member of the set A, this is written as $x \notin A$.
- *Subsets* – a set S is a subset of another set A if all the elements of S are also members of A. This is written as $S \subset A$. If S is not a subset of A, this is written as $S \not\subset A$.
- *Proper subsets* – a set P is a *proper subset* of a set A if P is a subset of A, but there are some elements of A that are not also members of P. For example, if $P = \{1,2,3\}$ and $A = \{1,2,3,4,5\}$, then P is a proper subset of A because the elements 4 and 5 are present in A but not in P.

Designing the set data structure   9.2

A set is a good example to use for defining a Java data structure, since it has a well-defined collection of operations that can be defined on it, so it is fairly easy to construct a class definition to represent it. To design a set class in Java, we need to identify the data fields and methods, and decide which fields should be public and which private (or protected, if we plan on using the class as a base class).

There are several ways we can implement sets in Java, so we need to consider carefully what we want our set class to achieve.

Ideally, we would like to declare sets for storing *any* data type: `ints`, `floats`, objects from user-defined classes, and so on. As we mentioned in section 8.4, Java allows the construction of generic classes, in which the data type is the fundamental `Object` class. However, we will see that the set class to be constructed in this chapter requires the elements to be sorted, which, in turn, requires that an element to be inserted into the set be compared with those elements already present. The comparison requires a 'less than' method or operator, which the `Object` class does not have. Therefore, we will construct the set class explicitly for `ints`, and postpone the construction of a generic set class to the end of this chapter.

We must now consider how we will store the elements in a set. From a mathematical point of view, if we know what elements are in the universal set, then to specify a subset of the universal set, all we need to do is say whether or not each element from the universal set is present in the subset. In other words, we could just define an array of `boolean` variables with a size equal to the size of the universal set, and then set those elements which are present in the subset to `true` and the others to `false`.

Doing things this way, though, means that we have to have some easy way to determine the array index corresponding to the set element we are interested in. If the set elements are consecutive integers, this is easy: we can just map the integers to the range 0...`ArraySize`. However, for other data types, a mapping to a sequence of integers isn't so easy.* Therefore, we will store the set elements as an array of the actual objects making up the set, rather than just a `boolean` array. For large data objects, this will require more memory, but it makes the coding a lot easier.

Finally, we need to consider how we are going to calculate things like unions and intersections. If we are storing the set elements in an array, then to calculate the union of two sets, we need to construct a third set whose elements contain all elements in the other two sets, but without any duplication. The last qualifier is what causes us some problems. If all we had to do was just copy the elements from the first two sets into the third, we could just pile the elements together into an array without any concern for their order or whether there were duplicate elements.

---

* Trying to do such a mapping leads us into the topic of hashing, which we cover in Chapter 12.

The easiest way to resolve this is to keep the set elements in *sorted order* within the array. That way, we could use the following algorithm to construct a union of two sets *A* and *B*:

- Initialize MarkerA to point to element 0 of set *A*, and MarkerB to element 0 of set *B*.
- While (MarkerA < Size of set *A*) and (MarkerB < Size of set *B*)
  - If A.Element[MarkerA] < B.Element[MarkerB], insert A.Element[MarkerA] into the union and increment MarkerA by 1.
  - Else if A.Element[MarkerA] == B.Element[MarkerB], insert A.Element[MarkerA] into the union and increment *both* MarkerA and MarkerB by 1.
  - Else insert B.Element[MarkerB] into the union and increment MarkerB by 1.
- Copy remainder of the set that has not been fully read into the union.

That is, we start at the beginnings of the two sets and step through them one element at a time, ensuring that we copy each element into the union only once. Try this algorithm yourself by hand for a couple of small sets with some common elements to convince yourself that it works.

The algorithm for intersection works similarly, except that we copy elements into the intersection set only if that element occurs in both sets.

The key point for both these algorithms is that we can rely on the set elements being sorted in increasing order. The routines for constructing a set and building unions and intersections must therefore ensure that this is always the case.

Although we haven't studied sorting algorithms yet, we will introduce a simple technique here so that we can guarantee that our set elements are sorted. The sorting algorithm we will use here is called *insertion sort*. It is not the most efficient general sorting algorithm around, but for sorting arrays that are almost in order already (as the set element array will be), it is one of the best. For a sorted array called `Element` containing `NumItems` elements, to which we wish to add one more item `NewItem`, insertion sort works as follows:

- Initialize Marker to NumItems (remember that arrays are indexed from 0, so element number NumItems is stored at location NumItems − 1).
- While Marker > 0 and NewItem < Element[Marker − 1]
  - Move Element[Marker − 1] to Element[Marker].
  - Decrease Marker by 1.
- Store NewItem in Element[Marker].

The elements in the array are shifted over one at a time until space is made at the correct location to insert NewItem. Insertion sort can be generalized to sort a completely unordered list, but we won't need that feature here.

Java code for sets   9.3

Having spent some time analyzing how we are to store a set and perform various operations on it, it is relatively easy to write the Java code for a set that stores integers. Since this class is a bit longer than those we have considered up to now, we will look at it in several parts.

First, the variable declarations and the constructor are shown.

```java
public class IntSet
{
   protected int Cardinality;
   protected int MaxSize;
   protected int[] Element;

   IntSet(int maxsize)
   {
      Cardinality = 0;
      MaxSize = maxsize;
      Element = new int[MaxSize];
   }
   // other methods
}
```

The Cardinality is the number of elements actually in the set (so an empty set has Cardinality zero, and so on). MaxSize is the size of the array in which the set elements will be stored, and Element is the actual array. Note that we allow the user to specify the array size as the argument to the constructor, so that the space for the array isn't allocated until the constructor is executed.

Next, we examine the code for the union operation.

```java
public IntSet Union(IntSet Set2) throws SetException
{
   IntSet UnionSet =
      new IntSet(MaxSize + Set2.MaxSize);
   int marker1 = 0, marker2 = 0;

   while (marker1 < Cardinality &&
      marker2 < Set2.Cardinality)
   {
      if(Element[marker1] < Set2.Element[marker2])
      {
         UnionSet.Insert(Element[marker1]);
         ++marker1;
      } else if
         (Element[marker1] == Set2.Element[marker2])
      {
         UnionSet.Insert(Element[marker1]);
```

```
          ++marker1;  ++marker2;
      } else
      {
         UnionSet.Insert(Set2.Element[marker2]);
         ++marker2;
      }
   }
   for (; marker1 < Cardinality; ++marker1)
      UnionSet.Insert(Element[marker1]);

   for (; marker2 < Set2.Cardinality; ++marker2)
      UnionSet.Insert(Set2.Element[marker2]);

   return UnionSet;
}
```

The `Union()` method will form the union of the set which calls the method (which we will refer to as `Set1`, even though its name never actually appears in the method code), with `Set2`, which is passed as an argument to the method.

We have defined a new exception called `SetException` to handle attempts to store more elements in a set than the array can hold. The exception is generated only by the `Insert()` method, which we consider below.

A new set called `UnionSet` is declared to hold the union as it is constructed. The size of `UnionSet` is set to be the sum of the `MaxSize` parameters from `Set1` and `Set2`, since this is as large as the union can possibly be.

Next, we declare and initialize the two markers (`marker1` and `marker2`) which will be used to step through the two sets. The `while` loop performs the union algorithm as given above. The set elements at the current marker positions are compared: if they are unequal, the smaller element is added to the union and the corresponding marker advanced by one; if they are equal, the element is added (once) to the union, and *both* markers advanced by one. This process continues until one of the markers reaches the last element in its set. Following the `while` loop are two `for` loops which pick up any remaining elements from whichever set contained more elements. Finally, the completed `UnionSet` is returned.

The `Union()` method (and several other methods) make use of the `Insert()` method, which inserts a single element into a set. Its code is as follows:

```
public void Insert(int NewElement)
   throws SetException
{
   if (Cardinality >= MaxSize)
      throw new SetException("Cannot insert -
         set full.");
   else if (!Contains(NewElement))
   {
      int marker = Cardinality;
      while (marker > 0 &&
```

```
            NewElement < Element[marker-1])
        {
            Element[marker] = Element[marker-1];
            ——marker;
        }
        Element[marker] = NewElement;
        ++Cardinality;
    }
}
```

First, a check is made that the array is not full – if it is, a `SetException` is thrown and the method terminates. Next, a check is made (by calling the `Contains()` method, considered below) that the element is not in the set already. If the set already contains the element, nothing further is done. No exception is thrown in this case, since no error has occurred.

If `NewElement` is to be added to the set, the insertion sort algorithm is used to find the correct insertion point. Starting at the largest element, each data item is moved over by one space until the correct location is found, at which point `NewElement` is inserted. Since the size of the set has increased, the `Cardinality` is incremented by 1.

The `Contains()` method checks whether an element is in the set:

```
public boolean Contains(int TestElement)
{
    int marker;
    for (marker = 0; marker < Cardinality; ++marker)
        if (TestElement == Element[marker])
            return true;
    return false;
}
```

Finally, there are three simple utility methods that we will find useful when designing the applet for testing the `IntSet` class:

```
public void Clear()
{
    Cardinality = 0;
}

public int getCardinality()
{
    return Cardinality;
}

public int getElement(int index)
{
    return Element[index];
}
```

The `Clear()` method clears a set by setting `Cardinality` to 0, effectively making it the empty set. The methods `getCardinality()` and `getElement()` merely retrieve data fields from the `IntSet` object.

The implementations of other set operations, such as intersection and difference, are left as exercises.

The applet designed to test the `IntSet` class is similar to those developed in Chapters 7 and 8 for testing lists, stacks and queues, so we will not dwell on the code here. The interface appears as shown in Fig. 9.1.

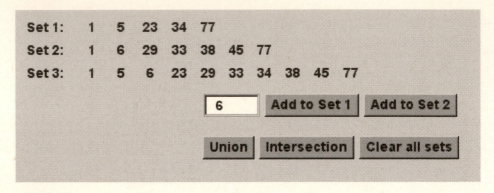

Figure 9.1.

The overall applet is split into three sub-panels: one for displaying the contents of the three sets, one for the first row of controls (the text box and buttons for adding elements to the two sets) and one for the second row of controls (union, intersection, and clearing the sets). Sets 1 and 2 can hold up to a maximum of 10 elements, and set 3 up to 20.

The user is allowed to enter an integer into the text box and add this integer to either of sets 1 or 2 by pressing the correct button. The union or intersection of sets 1 and 2 can be found by pressing the corresponding button, with the result being displayed as set 3. The 'Clear all sets' button resets all three sets to be empty, and clears the display. In addition, any error messages resulting from exceptions are displayed in a `Label` below the second row of buttons.

9.4 Generic classes using interfaces

In our introduction to generic classes at the end of Chapter 8, we mentioned that a generic class based on the `Object` data type is quite restrictive because of the lack of methods available in the `Object` class. A glance back at the `IntSet` class in this chapter shows, for example, that an element to be inserted into a set must be compared with the elements already present in the set so that we may store the set elements in sorted order. Since the `Object` class provides no methods for comparing data, we cannot use the same technique to produce a generic set class as we did in producing a generic stack.

However, we can use another feature of Java to define a set class that can serve as a generic class. It requires a bit more effort than that involved in the generic class for a stack, but the result is more general, and the technique can be used for any type of class.

The technique involves using the Java `interface`. An `interface` is a special type of abstract class, in which the prototypes of several methods can be declared, but not defined. Since an `interface` is an *abstract* class, it is not possible to define any instances of an `interface` using the `new` operator. An `interface` can only be used if another class `implements` it. The Java keyword `implements` is a bit like the `extends` keyword by which inheritance is performed. The main differences between `extends` and `implements` are as follows.

- `extends` applies to a class, but `implements` applies to an interface.
- A class which `extends` another class inherits all the data fields and methods of the class which is extended. Although methods of the base class may be overridden in the derived class, they need not be.
- A class which `implements` an interface *must* provide definitions for all the methods declared in the interface, since all interface methods are abstract.
- A class may extend at most one other class, but it may implement any number of interfaces.

An obvious question, given these conditions, is: since a class which `implements` an `interface` must provide definitions for all the methods declared in the `interface`, why bother with the interface at all? Why not just define all the methods for the first time in the class which you are actually going to use?

The answer to this question provides us with a technique for defining a generic class, so the easiest way to demonstrate this is to proceed with an example.

Since our aim in this chapter is to produce a class representing a set, and we have decided to store the set elements in sorted order, we need a method that will tell us whether or not one element is 'less than' another. We also need another method that tells us if two elements are equal in value. We can therefore define an `interface` which contains these two methods. Let us call this `interface` `Comparable`. The Java code for the `interface` definition might look like this:

```
public interface Comparable
{
   public boolean lessThan(Comparable other);
   public boolean equalTo(Comparable other);
}
```

Here, the `lessThan()` method accepts another `Comparable` object `other`, and returns `true` if the object that called the `lessThan()` method is, in some sense yet to be defined, 'less than' the other object `other`. We say 'in some sense yet to be defined', since the meaning of 'less than' depends on the class in which it is defined. If the class contains a single numerical field, for example, one object

```
        if (Cardinality >= MaxSize)
          throw new SetException("Cannot insert -
            set full.");
        else if (!Contains(NewElement))
        {
          int marker = Cardinality;
          while (marker > 0 &&
            NewElement.lessThan(Element[marker-1]))
          {
            Element[marker] = Element[marker-1];
            --marker;
          }
          Element[marker] = NewElement;
          ++Cardinality;
        }
    }

    public boolean Contains(Comparable TestElement)
    {
      int marker;
      for (marker = 0; marker < Cardinality; ++marker)
        if (TestElement.equalTo(Element[marker]))
          return true;
      return false;
    }

    public void Clear()
    {
      Cardinality = 0;
    }

    public int getCardinality()
    {
      return Cardinality;
    }

    public Comparable getElement(int index)
    {
      return Element[index];
    }
```

The alterations required are:

- Whenever two `Element` values are compared, the methods `lessThan()` and `equalTo()` must be used in place of < and ==, respectively.
- Set elements are of type `Comparable` rather than `int`.

This `Set` class can now be used to handle any class that implements the

`Comparable interface`. This means that we *cannot* use it with primitive data types such as `int` or `char`, just as with the generic stack. However, we also *cannot* use it with any of the Java library classes, since they do not implement `Comparable`. We will need to provide our own wrapper classes for any of these standard classes if we wish to store them using the `Set` class. Usually this involves nothing more than just defining a class with the `implement Comparable` clause, and then defining a single data field consisting of the Java library class we wish to wrap, followed by definitions for the methods in the `Comparable interface`. We have done this above with the `MyInteger` class.

This technique of producing generic classes may be used for all the remaining data structures covered in this book. In the interests of clarity, however, we won't be using generic classes for the remainder of the book. As you can see, though, it is fairly straightforward to produce generic classes for any data structure.

Exercises   9.5

1   Add methods to the `IntSet` class in the text to implement:
(a) set difference;
(b) a test that a set is a subset of another set;
(c) a test that a set is equal to another set;
(d) a test that a set is a *proper* subset of another set.

2   Derive a class from `IntSet` which includes a *universal set* field. The universal set should be the set of integers from 0 to `SetSize` − 1. Add a class method which implements the *set complement* operation.

3   (a) Write a set class that stores `chars` instead of `ints`. (You may do this either by rewriting `IntSet`, or by using the generic set class to store `chars` that have been wrapped in the `Character` class.)
(b) Write an applet which allows the user to enter some text in a `TextArea` and, using the set class you have written, generate a set of `chars` giving all the ASCII characters used in the text entered by the user.
(c) Add a second `TextArea` to the applet from part (b) and generate a set of `chars` containing those ASCII characters that are common to both `TextAreas`.

4   Define a set class in which a set of `ints` is stored using the other method described in the text. That is, a set is represented by an array of `boolean` values where each value in the array indicates whether the corresponding element is present or absent in the set. Define class methods for implementing union, intersection, reading, and writing for sets represented in this way.

5   (a) Write a class called `MyString` which implements the `Comparable` interface given in the text. This class should contain the same methods as the `MyInteger` class in the text, except that the data field should be a Java `String` object instead of an `int`. Use methods from the `String` class to

implement the `lessThan()` method (which should return `true` if the first `String` is alphabetically prior to the second), and the `equalTo()` method (which should return `true` if the two `Strings` contain the same text).

(b) Use the `MyString` class in the applet from question 3 to construct sets of the individual words in each `TextArea`. Provide an alphabetical list of (i) the words in each `TextArea`; (ii) a list of all words in *both* `TextArea`; (iii) a list of words common to the two `TextAreas`.

CHAPTER 10

SEARCHING ALGORITHMS

10.1 The study of algorithms

An *algorithm* is a precise set of instructions for achieving a particular goal. In a computer program, all data structures have associated algorithms which are used to access and modify the data they contain. Built-in data structures in Java, such as `ints` and `floats`, have built-in algorithms for such things as arithmetic and comparisons. User-defined classes have their associated algorithms encapsulated in their class methods.

For many operations performed on data structures, there are several different algorithms that may be used. Different algorithms make different demands on computer memory and running time. In an industrial setting, where the cost of commercial software and staff time become important, the availability and price of off-the-shelf routines that implement the algorithms, and the programming time required to implement the algorithm if no commercial package is available, must be considered.

Therefore, it is useful to know things like the running time and memory requirements of algorithms so that you can make an informed decision about which algorithm is best for your particular application. The theoretical study of algorithms, known as *complexity theory*, is a highly mathematical branch of computer science. It involves detailed analysis of the number of steps required by an algorithm to process varying amounts of data. For many algorithms, exact results have been derived, but for others, only approximations or averages are available.

Since this book assumes no significant mathematical knowledge on the part of the reader, we won't be going into any detailed studies of the complexities of the algorithms we will be studying. It is still important, however, for you to achieve an understanding of how the complexity of an algorithm is measured, and to develop techniques whereby you can measure these complexities experimentally by actually running programs to calculate them. This is one of the goals of this chapter.

We begin our study of algorithms by looking at a couple of methods for searching a list of items. We use searching algorithms as an introduction because they are commonly used as examples in an introductory course in programming, so there is a good chance you have met them before. They are also fairly simple algorithms, both to code and to analyze, so you shouldn't have to wrestle with the concepts behind the algorithms while you are trying to see how their efficiencies can be measured.

We will consider two searching algorithms: sequential search and binary search.

10.2 Sequential search

Both searching algorithms we will consider in this chapter work on one-dimensional lists of data. The data may be stored in an array or a linked list. The examples in this chapter all assume that the data are stored in an array.

A searching algorithm requires a *target* for which to search. The list is searched until either the target is located or the algorithm has determined that the target is not in the list. For simple data types, such as `ints`, a simple comparison is performed between the target and the data stored at each node in the list. For more complex data types such as user-defined classes, often one of the fields is chosen as a *key* field. The target is then compared only to the key field, with the other fields being ignored for the purposes of the search. For example, a database may store customer information for a company. A customer is represented by a class in which the surname, first name, address, phone number, and so on are stored. For searching purposes, an ID number unique to each customer may be defined. This number is then used as the key field in the class, and the searching algorithm would expect the target to be an ID number.

The sequential search is simple: we start at the first array element and compare each key with the target until we have either found the target or reached the end of the list without finding it. The index of the corresponding array element is returned if the search is successful, and an exception is thrown if the search fails. We can formalize the algorithm as follows:

1   Read in `Target`; initialize `Marker` to first array index (0).

2   While `Target != Key` at location `Marker` and not at the end of the list:

3   `Marker++`.

4   If `Target == Key` at location `Marker`, then return `Marker`.

5   Else, throw an exception.

Binary search   10.3

There are two forms of the binary search algorithm, both of which are designed to be applied to lists of *sorted* data. The condition that the data be sorted is a constraint not present for the sequential search, and could mean that extra computing is required to sort the list before the binary search is used. Since sorting algorithms are always less efficient than searching algorithms (as we will see in the next chapter), this could mean that even though binary search on its own is much more efficient than sequential search, the combination of (sort + binary search) may actually be less efficient than sequential search on its own. The binary search algorithm is best used on lists that are constructed and sorted once, and then repeatedly searched.

The first form of binary search we will look at here is sometimes called the *forgetful binary search* because it doesn't bother to check if the target node has been found until the very end of the algorithm. The forgetful algorithm looks less efficient than it needs to be, but as we will see, it is in most cases more efficient than the other form of the binary search.

The basic idea behind either binary search algorithm is to chop the list in half at each step, so that you only have half as many keys to search at each stage. The forgetful binary search continues to chop the list in half until there is only one ele-

```
      while (top > bottom)
      {
         middle = (top + bottom) / 2;
         if (Element[middle] < Target)
            bottom = middle + 1;
         else
            top = middle;
      }
      if (top == -1)
         throw new SearchException("List is empty.");
      if (Element[top] == Target)
         return top;
      else
         throw new SearchException("Target not found.");
   }

   int TargetSearch(int Target) throws SearchException
   {
      int top = ArraySize - 1, bottom = 0, middle;

      while (top >= bottom)
      {
         middle = (top + bottom) / 2;
         if (Element[middle] == Target)
            return middle;
         else if(Element[middle] < Target)
            bottom = middle + 1;
         else
            top = middle - 1;
      }
      throw new SearchException("Target not found.");
   }
}
```

This class deals with an array of `ints` – if you wished to sort a non-primitive data type, you would need to write your own methods for the comparison operators `==` and `<`. This class initializes the array by filling it with its index – in 'real life', of course, the array would contain more sensible data. This is a simple way of generating a list of sorted data on which the binary search can be tested.

We could test this class by writing an applet to allow the user to enter target values for which the class would search, but we will delay writing an applet until the next section.

10.5   Efficiency of searching algorithms – counting steps

The two searching algorithms presented in this chapter demonstrate that different methods require different amounts of work to achieve the same ends. The sequential search requires a number of comparisons (on average) that is roughly proportional to the size of the list being searched, while the binary search requires only one extra comparison (on average) when the list size is doubled.

Similar situations exist with the various algorithms that are used to perform other common computing tasks, such as sorting, dealing with trees and graphs, and so on. In order for you to make an intelligent choice of which algorithm to use in a given situation, you need to have some idea of how the efficiencies of algorithms are calculated. A full treatment of algorithm efficiency requires a proficiency in mathematics that we are not requiring of any reader of this book. We will try to convey a feel for how the efficiency of algorithms can be measured without using anything more than basic arithmetic, so that you can at least take an educated guess at the efficiency of an algorithm when you first meet it.

10.5.1 BEST, WORST, AND AVERAGE CASES

There are three main measures of efficiency that can be applied to most algorithms: the *best, worst,* and *average* cases. For example, in the sequential search algorithm, the best case occurs when the target for which you are searching is the first item in the list, since only one comparison needs to be done. The worst case is when the target is either the last item in the list or is not in the list at all, since the target must be compared with every list key in either of these cases. The average case is found by considering all possible outcomes of a search and averaging the number of comparisons over all these cases.

10.5.2 EFFICIENCY OF THE SEQUENTIAL SEARCH

Let us try to estimate the best, worst, and average number of comparisons for a list of length *n*. As just mentioned, the best case for the sequential search occurs when the target is the first item in the list, since only one comparison must be done. Thus the best case is always one comparison, independent of the list length *n*.

The worst case occurs when the target is either the last list item or is not present in the list, since both of these cases require *n* comparisons. Thus the worst case is proportional to the length of the list: double the length of the list and you double the amount of work you need to do.

The average case can be worked out by adding up the number of comparisons that you need to do for all possible outcomes and then dividing by the number of possible outcomes. However, it is more useful if we separate the efficiency estimates for the cases of *successful* and *unsuccessful* outcomes of the search. For an unsuccessful search, we know that we always require *n* comparisons, so the best, worst, and average efficiencies are all the same. For a successful search, the best case requires one comparison, and the worst case requires *n* comparisons.

What of the average number of comparisons required for a successful search? If we assume that any of the keys in the list is equally likely to be the target for which we are searching, then we would expect that, on average, we would have to look at half the list before we found the target. Thus we can estimate that the average number of comparisons is about $n/2$.

If you know a bit of algebra it isn't too hard to work out an exact formula for the average number of comparisons. Doing this shows that the value is $(n + 1)/2$, which is very close to our estimate of $n/2$, especially if the list is very long.

10.5.3 EFFICIENCY OF BINARY SEARCH

We know that the forgetful binary search looks first at the middle element in a sorted list. If the target lies in the upper half of the list, the lower half is ignored for the remainder of the search. Similarly, if the target lies in the lower half, the upper half is ignored. The process is repeated with the half-list and again with half of the half-list, and so on until we have only one element left. Finally, there is a comparison of this last element with the actual target to see if the target has been found.

We can get an estimate of how many comparisons are required by considering lists whose lengths are powers of 2 (2, 4, 8, 16, 32, and so on). The number of comparisons that is done in the first stage of the algorithm, where the list is being chopped in half at each stage, is equal to the number of times 2 divides the list length. For a list of length 8, for example, 3 divisions will be done, since $8 = 2 \times 2 \times 2 = 2^3$. The final comparison with the one remaining element makes a total of 4 comparisons for a list of length 8. For a list whose length is exactly the nth power of 2, there will be $n + 1$ comparisons required.

For lists with lengths that are not exact powers of 2, we would expect the number of comparisons to be close to that required for the list whose length is the nearest power of 2. For example, for a list of length 1000, we might expect that 10 comparisons would be needed to divide the list to the point where only one element remains (since the nearest power of 2 is $2^{10} = 1024$), with one further comparison to see if that element is the target we are looking for. We would predict therefore, that about 11 comparisons would be needed to locate an element in a list of length 1000. In addition, we would expect that the number of comparisons should be about the same whether the search is successful or unsuccessful.

For the targetted binary search, things are a bit different. If the search is unsuccessful, the same number of list-halvings is required as with the forgetful search, except that twice as many comparisons are done at each stage. For lists that are powers of 2 in length, we would therefore expect the number of comparisons to be twice the exponent of 2. For example, for a list of length $1024 = 2^{10}$, we would expect about 20 comparisons would be necessary.

The situation gets a bit more complicated for a successful search. If the target is found on the first attempt, for example, only 1 comparison is required. On the second try, we need to subdivide the list once, which incurs 2 comparisons, then we need to do the final comparison to verify that we have found the target, for a total of 3 comparisons. It's fairly easy to extend the argument to see that, if the target is found on the nth division of the list, a total of $2n + 1$ comparisons are done. Again considering lists that are powers of 2 in length, at most n subdivisions can be made before the list is reduced to length 1. If it were equally likely for the target to be found at each subdivision, we could find the average number of comparisons by dividing $(1 + 3 + 5 + \ldots + (2n + 1))$ by n, but unfortunately, things aren't quite that simple. To see why, try subdividing a list of length 8 by hand. On the first comparison, there is only one possible target: the `middle` element. After dividing the list in half, we might search either the lower half or the upper half, so there are two possible targets. Similarly, at the next stage there are four possible targets, and so on. Thus, it is more likely that the target will be found later in the process than earlier.

It is possible to work out the formula for this if you try hard enough, and the result is that, for fairly long lists, about twice as many comparisons as for the forgetful search are required for the successful search as well. However, the complexity of the calculation for this fairly simple algorithm should show you that a theoretical analysis of algorithm complexity is not often very easy.

10.5.4 COMPUTER EXPERIMENTS FOR FINDING COMPLEXITY

It is instructive to test these predictions by actually running the algorithms and counting the number of comparisons for a large number of searches. To this end, we will derive a new class from the `Search` class to test the efficiency of sequential search.

In doing our tests, we shall be concerned only with those comparisons between the target and a list element. In the program itself there are several other comparisons that are done (for example, testing termination conditions in `for` loops), but we shall ignore those. We want to find out how much work the algorithm itself is actually doing.

The new class will have some extra data fields for storing things like the number of comparisons done in a search, and the average numbers of comparisons for successful and unsuccessful searches. We will need to modify the various searching methods to have them count the comparisons.

To calculate an average for the number of comparisons required in a search, we need to run the search a large number of times for various targets and keep some statistics on the outcomes. Therefore, we will use the constructor for the new class to fill up the array with numbers (rather than reading them in from the keyboard), and then use a pseudo-random number generator to produce a stream of targets for which we shall search the list and record the number of comparisons required in each case. To separate successful from unsuccessful searches we will do a series of searches for numbers that we know to be in the list, and then another series of searches for numbers that we know are not in the list.

The new Java class for implementing these experiments is as follows:

```java
public class SearchEff extends Search
{
    static final int SEQSEARCH = 0;
    static final int FORGETSEARCH = 1;
    static final int TARGETSEARCH = 2;
```

```
int NumRuns, Comparisons, SearchType;
float AverageSuccess, AverageFail;

SearchEff(int arraysize, int numruns, int searchtype)
{
   super(arraysize);
   NumRuns = numruns;
   SearchType = searchtype;
   AverageSuccess = AverageFail = (float)0.0;
}

int SeqSearch(int Target) throws SearchException
{
   int index;
   Comparisons = 0;

   for (index = 0; index < ArraySize; ++index)
   {
      ++Comparisons;
      if (Element[index] == Target)
         return index;
   }
   throw new SearchException("Target not found.");
}

int ForgetSearch(int Target) throws SearchException
{
   int top = ArraySize - 1, bottom = 0, middle;

   Comparisons = 0;
   while (top > bottom)
   {
      middle = (top + bottom) / 2;
      ++Comparisons;
      if (Element[middle] < Target)
         bottom = middle + 1;
      else
         top = middle;
   }
   if (top == -1)
      throw new SearchException("List is empty.");
   ++Comparisons;
   if (Element[top] == Target)
      return top;
   else
      throw new SearchException("Target not found.");
}

int TargetSearch(int Target) throws SearchException
```

```
{
    int top = ArraySize - 1, bottom = 0, middle;

    Comparisons = 0;
    while (top >= bottom)
    {
        middle = (top + bottom) / 2;
        ++Comparisons;
        if (Element[middle] == Target)
            return middle;
        else if (Element[middle] < Target) {
            ++Comparisons;
            bottom = middle + 1;
        }
        else
            top = middle - 1;
    }
    throw new SearchException("Target not found.");
}

void TestSearch()
{
    int count;

    for (count = 0; count < NumRuns; ++count)
    {
        try
            switch (SearchType) {
            case SEQSEARCH:
                SeqSearch((int)(ArraySize * Math.random())
                    + ArraySize);
                break;
            case FORGETSEARCH:
                ForgetSearch((int)(ArraySize * Math.random())
                    + ArraySize);
                break;
            case TARGETSEARCH:
                TargetSearch((int)(ArraySize * Math.random())
                    + ArraySize);
                break;
            }
        catch (SearchException e);
        AverageFail += Comparisons;
    }
    AverageFail /= NumRuns;

    for (count = 0; count < NumRuns; ++count)
    {
        try
```

```
            switch (SearchType) {
            case SEQSEARCH:
                SeqSearch((int)(ArraySize * Math.random()));
                break;
            case FORGETSEARCH:
                ForgetSearch((int)(ArraySize
                    * Math.random()));
                break;
            case TARGETSEARCH:
                TargetSearch((int)(ArraySize
                    * Math.random()));
                break;
            }
        catch (SearchException e);
        AverageSuccess += Comparisons;
    }
    AverageSuccess /= NumRuns;
}

float getFail()
{
    return AverageFail;
}

float getSuccess()
{
    return AverageSuccess;
}

}
```

The class `SearchEff` inherits the `Search` class and overrides its searching methods to include a counter for the number of comparisons. Note that only comparisons between `Target` and one of the data stored in the `Element` array are counted for the purposes of these experiments. Apart from the inclusion of the comparison counts, the three searching methods are identical to their counterparts in the `Search` class.

The actual experiment is run by calling the `TestSearch()` method. The type of search (sequential, or one of the binary searches) is assumed to have been specified in the constructor, and the corresponding method is called depending on the `SearchType` flag. The number of searches is also specified in the constructor by setting the parameter `NumRuns`. The `for` loop generates `NumRuns` random numbers using the `random()` method in the Java `Math` library. This method generates a `double` value between 0.0 and 1.0, so it must be scaled to give the required range of values. Since the `Element` array was initialized with the values from 0 to `ArraySize` − 1, we know that any number in that range will result in a successful search, and any number outside that range will result in an unsuccessful search. The unsuccessful searches are done first, and the numbers are chosen by generating a number between 0 and `ArraySize` − 1 and then adding `ArraySize` to it. The second `for` loop simply generates values in the range 0 to `ArraySize` − 1. The variables `AverageFail` and `AverageSuccess` keep a running total of the number of comparisons done in each run, and after all runs have been completed, the average values are found by dividing the totals by `NumRuns`. The last two methods return these values to an external class.

We can run these experiments for a range of array sizes and plot the results to get a feel for how the efficiencies of these algorithms depend on the length of the list. The result for the sequential search is shown in Fig. 10.1.

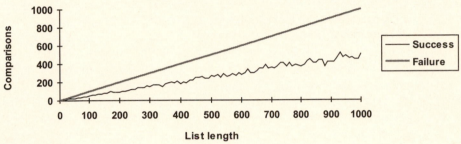

Figure 10.1.

As expected, both curves increase in direct proportion to the length of the list, and the number of comparisons required for an unsuccessful search is about twice that for a successful search.

The results for the forgetful binary search are shown in Fig. 10.2. As expected, the number of comparisons is roughly the same for successful and unsuccessful searches.* However, the main thing to notice is that the overall number of comparisons is much smaller than for the sequential search. This seems to indicate that there is some fundamental difference between the two algorithms. We shall explore this idea in the next section.

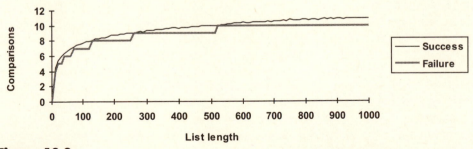

Figure 10.2.

* You may notice that the 'Success' curve is fairly smooth, whereas the 'Failure' curve goes up in a series of steps. This is due to the method used for measuring the unsuccessful search. Try to figure out why this happens and rewrite the corresponding method to get a smoother curve.

10.6   Efficiency of algorithms – general

10.6.1 CLASSIFYING ALGORITHMS BY THEIR EFFICIENCY

We saw in the last section that two algorithms for achieving the same result (locating an item in a list) can have very different efficiencies. It is natural to ask whether such differences exist for algorithms in other areas, and whether there is any systematic way of finding and classifying efficiencies.

As you might expect, the answer to all these questions is 'Yes'. There are various approaches to the study of algorithm efficiency, but since we are not assuming any great mathematical proficiency on the part of the reader, we must stick with heuristic and experimental methods. The general sorts of arguments and methods that we will use were illustrated in the last section, where we gave a simple argument to estimate the efficiencies of both the sequential and binary search algorithms. For some algorithms, such arguments are fairly easy to construct; for others, considerably more difficult. One thing we can always do, though, is a series of computer experiments in which we count the number of steps required to run the algorithm on data sets of varying sizes. We used this method in the last section as well, and managed to produce some plots of the number of steps as a function of the length of the list being searched.

We discovered, both by heuristic argument and by computer experiment, that the average number of comparisons required in using sequential search is directly proportional to the length of the list. Using the same methods, we discovered that the average number of comparisons required in the binary search is proportional to the power to which 2 must be raised to obtain the length of the list (that is, if the list length is 2^n, the number of comparisons is proportional to n).

We usually find, either by theoretical argument or by computer experimentation, that the number of steps required by an algorithm depends on some simple expression involving the amount of data being processed. For example, in the case of sequential search, we can say the number C of comparisons is (roughly) equal to half the length L of the list: $C = L/2$. In the case of the forgetful binary search, if the length L of the list can be written as $L = 2^n$, then the number of comparisons is roughly equal to n: $C = n$.

The most important thing to notice about the efficiency of the sequential search is that C is *directly proportional* to L. The fact that the scaling factor is 1/2, although useful to know, is not the most important bit of information. Knowing that C is directly proportional to L means that we know that if the length of the list is doubled, the number of comparisons required will double also; if the length is tripled, the number of comparisons also triples, and so on. In other words, what is important is that C is directly proportional to L, and not what the actual proportionality constant is. The main point of working out the efficiency of an algorithm is to know how it behaves for large amounts of data; in particular, how fast the amount of work increases as the amount of data increases.

We can therefore make an argument for classifying together all algorithms in which the number of steps increases in direct proportion to the amount of data.

Such algorithms are called *linear* algorithms (since the graph of the amount of work versus the amount of data is a straight line, as we saw for the sequential search in the last section).

In a similar way, we can classify together all algorithms that behave like the binary search. These sorts of algorithms are called *logarithmic* algorithms. If you know how logarithms are defined in mathematics, you will see why this is true. If you don't know what logarithms are, a brief description is in order.

Consider an expression like the one we used above for the length of a list in terms of a power of 2: $L = 2^n$. The *logarithm* of L (to base 2) is *defined* to be n. That is, log $L = n$, if $L = 2^n$. In words, the (base 2) logarithm of a number is the power to which 2 must be raised to give that number. The logarithm of 2 is therefore 1 (since $2^1 = 2$), the logarithm of 4 is 2 (since $2^2 = 4$), the logarithm of 8 is 3 (since $2^3 = 8$), and so on.

Logarithms of numbers that aren't exact powers of 2 can also be defined using some mathematical trickery. For example, we can define the logarithm of 5 to be the power to which 2 must be raised to give 5. Since 5 isn't an exact power of 2, but lies between 4 and 8, you would expect that the logarithm of 5 is somewhere between 2 and 3, and you would be right (it is 2.322, to 3 decimal places). For the purposes of this book, don't worry about how such 'weird' logarithms are calculated, since that requires a fair bit of mathematical knowledge. If you remember that a base 2 logarithm of a number is the power to which 2 has to be raised to get that number, that's all you need.

The forgetful binary search algorithm has an efficiency that can therefore be written as $C = \log L$, where C is the number of comparisons, and L is the length of the list.

One final note about logarithms: if you want to use a calculator to evaluate a base 2 logarithm, you may have to use a two-step procedure. Most calculators don't have a button for working out base 2 logarithms directly. The most common logarithm buttons are labelled 'log' or 'ln'. The 'log' button gives you a *base 10* logarithm, which is the power to which 10 (not 2) must be raised to give a number. For example, the base 10 logarithm of 100 is 2, since $10^2 = 100$, and so on. To get a base 2 logarithm from a base 10 logarithm, divide the base 10 logarithm of the number by the base 10 logarithm of 2. For example, to get the base 2 logarithm of 5, find the base 10 logarithm of 5 by pressing the 'log' button on your calculator. The calculator will show the answer as 0.69897. Now divide this number by the base 10 logarithm of 2 (which is 0.30103) to get the base 2 logarithm of 5, which is 2.32193.

10.6.2 THE BIG-OH NOTATION

Once you get used to the idea of classifying algorithms by the general way they depend on the amount of data, you will find a shorthand notation for efficiency to be quite handy. We can borrow such a notation from mathematics. We can represent a linear algorithm (one where the number of steps increases in direct proportion to the amount of data) by the notation $O(n)$, which is read 'order n'. This notation means that, for 'large' values of n (where n is a quantity that measures the amount of data being processed by the algorithm; n was equal to L when we were discussing list lengths above, for example), the number of steps taken by the algorithm is directly proportional to the amount of data being processed.

The restriction of this definition to 'large values of n' is imposed because in some cases the exact form of the dependence of the number of steps on the amount of data implied by the notation $O(n)$ doesn't become accurate until n gets quite large. For example, we mentioned above that the average number of comparisons required by sequential search on a list of length L is $(L + 1)/2$, which expands to $L/2 + 1/2$. The extra term of $1/2$ means that the number of comparisons isn't strictly proportional to L. However, when the list gets very long, so that L gets very large, the extra $1/2$ fades into insignificance and saying that the number of steps is proportional to L becomes more and more accurate. The notation $O(n)$ thus means that the term that increases the fastest is the one proportional to n. There could be other 'lower order' terms (that is, terms that don't change as fast as n increases), but these will become negligible as n gets large.

In the case of the binary search, the highest order term (the term that increases the fastest) is the logarithmic term, so we say that the binary search is an $O(\log n)$ algorithm.

Therefore, all algorithms can be classified by giving their order, in the form of big-oh notation. To do this, of course, we must first find an expression for the dependence of the number of steps in the algorithm on the amount of data being processed. This is the hard bit. We may be able to do it by working out a formula analytically, by some form of heuristic argument, or by computer experimentation. However, we do it, we are interested mainly in the term in this expression that increases the fastest as the amount of data becomes larger.*

The most common orders of algorithms are the following, listed in increasing order of complexity:

- Constant ($O(1)$) – the number of steps is independent of the amount of data. The best case result for the sequential search is $O(1)$, since if the element for which we are searching is the first element in the list, only one comparison is required no matter how long the list is. Remember, though, that $O(1)$ means that a *constant* number of steps is required, where the constant number can be any number, not necessarily just one. An algorithm that always requires 15 steps is still an $O(1)$ algorithm.
- Logarithmic ($O(\log n)$) – algorithms like the binary search.
- Linear ($O(n)$) – algorithms like the average case of the sequential search.

* It should be pointed out that, from a strictly mathematical point of view, the only way that the order of an algorithm can be determined is by mathematical analysis. The 'heuristic argument' and 'computer simulation' approaches do not provide a rigorous proof that the order of an algorithm is what it may seem from the argument or simulation. However, since the main reason for our doing efficiency measurements of algorithms is to get a rough idea of how they behave, there is no need for us to pursue the rigorous mathematical approach.

- Log-linear ($O(n \log n)$) – algorithms where the leading term is proportional to the product of the amount of data n by the logarithm of the amount of data ($\log n$). The most efficient sorting algorithms are of this type, as we will see in the next chapter.
- Quadratic ($O(n^2)$) – algorithms where the number of steps depends on the square of the amount of data. In such algorithms, doubling the amount of data quadruples the amount of work that must be done. Some sorting algorithms are of this type.

Other forms of algorithms exist, but these are the only varieties that we shall meet in this book.

Exercises   10.7

1 (a) Rewrite the classes that we used in this chapter to implement the sequential and forgetful binary search algorithms so that the data are stored in a linked list rather than in an array.
  (b) Derive a class from the class in part (a) and use it to calculate the efficiency of the two searching algorithms in a manner similar to that in the text. Compare your results with those in the text where the data are stored in an array. Are linked lists or arrays more efficient in either algorithm?

2 Redesign the experiment used in the text for calculating the efficiency of the forgetful binary search so that, for unsuccessful searches, numbers less than the smallest number in the list, numbers between numbers in the list, and numbers greater than the largest number in the list are all used. Plot a graph of your results and compare it with the graph given in the text. Do you get a smoother curve?

3 As you will have noticed in question 1, implementing the binary search on a linked list requires many traversals of the list to locate the various elements to use in the comparisons. An alternative algorithm for searching a sorted linked list is as follows:

1 Set pointers `Marker` and `OldMarker` to the first data node in the list.
2 While `Marker != 0`
      3 Compare data at location `Marker` with `Target` data.
      4 If `Target == Marker`, return indicating target found.
      5 Else if `Target > Marker`, save current `Marker` in `OldMarker`, advance `Marker` by `step` nodes (`step` is usually `>= 2`; if `step == 1`, this algorithm is equivalent to sequential search) and repeat from step 2.
6 Else if `Target < Marker`, return to location `OldMarker` and compare the `step - 1` nodes forward from that location with `Target`. If a match is found, return indicating that `Target` has been found; if no match is

found, or a zero pointer is encountered, return indicating that `Target` has not been found.

The idea behind this algorithm is to use larger steps to do a crude initial search through the list. Once a pair of markers localizing the section of the list where `Target` may be found are identified, that section of the list is searched in detail.

Implement this algorithm for a linked list and run some experiments to calculate its efficiency. Try several values of `step`, and compare your results with the binary search.

4 Implement the targetted form of the binary search for an array, and run an experiment to calculate its efficiency. How does it compare with the forgetful binary search? The result is surprising, since it would seem that by checking for the target at each stage of the algorithm rather than only at the end, you should be able to shorten the search for a large number of targets. However, for any list of reasonable size, most of the elements will not be found until you have reduced the list to one or two elements anyway. The gain for a few list elements is more than offset by the fact that you must do two comparisons, rather than one, at each step.

CHAPTER 11

SORTING
ALGORITHMS

11.1   Introduction

Since one of the most common uses to which computers are put is the storage and retrieval of information, it is important to use algorithms that maximize the efficiency of such data manipulation. As we saw in the chapter on searching algorithms, the binary search algorithm is, for any but the smallest lists, a much more efficient searching technique than the sequential search. The binary search, however, requires that its data be sorted first. Many other algorithms either require sorted data, or are much more efficient when their data are sorted. Since sorting is such a common operation in computing, it is not surprising that there are a great many algorithms for doing it.

We shall examine four sorting algorithms in this chapter. The first two (insertion sort and selection sort) appear to have much poorer efficiency than the last two (mergesort and quicksort). However, this is only true for data of a particular initial ordering. For example, although insertion sort is an $O(n^2)$ algorithm for randomly ordered initial lists, it is closer to an $O(n)$ algorithm for lists that are almost fully sorted to begin with. Therefore, it is a very efficient algorithm for checking that lists are correctly sorted. The quicksort algorithm is, on average, an $O(n \log n)$ algorithm for randomly ordered lists, but its efficiency actually *degenerates* to $O(n^2)$ for fully sorted lists. Therefore, quicksort is an efficient algorithm for sorting lists whose ordering is random, but hideously inefficient for checking that a sorted list is actually in the right order.

As with our treatment of searching algorithms in Chapter 10, we will take an experimental approach to determining the efficiency of sorting algorithms. We will motivate these experiments with some heuristic arguments along the way.

11.2   Insertion sort

The insertion sort algorithm is copied directly from a commonly used technique for hand-sorting objects, such as index cards or forms. If we are presented with a pile of cards, on each of which is printed someone's name, and told to sort them into alphabetical order, with the As on the top and the Zs on the bottom, one way we might proceed is as follows.

Take the first card to form the beginning of our sorted pile. Take the next card and compare it with the first card: if it comes before the first card, place it on top of the first card, otherwise place it underneath the first card. Take the third card and compare it with the top card in our sorted pile. If it doesn't come before the top card, compare it with the next card in the pile, and so on, until you find a card which comes after it. In other words, insertion sort inserts the items into the sorted list one at a time by beginning at the beginning of the list and stepping through the list one item at a time until the correct position is found.

The algorithm can be implemented pretty much as described in the previous paragraph if we use linked lists to represent our data. If we wish to use an array to store the sorted list, perhaps because we wish to use a binary search on the list later on, we need to make a few alterations. Because of the nature of an array, if we wish to insert an item at some point in an array, we need to move over by one space all the items to one side of that point in order to create a space for the new item.

We will see the complete code for implementing insertion sort later, when we give a Java example. For now, we summarize it in words.

We assume we are given a list with `numarray` elements in some arbitrary order. We take element 0 (since Java arrays start at zero) to be the first element in the sorted list. To facilitate the shifting/insertion process, we examine the first element after the end of the sorted part of the list, and search *backwards* through the sorted list (rather than forwards from the first element). The reason for this is that we can do the shifting at the same time as the searching. We are using a sequential search here to locate the correct location for each item.

Our algorithm is therefore as follows, for a list `Element` of `L` items stored in an array with elements numbered from 0 to $L - 1$:

1   Initialize `marker1` to 1 (the second element in the list).

2   While `marker1 < L`.
   3   If `Element[marker1] < Element[marker - 1]`, store `Element [marker1]` in a temporary location `temp`. Initialize `marker2` to `marker1 - 1` (the location just before `marker1`).
        4   While `Element[marker2] > temp` and `marker2 >= 0`, shift `Element[marker2]` to location `marker2 + 1`. (This slides the element over to make room to its left.) Decrease `marker2` by 1.
        5   Insert `temp` into the location last vacated by a shift.
   6   Increase `marker1` by 1.

Notice that steps 4 and 5 are only done if a shift needs to be performed. If an element is already in the correct location relative to its neighbor, nothing is done. It is this fact that makes insertion sort so efficient for checking that a list is correctly ordered. Each element is compared only with its immediate predecessor, and if these two elements are in the correct relative order, no shifting of data is done.

An example of insertion sort is shown in Fig 11.1.

The arrow shows the location of `marker1` as we progress through the algorithm. Beginning with array element 1 (the number 9), we compare the element with its immediate predecessor. In this case, 9 > 3 so no data shifting needs to be done. We move `marker2` along to element 2 (the number 1). In this case, 1 < 9 so we need to shift some elements over to the right to make a space into which we can insert 1. We store the 1 in the `temp` location, and then shift the 9 and the 3 over to make a space for 1, into which it is inserted. The process is repeated for the remaining elements in the array (7 and 2) until we achieve a fully sorted list.

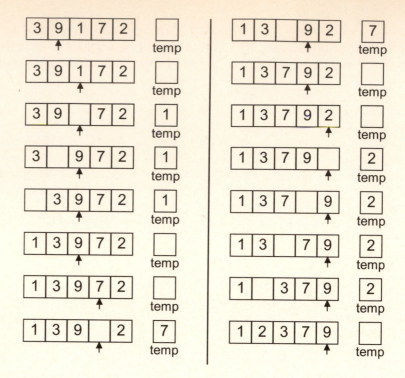

Figure 11.1.

11.3 Selection sort

Although insertion sort is a straightforward algorithm which is easy to program, it requires a large amount of shifting within the array (although if it is implemented using linked lists, this disadvantage disappears). For large lists, this shifting can be the dominant operation, especially if each item contains a large amount of data that must be moved (as in a personal record with name, phone number, and other data, for example). We will quantitatively analyze the various sorting methods for efficiency later, but for now, it appears that an alternative algorithm in which the amount of shifting was reduced would be an advantage. Selection sort was designed with this in mind.

The idea behind selection sort is that each shift of data moves an item directly into its final, correct place. This is done by starting with a list with `numarray` elements. In the first step, the largest element in the array is located and swapped with the element at the high end of the list. Then the largest element in the remaining `numarray` - 1 elements is located and swapped into the second-highest location, and so on. Because selection sort involves accessing the list at various points in a more-or-less random fashion, it is not a good algorithm to use with data stored as a linked list, since a great deal of time will be used traversing the list trying to locate the correct elements at each step, and then reassigning the pointers. It was designed primarily to avoid the excessive number of shifts that occur when insertion sort is used on an array, and so should be used only with arrays.

Selection sort will shift only (at most) two items at each step, and possibly none, if the item is already in the correct location. Its main overhead is in the determination of the maximum element in each sublist. This requires a scan of all remaining unsorted elements at each iteration, but this scanning does not actually move any data and so should be relatively fast.

For a list with L elements numbered from 0 to L – 1, the selection sort algorithm is:

1 Set marker to L – 1 (begin with the last element in the list).

2 While marker > 0.

   3 Find the largest element in the range numbered from 0 to marker.

   4 Swap that element with the element at location marker.

   5 Increase marker by 1.

An example of selection sort is shown in Fig 11.2. The position of the arrow indicates the location of marker at each step. In the first step, marker points to the end of the list, and the maximum value in the entire list is found (9). In the next step, the 9 is swapped with the 2. Note that a swap requires an auxiliary storage location (not shown in the diagram). To swap two values a and b, for example, we must define an extra location temp. Then a is copied into temp, b is copied into a, then temp is copied into b. Thus each swap requires three shifts of data.

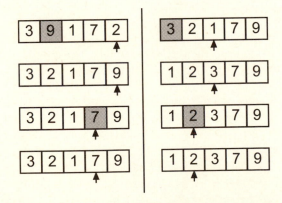

Figure 11.2.

In the next step, `marker` is moved back one step in the list, so that it now points to the second last element (7). The largest element from the beginning of the list up to `marker` is now found. This turns out to be the value at which `marker` is currently pointing. We have also not bothered to ask the algorithm to detect when the largest element coincides with `marker`, so 7 is swapped with itself. This decision is a trade-off between the extra comparison that would need to be done at each stage in the algorithm and the extra swap that may need to be done occasionally if the largest element in the unsorted part of the list happens to be at location `marker`.

11.4 Java code for insertion sort and selection sort

11.4.1 AN ABSTRACT PARENT CLASS FOR TESTING SORTING ALGORITHMS

We will now consider the implementation of insertion sort and selection sort in Java. We will find that the four sorting algorithms that we consider in the chapter all have certain methods in common, so in order to test the algorithms we can define an abstract parent class which contains these common methods. Each sorting algorithm will then be tested by deriving a specialized class from this parent class.

In 'real life', of course, you will probably only use one sorting algorithm as part of a larger program, so you will need to embed the sorting code within whatever class you are using at the time.

A suitable abstract sorting class that can be used to test all four sorting algorithms in this chapter (and most other sorting algorithms as well) is:

```java
abstract class AbstractSort
{
    static final int MAXELEMENT = 1000;
    int ArraySize;
    int[] Element;

    AbstractSort(int arraysize)
    {
        int index;

        Element = new int[arraysize];
        ArraySize = arraysize;
        for (index = 0; index < arraysize; ++index)
            Element[index] =
                (int)(MAXELEMENT * Math.random());
    }

    void Swap(int marker1, int marker2)
    {
```

```
        int temp = Element[marker1];
        Element[marker1] = Element[marker2];
        Element[marker2] = temp;
    }

    int getElement(int index)
    {
        return Element[index];
    }

    int getArraySize()
    {
        return ArraySize;
    }

    abstract void Sort();
}
```

The class sets up an array of a size determined by the user when the constructor is called, and initializes the array by filling it with random integers in the range 0 to MAXELEMENT. The other three methods are utility methods which allow two elements to be swapped, and allow retrieval of a specific array element and the array size. Finally, an abstract method Sort() is declared which must be implemented separately in each class derived from this abstract class.

Before we move on to consider the individual sorting algorithms, we urge the reader to keep in mind that some of the following code will have to be altered slightly if you want to use it to sort non-primitive data types. The methods defined in the abstract class above should be independent of the data type (beyond replacing the array of ints by an array of whatever type you are using, and changing the initialization of the array in the constructor). There is one subtle difference in the way the Swap() method works for primitive data types and classes, since primitive data types are *copied* by an assignment operation, while for classes, only a reference to an object is assigned by the = operator. You should convince yourself that the Swap() code above will work in both cases.

11.4.2 JAVA CODE FOR INSERTION SORT

The insertion sort class follows the algorithm above exactly:

```
public class InsertSort extends AbstractSort
{
    InsertSort(int arraysize) { super(arraysize); }

    void Sort()
    {
        int temp, marker1, marker2;
```

```
      for (marker1 = 1; marker1 < ArraySize; ++marker1)
      {
        if (Element[marker1] < Element[marker1 - 1])
        {
          temp = Element[marker1];
          for (marker2 = marker1 - 1; marker2 >= 0;
            --marker2)
          {
            Element[marker2 + 1] = Element[marker2];
            if (marker2 == 0 ||
              Element[marker2 - 1] < temp)
              break;
          }
          Element[marker2] = temp;
        }
      }
    }
  }
```

The `InsertSort` class calls the `AbstractSort` constructor to initialize the array. The `Sort()` method implements the algorithm. Note that if this method is to be used with user-defined data types, a special `lessThan()` method must be defined to replace the < operator used here to compare the `Element` data to each other.

11.4.3 JAVA CODE FOR SELECTION SORT

The class implementing selection sort is as follows.

```
public class SelectionSort extends AbstractSort
{
  SelectionSort(int arraysize) { super(arraysize); }

  private int MaxKey(int low, int high)
  {
    int marker1, max = low;

    for (marker1 = low + 1; marker1 <= high; ++marker1)
      if (Element[max] < Element[marker1])
        max = marker1;
    return max;
  }

  void Sort()
  {
    int marker1, marker2;

    for (marker1 = ArraySize - 1; marker1 > 0;
```

```
        --marker1)
    {
        marker2 = MaxKey(0, marker1);
        Swap(marker2, marker1);
    }
  }
}
```

Again, the code follows the algorithm precisely. In addition to the `Sort()` method, we have defined a subsidiary method `Max()` for finding the maximum element value between array elements `low` and `high`.

Efficiency of insertion sort and selection sort   11.5

11.5.1 COMPARISONS AND ASSIGNMENTS

We can do a similar sort of experiment as we did for the searching algorithms in the last chapter to determine their efficiencies. In the case of a searching algorithm, we evaluated its efficiencies for successful and unsuccessful outcomes separately. With a sorting algorithm we always expect the outcome to be successful (otherwise we have made a mistake coding the algorithm!). However, there are two types of operations involved in sorting a list of data: comparisons and assignments. Since these two operations require different resources in terms of computing, we need to evaluate them separately.

A comparison requires that those parts of the data structure being used for sorting are compared to determine whether they are in the correct order. Depending on the complexity of the data structures being compared, this can take varying amounts of time. If we are sorting lists of integers (or only using an integer field of a more complex data structure to determine the sorting order) a comparison is relatively fast. If we must compare several fields in a complex data structure, comparisons can take considerably longer.

An assignment requires that data be physically moved within the computer's memory. Therefore, assignments are almost always more time-consuming than comparisons. In general, algorithms that minimize the number of assignments are to be preferred.

11.5.2 INSERTION SORT

Before doing the computer experiment, let us see if we can get a heuristic estimate of what order insertion sort will be. For a randomly ordered list, we might expect that we must compare each element with about half of those already sorted before we insert it into its proper place. This, in turn, means that we have to shift about half the data in that portion of the list that has been sorted to insert each new element. This should give us a clue that we expect the number of comparisons and assignments to be about the same. Certainly they should be the same order, even if the constant of proportionality isn't quite the same.

What order will this be? Let us look at the amount of work that is required to insert the *last* element into its proper place. If the list length is L, we expect about $L/2$ comparisons *and* $L/2$ assignments to be made. For the first element to be sorted (remember that the first element that actually needs sorting is the second element in the list), we expect that 1 comparison and either 0 or 1 assignments must be made. The average of these two extremes gives us about $L/4$ comparisons and $L/4$ assignments (very roughly) as an *average* number of comparisons and assignments *per element*. Since we have $L-1$ elements to sort (remember that the first element in the list is not actually sorted on its own), we would expect about $(L - 1)L/4$ comparisons and assignments to be made in total. The leading term in this expression is $L^2/4$, so we can predict that insertion sort is an $O(n^2)$ algorithm for both comparisons and assignments, with a proportionality constant of about 0.25 in both cases.

We can test this prediction by writing a program similar to the one that we wrote for testing the searching algorithms in Chapter 10. The program will generate a number of lists of a given length, fill the lists up with randomly ordered numbers, and then apply the insertion sort algorithm to sort the list, keeping track of the number of comparisons and assignments that are made. We will not give the details of the program here, but merely present the results in Fig. 11.3.

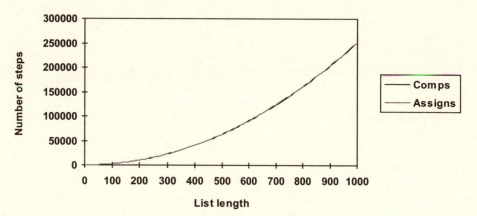

Figure 11.3.

At first glance, it looks as though our predictions are quite good. The two curves (for comparisons and assignments) are so close that they cannot be distinguished in the graph, and a few checks seem to indicate that the number of steps in each is about $L^2/4$. The curve looks roughly like a parabola, which is what it should be if we have an $O(n^2)$ relationship.

However, we can do better than this. If we believe that the relationship between the number of steps and the list length really does depend on L^2, then we can try drawing a graph of the ratio of the number of steps to L^2 as a function of the list length. If our prediction is right, we should get (at least as L gets larger) a horizontal line, and the horizontal level of this line should be close to 0.25. If we do this, we get Fig. 11.4.

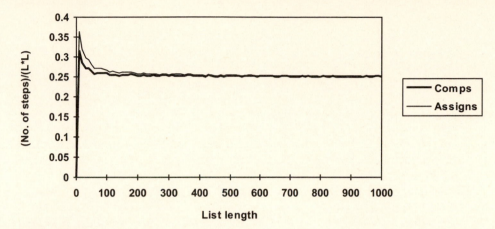

Figure 11.4.

We can see from this graph that our prediction is definitely true.* After an initial flurry above the 0.25 level, the ratios settle down nicely by the time the list length is about 100.

11.5.3 SELECTION SORT

Selection sort is unusual amongst sorting algorithms in that, for a given list length, it always performs exactly the same number of both assignments and comparisons. With a bit of elementary algebra it is possible to work out the exact formula, but in keeping with the spirit of this book, we will arrive at an approximate answer through a heuristic argument.

First, consider the number of comparisons. In the first iteration of the algorithm, we must find the largest element in the entire list. With a list of length L, we must therefore do $L - 1$ comparisons. To see this, look at it this way. We first compare elements 1 and 2. Then we pick whichever is the larger of these two elements and compare it with element 3, and so on, until we compare the largest element in the first $L - 1$ elements with the last element. This makes one comparison for the first two elements, and then another comparison for all the remaining elements, for a total of $L - 1$.

In the last iteration of the algorithm, we have a list of length 2 to sort, which requires only a single comparison. Therefore, the average number of comparisons *per element* is the average of $L - 1$ and 1, which is $L/2$. The overall average should

* To repeat our comment in Chapter 10, it is not possible to *prove* that the order of an algorithm is anything in particular just by drawing a graph – a mathematical proof is required for that. However, for our purposes, it should be obvious that the behavior of the algorithm is at least approximately $O(n^2)$ from the graph

therefore be $L(L/2)$ or $L^2/2$. Therefore, selection sort is an $O(n^2)$ algorithm for comparisons, with the proportionality constant equal to 0.5. It requires twice as many comparisons, on average, as insertion sort.

Now consider the number of assignments. If we don't do any checking to avoid swapping an element with itself (as discussed in the previous section), then there will be $L - 1$ swaps. Each swap (as explained earlier) requires 3 assignments, so there will be a total of $3(L - 1) = 3L - 3$ assignments. Therefore, selection sort is an $O(n)$ algorithm for assignments, with a proportionality constant of 3. It is a *linear* algorithm for assignments, which is a vast improvement over insertion sort.

To test these predictions, we can try selection sort on lists of various lengths. The results are as shown in Fig. 11.5.

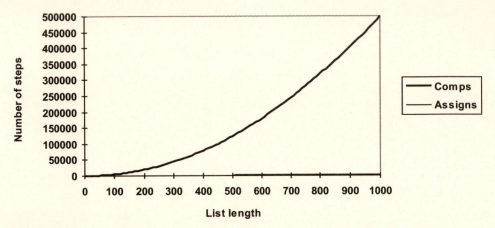

Figure 11.5.

The plot dramatically shows the difference between an $O(n^2)$ and an $O(n)$ algorithm. The number of comparisons curves up quickly, while the number of assignments is scarcely distinguishable from the horizontal axis. The accuracy of our predictions for the two efficiencies could be further verified by plotting the ratio (number of comparisons)/(L^2) versus list length L, and (number of assignments)/L versus L, but we trust that the point has been made with the above graph.

11.6 More efficient sorting methods

In our study of searching algorithms in Chapter 10, we saw that with a little ingenuity, we could vastly improve the efficiency of the sequential search algorithm by using the binary search. It is natural to ask if a similar improvement can be obtained with sorting algorithms.

How efficient can we expect the best sorting algorithm to be? A full analysis requires a fair bit of mathematics, but we can get a rough idea from the following argument.

Suppose we start by asking: how many different ways can a list of length L be arranged? We can work this out by placing the elements of the list in an array one step at a time. For the first element, we may choose any of the L elements, so there are L ways of filling the first array element. For the second array element, we may choose from any of the remaining $L - 1$ elements, so there are $L - 1$ ways of filling the second array element. However, for each of these $L - 1$ ways, there were L ways of filling the first element, so the total number of ways of filling the first *two* elements of the array is $L(L - 1)$. We can continue the argument in the same fashion for the remaining elements of the array so that we find that there are $L(L - 1)(L - 2)(L - 3)...(3)(2)(1)$ ways of ordering the entire list. There is a shorthand notation for this expression: we can write $L(L - 1)(L - 2)(L - 3)...$ $(3)(2)(1) = L!$ (pronounced 'L factorial').

For example, if $L = 2$, there are $2! = (2)(1) = 2$ ways of ordering a list of 2 elements (either *ab* or *ba*). If $L = 3$, there are $3! = (3)(2)(1) = 6$ ways (*abc, bac, acb, bca, cab, cba*), and so on.

At each stage in a sorting algorithm, a comparison between two elements in the list is made and, as a result of this comparison, one of two things is done. Either the two elements are left in the same places in the list, or else they are swapped. Now suppose that, with each swap, the number of final orderings of the list that needed to be considered was reduced by a factor of 2 (in much the same way that the number of elements being considered was reduced by a factor of 2 at each stage in a binary search). This is the largest factor by which the number of choices could be reduced, since there are only two options (to swap or not to swap) at each step in the algorithm. If the total number of possible orderings is a power of 2 (say, $L! = 2^n$), then the number of steps we need to completely sort the list is n.

This argument is necessarily a bit vague and imprecise because we are not using a proper mathematical formalism to do the calculation, but the basic assumption that we are making is that there is a sorting algorithm that is capable of eliminating half of the possible orderings of the list at each step in the algorithm. If such an algorithm exists, the number of steps that it should require is around log $(L!)$, for the same reason that the binary search algorithm is an $O(\log n)$ algorithm: each step in the algorithm cuts the amount of remaining work in half. Using results from mathematics, the logarithm of a factorial may be approximated by the expression $\log (n!) \approx n \log n$. In other words, the most efficient sorting algorithm should be an $O(n \log n)$ algorithm. Since log n increases much more slowly than n, an $O(n \log n)$ algorithm is considerably more efficient than an $O(n^2)$ algorithm, which, as you remember, was the efficiency of both the insertion and selection sort algorithms for sorting random lists.

In the remainder of this chapter, we will examine two $O(n \log n)$ sorting algorithms: mergesort and quicksort. Both of these algorithms rely on the 'divide and conquer' technique. The list is split into two parts and the same algorithm is recursively applied to each part until the entire list is sorted.

11.7 Mergesort

11.7.1 THE MERGESORT ALGORITHM

Mergesort is based on another simple idea: if you are given a pile of cards to sort, divide the pile in half, sort each half independently, and then merge the two piles. This statement looks innocent enough, until we notice that part of the algorithm is to 'sort each half independently'. How? Do we use selection sort or some other method to sort these smaller piles and then merge the result? We could, but we could also apply the mergesort algorithm again to each half pile. In other words, we apply mergesort recursively to each half pile until we encounter the smallest possible pile: a pile of one object. We then 'merge' the sub-piles together one stage at a time until we reach the top level again, at which point the entire list is sorted.

Therefore, mergesort has two stages: the initial division of the list into sublists of a single element each, and the merging of these sublists to produce the final sorted list. The first stage of mergesort is illustrated in Fig. 11.6.

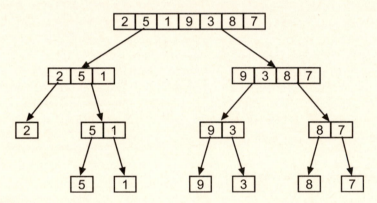

Figure 11.6.

The second stage merges each of the sublists, starting at the bottom level and working upwards, sorting each pair of sublists to an ordered list at the next higher level at each stage (see Fig. 11.7).

Despite the appeal of mergesort, it has its problems when we attempt to implement it. Suppose first that we try to implement it on data stored in arrays. Since we are dividing the original list in half and sorting each half before we merge the results to produce the final sorted list, we will be (potentially) changing the positions of all the elements in the array before the final merge. This means we need some place to store these sublists while they are being sorted, which means we need to declare a temporary array of the same size as the original list to use as working space.

If we attempt to use mergesort for a linked list, we don't need any extra space since we can perform the sorts by redirecting pointers. However, we need to be

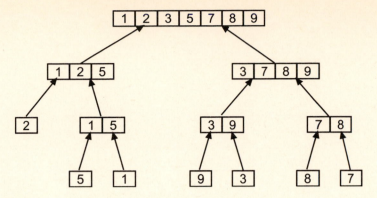

Figure 11.7.

able to divide a linked list in half, which means we must be able to access the central node. Since the only way we can do this is to follow a chain of pointers from one end of the list, we use a lot of time in continually locating the center of a linked list.

11.7.2 JAVA CODE FOR MERGESORT

The Java class for implementing mergesort on an array of ints is as follows.

```java
public class MergeSort extends AbstractSort
{
    int TempArray[];

    MergeSort(int arraysize)
    {
        super(arraysize);
        TempArray = new int[arraysize];
    }

    private void RecursiveSort(int list1, int size)
    {
        int list2, size1, size2;

        if (size > 1)
        {
            list2 = list1 + size / 2;
            size1 = list2 - list1;
            size2 = size - size1;
            RecursiveSort(list1, size1);
            RecursiveSort(list2, size2);
            Merge(list1, size1, list2, size2);
        }
```

```
      }

      private void Merge(int list1, int size1, int list2,
         int size2)
      {
         int i = list1, j = list2, k = list1;

         while (i < list1 + size1 && j < list2 + size2)
         {
            if (TempArray[i] < TempArray[j])
               Element[k++] = TempArray[i++];
            else
               Element[k++] = TempArray[j++];
         }

         while (i < list1 + size1)
            Element[k++] = TempArray[i++];
         while (j < list2 + size2)
            Element[k++] = TempArray[j++];
         for (k = list1; k < list1 + size1 + size2; k++)
            TempArray[k] = Element[k];
      }

   void Sort()
   {
      int index;

      for (index = 0; index < ArraySize; ++index)
         TempArray[index] = Element[index];
      RecursiveSort(0, ArraySize);
   }
}
```

This class introduces a technique we shall be using frequently with recursive algorithms. The protected method `RecursiveSort()` has two arguments:

- `list1` – the array index of the first element in the list (or sublist, in recursive calls) to be sorted.
- `size` – the number of elements in the list or sublist to be sorted.

To keep with the philosophy of OOP, the user should not have to be bothered with these arguments when calling the sorting method. A simple call like `MessyList.Sort()` should be all that is required. The `Sort()` method should then call some internal method which does the actual work. The best way to implement this is as we have done here: a public `Sort()` method is declared which (as we shall see) calls the protected `RecursiveSort()` method which starts the recursion off.

The other protected method `Merge()` is non-recursive, and performs the merging operation on the two sublists.

Look first at the third method `Sort()`, which is the method called by an external user. It declares an auxiliary array `TempArray`, and copies the data from the `Element` array into it. The idea is that successive splits and merges of the list alternate between the `TempArray` array and the original `Element` array. The `RecursiveSort()` method is called with the `temp` array and told to sort a list of size `ArraySize` beginning at element 0 (the first element).

The `RecursiveSort()` method uses the marker `list2` to record the position of the first element of the second half of the list. `size1` and `size2` store the sizes of the two sublists. The first sublist is sorted by a recursive call to `RecursiveSort()`, followed by the second sublist. After the two sublists have been sorted, they are merged using the `Merge()` method. Notice that the bottom of the recursion is reached when the list contains only one element.

The `Merge()` method takes the `TempArray` array and the starting points and sizes of the two sublists that it is to merge. The first `while` loop merges the two sublists until the end of one of the sublists is reached. At this point, either `i == list1 + size1` or `j == list2 + size2`, depending on which sublist was finished first. Thus only one of the two `while` loops following the main loop will actually do anything. This loop simply copies those elements from the unfinished subloop into the `Element` array.

After the merge of the two sublists, the elements are copied back into the `TempArray` array since the merge that has just occurred may have been at some point deep in the recursion, so further merges are necessary as we climb out of the recursion. This copying operation is unnecessary at the top level where the two sublists each consist of half the original list, but rather than putting in a special check for this one case, it is easier to just do the extra copying anyway.

Efficiency of mergesort   11.8

We can run an experiment to count up the numbers of comparisons and assignments in the same fashion as for insertion sort and selection sort earlier in this chapter. The results are shown in Fig. 11.8.

The results are averages over 100 runs for each list length. The first thing we notice is that mergesort does about twice as many assignments as comparisons, which is bad news, since assignments are usually more costly in terms of computer time. However, the actual numbers of each of these operations is considerably less than for insertion sort (where about 250,000 each of comparisons and assignments were done for a list of 1000 items), so we definitely have a more efficient algorithm in mergesort.

To see if we have indeed found the holy grail of an $O(n \log n)$ algorithm, we can plot the ratio of the number of steps required in a list of length L against $L \log L$ for each of comparisons and assignments. The results are shown in Fig. 11.9.

We can see that the number of assignments levels off at around 1.9 $L \log L$,

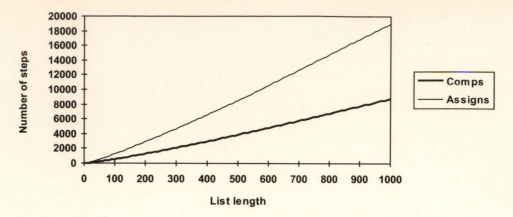

Figure 11.8.

and the number of comparisons at around $0.9 \, L \log L$. Theory predicts that, in the worst case, the number of comparisons should be $L \log L$, and the number of assignments should be $2 \, L \log L$. Since our experiments would give results closer to the average case than the worst case, we can see that the average case is not far off the worst case for the mergesort algorithm.

Therefore, we see that mergesort is an $O(n \log n)$ algorithm overall. Actually, the version we have studied here, using arrays, is not the most efficient form. Mergesort is more efficient if used with linked lists, in which case it comes very close to the theoretically most efficient sorting algorithm possible.

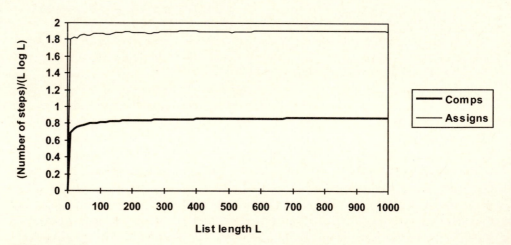

Figure 11.9.

Quicksort 11.9

11.9.1 THE QUICKSORT ALGORITHM

The final sorting algorithm we shall consider is another one that relies on recursive subdivision of the list. The main difference between mergesort and quicksort is that in quicksort, the list is divided into two parts in such a way that all the elements in the first sublist are less than all the elements in the second. The two sublists are then sorted independently as in mergesort, but because of the condition used to separate the list in the first place, the final merge is not required.

The list is divided by choosing one of the list elements and using it as a *pivot*. If we are dealing with lists initially in random order, we can simply choose the first element in the list as the pivot. If the list is known to have some partial order, a different choice may be more appropriate. Ideally, the pivot should be chosen so that it divides the list exactly in half, according to the relative sizes of the keys. For example, if we had a list of the integers from 1–10, 5 or 6 would be the ideal pivots, while 1 or 10 would be poor pivots.

Once the pivot has been chosen, it is used to sort the remainder of the list into two sublists: one where all keys are less than the pivot, and the other where all elements are greater than or equal to the pivot. These two partial lists are then sorted recursively using the same algorithm. The final sorted list is then produced by concatenating the first sublist, the pivot, and the second sublist, in that order, into a single list. The first stage in quicksort is the recursive partitioning of the list until all sublists consist of only a single element. This stage is illustrated in Fig. 11.10.

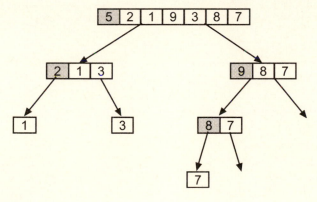

Figure 11.10.

In this example, we use the first element in each list (or sublist) as the pivot for that list (the pivot element is shaded in each sublist). In the first step, the element 5 is used as the pivot, so the list is to be partitioned into two sublists, the first containing elements less than 5, and the second, elements greater than or equal to 5. These two sublists are shown on the second level in the diagram. Note that the pivot itself does not form part of either sublist.

In the second stage of the partitioning, each sublist is partitioned in the same way. The lower sublist uses the element 2 as the pivot and is partitioned into two sublists, each containing a single element, so the partitioning of that portion of the list is now complete. In the upper list (9, 8, 7), 9 is used as the pivot. Since all the other elements of this sublist are less than 9, only one sublist is formed, consisting of the elements 8 and 7. The arrow pointing into empty space at this stage shows that no upper sublist is produced when 9 is used as the pivot.

The upper sublist requires an extra stage in the partitioning process, with 8 used as the pivot, before the size of the sublist is reduced to a single element. When all sublists have been reduced to this stage, they are concatenated with their respective pivots until the original list is reconstructed in sorted order. This concatenation process is shown in Fig. 11.11.

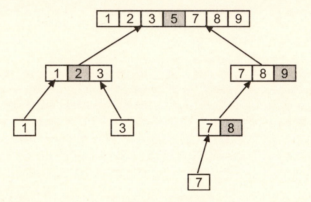

Figure 11.11.

As we will see when we consider the Java code for quicksort, the concatenation process does not need to be explicitly programmed, since the partitioning process automatically places the pivot between its respective sublists at each stage, so that when the list has been partitioned to the point where all the sublists contain only a single element, it is already sorted.

This simple example illustrates why it is best to choose the pivot so as to divide the list as nearly in half as possible. The first pivot in the example (5) does just that. In the partitioning of the two sublists resulting from this initial partition, however, we see two contrasting cases. In the lower sublist, the pivot (2) also divides its sublist in half, with the result that this partition is the last one required for that sublist, since both sublists (the 1 and the 3) now contain a single element. In the other sublist, the pivot (9) is the largest element in the sublist, with the result that no division of the list takes place. The only sublist contains two elements, which must be partitioned again.

In the extreme case where the pivot at each stage is always either the largest or smallest element in the sublist, quicksort is actually a very poor algorithm, being even less efficient than some $O(n^2)$ algorithms. For this reason, some variants on quicksort put in a few extra comparisons before each partitioning to ensure that the pivot will actually divide the list as nearly in half as it can.

11.9.2 IMPLEMENTING QUICKSORT IN AN ARRAY

In order to continue building our library of sorting routines we will consider the implementation of quicksort for a list of data stored in an array. The only slightly tricky part of the algorithm is how to partition the array into the two lists separated by the pivot, without having to declare any auxiliary storage space. Let us suppose that we are using the first element in the list as the pivot. (If we are using some other element, then simply swap it with the first element before proceeding.) We would like to partition the list so that all keys less than the pivot are followed by all those greater than or equal to the pivot. Starting from the element in the array immediately following the pivot, we search for the first element that is greater than or equal to the pivot. We mark this location (call it s) as the beginning of the second sublist (the one that will follow the pivot). Now define a marker variable m which will be used to point to each location after s. For each key after s, we compare it with the pivot. If it is greater than or equal to the pivot, we leave it where it is and advance the marker m by 1. If it is less than the pivot, we swap it with the key at location s and advance s by 1 so that it points to the new start of the second list. We continue this process until we reach the end of the list. At this stage, the pivot is still the first element in the array, but we know that the second element is the beginning of the sublist containing elements less than the pivot, and the location marked by s is the beginning of the sublist containing elements greater than or equal to the pivot. (If the lower sublist does not exist, then s will point to the second list element. If the upper sublist does not exist, s should have a value one larger than the sublist length, in order that the next step will work properly.)

Since we would like the pivot to be between the two lists, we swap the pivot with the key immediately before the position s. This completes the partitioning of the list. An example of this algorithm which illustrates the first partition in the previous example is shown in Fig. 11.12.

In the first three steps in this diagram, the marker m is moved along the array until the first element larger than the pivot is found. This element is labelled with the marker s to indicate it is the starting point of the upper sublist. The marker m is then moved along from s. The next element (3) is less than the pivot, so it is swapped with the element at location s (first step in the second column in the diagram) and s is advanced by one. In the next two steps, m is advanced further, but the remaining two elements (8 and 7) are both larger than the pivot so no further swaps are required. In the final step, the pivot (5) is swapped with the element just prior to s. This swap places the pivot between the two sublists, so when these sublists are sorted recursively, it will be in the correct place relative to the sublists. It is this swap of the pivot into the correct location which ensures that the final concatenation step is not required. Note, however, that swapping the pivot into this location alters the order in the lower sublist. In our example above, the

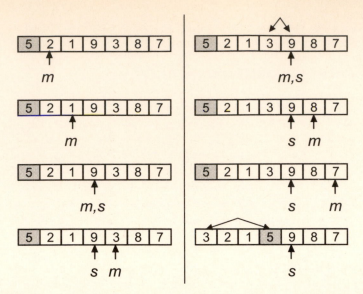

Figure 11.12.

lower sublist had the order 2, 1, 3, while here it has the order 3, 2, 1. This will, of course, affect the pivot that is chosen for partitioning the sublist in the next stage of the algorithm. In our case, it will make the second partition less efficient than in our original example, but in other cases, of course, it may improve the efficiency so on average, this step will not adversely affect the efficiency of the algorithm overall.

11.9.3 JAVA CODE FOR QUICKSORT

The Java class for implementing quicksort in an array is as follows.

```
public class QuickSort extends AbstractSort
{
   QuickSort(int arraysize) { super(arraysize); }

   private int Partition(int low, int high)
   {
      int pivotloc, i, pivotkey;

      // May need to swap pivot into first position here
      pivotkey = Element[low];
      pivotloc = low;
      for (i = low + 1; i <= high; i++)
         if (Element[i] < pivotkey)
            Swap(++pivotloc, i);
      Swap(low, pivotloc);
      return pivotloc;
   }
```

```
private void RecursiveSort(int low, int high)
{
   int pivotloc;

   if (low < high)
   {
      pivotloc = Partition(low, high);
      RecursiveSort(low, pivotloc - 1);
      RecursiveSort(pivotloc + 1, high);
   }
}

void Sort()
{
   RecursiveSort(0, ArraySize - 1);
}
}
```

The code for quicksort follows our written algorithm fairly closely, except for a few minor points. The variable `pivotloc` in the `Partition()` method is the location immediately *previous* to our variable s, which means that it is the location to which the pivot will be swapped at the end of the partitioning (hence the name `pivotloc`). Also, the partitioning algorithm does not do a distinct search for elements after the first which are less than the pivot. Rather, it swaps every element which is less than the pivot to location `pivotloc + 1` (which is s). This means that if the first few keys immediately after the first element are less than the pivot, they will be swapped into themselves. This is not particularly efficient, especially if we are unfortunate enough to choose a large pivot, so that most of the keys are less than the pivot value. However, adding the extra check would serve to complicate the code for what should be, for most lists, minimal gain.

The `Partition()` method returns the location of the pivot after the partitioning so that the `RecursiveSort()` method knows the locations of the endpoints of the two sublists, which it then sorts recursively. Since all sorting takes place within the original array, there is no need to explicitly concatenate the sorted sublists: they will automatically be in the correct locations.

Finally, the initial call to the `RecursiveSort()` method is made by the public `Sort()` method as with the mergesort code, in order to hide the internal workings of the class from external users.

Efficiency of quicksort   11.10

As with other sorting algorithms we will investigate the efficiency of quicksort by running a computer experiment to count the number of comparisons and assignments for various list lengths. The results are shown in Fig. 11.13.

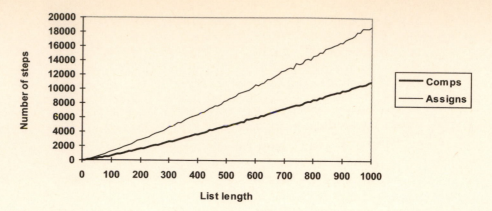

Figure 11.13.

The results look very similar to those for mergesort, where the number of assignments is roughly twice the number of comparisons. We can check that quicksort is an $O(n \log n)$ algorithm by plotting the ratio (number of steps)/($L \log L$) (see Fig. 11.14).

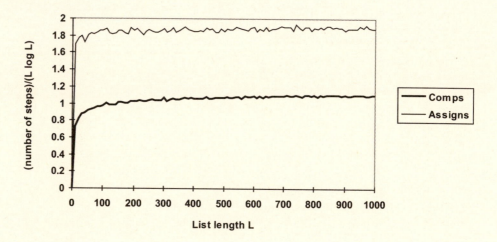

Figure 11.14.

For random sequences, quicksort behaves as approximately $O(n \log n)$ for comparisons, and $O(1.8n \log n)$ for assignments. (Theoretical estimates place the order for comparisons around $1.4 \ n \log n$ and for assignments at around $2 \ n \log n$.) However, quicksort is inordinately sensitive to the initial ordering of the list. In particular, if the initial list is already ordered (or nearly so), quicksort is effectively an $O(n^2)$ algorithm, unless extra comparisons are done to ensure that the pivot divides the list in half at each stage.

Summary   11.11

We have examined four sorting algorithms in this chapter and have seen that they give very different behaviors. Insertion sort and selection sort are both $O(n^2)$ algorithms, while mergesort and quicksort are, for random lists, both $O(n \log n)$ algorithms. However, this doesn't necessarily mean that either mergesort or quicksort is best for all your sorting problems. For example, if you want an algorithm that will check to see if a list is already in order, insertion sort is one of the best algorithms around because it doesn't move any data at all. For initially ordered data, quicksort is one of the worst algorithms because the pivot is always the lowest element in the sublist being partitioned, so no partitioning takes place.

If the elements of the list contain large data records, so that movement is very expensive in terms of computing time, selection sort is probably your best bet, since it is linear ($O(n)$) for assignments. If your data are stored as a linked list rather than an array, mergesort is one of the most efficient algorithms for sorting linked lists.

There are many other sorting algorithms in existence, but hopefully the introduction given here has demonstrated that you should investigate which algorithm is best suited to the type and amount of data you wish to process.

Exercises   11.12

1   Sort the following list of numbers:

    23 19 5 78 12 66 47 32 98 32 24

    by hand using
    (a) insertion sort;
    (b) selection sort;
    (c) mergesort;
    (d) quicksort.

    In each case, count the number of comparisons and assignments that are done. For mergesort and quicksort, draw a tree diagram similar to those in the text (Figs. 11.6, 11.7, 11.10 and 11.11) to show the various levels in the recursive algorithm.

2   Design and write versions of insertion sort and selection sort for linked lists. Construct computer experiments to measure the efficiencies of these two algorithms when used on linked lists, and draw graphs similar to those in the text to illustrate your results.

3   Write a version of mergesort that operates on a linked list. You should handle all assignments by redirecting pointers rather than copying any data elements. Design and run a computer experiment to calculate the efficiency of mergesort when applied to a linked list.

4   Run a computer experiment on the quicksort algorithm when it is applied to fully ordered lists to verify that it is an $O(n^2)$ algorithm in this case. (If your mathematical skills are up to it, you could also try proving this analytically.)

5   Alter the quicksort algorithm so that the pivot is chosen to divide the list as nearly in half as possible at each step. Design and run a computer experiment to test the effect of this refinement on the efficiency of quicksort. Run your experiment for both randomly ordered lists and fully sorted lists.

6   One of the simplest sorting algorithms is known as *bubblesort*. The algorithm is as follows.

Beginning at the first element of the list, compare each element with the next element in the list. If an element is greater than its successor, swap the two elements. To completely sort the list, you need to perform this process $n - 1$ times on a list of length n.

(a) Run through the bubblesort algorithm by hand on the list

   4 9 2 1 5

(b) Write a Java program implementing the bubblesort algorithm on an array. Use your program to count the numbers of assignments and comparisons done by the algorithm on lists of lengths from 10 up to 1000, and draw graphs similar to those in the text. Use these graphs to deduce the complexity of the algorithm, and give your answer using the big-oh notation.

(c) The bubblesort algorithm may be improved by noticing the following points:

• It is easy to detect when the list is completely sorted, since no swaps will be done on a given pass through the list. You can therefore reduce the number of comparisons required if you stop the algorithm after the first pass where no swaps are done.

• On the first pass, the largest element will be moved to its correct location in the list; on the second pass, the second largest element will be moved to its correct location, and so on. You therefore do not need to scan the entire list after the first pass; rather, on pass m, you need compare only elements 1 through $n–m$ with their successors.

Modify your bubblesort program to implement these improvements and do the efficiency checks again. What effects do the changes have?

CHAPTER 12

TABLES AND HASHING

12.1 Alternative methods of storing data

In the last two chapters, we have examined several ways of sorting and searching lists of data. All of the methods we studied required, on average, more computation (comparisons and assignments) to deal with longer lists. You might not be surprised at this, but in fact there is a way of storing data so that the amount of work required to retrieve a particular item is more or less independent of the length of the list. This technique is known as *hashing*.

You have already seen an example of this method of data storage and retrieval, as it is essentially the way arrays are stored and used. The array data type stores data at a location given by the array index. The location at which element *i* of an array is stored is calculated by starting at the base address of an array (the memory address at which the first array element is stored) and adding the size of each element of the array multiplied by *i* to this base address to find the correct location. This method of 'base plus offset' means that the time required to locate any array element is a constant, independent of its location in the array, or even of the overall size of the array.

The important point to remember here is that some formula for converting the array index *i* into a memory location inside the computer must be used to find any given array element. This formula must take the same time to calculate regardless of which array element is sought, or how many elements the array contains. This idea is used in hashing to find efficient ways of storing various types of data.

12.2 The `table` data structure

We can generalize the idea behind storing array elements to allow any data to be stored in a one-dimensional form. As an example, suppose we wish to count the number of times each word occurs in a file. We would like to define an array where each element in the array stores the count for a particular word. In doing so, we are faced with two problems:

- The character string forming a word is not an integer and, in Java, cannot be used as an array index.
- There are more than 400,000 words in the English language, only a small fraction of which will be used in any file of moderate length. We do not want to define an array with 400,000 elements; we would rather define an array of a size near, or slightly larger than, the number of different words we expect to encounter in an average file. We will not, in general, know in advance what these words will be.

Therefore, we need to consider how to transform non-integer data into integer form so that it may be used as an array index. We also need to consider how to map this data into a fairly restricted set of integers. In the word-counting problem, we might define an array of, say, 1000 elements, numbered from 0 to 999.

We are then faced with the problem of mapping any of the 400,000 words in English into the integer range 0...999.

To cope with these problems, a new data structure called a *table* is defined. Tables are superficially similar to arrays, but we will reserve the word *array* to refer to the actual data structure found in the Java language.

A table consists of a function or formula which maps members of one data type *D* (for example, the words in the word-counting problem) onto another type, called the *index I* (usually non-negative integers), which is used to store and access the original data. The properties required of a table data type are:

- A function which calculates the value of the index *I* given the data *D*. (Such a function in the word-counting problem would calculate the array index at which a particular word is stored.)
- Table insertion – a new data item (for example, a word) may be inserted into the table.
- Table retrieval – a table may be searched for a data item and, if present, it, and associated values, may be retrieved. (Given a word, the table is searched to see if that word is present and, if so, the count of the number of times it has been used may be retrieved.)
- Table deletion (optional) – a data item may be deleted from the table.

Provided the function which converts the original data into the table index *I* is efficient, a table can, ideally, represent a considerable increase in efficiency over the searching routines we studied earlier. Given the data for which you are searching, its location (if present) is calculated directly from the data, so you need only look in one place in the table to see if the word is there. For example, if the word 'thing' was calculated to have index 39, you need only look at location 39 in the table. If this location is empty, you know immediately that the word 'thing' is not in the table, while if location 39 is occupied, it will be by the word 'thing' and its associated count will be found at that location.

In practice, such clean access to the table is rarely found. This is because you are usually trying to map data from a very large set (such as the 400,000 words in English) into a much smaller space (say, 1000 array elements). Since you don't know in advance what data items will occur, it is very difficult to find a transformation function which will map all the different data items that actually occur into different locations in the array. For example, if the word 'thing' maps into location 39, another word, such as 'computer', might also map into location 39. When this happens, a *collision* is said to occur. We need to establish some method of handling collisions in such a way that both these words can be stored in the array and, of course, can both be retrieved.

Now that we have some idea of the techniques we intend to use and of some of the problems that may arise, we can get down to a more systematic study of the solutions that have been proposed.

12.3   Hashing

12.3.1   PRINCIPLES

The process of mapping large amounts of data into a smaller table is called *hashing*, because in the processing the original data gets mixed up, or hashed, as it is stored in the smaller array. The function which provides the map between the original data and the smaller table in which it is finally stored is a *hash function*, and the table itself is called a *hash table*.

The operations defined above in the definition of the table data type are implemented in hashing as follows:

- The hash function provides the map which translates the data D into the index I.
- A new data item D is inserted into the table by using the hash function to calculate its index I. If this location is free, the item is inserted directly into the table. If not, a procedure for resolving the collision must be given.
- A specific item of data D may be retrieved by using the hash function to calculate its index I. Position I in the table is checked. If it is empty, item D is not present. If it is occupied, its contents must be tested to see if they match item D. If so, D has been found. If not, the item at index I has the same value given by the hash function as item D and there are two possibilities: (i) item D is not present in the table; (ii) item D is present in the table, but when it was inserted, the other item at index I was already there, causing a collision. In either case, the same procedure used for resolving a collision during insertion of an item must be followed to see if D is located somewhere else in the table. With a properly chosen hash function and collision resolution procedure, there should not be many searches required to resolve the question.
- Item deletion may proceed in a similar manner to insertion, in the sense that the hash function is called to determine the location of the item and if it is present, it may then be deleted. However, if a collision occurred when the item was originally inserted, care must be used in deleting it, as will become apparent later.

In Fig. 12.1, several ice cream flavors are mapped into an array using an unspecified hash function. Note that the two flavors 'raspberry' and 'strawberry' map to the same location, resulting in a collision.

12.3.2   CHOOSING A HASH FUNCTION

A good hash function should satisfy two criteria:

1   It should be quick to compute.

2   It should minimize the number of collisions.

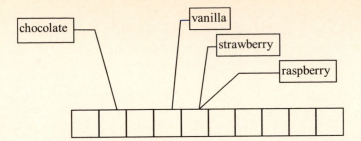

Figure 12.1.

Speed of computation means that the function should be fairly simple, and minimize time-consuming operations such as multiplication, division, or more complex functions such as square roots. Speed is an important consideration, because you must remember that the hash function must be used every time the table is accessed for any reason. (For example, look at any program that uses arrays and count up the number of times an array element is accessed.)

Minimization of collisions can best be achieved by choosing a hash function that spreads the incoming data as evenly as possible over the hash table. As an example of a bad hash function from this point of view, in the case of counting words, suppose we have a hash table of 1000 elements, and we choose a hash function that takes the ASCII code of the first character in the word and uses that as an array index. This method would provide only 26 different indexes, so that 974 sites in the table are not directly accessible by the hash function. Any two words beginning with the same letter would result in a collision.

A few examples of commonly used hash functions follow.

- *Truncation* – part of the key is simply ignored, with the remainder truncated or concatenated to form the index. For example, if we are storing 7-digit phone numbers in a hash table with 1000 elements, we may ignore all but the 2nd, 4th, and 7th digits in the phone number, so that a number such as 731-3018 would be indexed at location 338. This method is quick, as it simply involves accessing a few digits in the input data, but the number of collisions it produces depends on how uniform the input data are. If the table is to contain phone numbers from people all living within a small area, for example, the exchange part of the number (the first three digits) may be the same for all the numbers. In this case, that would mean that all phone numbers would be hashed into indexes beginning with 3 in the table, so that 900 locations would remain unused. This problem could be solved in this case by choosing, say, the last three digits in the phone number instead. In general you should consider what regularities may be present in the data before deciding on a hash function.
- *Folding* – the data can be split up into smaller chunks which are then folded together in some form. For example, a 7-digit phone number could be split into three groups of 2, 2, and 3 digits, which are then added together and truncated to produce an index in the range 000 to 999. For the number 731-3018,

we produce the three numbers 73, 13, and 018, which add up to 104, which may be used as the index. Another number such as 899-6989 would split into 89, 96, and 989, which add up to 1174. Since this number is larger than the highest allowed index in the hash table, we truncate it by saving only the last three digits, giving an index of 174.

- *Modular arithmetic* – convert the data into an integer (using truncation, folding, or some other method), divide by the size of the hash table, and take the remainder as the index (for example, by using the % operator in Java). For example, modular arithmetic was used in the second example under 'folding' above: the phone number 899-6989 produced the index 1174 under the folding procedure, so this number was taken modulo the hash table size (1000) to produce the final index of 174.

There are, of course, many other hash functions that could be used, so you may well think of others on your own. Before using one of your own hash functions, it is a good idea to consider the following points:

- Is it fast and easy to compute?
- Will it spread the data to be hashed fairly evenly over the hash table, and therefore minimize the number of collisions?
- Do you have a collision resolution method available? If not, read on...

12.3.3 COLLISION RESOLUTION WITH OPEN ADDRESSING

We now examine a few ways in which collisions may be resolved. There are two main ways this can be done: *open addressing* and *chaining*. In open addressing, the amount of space available for storing data is fixed at compile time by declaring a fixed array for the hash table. With chaining, an array is also declared for the hash table, but each element in the array is a pointer to a linked list which holds all data with the same index.

If we are using open addressing, we must deal with a collision by finding another, unoccupied, location elsewhere in the array. In deciding how to do this, we are faced with the same two requirements as in deciding on the hash function in the first place: we would like a method of choosing an alternative location that is fast, and that minimizes the number of additional collisions that will occur as more data are added to the table.

Linear probing   The simplest method is known as *linear probing*. If a collision occurs when we are inserting a new item into the table, we simply probe forward in the array, one step at a time, until we find an empty slot where we can store our new data. When we wish to retrieve this data, we start by calculating the hash function, test the location given by the index to see if the required data item is there and, if not, examine each array element from the index location until the item is found, or until we encounter an empty site or examine all locations in the table, at which point we know the item is not in the table.

When using linear probing, we assume the array is circular, so that if we search past the end of the array, we start again at element 0.

The disadvantage with linear probing is that data tend to cluster about certain points in the table, with other parts of the table not being used. This gives rise to lengthy sequential searches through the table when attempting to retrieve data. To see why this happens, suppose we have a hash function that distributes data uniformly over a hash table of size n. When we insert the first element, the hash table is empty so the first item to be hashed will be placed at exactly the location specified by the hash function. Suppose it is placed at location i. For this initial element, all sites in the hash table will be equally likely to be targeted by the hash function, so there is no problem. Consider what happens when the next element is inserted into the table. If it is equally likely to be mapped to any of the table locations by the hash function, then there is equal likelihood that it will be mapped to locations i and $i + 1$. However, site i is full, having been occupied by the first element. Therefore, if the hash function maps the second element to either location i or $i + 1$, the element will be stored in location $i + 1$. Therefore, site $i + 1$ has twice the chance of being filled by the second element as any other site in the hash table. If sites i and $i + 1$ are filled by the first two elements, then site $i + 2$ will have three times the chance of any other element of being filled by the third element, and so on. The problem is that any empty site at the end of a sequence of filled sites will receive any item that is hashed to any of the filled sites *as well as* an item that is hashed to that site directly. Thus once a chain of filled sites has started to form, the effect snowballs, causing longer and longer clusters to appear. These long chains of filled sites require long sequences of comparisons in the retrieval process, reducing efficiency.

Fig. 12.2 shows an item being inserted into a hash table using linear probing to resolve the collision. The item is mapped to location 4 by the hash function, but locations 4, 5, and 6 are already full, so the collision resolution method eventually places the item in location 7.

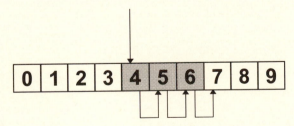

Figure 12.2.

Quadratic probing   One way of resolving the clustering problem is to use a collision resolution function that depends on the index value, or on the number of previous attempts made to resolve the collision. An example of the latter is *quadratic probing*. In this case, if a collision occurs at position i, locations $i + 1$, $i + 4$, $i + 9$, and so on, are tested until an empty site is found. Although this method reduces clustering, it does not probe every site in the table. It can be shown that if the table size is a prime number, the maximum number of probed sites in a hash table of size n is $(n+1)/2$, so that approximately half the table is probed. For example, if the table size is $n = 11$, then for an element mapped to location 0, the six sites 0, 1, 4, 9, 5 (16 mod 11), and 3 (25 mod 11) will be probed. The next location to be probed by the quadratic probing algorithm would be site 3 again (36 mod 11), and all further sites produced by this algorithm will be one of the six already visited. For table sizes that are not prime numbers, the number of different sites probed by the quadratic probing algorithm can be less or more than $(n+1)/2$. For example, if the table size is $n = 10$, six sites are still probed (for example, starting at location 0, sites 0, 1, 4, 9, 6, and 5 are probed). For a table size that is a perfect square, very few sites will be probed. For example, if the table size is 16, only the four sites 0, 1, 4, and 9 are probed. Therefore, it is a good idea to avoid choosing table sizes that are perfect squares (or are divisible by perfect squares), in order to maximize the number of items with the same hash function value which can be stored. A good guide is to choose your table size as either a prime number or a product of two different prime numbers.

Other collision resolution methods   One way of resolving collisions by using an item-dependent probe distance, is to truncate the data and use the truncated form to calculate the increment. For example, we could take the last digit of a phone number and use that as an increment. Another possibility is to use a *pseudo-random number generator* to generate a 'random' increment. A pseudo-random number generator uses a *seed* value to generate a sequence of integers that appear random, but are actually calculated using a deterministic rule. (We have used pseudo-random number generators in our computer experiments in previous chapters.) However, the property of the random number sequence that makes it useful for generating probe increments is that, provided the same seed is used for successive runs, the same sequence of numbers will be generated. As long as we keep track of the seed and where we are in the sequence of numbers we will always know where to probe next.

12.3.4 DELETING ELEMENTS FROM HASH TABLES

Having considered several ways of resolving collisions, we will briefly consider the problem of deleting an item from a hash table where open addressing is used. Deletion is very difficult to do efficiently in such a table. The reason is that in any table where collisions have occurred during the insertion of data, there is a chain of items with the same index. If we want to delete any item that is not at the end of the chain, we will remove a link in the chain, thus disconnecting the elements beyond that link. For example, suppose we have stored four items with the same index at sites i, j, k, l, and we wish to delete item j. We must first locate the item by using the hash function to calculate its index. This will direct us to site i, where the first item with that index is stored. This is not the correct item, so we apply whatever collision resolution system we are using to locate the next site, which contains item *j*, the one we are looking for. If we simply delete *j* from that site, then the site will be empty. A subsequent search for items *k* or *l* will start by using the hash function to find their index, which, as before, will start us off in site *i*. Applying the collision resolution system will lead us to the site formerly occupied by *j*. However, since *j* has been deleted, we will be confronted with an empty site, which is the signal that no more items of that index are present, so the search will terminate with the conclusion that *k* and *l* are not present in the table.

There are several solutions to this problem, including shifting the remaining items forward in the list when an item is deleted, or using a special flag which marks an empty cell as 'deleted' rather than just 'empty' so that searches will continue through this cell to see if any more items with that index are present. However, all these methods are rather slow and cumbersome. If you are likely to require item deletion from a hash table, it is better to resolve collisions using the chaining technique, as described in the next section.

12.3.5 COLLISION RESOLUTION WITH CHAINING

The second method of resolving collisions involves using dynamic data allocation and linked lists. The hash table and associated hash function are defined in the usual manner, except that now the array is an array of pointers to linked lists, one list for each index. If no data are stored at an index site, the corresponding pointer is set to 0. If an item is to be inserted, the hash function is used to find the list to which the item is to be added, and the standard insertion procedures for a linked list are used to insert the item. If a collision occurs, we simply add another node to the end of this list at the corresponding index. When an item is to be retrieved, we use the hash function to calculate its index as usual, and look at the corresponding pointer. If the pointer is 0, the item is not present. If the pointer points to a list, that list is traversed sequentially to see if the desired item is present. With a properly designed hash function, none of these lists should contain more than a few items, so sequential search is an efficient way to search them.

Deletion of an item from a table constructed this way is also quite simple. The hash function is called to determine the index of the item to be deleted. The linked list at that index is searched and, if the item is present, its node is simply spliced out of the list in the usual way. We need not worry about isolating other parts of the table.

The only disadvantage to using chaining is that a linked list requires extra storage space for the pointers connecting the list elements. If the amount of data to be stored consists of a large number of fairly small items, the extra memory required for the pointers could be substantial.

In Fig. 12.3, the array of pointers is shown as the vertical column of boxes on the left, with each box labeled with its hash function value. When a data item (single characters are being stored in this hash table) maps to a particular location, an extra node is allocated and added to the corresponding list. Note that a chained hash table can store more data items than the number of cells in the table. In this case, seven items are stored in a table with six cells.

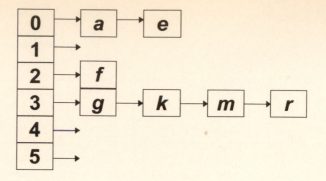

Figure 12.3.

12.4 Java code for hash tables

12.4.1 JAVA CODE FOR HASHING WITH OPEN ADDRESSING

The following Java class implements hashing with open addressing, using quadratic probing to resolve collisions.

```java
public class OpenAddress
{
   private int[] Element;
   private int TableSize;
   private int EmptyCell;

   OpenAddress(int tablesize)
   {
      int index;

      TableSize = tablesize;
      EmptyCell = 0;
      Element = new int[tablesize];
      for (index = 0; index < tablesize; ++index)
         Element[index] = EmptyCell;
   }

   OpenAddress(int tablesize, int emptycell)
   {
      int index;

      TableSize = tablesize;
      EmptyCell = emptycell;
      Element = new int[tablesize];
      for (index = 0; index < tablesize; ++index)
```

```java
      Element[index] = EmptyCell;
}

private int HashFunc(int newElement)
{
   return newElement % TableSize;
}

public void Store(int newElement)
   throws OpenAddressException
{
   int probe, baseIndex = HashFunc(newElement),
      index = baseIndex;

   for (probe = 1; probe <= (TableSize + 1)/2 + 1;
      ++probe)
   {
      if (Element[index] == EmptyCell)
      {
         Element[index] = newElement;
         return;
      }
      else if (Element[index] == newElement)
         throw new OpenAddressException("Element already
            in table.");
      else
         index = (baseIndex + probe * probe) %
            TableSize;
   }
   throw new OpenAddressException("Cannot insert:
      table is full.");
}

public int Retrieve(int searchElement)
   throws OpenAddressException
{
   int probe, baseIndex = HashFunc(searchElement),
      index = baseIndex;

   for (probe = 1; probe <= (TableSize + 1)/2 + 1;
      ++probe)
   {
      if (Element[index] == EmptyCell)
         throw new OpenAddressException("Element not
            found in table.");
      else if (Element[index] == searchElement)
         return searchElement;
      else
         index = (baseIndex + probe * probe) %
```

```
                    TableSize;
        }
        throw new OpenAddressException("Element not found
            in table.");
    }
}
```

We have provided two constructors for this class, which is designed to store `ints` in a hash table. The `OpenAddress` class allows the user to specify the size of the hash table through either constructor. A special value which marks a hash table cell as empty must also be provided. The first constructor uses the value 0 as the default, while the second constructor requires the user to specify the value.

The hash function used here determines the cell location by taking the element to be added and calculating its modulus with respect to `TableSize`.

The `Store()` method calculates a `baseIndex` by using `HashFunc()`, and initializes an `index` parameter to `baseIndex`. The variable `index` will be used as the array index in the event of a collision, when quadratic probing must be used.

The `for` loop first tests the `baseIndex` to see if it is empty, and if so, `newElement` is stored there. If not, the `Element` is tested to see if it already contains the same element as the one which is being inserted. If so, an exception is thrown and the method ends. This test is, of course, optional – you may wish to allow more than one copy of each element in the hash table.

Finally, if the `baseIndex` is occupied and `newElement` is different from what is stored there, the quadratic probing algorithm is used to find the next location to examine.

The `for` loop examines up to `(TableSize + 1)/2 + 1` locations in the hash table. As described above, if `TableSize` is a prime number, this is the maximum number of different locations that will be searched by the quadratic probing algorithm. If `TableSize` is not prime, there may be more or less locations that could be probed, but `(TableSize + 1)/2 + 1` will still provide a reasonable number of sites in these cases as well.

The `Retrieve()` method follows much the same set of steps as the `Store()` method. The same cells in the `Element` array are probed in the same order, and if `searchElement` is found during the course of these probes, it is returned. If the `for` loop is allowed to finish, `searchElement` is not in the hash table and an exception is thrown informing the user of this.

12.4.2 JAVA CODE FOR HASHING WITH CHAINING

The Java code for hashing with chaining is very simple if we use the `IntList` class defined in Chapter 7. In addition to the routines for inserting and deleting elements provided there, we also need a method for searching a list. We can either add this method directly to the `IntList` class, or define a new class derived from `IntList`. A possible method is:

```
public int Search(int SearchElement)
   throws ListException
{
   ListNode Marker;
   for (Marker = Head; Marker != null; Marker =
     Marker.Next)
     if (Marker.Element == SearchElement)
        return SearchElement;
   throw new ListException("Element not found in
     list.");
}
```

This method returns the element if it is found; otherwise it throws an exception. This may seem a bit pointless in the case where we are searching for a single int, since there is little benefit from returning the same element as that for which we are searching. However, this method is easily generalizable to lists which store more complex data types. In this case, we can use one of the data fields from this data type as a *key* field which is used to do the searching. The Search() method can then return the entire data object, if it is found.

Having provided this Search() method, the Chaining method is quite straightforward:

```
public class Chaining
{
   private IntList[] Bucket;
   private int TableSize;

   Chaining(int tablesize)
   {
      int index;

      TableSize = tablesize;
      Bucket = new IntList[tablesize];
      for (index = 0; index < tablesize; ++index)
         Bucket[index] = new IntList();
   }

   private int HashFunc(int newElement)
   {
      return newElement % TableSize;
   }

   public void Store(int newElement)
   {
      Bucket[HashFunc(newElement)].InsertEnd(newElement);
   }

   public int Retrieve(int searchElement)
```

```
        throws ChainingException
    {
        try {
          Bucket[HashFunc(searchElement)].
             Search(searchElement);
          return searchElement;
        } catch (ListException e)
          throw new ChainingException("Element not in
             table.");
    }
}
```

The constructor initializes the array of `IntLists` which is used to store the elements in the hash table. Note that no special `EmptyCell` parameter is needed for this case. The `HashFunc()` method is the same as in the open addressing case.

The `Store()` method is reduced to a single line. The `HashFunc()` method is called to determine in which bucket the new element should be placed, and the `InsertEnd()` method for that list is called to do the insertion. In most hash tables, there will not be many elements stored in each list, so there is no point in sorting the elements as they are inserted.

The `Retrieve()` method uses the `Search()` method of the `IntList` class. If the `searchElement` is found, it is returned; otherwise an exception is thrown.

12.5 Efficiency of hashing

The main motivation for studying hashing is that it is supposed to give us a method of storing and retrieving data that is equally efficient for any size of hash table. The time has come to see if the method lives up to its promises.

We can do the usual computer experiments to see how the number of comparisons for successful and unsuccessful searches vary with the amount of data stored, but in addition to this there is another factor that we should consider. What is important in hashing is not so much the overall size of the table, but the fraction of sites within this table that are occupied. This fraction, defined as the ratio of the number N of objects in the hash table to the number of buckets T in the table, is called the *load factor L* of the table: $L = N/T$.

For hash tables using open addressing, the maximum load factor is $L = 1$, since each bucket in the table can store only one object. If chaining is used, the load factor can be larger than 1, since each bucket is a pointer to a linked list that can, in principle, store any number of objects. For both methods (chaining and open addressing), we would expect the number of comparisons required for both successful and unsuccessful searches to increase as the load factor increases. The reason is simply that the more objects there are in the table, the more likely it is that collisions have occurred during the storage process, so the more likely it is that more than one comparison will be required to locate an object in the table (or to determine that the object is not present).

Therefore, we will examine the efficiency of hashing from two viewpoints. In the first, we will show plots of the number of comparisons required for successful and unsuccessful searches on hash tables of various sizes, but with a constant load factor. We expect that the number of comparisons required should be constant for all sizes of hash table in this case.

In the second experiment, we will examine the number of comparisons required for a hash table of a fixed size, but with various load factors. In this case, we expect the number of comparisons to increase as the load factor increases.

First, let us consider the hash table using open addressing, with the linear and quadratic probing methods of resolving collisions. The number of comparisons required is shown in Fig. 12.4.

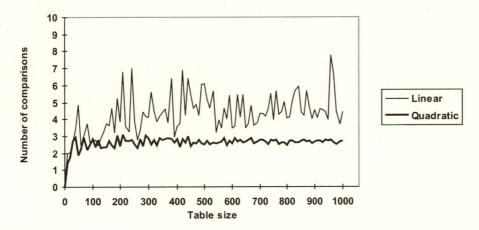

Figure 12.4.

The graph shows the results of a series of experiments run on tables of various sizes (values at every 10 from 10 to 1000). All tables were filled to load factor $L = 0.9$ before the searching experiments were done. It can be seen that quadratic probing requires significantly fewer comparisons to retrieve an item from the table. The number of comparisons is roughly constant over the range of table sizes used in the experiments, though considerable variation is shown for the linear probing method. This is probably due to the formation of clusters in the linear probing method, something which does not occur to the same extent with quadratic probing.

Next, we consider the number of comparisons required for unsuccessful searches using these two collision resolution methods (Fig. 12.5). Again, the quadratic probing method requires fewer comparisons and shows less fluctuation than the linear probing method.

If we examine the number of comparisons for a table of fixed size, but with various load factors, we get the results shown in Figs. 12.6 and 12.7.

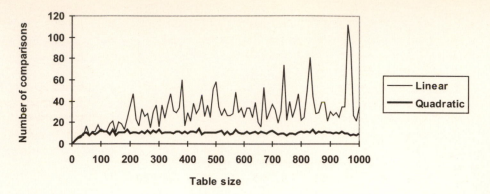

Figure 12.5.

These graphs show that quadratic probing performs better than linear probing, especially at high load factors. (The number of comparisons required for a fully loaded hash table using linear probing is, of course, equal to the table size since all locations in the table must be probed. This gives a value of 1000 for the graph in Fig. 12.7, which is off scale in order to allow the other values to show up on the graph.) Perhaps the most striking thing about these plots is the dramatic increase in the number of comparisons when the tables become fully loaded. The moral is that if you plan on using open addressing, you should ensure that the table size is large enough so that you do not approach full loading in practice. If you keep the load factor below about 0.8, the performance of the hash table should be quite good.

We can do similar experiments for hashing using chaining to resolve collisions. The results are shown in Fig. 12.8.

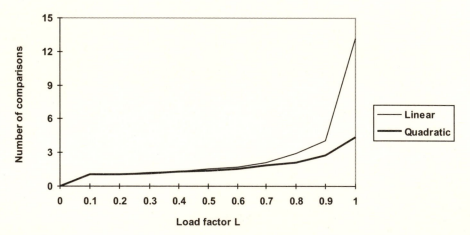

Figure 12.6.

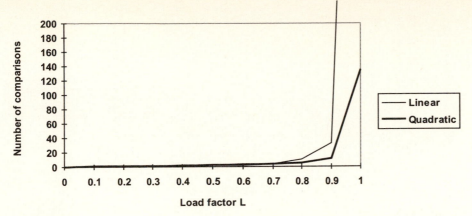

Figure 12.7.

The graph shows the number of comparisons required for successful and unsuccessful searches on tables of various sizes. The load factor on all tables was $L = 1$. This does not mean that the table was fully loaded since, with chaining, there is in principle no limit to the number of objects that can be stored in the table. It can be seen that significantly fewer comparisons are required using the chaining method, than with either of the open addressing methods considered above. This is because the chaining method keeps objects with the same hash function value strictly separate in their own linked lists, so that only those values need be searched. All open addressing collision resolution methods of necessity must store objects in sites other than those to which they are mapped by the hash function if a collision occurs, so that even if *no* items with a particular hash function value are present in the table, some searching may be required to demonstrate this.

The behavior of chaining as we increase the load factor is illustrated in Fig. 12.9.

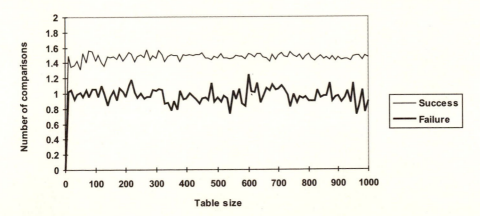

Figure 12.8.

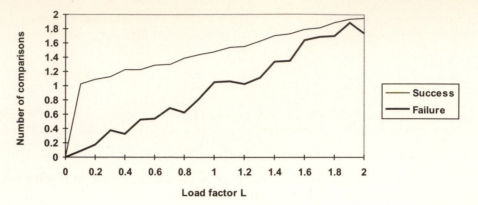

Figure 12.9.

We see that the number of comparisons increases as the load factor increases, just as with the open addressing methods. However, the number of comparisons, even at load factor $L = 2$, is still very small compared with those for open addressing methods at high load factors.

Given the significant advantages of chaining over open addressing in all our efficiency experiments, why would you ever use open addressing? The main reason is space; because chaining uses linked lists to store its objects, each object must have an extra field provided for storing its associated pointer. Also, there are some languages (such as most versions of BASIC, including the currently very popular Visual Basic) which do not support pointers as part of the language, so implementing a hash table using chaining is not easy with these languages. If you are using a language that supports pointers easily and are not severely restricted in terms of memory, then chaining is certainly the best method for implementing a hash table.

12.6 Summary

In this chapter we have introduced the idea of *hash tables* for storing data in a form in which a search of the table is essentially independent of the table size. Hashing is used primarily for storing data which cannot be used directly as array indices, or for storing samples of data chosen from very large data sets. Each item of data is mapped to an *index* by using a *hash function*. The index is used to determine the cell in which the data item is stored. If the cell determined by the hash function is already occupied, a *collision* occurs, and some method of *resolving* the collision must be used. Two main methods of resolving collisions are in use: open addressing and chaining. In open addressing, alternative cells in the array are chosen according to some algorithm (such as linear or quadratic probing). In chaining, each cell in the hash table is a pointer to a linked list. Different items with the same index are simply added to the linked list.

Chaining is more efficient than most forms of open addressing, although it requires extra memory to store the pointer associated with each data item.

Exercises   12.7

1   (a) The integers given below are to be stored in a table with 10 locations (numbered 0–9 inclusive) using open addressing. As a hash function use

location = number % tablesize

where % is the modulus operator. Use quadratic probing to resolve collisions. The numbers to be stored are:

145 87 477 990 797 878 556 551 965 52

(b) For the hash table constructed in part (a), calculate (i) the average number of comparisons necessary for a successful search of the table; (ii) the average number of comparisons necessary in an unsuccessful search of the table.

(c) Insert the same integers into a hash table with ten locations using the same hash function, but use chaining to resolve collisions. Calculate the average number of comparisons for (i) a successful search and (ii) an unsuccessful search in this case.

2   Write a Java abstract class for a hash table in which the collisions are resolved using open addressing with quadratic probing. Test your class by deriving another class from it which stores `ints` in the hash table using a suitable hash function of your choice.

3   (a) Write a Java abstract class for a hash table in which the collisions are resolved using open addressing with a pseudo-random number generator (RNG). The RNG should generate integers which are used as offsets from the starting position, in the same manner as in quadratic probing. Test your class by using it to store integers and retrieve them.

In order to use random numbers for collision resolution, you must ensure that the same sequence of random numbers is generated each time the hash table is accessed. The `random()` method in the Java `Math` class cannot be used for this, as there is no way to specify the initial number generated. However, the `Random` class in the `java.util` package does allow you to specify the seed used to generate the random numbers. Read the Java documentation to learn more about the `Random` class.

(b) Run a computer experiment to test the efficiency of using an RNG to resolve collisions. Follow the examples in the text by finding the number of comparisons required for successful and unsuccessful searches of the table, as a function of table size for a fixed load factor, and as a function of load factor for a fixed table size. Compare your results with the graphs in the text.

4 Using one of the hash classes in the chapter, or one of those from questions 2 or 3 above, write a Java program which counts the number of times various words occur in a text file. You must first define a class containing a `String` field and an integer field for storing the word count, together with any overloaded operators required by the hashing class and hash function you are using. A convenient hash function to use for storing a character string adds up the ASCII codes of the characters in the string and uses this sum, modulo the table size, as the array index. The output from your program should be a list of the words in the file followed by the count of the number of times each word occurred. (If you are feeling ambitious, you may want to use one of the sorting algorithms from the previous chapter to sort the list into (i) alphabetical order; (ii) descending order of frequency of occurrence.)

5 The `java.util` package provides an abstract class called `Dictionary` and a class derived from it called `Hashtable`. The `Hashtable` class will store data of any (non-primitive) type in a hash table. Any object stored in a `Hashtable` must be instances of a class in which overriden versions of the `hashCode()` and `equals()` methods of the basic `Object` class are provided. The `hashCode()` method provides a hash function, and the `equals()` method returns a `boolean` stating whether two objects are equal. Read the Java documentation on the `Hashtable` class and use it to provide an alternative solution to question 4. (Note that the `String` class already contains overridden versions of `hashCode()` and `equals()` and so may be used directly in a `Hashtable`.)

CHAPTER 13

TREES

13.1　Binary search trees

13.1.1　DEFINITIONS

A *tree* is a data structure consisting of data nodes connected to each other with pointers, in much the same spirit as a linked list. However, each node in a tree may be connected to two or more other nodes, rather than the single node allowed in a linked list. The maximum number of nodes to which any single node may be connected is called the *order* of the tree. The simplest tree is of order 2, and is called a *binary tree*. A diagram of a binary tree is shown in Fig. 13.1.

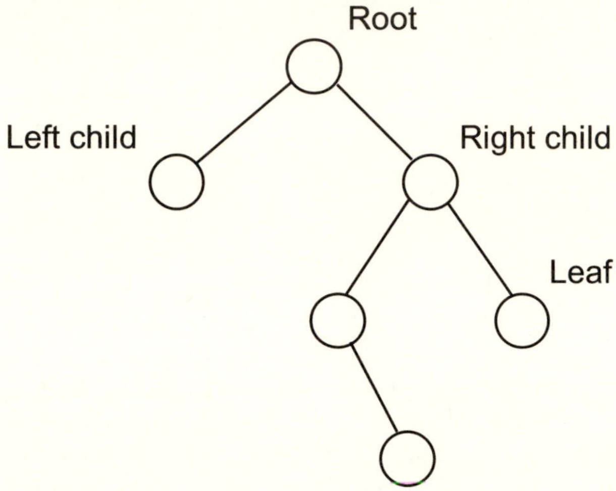

Figure 13.1.

Each node in this diagram contains one or more data fields, and two pointers: one to the left child and the other to the right child. The topmost node in the tree is called the *root node*. A node with no children is called a *leaf*. If we redraw the tree shown above to illustrate the internal structure of its nodes, it would look as shown in Fig. 13.2.

Here, each node is shown with its three main components: the data area, and the pointers to the left and right children. These pointers are used in the same way as pointers in the linked list. When a new node is to be added to the tree, memory is allocated for the new node using the `new` operator in Java, and the address of this location is loaded into the appropriate pointer (left or right) in the new node's parent. Just as a null pointer indicates the end of a linked list, a null pointer in a tree indicates the end of a branch in that direction. Therefore, a leaf is a node, both of whose pointers are null.

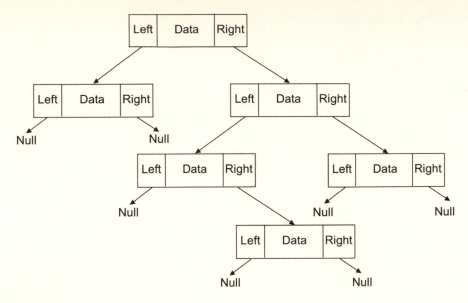

Figure 13.2.

13.1.2 TREE OPERATIONS

A binary tree as defined above can contain any type of data in any order, depending on the use to which the tree is to be put. Probably the most common use of trees, however, is as yet another method for sorting and searching data. Trees which are used for this purpose are called *search trees*, and binary trees used for sorting and searching data are called, not surprisingly, *binary search trees*.

Trees (binary and otherwise) have much the same basic types of operations as other data structures:

- Inserting a new node.
- Deleting a node.
- Listing or visiting the nodes of the tree.

One way that a binary search tree can be used to sort data is as follows. Let us suppose that we have a list of integers, such as 5, 2, 8, 4, and 1, that we wish to sort into ascending order. We can perform a two-stage sorting algorithm. The first stage involves inserting the integers into a binary search tree:

1   If the current pointer is 0, create a new node, store the data, and return the address of the new node.

2   Otherwise, compare the integer to the data stored at the current node. If the new integer is less than the integer at the current node, insert the new integer into the left child of the current node (by recursively applying the same algorithm). Otherwise, insert it into the right child of the current node.

We illustrate the process by inserting the integers as shown in Fig. 13.3.

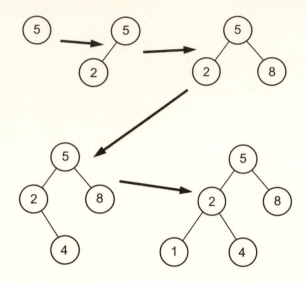

Figure 13.3. Inserting the integers 5, 2, 8, 4, and 1 into a binary search tree.

The first integer (5) is inserted into an empty tree (where the root pointer is 0), so the root node is created and the integer 5 is stored there. The next integer (2) is compared with the value at the root node, found to be less than it, and inserted as the left child of the root. Similarly the third integer (8) is inserted as the right child of the root since it is larger than 5. The fourth integer (4) is compared with the root and found to be less than 5, so the algorithm tells us to insert 4 into the left child. The left child is already occupied, however, so we simply apply the algorithm recursively starting at the left child of the root. The integer 4 is compared with 2, found to be greater than 2, so it is inserted as the right child of 2. The process can be continued as long as we have more data to add to the tree.

Having inserted the numbers into the binary search tree, it may not be immediately obvious how that has helped us. In order to produce a sorted list of the data, we need to *traverse* the tree, that is, list the nodes in some specific order.

Various types of tree traversal exist, but the most common is *inorder* traversal, which means that we follow the algorithm:

1 If the current pointer is not 0, then:

2 Traverse the left child of the current pointer.

3 Visit (or print) the data at the current pointer.

4 Traverse the right child of the current pointer.

Steps 2 and 4 in this algorithm use recursion: they call the same algorithm to process the left and right children of the current pointer.

To see how the traversal produces a sorted list, consider the binary search tree that we produced in Fig. 13.3 above. We begin the traversal algorithm, as usual, with the root node. The root pointer is not 0, so we must traverse the left child. Its pointer isn't 0 either (it contains the value 2), so we must visit *its* left child. This child's pointer still isn't 0 (it contains the value 1), so we call the algorithm again for the node containing the value 1. The pointer to the left child of this node is now 0, so the recursive call to this node will return without doing anything. We have now completed step 2 in the algorithm for the node 1, so we can now proceed to step 3 for that node, which prints out the number 1. This looks promising, since the first value actually printed from the traversal algorithm is, in fact, the smallest number stored in the tree.

We then complete the algorithm for node 1 by traversing its right child. Since the pointer to its right child is 0, the algorithm is complete for node 1. We can now return to the processing of the next node up, which is node 2. Its left child has been fully traversed, so we now print its value, which is 2. We then traverse the right child of node 2, which takes us to node 4. Since node 4 is a leaf (it has no children) it is printed after node 2.

The entire left subtree of the root node has now been traversed, producing the list 1, 2, 4. The root node may now be printed, giving the value 5. Finally, the right child of the root is traversed, printing out the value 8. The completed list is 1, 2, 4, 5, 8, which is the correctly sorted list.

Java code for a simple binary search tree   13.2

13.2.1 BUILDING THE TREE

The development of Java code for a binary search tree is very similar to that for the linked list that we considered in Chapter 9. Since each node in the tree must store not only some data, but also pointers to the node's left and right children, we first define a class called `TreeNode` which contains all these fields.

```java
public class TreeNode
{
   int Element;
   TreeNode Left, Right;

   TreeNode(int newElement)
   {
      Element = newElement;
   }
}
```

Since a new node is always added at the end of a branch, we do not bother to explicitly initialize the `Left` and `Right` pointers. Remember that Java guarantees that all objects are initialized to `null` unless the program explicitly provides a value for them.

We can now use `TreeNode` to construct a class for a simple binary search tree.

```
public class BinTree
{
   private TreeNode Root;

   private TreeNode Insert(TreeNode tree,
      int newElement)
   {
      if (tree == null)
        return new TreeNode(newElement);
      else if (newElement < tree.Element)
        tree.Left = Insert(tree.Left, newElement);
      else
        tree.Right = Insert(tree.Right, newElement);
      return tree;
   }

   public void Insert(int newElement)
   {
      Root = Insert(Root, newElement);
   }
}
```

The class so far contains only methods for inserting an element into the tree. We will worry about other methods later.

Note that the `BinTree` class contains only a single data field: `Root`. This represents the root node of the tree, and is initialized automatically by Java to `null`, representing an empty tree. There is no constructor, since all insertion of data into the tree is handled by the `Insert()` methods.

The public `Insert()` method provides the public interface to the tree, and calls the recursive `Insert()` method internally. This is the same technique as we used with the sorting classes in Chapter 11. When a user wishes to insert a new item into a tree, they only wish to pass the element to be inserted. Since the recursive `Insert()` method also requires the root of the tree to begin its recursion, we hide this from the user by calling it from the public `Insert()` method.

The internal `Insert()` method follows the algorithm given above quite closely. Consider what happens if the method is called when the tree is empty, so that `Root` is null. In this case, the `if (tree == null)` condition is true, so the method allocates a new `TreeNode`, stores `newElement` in it, and returns this `TreeNode` object. `Root` is therefore assigned this new object by the `Root = Insert(Root, newElement)` statement in the public `Insert()` method.

You might wonder why this final assignment is necessary. That is, couldn't we just write the public `Insert()` method as follows?

```
public void Insert(int newElement)
{
    Insert(Root, newElement);
}
```

Since `Root` is passed by reference to the recursive `Insert()` method, you might think that the assignment of a new `TreeNode` to `Root` inside the recursive `Insert()` method would be passed back to the public `Insert()` method, and thus provide a permanent new home for `Root`. However, remember that passing by reference means that only changes in the object *pointed to* by `Root` are permanent – any change to the address pointed to by `Root` is *not* permanent, and will be lost when the recursive `Insert()` method ends. Since `Root` points to `null` when it is passed to the recursive `Insert()` method, it will still be pointing to `null` when that method finishes, regardless of what changes are made to it in the meantime. The only way we can make the assignment of a new `TreeNode` to `Root` permanent is to pass the new `TreeNode` back to the public `Insert()` method and assign it to `Root` there.

It is for this reason that we also use assignment statements in the recursive calls to assign locations to `tree.Left` and `tree.Right`. Consider what happens if we have just stored the number 5 at location `Root` and we now wish to insert 3 into the tree. Since 3 is less than 5, the first call to the recursive `Insert()` method drops down to the line `else if (newElement < tree.Element)`, and a recursive call is made with the statement `tree.Left = Insert(tree.Left, newElement)`. Since `tree.Left` is null at this point, a null `TreeNode` is passed to the `Insert()` method, resulting in a new `TreeNode` being allocated and returned. In the top level call, this `TreeNode` is assigned to `tree.Left`, thus making the assignment permanent and adding an extra node to the tree. Note that the last action of the `Insert()` method is then `return tree`, which passes the `Root` pointer back to the public `Insert()` method. This last step simply reassigns `Root` to the same place it was before and might seem a bit of wasted effort, but it is the simplest way to make the insertion process work consistently. The important point is that the bottom level of the recursion (where the new `TreeNode` is allocated) *must* pass this `TreeNode` up to the next higher level of recursion so that it can be assigned to the correct pointer. All higher levels in the recursion simply reassign `TreeNode`s to pointers that already pointed to them, thus they don't change anything in the tree structure.

13.2.2 TRAVERSING THE TREE

Having inserted some data into the binary search tree, the next question is obviously, 'How do we extract the information from the tree?' This depends to a large extent on the use to which the information is to be put. In previous chapters, we have used a small applet to display the results of using a data structure, so an obvious application might be to traverse the tree (visit all its nodes in some definite order) and display the data stored at each node in a `Label` within an applet.

We have done this with arrays (in data structures such as stacks, queues, and sets) and with linked lists. To traverse an array, we provided a `getElement()` method which retrieved a specified array element. For a linked list, we provided a list iterator which kept track of where we were within the list and returned the next item on command.

Arrays and lists are inherently non-recursive structures* however, so the same methods do not work easily with a binary search tree. Since we used recursion to insert new data into the tree, we might try a recursive method to traverse the tree as well.

Suppose we have a `Panel` containing an array of `Labels`, each of which is to display the `int` stored at a node of the tree. The following methods, which are part of the `BinTree` class, will update the display in this `Panel`:

```
private int Update(ResultsPanel Results,
    TreeNode tree,
    int index)
{
    if (tree != null) {
        index = Update(Results, tree.Left, index);
        Results.setLabel(index++,
            Integer.toString(tree.Element));
        index = Update(Results, tree.Right, index);
    }
    return index;
}


public void Update(ResultsPanel Results)
{
    Results.clearLabels();
    Update(Results, Root, 0);
}
```

As with the `Insert()` methods, we have here a pair of `Update()` methods, one recursive, the other non-recursive and public. The public `Update()` method calls one of the `Panel`'s methods `clearLabels()`, which removes all text from the array of `Labels`. Then it calls the recursive `Update()` method to traverse the tree and update the `Labels`.

The recursive `Update()` method accepts the `Panel` as one of its arguments, followed by a `TreeNode` argument, and an `int`. The `int index` is the index in

---

* It is *possible* to write a recursive list traversal method (examine the first list element, then recursively examine the remainder of the list, for example), but much less efficient to do so. However, in some computer languages such as LISP and Prolog, this is the only way lists can be traversed.

the array of `Labels` to be updated. It is initialized in the first call to 0. The `TreeNode` is the node in the tree being considered.

The recursive `Update()` method first tests the `TreeNode  tree` to see if it is `null`. If so, the method returns `index` and stops. If not, then the left branch of the tree is traversed by the recursive call `index  =  Update(Results, tree.Left,  index)`. Then the current `TreeNode` is used in the statement:

```
Results.setLabel(index++,
   Integer.toString (tree.Element));
```

This statement calls the `Panel`'s `setLabel()` method with the current `index` value and the data at the current `TreeNode` (converted to a `String`). This method then just sets the text of that `Label` to the indicated text. The `++` operator then increments the `index`. After this, the right branch of the tree is traversed recursively.

Note that in order for the altered `index` counter to be passed between the various recursive layers, it must be returned by each recursive call after it finishes. The reason for this is that `ints` are always passed by value between methods, so in order to save the change to `index` in one method, it must be returned to the layer above it.

Although this particular example illustrates how the data in a tree can be retrieved for one specific purpose – display in an array of `Labels` – the same idea is used in any traversal method. First, check if the current node is `null`. If not, traverse the left branch of the tree, process the current node, and traverse the right branch.

13.2.3 DELETION FROM A BINARY SEARCH TREE

We now consider an algorithm for deleting a node from a binary search tree in such a way that the remaining nodes still have the same inorder traversal.

There are three categories of nodes we may wish to delete:

1   Leaves – these are the easiest, since all we need to do is delete the leaf and set the pointer from its parent (if any) to 0.

2   Nodes with a single child – these too are fairly easy, since we just redirect the pointer from the node's parent so that it points to the child.

3   Nodes with both children – these can be fairly tricky, since we must rearrange the tree to some extent. The method we shall use is to replace the node being deleted by the *rightmost* node in its *left* subtree. (We could equally well have used the leftmost node in the right subtree.) Because of the rules for inorder traversals, this method guarantees the same traversal.

The actual implementation in Java rearranges only the pointers to nodes, and thus avoids any actual copying of the data stored at the nodes. A method which accepts a single data argument `item`, searches for the item in the tree, and then

deletes the node (if found) is given below. This method can be added to the
BinTree class above:

```java
public void Delete(int item) throws TreeException
{
    TreeNode marker = Root, parent = null,
        child = Root, temp;

    while (marker != null && marker.Element != item)
    {
        parent = marker;
        if (item < marker.Element)
            marker = marker.Left;
        else
            marker = marker.Right;
    }
    if (marker == null) throw new TreeException
        ("Cannot delete: item not in tree.");

    // Delete root node
    if (parent == null)
    {
        if (marker.Right == null)
            Root = marker.Left;
        else if (marker.Left == null)
            Root = marker.Right;
        else
        {
            for (temp = marker, child = marker.Left;
                child.Right != null;
                temp = child, child = child.Right);
            if (child != marker.Left)
            {
                temp.Right = child.Left;
                child.Left = Root.Left;
            }
            child.Right = Root.Right;
            Root = child;
        }
    }

    // Delete internal node
    else if (marker.Right == null)
    {
        if (parent.Left == marker)
            parent.Left = marker.Left;
        else
            parent.Right = marker.Left;
    }
```

```
        else if (marker.Left == null)
        {
           if (parent.Left == marker)
              parent.Left = marker.Right;
           else
              parent.Right = marker.Right;
        }
        else
        {
           for (temp = marker, child = marker.Left;
              child.Right != null;
              temp = child, child = child.Right);
           if (child != marker.Left)
           {
              temp.Right = child.Left;
              child.Left = marker.Left;
           }
           child.Right = marker.Right;
           if (parent.Left == marker)
              parent.Left = child;
           else
              parent.Right = child;
        }
     }
  }
```

This method looks rather complicated, but isn't really, since it just treats all possible cases. The actual steps within each case are fairly simple. The description below is much more easily followed if you draw a binary search tree and trace the steps as this method proceeds.

The first thing to note about this method is that it is *non-recursive*, which in itself is something of an oddity for binary search tree routines. Recursion works well if we are attempting to locate one site in a tree and restrict our activities to that site once it is found. Node deletion, however, requires action at various places within the tree, so we need to be able to store several locations in memory. This is most easily done with a non-recursive method.

The first part of the method (the `while` loop) does a non-recursive search for the first node whose `Element` field matches the argument `item`. The search is straightforward, except that we also keep track of the `parent` of each node checked. We need the parent since one of its pointers must be redirected if its child is being deleted. If the required node is not found, `marker` will be `null` after the `while` loop finishes, and the method throws an exception to indicate the node is not in the tree.

Assuming the node to be deleted is present in the tree, we are faced with two possibilities: the required node is the root node, or it is some other node. These must be treated as separate cases, since the root node has no parent.

Let us consider deletion of the root node first. In this case `marker` will be pointing to the root node. We must now deal with the three cases listed above: the root node has (i) no children, (ii) one child, or (iii) both children. The cases of either no children or only a left child are handled by the first section of the `if` statement. In this case, the `Root` of the tree is set to the left child of the old root.

If the right child of the root exists, we next check to see if there is a left child. If not, the second section of the `if` statement assigns `Root` to the right child of the old root.

The final `else` deals with the case where the root has both children. Two temporary pointers are used to keep track of things here. The `temp` pointer starts off pointing to the root, and `child` points to the root's left child. The termination condition of the `for` loop tests whether `child` has a right child itself. If not, we have found the rightmost node in the left subtree of the root. If a right child *does* exist, we move both `temp` and `child` one step down the right side of the left subtree. We continue until the rightmost node in the left subtree is found. This node is the one we want to move up to replace the root node.

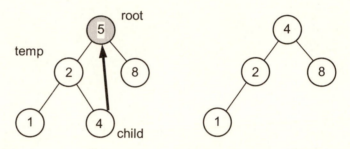

Figure 13.4.

To do this, we need to redirect several pointers (much more easily visualized if you draw a picture – see Fig. 13.4). Exactly which pointers are redirected depends on whether or not the left child of the root has a right child. If it doesn't, it will be the node that is moved up to the root position. In this case, (where `child` is still `marker.left` after the `for` loop has finished) we must assign `child.right` to point to the same node that the old right child of the root (`Root.right`) did, and assign `Root` to be `child`. No other redirections are necessary. In particular, we do *not* need to redirect any pointers from `child`'s parent, since that parent is the old root node, and is going to be deleted anyway.

If the search for `child` progressed past `marker.left`, however, we *do* need to redirect the pointer from `child`'s parent, since that parent will still be in the tree after `child` is relocated to become the new root node. We know that `child` must have been the right child of its parent (because we are finding the *rightmost* node in the left subtree), and that `child` can have at most a left child (since it is the rightmost node in its subtree) we must redirect the *right* pointer of its parent to point to its *left* child, which is done by the statement `temp.right = child.left`. Finally, we need to ensure that `child`'s left pointer is also correctly assigned. An example of deleting the root node is shown in Fig. 13.4.

The remainder of the method deals with the case where a node other than the root is deleted. The steps are very similar, except now we must make sure that the parent of the deleted node has its pointers correctly reset. You are urged to trace this method through for several test binary search trees to see how it works. An example of what happens in this case is shown in Fig. 13.5.

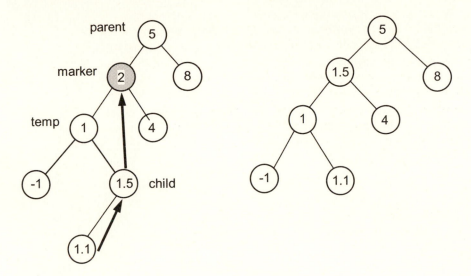

Figure 13.5.

13.2.4 EFFICIENCY OF BINARY SEARCH TREES

The binary search tree routines above illustrate a way of using trees to sort and search data. The treesort and treesearch algorithms work well if the initial data are in a jumbled order, since the binary search tree will be fairly well *balanced*, which means that there are roughly equal numbers of nodes in the left and right subtree of any node. Balanced trees tend to be 'bushy': they have few levels and spread out width-wise. This makes for efficient sorting and searching routines, because both these routines work their way vertically through the tree to locate nodes. Trees that are wide and shallow have only a few levels, so the insertion and searching routines have relatively few steps. In fact, in these cases, the sorting routine is $O(n \log n)$, so it is of comparable efficiency to mergesort and quicksort. The searching routine is essentially a binary search, and so is $O(\log n)$. (We will leave it up to the reader to construct some computer experiments to verify these results.)

However, if the list is already in order (or very nearly so), the tree formed by this insertion algorithm will be essentially linear, meaning that any searches performed on the tree will be essentially sequential. This simple insertion routine is, therefore a disaster if fed a list that is already sorted, or contains a significant amount of order. If we wish to use a binary tree in searching and sorting, we would therefore like a way to ensure that the tree is reasonably balanced, no matter what the order of the input data.

You may be wondering why, with all the searching and sorting algorithms we have studied, we need to consider yet another way of doing these operations. The treesort and treesearch routines, however, offer distinct advantages over other methods in certain circumstances. We see from the above routines that it is easy to insert items into a binary search tree, and equally easy to use binary search to look for them. Insertion of items into an already sorted list is slow and painful if we have used mergesort or quicksort, since these methods operate on the list as a whole, and if more data are added, the methods must be reapplied to the entire data set again. Mergesort also works best on linked lists, on which it is difficult to use binary search, while quicksort works best on arrays, where it is difficult to insert items into a sorted list efficiently. Thus the tree algorithms are suited to cases where data are continually arriving and we want to maintain a sorted list (which can be searched efficiently) at all times.

There are two main approaches which may be taken to decrease the depth (the number of layers) of a binary search tree:

1   Insert a number of elements into a binary search tree in the usual way (using the algorithm given in the previous section). After a large number of elements have been inserted, copy the tree into another binary search tree in such a way that the tree is balanced. This method of 'one-shot' balancing works well if the tree is to be fully constructed before it is to be searched. However, if data are to be continually added to the tree, and searching takes place between additions, the second method is to be preferred.

2   Balance the tree after each insertion. The *AVL tree* is the most popular algorithm for constructing such binary search trees. It is considered in the next section.

13.3 AVL trees

13.3.1 CONSTRUCTION OF AN AVL TREE

An algorithm for constructing balanced binary search trees in which the trees remain as balanced as possible after every insertion was devised in 1962 by two Russian mathematicians, G. M. Adel'son-Vel'sky and E. M. Landis (hence the name *AVL tree*). An AVL tree is a binary search tree in which the left and right subtrees of any node may differ in height by at most 1, and in which both the subtrees are themselves AVL trees (the definition is recursive). Fig. 13.6 shows some examples of trees that are and that are not AVL trees. In these diagrams, the number in each node is equal to the height of the right subtree minus the height of left subtree. An AVL tree must have only the differences −1, 0 or 1 between the two subtrees at any node.

An AVL tree is constructed in the same manner as an ordinary binary search tree, except that after the addition of each new node, a check must be made to ensure that the AVL balance conditions have not been violated. If all is well, no

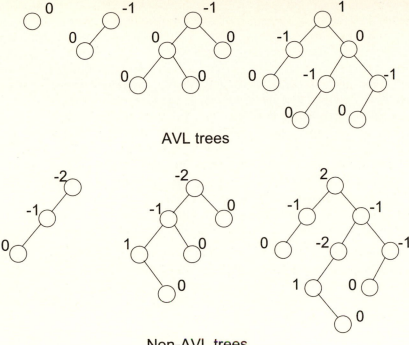

AVL trees

Non-AVL trees

Figure 13.6.

further action need be taken. If the new node causes an imbalance in the tree, however, some rearrangement of the tree's nodes must be done. The insertion of a new node and test for an imbalance are done using the following algorithm:

1   Insert the new node using the same algorithm as for an ordinary binary search tree.

2   Beginning with the new node, calculate the difference in heights of the left and right subtrees of each node on the path leading from the new node back up the tree towards the root.

3   Continue these checks until either the root node is encountered and all nodes along the path have differences of no greater than 1, or until the *first* difference greater than 1 is found.

4   If an imbalance is found, perform a *rotation* of the nodes to correct the imbalance. Only one such correction is ever needed for any one node. (We will describe rotations below.)

To see how these modifications work, it is easiest if we give an example of the construction of an AVL tree. We will therefore construct a tree by inserting integers into it. We begin by inserting the integer 10 into the root:

Since this node has no children, the difference in height of the two subtrees is 0, and this node satisfies the AVL conditions.

We now add another node (20):

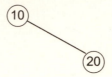

Beginning at the new node (20) we calculate differences in subtree heights. The node 20 has a difference of 0, and its parent (10) has a difference of +1. This tree is also an AVL tree.

We now insert a third node (30):

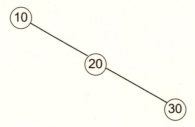

Beginning at the new node (30), we find a difference of 0. Working back towards the root, the node 20 has a difference of +1, which is OK, but the root node 10 has a difference of +2, which violates the AVL conditions. Therefore, we must rearrange the nodes to restore the balance in the tree.

As mentioned above, we perform an operation known as a *rotation* when the tree goes out of balance. There are two types of rotation used in AVL trees: *single* and *double* rotations. The rules for deciding which type of rotation to use are quite simple:

1   When you have found the first node that is out of balance (according to the algorithm above), restrict your attention to that node and the two nodes in the two layers immediately below it (on the path you followed up from the new node).

2   If these three nodes lie in a straight line, a *single rotation* is needed to restore the balance.

3   If these three nodes lie in a 'dog-leg' pattern (that is, there is a bend in the path), you need a *double rotation* to restore the balance.

In our example here, the three nodes to consider are the only three nodes in the tree. The first node where an imbalance was detected was the root node (10). The two layers immediately below this node, and on the path up from the new node, are the nodes 20 and 30. These nodes lie in a straight line, so we need a single rotation to restore the balance.

A single rotation involves shifting the middle node up to replace the top node and the top node down to become the left child of the middle node. After performing the rotation on this tree, we obtain:

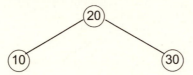

A check shows that the AVL structure of the tree has been restored by this operation.

We continue by adding two more nodes: 25 and 27. After adding 25, a check shows that the AVL nature of the tree has not been violated, so no adjustments are necessary. After adding 27, however, the tree looks like this:

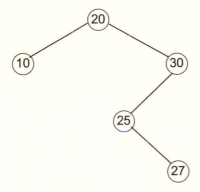

Tracing a path back from the node 27, we find height differences of 0 at 27, +1 at 25, and −2 at 30. Thus the first imbalance is detected at node 30. We restrict our attention to this node and the two nodes immediately below it (25 and 27). These three nodes form a dog-leg pattern, since there is a bend in the path at node 25. Therefore, we require a double rotation to correct the balance. A double rotation, as its name implies, consists of two single rotations. These two rotations are in opposite directions. The first rotation occurs on the two layers below the node where the imbalance was detected (in this case, it involves the nodes 25 and 27). We rotate the node 27 up to replace 25, and 25 down to become the left child of 27. The tree now looks like this:

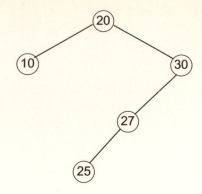

This operation obviously has not corrected the imbalance in the tree, so we must perform the second rotation, which involves the three nodes 25, 27, and 30. Node 27 rotates up to replace 30 and node 30 rotates down to become the right child of 27:

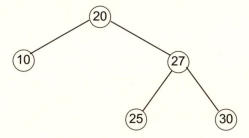

The AVL structure of the tree is now restored. We continue by adding the nodes 7 and 4 to the tree. Adding the 7 doesn't upset the balance, but adding the 4 does:

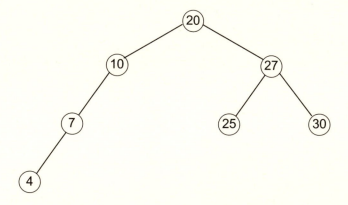

In this case, the first imbalance is detected at node 10, where a difference of −2 occurs. Considering this node and the two immediately below it, we see that the nodes 10, 7, and 4 lie in a straight line, so a single rotation is needed. Applying the rotation balances the tree:

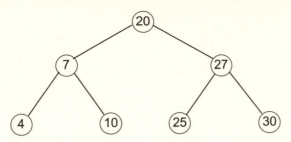

One final example, before we consider the general case. We add the nodes 23, 26, and 21 to the tree (the 23 and 26 do not disturb the balance, but the 21 does):

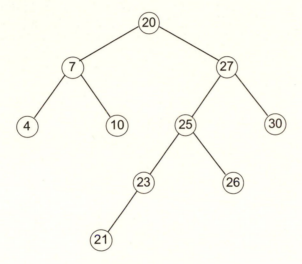

Working back from node 21, we find differences of 0 at 21, −1 at 23, −1 at 25, and −2 at 27. Therefore, node 27 is the first node where an imbalance occurs. We examine this node and the two layers immediately below it on the path to the new node. This gives us the three nodes 27, 25, and 23, which lie in a straight line, so a single rotation is indicated. The middle node (25) rotates up to replace node 27 and node 27 rotates down to become the right child of 25. What happens to node 26, which is the old right child of 25? It must swap over to become the new *left* child of node 27. Making these modifications, we obtain:

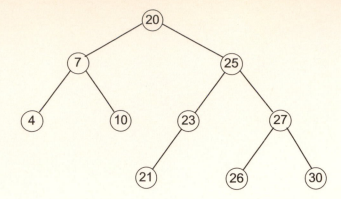

In summary, the steps involved in inserting a new node in an AVL tree are:

1   Insert the node in the same way as in an ordinary binary search tree.

2   Beginning with the new node, trace a path back towards the root, checking the difference in height of the two subtrees at each node along the way.

3   If you find a node with an imbalance (a height difference other than 0, +1, or −1), stop your trace at this point.

4   Consider the node with the imbalance and the two nodes on the layers immediately below this point on the path back to the new node.

5   If these three nodes lie in a straight line, apply a single rotation to correct the imbalance.

6   If these three nodes lie in a dog-leg pattern, apply a double rotation to correct the imbalance.

The single rotation can occur towards either the left or the right: one is just the mirror image of the other. Which direction to go should be obvious from the nature of the imbalance. Similarly, double rotations can be either left first, then right, or right first, then left. The first rotation should always be *into* the bend in the dog-leg.

We may describe single and double rotations in general as follows. First, consider the single rotation. Suppose the state of the tree before the new node which causes the imbalance is as shown in Fig. 13.7. The capital letters indicate nodes in the tree, and the rectangular boxes indicate subtrees whose structure doesn't concern us. The letter h indicates the height of the subtree. It is possible that $h = 0$, in which case the nodes B, D, and E are zero pointers. If $h > 0$, then these three nodes are actually present in the tree.

The structure of this tree satisfies the AVL conditions if all the subtrees in the rectangular boxes are AVL trees, since the height difference is 0 at node C and +1 at node A.

Now suppose that we insert a node into the subtree under node E, in such a way that the height of this subtree increases. We now have the situation shown in Fig. 13.8.

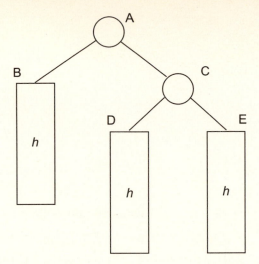

Figure 13.7.

The tree is now unbalanced at node A, since the height difference there is now +2. Following the rules that we outlined above, we examine the node where the imbalance first occurs (A), and the two nodes immediately below it, on the path to the new node. This gives us the nodes A, C, and E. These three nodes are in a straight line, so we need a single rotation. We rotate C up to replace A and A down to become the left child of C. Node D must swap over to become the new right child of A. The situation after the rotation is shown in Fig. 13.9.

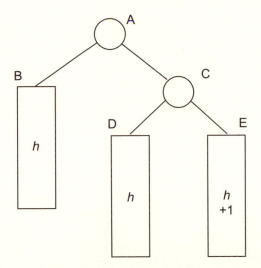

Figure 13.8.

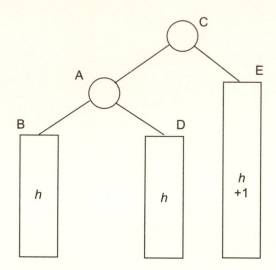

Figure 13.9.

The balance is now restored, as can be checked by calculating the differences at each node. Note that a single rotation might involve two or three nodes, depending on whether the value of h is zero or greater than zero. The same technique works in both cases. The example shown here was a single rotation to the left. An example of a single rotation to the right can be obtained by looking at the diagrams in a mirror!

The double rotation *always* involves three nodes. Suppose a binary search tree looks like Fig 13.10 before an insertion. This tree is an AVL tree, assuming all subtrees in the rectangular boxes are AVL trees. The height differences are 0 at node D, 0 at node C, and +1 at node A. The value of h must be at least 1, in which case the two subtrees F and G are empty, and node D is a leaf. If $h > 1$, then all four subtrees in the rectangular boxes are actually present in the tree.

Now suppose we insert a new node into subtree F or G (it doesn't matter which) in such a way that the height of the corresponding subtree increases. Suppose we choose subtree G. The situation is now as shown in Fig. 13.11.

The tree is now unbalanced, since the height differences are +1 at D, −1 at C, and +2 at A. Therefore, node A is the first node where an imbalance is detected. Considering this node and the two nodes immediately below it, on the path to the new node, gives us nodes A, C, and D, which form a dog-leg pattern. Therefore, a double rotation is needed.

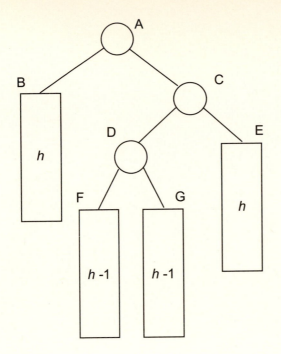

Figure 13.10.

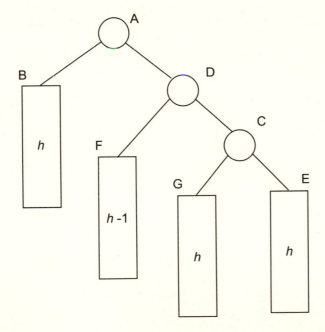

Figure 13.11.

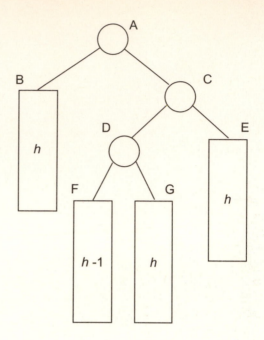

Figure 13.12.

The first rotation involves nodes C and D: node D rotates up to replace C and C rotates down to become the new right child of D. Subtree G swaps over to become the left child of C. The result of this is shown in Fig. 13.12. As can be checked from the diagram, this first rotation does not solve the imbalance problem, since the height differences are still +2 at both nodes A and D.

Therefore, we perform the second rotation, which is in the opposite direction to the first one, and involves nodes A, D, and C. Node D rotates up to replace node A, node A rotates down to become the left child of D, and subtree F swaps over to become the new right child of node A. The result of this is shown in Figure 13.13.

Note that the first rotation of the double rotation involves a single rotation with two nodes, and the second rotation involves a single rotation with three nodes.

The final tree is now balanced, since the height differences are now 0 at node C, −1 at node A, and 0 at node D.

Although both of these examples (the single and double rotations) were done with trees where the first imbalance occurs at the root node, exactly the same procedures would be applied in those cases where an imbalance occurs within a tree. The structure of the tree above the node where the first imbalance occurs is irrelevant: all the changes occur at the level of that node and in the two layers immediately below.

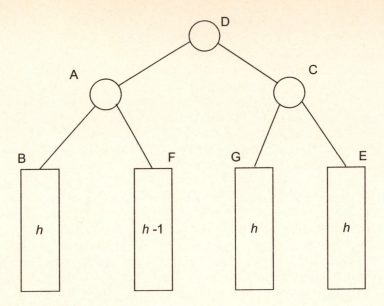

Figure 13.13.

13.3.2 JAVA CODE FOR AVL TREES

As the AVL tree is essentially an ordinary binary search tree with a balancing operation added to the insertion routine, it may seem logical to design an AVL tree
template by inheriting the classes we designed earlier for the binary search tree
and its node, and overloading the `Insert()` methods. However, there is more to
it than this. The balancing operation requires that we calculate the heights of the
two subtrees arising from each node on the path from the newly inserted node
back up to the root. The height (or depth, as it is sometimes called) of a binary
search tree is a fairly easy thing to find using a recursive method, but it is also
quite costly in terms of computing time. The reason for this is that a *doubly recursive* algorithm is required for finding the height of a tree: we must explore both
the left and right branches of all nodes to be sure we find the deepest branch, so
if all nodes from the starting point to the leaves have two children, the number of
branches that must be explored increases exponentially with the depth of the tree.

Therefore, it is highly inefficient to calculate the depth of each subtree every
time we add a new node. It is a better plan to store some information about the
relative sizes of a node's two subtrees as a field in the node itself, so that we don't
have to recalculate the information every time a new node is added.

Let us consider what information we need to store. In an AVL tree, each node
can be in one of three balance states. The height difference between the left and
right subtrees can be 0, -1, or +1. We will refer to these states as balanced, left-
high, and right-high, respectively. Given this information, there are two cases in
which action must be taken to rebalance the tree after a new node is added: if a

left-high node's left subtree increases in height, or if a right-high node's right sub-tree increases in height. All other possibilities will result in the state of a node changing, but without any balancing being necessary.

The conditions are summarized in Table 13.1. How do we implement these conditions in Java code? The recursive method for node insertion that we used in constructing ordinary binary search trees offers an almost ready-made solution to this problem. Recall that the way we determine where a rotation is necessary to restore balance is by starting with the node that has just been inserted and working our way up the tree towards the root, checking the balance of each node along the way. This path is stored automatically for us by the recursive insertion routine when it is locating the position where the new node is to be inserted. When a new node is to be inserted in a binary search tree, the insertion routine begins by examining the root node and comparing its value with that of the new node. If the new node is, say, less than the root node, the insertion routine pushes the root node onto a stack and recursively calls itself to examine the root's left child. That node in turn is pushed onto the stack and one of its children is then examined by another recursive call to the insertion routine. In this way, a complete record of all the nodes visited by the insertion routine on its way to finding the correct position for insertion of the new node is stored on the stack. In an ordinary binary search tree, this information is never used: once the node is inserted, the job is finished and the chain of recursive calls simply returns without doing anything else.

TABLE 13.1.
AVL tree actions

State of node	Effect of new node	Action or new state
Balanced	Increase left subtree height	Left-high
Balanced	Increase right subtree height	Right-high
Left-high	Increase left subtree height	**Left balance**
Left-high	Increase right subtree height	Balanced
Right-high	Increase left subtree height	Balanced
Right-high	Increase right subtree height	**Right balance**

In constructing an AVL tree, however, we can make use of this information. After the new node has been inserted into the tree, we can examine each node as we climb out of the recursion to check its balance and adjust it, if necessary, to take account of the effect of adding the new node. If an imbalance occurs, we can then apply a rotation routine.

The Java routines we present here make use of this idea. We modify the `TreeNode` data type to include a field for storing information on the balance state of each node. We then modify the insertion routine so that it checks the state of each node after a new node has been inserted. If an imbalance is found, the appropriate rotation routine is called to restore the balance.

We first present the `AVLNode` class, which contains the definition of the data structure to be used as a node in an AVL tree.

```
class AVLNode
{
    static final int LEFTHIGH = 0;
    static final int BALANCED = 1;
    static final int RIGHTHIGH = 2;

    int Element;
    int Balance;
    AVLNode Left, Right;

    AVLNode(int newElement)
    {
        Element = newElement;
        Balance = BALANCED;
    }
}
```

We define three constants which are used to describe the balance situation at the node in question. The data fields themselves contain the `Element`, `Left` and `Right` data fields familiar to us from the ordinary binary search tree, with the addition of the `Balance` field, whose value will always be one of the three constants defined in this class. The constructor for `AVLNode` requires the `newElement` to be inserted at that node. The initial `Balance` is set to BAL-ANCED, since a new node is always inserted as a leaf.

The code for insertion of a new node into an AVL tree is fairly involved, consisting of the initial `Insert()` method, together with all the 'helper' methods which check the balance and perform the rotations. We will take these routines one at a time.

First, the class definition, together with the `Insert()` method, and its recursive counterpart, are as follows:

```
public class AVLTree
{
    private AVLNode Root;
    private boolean Taller;

    AVLTree()
    {
        Taller = false;
        Root = null;
    }

    public void Insert(int newElement)
    {
        Root = Insert(Root, newElement);
    }
```

```
private AVLNode Insert(AVLNode tree, int newElement)
{
    if (tree == null)
    {
        tree = new AVLNode(newElement);
        Taller = true;
    }
    else if (newElement < tree.Element)
    {
        tree.Left = Insert(tree.Left, newElement);
        if (Taller)
            switch (tree.Balance) {
            case AVLNode.LEFTHIGH:
                try
                    tree = LeftBalance(tree);
                catch (TreeException e);
                break;
            case AVLNode.BALANCED:
                tree.Balance = AVLNode.LEFTHIGH;
                break;
            case AVLNode.RIGHTHIGH:
                tree.Balance = AVLNode.BALANCED;
                Taller = false;
                break;
            }
    }
    else
    {
        tree.Right = Insert(tree.Right, newElement);
        if (Taller)
            switch (tree.Balance) {
            case AVLNode.LEFTHIGH:
                tree.Balance = AVLNode.BALANCED;
                Taller = false;
                break;
            case AVLNode.BALANCED:
                tree.Balance = AVLNode.RIGHTHIGH;
                break;
            case AVLNode.RIGHTHIGH:
                try
                    tree = RightBalance(tree);
                catch (TreeException e);
                break;
            }
    }
    return tree;
}
```

The class contains two data fields: `Root` represents the root node of the tree, and `Taller` is a `boolean` flag that is set at a node when a new node is added to the tree. It indicates whether or not a branch of the tree has become taller.

The constructor for the tree initializes `Taller` to be `false` and `Root` to be `null`. (Java would initialize these variables to these values anyway, but it sometimes reassuring to see it done explicitly.) The first `Insert()` routine is the public interface to the AVL tree – it requires only the value of the new node to be inserted into the tree. It then calls the recursive `Insert()` method. Note that `Root` is assigned to the return value of this method for the same reason as with the ordinary binary search tree. Since we cannot change the actual value of the memory to which an object points by passing it as an argument to a method, we must set this value by returning the new object from the method.

The structure of the recursive `Insert()` method is similar in outline to that of the ordinary binary search tree that we have seen earlier. The `tree` node passed to the method is tested to see if it is `null`, and if so, a new node is allocated. Otherwise, if the new node is less than the root node, the left branch is recursively explored. If the new node is greater than the root node, the right branch is explored.

However, there are quite a few new statements mingled in with those that are familiar to us from the ordinary binary search tree method. The recursive `Insert()` method implements the idea we described earlier: using the recursive nature of the insertion to check the balance of each node as we climb out of the recursion. If `Insert()` is passed a `null` node, it creates a new node and stores the data there. The parameter `Taller` is set to `true`. This flag is set to indicate that the subtree of which this node is a member has increased in height. Clearly this must be true for the branch onto which the new node is added, so the `Taller` flag is set to `true` when a new node is added.

To see how the balance is checked by the `Insert()` routine, we will examine what happens in the first `else` block, which handles the case of `newElement` being less than the current `Element`. The first thing that happens in this block is that `Insert()` is called recursively to explore the left child of the current node. This part is exactly the same as in the ordinary binary search tree. The recursion will explore the tree until it finds the correct location to insert the new node. Then, starting from the new node itself, the recursion will start to return. On the first level up from the new node, `Taller` will be `true`. The `if (Taller)` statement handles what to do in this case. It examines the current state of the `Balance` field for that node and takes the action specified in the table above: if the node is `LEFTHIGH`, the tree must be balanced, so it calls the `LeftBalance()` method (to be defined in a minute). Otherwise, it simply adjusts the `Balance` label of the current node. The exploration of the right branch is done in the same way.

```
private AVLNode LeftBalance(AVLNode tree)
   throws TreeException
{
   AVLNode leftsub = tree.Left, rightsub;
```

```
            switch(leftsub.Balance) {
            case AVLNode.LEFTHIGH:
               tree.Balance = leftsub.Balance =
                  AVLNode.BALANCED;
               tree = RotateRight(tree);
               Taller = false;
               break;
            case AVLNode.BALANCED:
               throw new TreeException("AVL tree error:
                  tree already balanced.");
            case AVLNode.RIGHTHIGH:
               rightsub = leftsub.Right;
               switch (rightsub.Balance) {
               case AVLNode.LEFTHIGH:
                  tree.Balance = AVLNode.RIGHTHIGH;
                  leftsub.Balance = AVLNode.BALANCED;
                  break;
               case AVLNode.BALANCED:
                  tree.Balance = leftsub.Balance =
                     AVLNode.BALANCED;
                  break;
               case AVLNode.RIGHTHIGH:
                  tree.Balance = AVLNode.BALANCED;
                  leftsub.Balance = AVLNode.LEFTHIGH;
                  break;
               }
               rightsub.Balance = AVLNode.BALANCED;
               tree.Left = RotateLeft(leftsub);
               tree = RotateRight(tree);
               Taller = false;
            }
         return tree;
      }
```

The LeftBalance() method is called when a LEFTHIGH node's left subtree increases in height. At the time that LeftBalance() is called, it is not known whether a single or double rotation is required, so that is the first thing that LeftBalance() must discover. Remember that to discover which type of rotation is needed, you must examine the node at which the imbalance occurs, and the two layers below that. If those three nodes are in a straight line, a single rotation is needed, while if they are in a dog-leg formation, a double rotation is needed.

LeftBalance() sorts this out by examining the Balance condition of the current node's left child, since it is known that the new node was inserted into either the left or right subtree of the left child. If the new node was inserted into the left subtree of the left child, then the three nodes (current node, left child, and left subtree) all lie in a straight line, so a single rotation is needed. This is handled by the case AVLNode.LEFTHIGH section. The RotateRight() method (see below) is called, the balance of the two nodes involved in the rotation is restored, and the `Taller` flag is switched off to prevent any further rotations later on.

The current node's left child cannot be in the `BALANCED` state (you should convince yourself this is true), so an exception is thrown if this option is ever chosen.

Finally, if the current node's left child is in the `RIGHTHIGH` state, this means that the new node was inserted into the right subtree of the current node's left child, so that the current node and the two layers immediately below it form a dog-leg. Therefore, a double rotation is required. Before the double rotation is actually done, the `Balance` labels must be adjusted, and this depends on which actual branch of the tree the new node was inserted into (you should draw out a few examples to convince yourself that the code is correct). Finally, the double rotation is done by calls to `RotateLeft()` and `RotateRight()`.

The `RightBalance()` method is identical to `LeftBalance()` except all lefts and rights are interchanged.

```
private AVLNode RightBalance(AVLNode tree)
   throws TreeException
{
   AVLNode rightsub = tree.Right, leftsub;

   switch(rightsub.Balance) {
   case AVLNode.RIGHTHIGH:
      tree.Balance = rightsub.Balance =
         AVLNode.BALANCED;
      tree = RotateLeft(tree);
      Taller = false;
      break;
   case AVLNode.BALANCED:
      throw new TreeException("AVL tree error:
         tree already balanced.");
   case AVLNode.LEFTHIGH:
      leftsub = rightsub.Left;
      switch (leftsub.Balance) {
      case AVLNode.RIGHTHIGH:
         tree.Balance = AVLNode.LEFTHIGH;
         rightsub.Balance = AVLNode.BALANCED;
         break;
      case AVLNode.BALANCED:
         tree.Balance = rightsub.Balance =
            AVLNode.BALANCED;
         break;
      case AVLNode.LEFTHIGH:
         tree.Balance = AVLNode.BALANCED;
         rightsub.Balance = AVLNode.RIGHTHIGH;
         break;
      }
```

```
            leftsub.Balance = AVLNode.BALANCED;
            tree.Right = RotateRight(rightsub);
            tree = RotateLeft(tree);
            Taller = false;
        }
        return tree;
    }
```

We now consider the code for performing the actual rotations.

```
    private AVLNode RotateLeft(AVLNode tree)
    {
        AVLNode newTree = tree.Right;
        tree.Right = newTree.Left;
        newTree.Left = tree;
        return newTree;
    }

    private AVLNode RotateRight(AVLNode tree)
    {
        AVLNode newTree = tree.Left;
        tree.Left = newTree.Right;
        newTree.Right = tree;
        return newTree;
    }
```

The nodes are swapped in the correct order to implement the rotation. Note that the argument in each method is the topmost node in the group of two or three pointers to the nodes being rotated. Since the memory location to which this node points is changed inside the method, the new location is returned by the method so it can be reassigned in the calling routine. As usual, if this were not done, the changes made within the two rotation methods would be lost after they finished.

A useful routine for comparing the AVL tree with its unbalanced counterpart is a method for calculating the depth of the tree:

```
    public int Depth(AVLNode tree)
    {
        if (tree != null)
        {
            int DepthLeft = Depth(tree.Left);
            int DepthRight = Depth(tree.Right);
            if (DepthLeft > DepthRight)
                return 1 + DepthLeft;
            else
                return 1 + DepthRight;
        }
        return 0;
    }
```

This method uses recursion to find the maximum depth of the left and right subtrees of the root node, and returns 1 plus this value as the total number of layers in the tree. The same method (except with an argument of data type `TreeNode`) can be used to find the depth of an ordinary binary search tree. When the same data (in the same order) are fed into the two types of tree, the AVL tree will usually have a smaller depth.

13.3.3 EFFICIENCY OF AVL TREES

As you can see, the improved efficiency of AVL trees comes at a rather severe cost in terms of the amount of effort required to program them. However, once you have written the code for one type of AVL tree (or copied it from this book), it is relatively easy to implement the tree for other data types (or else define a generic AVL tree using interfaces).

The AVL insertion algorithm is sufficiently complicated that it is difficult to do much in the way of quantitative analysis of such things as running time or average behavior, except by running simulations. As with the ordinary binary search tree, we leave it as an exercise to run these experiments and produce a plot of the average depth of an AVL tree for various numbers of nodes. A theoretical analysis shows that, in the worst case, the height h of an AVL tree containing N nodes should be about $1.44 \log N$. A perfectly balanced tree should have a height of around $\log N$, so we see that, even in the worst case, an AVL tree is still quite good. Running actual simulations shows that most AVL trees have depths that are only 2 or 3 greater than a perfectly balanced tree, even for several hundred or thousand nodes.

The computational overhead involved in using the AVL algorithm as opposed to the simple insertion algorithm is small enough to justify its use if the resulting tree is expected to be large and data accesses frequent. Most new nodes do not require rebalancing, and even if they do, there can be at most one rebalancing of the tree (using either single or double rotation) for each item added, since the first balancing restores the balance in the subtree containing the new node, and the rest of the tree was balanced from previous insertions. Thus besides the possible single call to one of the balancing functions, the only extra work is a few comparisons to test that the tree is properly balanced.

Before we leave AVL trees, we should say a few words about deleting nodes from them. You may recall that, even for a simple binary search tree, the computer code for deleting a node was fairly involved. The situation with AVL trees is even worse. Due to the requirement that the AVL tree be balanced at all nodes, the deletion of a node presents us with the dual problem of maintaining the same inorder traversal of the remaining nodes, and of retaining the AVL structure of the tree.

Faced with these problems, many authors recommend that if deletions are fairly infrequent (they may be due to an error in typing in a node, for example), the best method to use is so-called *lazy deletion*. Using this method, the deleted node is not actually removed from the tree; rather it is *marked* by either changing the data stored at that node to some value recognized as an indication that the node should be ignored, or by adding an extra field to the data node class which can be used as a flag to indicate that the node has been deleted. Any functions which access data in the tree would then have to be modified to ignore deleted nodes, but this usually requires only a single `if` statement.

Lazy deletion obviously preserves the traversal of the tree, but it does not preserve the AVL structure. However, provided that deletions are uncommon, this is a small price to pay to avoid having to understand and code the 'proper' AVL deletion algorithm.

13.4   Heaps, heapsort, and priority queues

13.4.1 THE HEAP DATA STRUCTURE

The final application of a purely binary tree that we shall examine is a data structure called a *heap*. Heaps are unusual in the menagerie of tree structures in that they represent trees as arrays rather than linked structures using pointers. To see how a binary tree can be represented as an array, consider Fig. 13.14. Here we have drawn a binary tree and numbered the nodes in order starting with the root node as node 1 and progressing across each level in turn. This numbering is not the order in which the nodes are traversed in any standard traversal pattern, but the purpose of a heap is not to traverse a tree, so this doesn't matter.

If we use the number of a node as an array index, this technique gives us an order in which we can store tree nodes in an array. The tree may be easily reconstructed from the array by noticing that the left child of node number k has index $2k$ and the right child has index $2k + 1$. Thus the root node is always stored in position 1 (the 0 element with which all Java arrays begin is not used), and its two children are in positions 2 and 3. The children of node 2 are in locations 4 and 5, and so on.

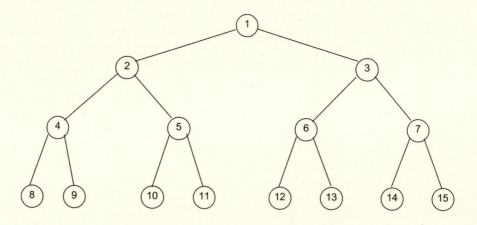

Figure 13.14.   Numbering of a tree's nodes for storage in an array.

Any binary tree can be represented in an array in this fashion if we leave blank those array elements where no corresponding tree nodes exist. This is not an efficient way to store just any binary tree, however, since for most trees there would be many array elements that are left empty, wasting a great deal of space. A heap, however, is a special kind of binary tree that leaves no gaps in an array implementation.

The definition of the heap data type is as follows. A heap is a binary tree satisfying the restrictions:

1   All leaves are on two adjacent levels.

2   All leaves on the lowest level occur at the left of the tree.

3   All levels above the lowest are completely filled.

4   Both children of any node are again heaps.

5   The value stored at any node is at least as large as the values in its two children.

The first three conditions ensure that the array representation of the heap will have no gaps in it. The last two conditions give a heap a weak amount of order, in that in progressing from the root down to a leaf, the keys must not get any larger, and may get smaller. However, the order in which the elements are stored in the array will, in general, not be a sorted representation of the list, although the largest element will be stored at location 1. An example of a heap is shown in Fig. 13.15.

In this figure, note that the largest element (50) is the root node, and that the value stored in each node is larger than both of its children. The leaves of the heap occur on two adjacent levels (the third and fourth), and the nodes on the lowest layer fill that layer from the left. We could remove node 9, for example, and still preserve the heap property, but if node 9 remains where it is, we cannot remove any other node in the bottom layer without violating heap property 2 in the list above.

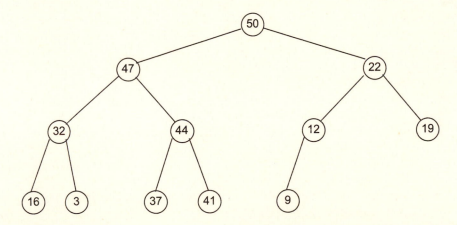

Figure 13.15.   A heap.

The elements of this heap would be stored in an array in the order 50, 47, 22, 32, 44, 12, 19, 16, 3, 37, 41, 9.

Since heaps have only weak ordering of their elements and their traversals don't, in general, give us any useful information, you might wonder what heaps are used for. The most useful property of a heap is that the largest node in the tree is always at the root. If the root is extracted from the heap, there is a simple algorithm (which we will examine below) which can be used to restore the heap condition in the remaining nodes, so that the largest of the remaining nodes is again at the root position. In other words, a heap offers us a way to process its contents in a sorted order by extracting one element at a time and not bothering to fully sort the remainder of the data until it is needed. The most common application of a heap is as a *priority queue*.

Recall that a queue is a data structure in which items are inserted at the tail of the queue and extracted from the head, in first-in-first-out, or *FIFO*, order. A priority queue is similar in spirit to an ordinary queue, except that each item in the queue has an associated *priority*. Items with higher priority will get processed before items with lower priority, even if they arrive in the queue after them.

We could implement a priority queue by using one of the sorting methods from Chapter 11, but since we only need to process one item at a time, a heap turns out to be more efficient. When the current item is being dealt with, we don't care what order the other items in the queue are in: when we make a request for the next item it just has to be the one with the highest priority. Although heaps are fairly sloppy in keeping their members in strict order, they are very good at finding the maximum member and bringing it to the top of the heap.

13.4.2 CONSTRUCTING A HEAP

In practice, a priority queue may begin with a list of unsorted data. The first step, then, is to organize this initial data so that it has the heap properties. Once we have made our initial heap, we may deal with the priority queue in a continuous fashion by extracting the item at the top and processing it, or inserting another item into the queue while maintaining the heap property. Let us begin by inserting some integers into a binary tree in random order (Fig. 13.16).

This tree is clearly not a heap, since there are several nodes that are smaller than one or both of their children.

The method of constructing a heap from this scrambled tree begins by considering the last node that is not a leaf. Remember that these numbers are stored in an array by reading across each layer in the tree from left to right, so the last non-leaf node is 50. We compare this node to its children (or child, in this case). If the node is larger than its children (as it is in this case) then it satisfies that heap condition, so no change is required.

We move backwards through the tree, examining each node in turn. Looking at node 16, we see that it is larger than 9, but smaller than 19, so it does *not* satisfy the heap condition. To correct this, we swap the node with the larger of its two children, to obtain the tree shown in Fig. 13.17.

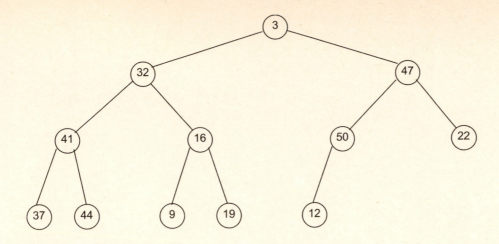

Figure 13.16.

Proceeding backwards, we see that we must swap the nodes 41 and 44. We then consider the node 47. Comparing it with its two children, we see that it must be swapped with 50, giving the result shown in Fig. 13.18.

We must also check that 47 is acceptable in its new position by comparing it with its children at that location. We see that 47 is larger than 12, so we are OK here.

Proceeding back to node 32, we must swap it with 44. Having done that, we now see that the two children of 32 are 37 and 41, both of which are larger than

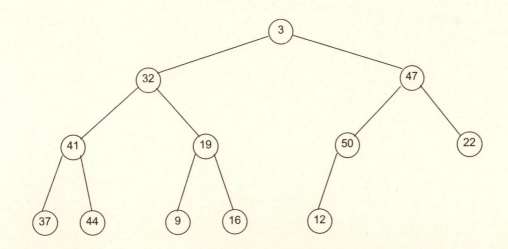

Figure 13.17.

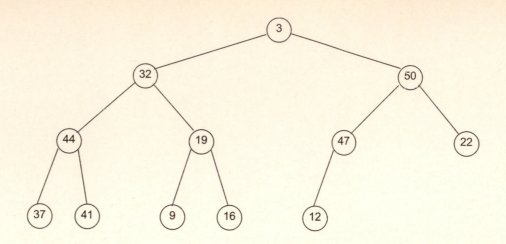

Figure 13.18.

32. Therefore, we must swap 32 with the larger of its children (41), giving the result shown in Fig. 13.19.

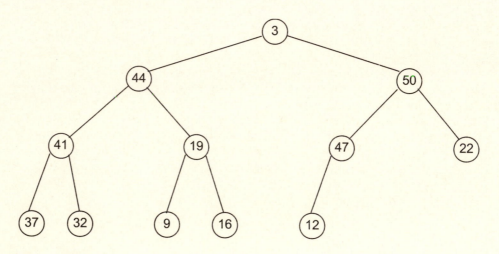

Figure 13.19.

Finally, we must consider node 3. It is swapped with the larger of its two children (50), then with 47, and finally with 12, giving the final, properly constructed heap (Fig. 13.20).

13.4.3 HEAPSORT AND PRIORITY QUEUES

Having created the heap, we may now use it in applications. As mentioned above, the main use of a heap is as a priority queue, in which the largest element is

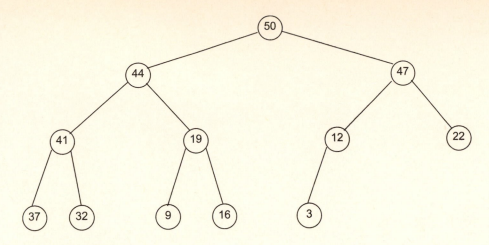

Figure 13.20.

extracted from the root node (and used externally), with the remaining elements being rearranged to form a smaller heap.

A variation on the priority queue provides us with yet another sorting method, known as *heapsort*. Heapsort makes use of the fact that a heap is stored in an array. With the heap shown above, the numbers are stored in the array in the order 50, 44, 47, 41, 19, 12, 22, 37, 32, 9, 16, 3 (a total of 12 numbers). In heapsort, the last number in the array (3) is stored in a temporary variable, the root of the heap is transferred to this vacated location, and the temporary variable is reinserted into the heap starting at the root position. This reinsertion follows the same procedure as that used in constructing the original heap above: when the 3 is inserted at the root position, its two children are 44 and 47. It is swapped with the larger of the two children, which places 47 at the root and moves 3 down to be the right child of 47. Here, 3 is compared with its two children (12 and 22), and the larger of these two is swapped with 3 to give the final heap shown in Fig. 13.21. The size of the heap is reduced by 1.

The contents of the array are now 47, 44, 22, 41, 19, 12, 3, 37, 32, 9, 16, 50, and the heap size is reduced to 11. Note that the last array element now contains the largest number (50) in the array, and that this number has been removed from the heap.

If we repeat the process with the new root (47), we obtain the heap shown in Fig. 13.22.

The last element in the previous heap (16) was stored in a temporary variable, the 47 was removed and placed just after the end of the heap in the array, and the 16 was reinserted from the root position. The array contents are now 44, 41, 22, 37, 19, 12, 3, 16, 32, 9, 47, 50, with a heap size of 10. The last two numbers in the array are no longer part of the heap, and contain the two largest numbers in sorted order.

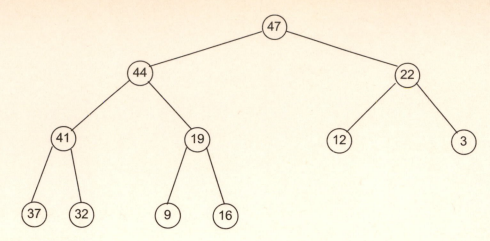

Figure 13.21.

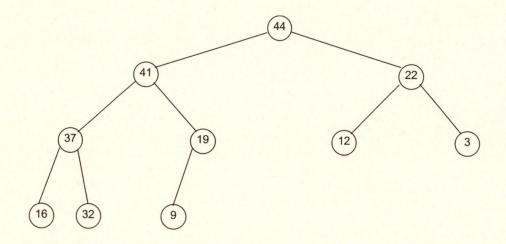

Figure 13.22.

The process continues in the same manner until the heap size has been reduced to zero, at which point the array contains the numbers in sorted order.

If a heap is used purely for sorting, the heapsort algorithm turns out to be an $O(n \log n)$ algorithm, although it is only about half as efficient as quicksort or mergesort for randomly ordered initial lists. However, we may use the same technique to implement a priority queue. Rather than carry the sorting process through to the bitter end, we can extract the root node (which is the item with highest priority) and rearrange the tree as we did above so that the remaining nodes form a heap with one less element. We need not process the data any further until the next request comes in for an item from the priority queue, at which point we perform the second step in the heapsort, and so on. The heap guarantees that the item with highest priority is always ready and waiting, but makes no promises about the ordering of the remainder of the tree.

A heap is an efficient way of implementing a priority queue since the maximum number of nodes that need to be considered to restore the heap property when the root is extracted is about twice the depth of the tree. This is so because we need to examine the two children of a node in each layer in the tree to decide which number to promote to the next higher level. If we located the largest number in the list by straightforward comparisons, we would need to do $N - 1$ comparisons for a list of size N, as we saw when we studied selection sort in Chapter 11. A heap reduces the number of comparisons to around $2 \log N$, which is a significant improvement.

Java code for heaps   13.5

The Java code that implements the algorithms described above is fairly straightforward. Although a heap is really a binary tree, we can't really make use of any of the tree code developed earlier, since a heap is implemented by representing the tree as an array, and not a linked structure as with the binary tree and the AVL tree. The entire class is as follows:

```
public class Heap
{
   private int[] Element;
   private int HeapSize;

   Heap(int heapsize)
   {
      HeapSize = heapsize;
      Element = new int[heapsize + 1];
   }

   private void MakeHeap()
   {
      int index;

      for (index = HeapSize/2; index >= 1; --index)
         Insert(Element[index], index, HeapSize);
   }

   private void MakeRandomHeap(int upperLimit)
   {
      int index;

      for (index = 1; index <= HeapSize; ++index)
         Element[index] = (int)(upperLimit *
            Math.random());
   }
```

```
    private void Insert(int newElement, int start,
      int maxheap)
    {
      int marker = 2 * start;

      while (marker <= maxheap)
      {
        if (marker < maxheap &&
           Element[marker] < Element[marker + 1])
           marker++;
        if (newElement >= Element[marker])
           break;
        else {
           Element[start] = Element[marker];
           start = marker;
           marker = 2 * start;
        }
      }
      Element[start] = newElement;
    }

    public void Sort()
    {
      int tempItem;
      int maxheap = HeapSize;

      while (maxheap > 0)
      {
        tempItem = Element[maxheap];
        Element[maxheap] = Element[1];
        Insert(tempItem, 1, --maxheap);
      }
    }

    public int getElement(int index)
    {
      return Element[index];
    }

    public int getHeapSize()
    {
      return HeapSize;
    }
}
```

The size of the array in which the heap elements are to be stored is determined dynamically by the constructor. Note that the array size is one greater than HeapSize, since we shall not be using element 0. The heap is stored in locations 1 through HeapSize.

In a Java applet that might be written to test the heap code, we would first fill up the array with data and then call the various class methods to construct the heap and apply the heapsort algorithm. We have provided an extra method called MakeRandomHeap() which fills the array with random ints in the range 0 through upperLimit. After calling this method, the class method MakeHeap() would be called to rearrange the initial data into a heap.

Since the first node we must consider when constructing the initial heap is the last non-leaf node in the tree, we can begin with the node HeapSize/2 (using integer division). Recall that the two children of node k occupy array locations $2k$ and $2k + 1$, so the first non-leaf node will be at location HeapSize/2. For each node from this point back to the root, we are using the insertion algorithm to place it in its proper place in the heap. Thus MakeHeap() simply calls Insert() for each of these nodes.

The Insert() function's arguments are:

- newElement – the item to be inserted into the heap.
- start – the first node in the array into which newElement will try to be placed.
- maxheap – the highest element in the array that can be used for storage.

The Insert() function follows the insertion algorithm above quite closely. If we are inserting newElement beginning at location start, we must compare it to its two children, which are located at positions 2*start and 2*start + 1. We define marker as 2*start, so that it points to the location of the left child of start. To see if newElement is the largest, we first locate the larger of its two children, using the first if statement inside the while loop. This is done by assigning marker to point to the larger child, after first checking that the node has two children rather than just one.

With the larger child identified, we check to see if newElement is larger than (or equal to) this child. If so, it is already in the correct place, so we break out of the while loop. If not, we move the larger child up to position start. We now redefine start to point to the position formerly occupied by the larger child, set marker to point to the left child of this new location, and continue the process until either newElement is placed correctly, or we reach a leaf in the tree. When either of these two things happens, we have found the correct location at which newElement should be inserted, so the final statement in Insert() performs this insertion.

The Sort() routine is elegantly simple, since it can make use of the Insert() routine to do most of the work. It follows the algorithm described above very closely. The item at position maxheap is stored in a temporary variable tempItem, the item at position 1 (the root) is shifted to location maxheap, and tempItem is reinserted into the tree starting at the root position, after decrementing `max-heap` by 1. The process continues until the heap is empty, and the list is sorted.

13.6 B-trees

13.6.1 MULTIWAY SEARCH TREES

The trees that we have considered so far in this chapter have all been binary trees: each node can have no more than two children. Since the main factor in determining the efficiency of a tree is its depth, it is natural to ask if the efficiency can be improved by allowing nodes to have more than two children. It is fairly obvious that if we allow more than one item to be stored at each node of a tree, the depth of the tree will be less, but does this necessarily mean that fewer comparisons will be required to insert or locate an item in the tree?

Let us consider an extreme case where we allow, say, 127 items to be stored at each node in the tree. Then the second layer of the tree will contain up to 128 nodes, since a branch is possible on either side of any item in the root node. Then we can store 127 items in a tree of depth 1, $128 \times 127 + 127 = 16383$ items in a tree of depth 2, and so on. However, to locate an item in the root node will require searching a list of 127 objects. The number of comparisons required for this search depends on how the items are stored: if they are sorted as they are stored, we could use a binary search, but if they are stored in unsorted order, a sequential search is needed. The same process must be repeated at each layer in the tree.

In general, then, any attempt to increase the efficiency of a tree by allowing more data to be stored in each node is compromised by the extra work required to locate an item within the node. To be sure that we are getting any benefit out of a multiway search tree, we should do some calculations or simulations for typical data sets and compare the results with an ordinary binary tree.

All of this assumes that we are dealing with a program which runs entirely within main memory. That is, when the program is started, it and all the data on which it operates are loaded into RAM, and no disk accesses are required from that point on. In many large-scale databases, however, such as those maintained by governments or libraries, the amount of data being stored is so great that it would not be feasible to load all the data into RAM. These databases may contain hundreds or thousands of megabytes of data. In these cases, the data are stored on other media, such as hard or floppy disks, or magnetic tape. The access time for such media is many times slower than for dynamic memory, such as RAM chips.* Since disk accesses are so slow, we would like some form of data storage that minimizes the number of times such accesses must be made.

---

* Anyone with a home computer whose only external storage is on floppy disk will verify this point. One way of speeding up access is to install a *ramdisk* on your home computer. A ramdisk is a section of your computer's RAM that is reserved for storing files in the same way as on a floppy disk, except that the memory is in a chip rather than on a plastic disk. If you have ever used a ramdisk, you will know how much faster they are.

A single disk access allows a certain amount of data, called a *block*, to be read into RAM. A typical block size is usually fairly large compared to the size of a single data item stored in the database. If the total amount of data is large enough that it cannot all be loaded into RAM at once, we therefore want a way of searching through the data on disk while satisfying two conditions:

- The amount of data read by each disk access should be close to the block size.
- The number of disk accesses should be minimized.

If we use a binary tree to store the data on disk, we must access each item of data separately since we do not know in which direction we should branch until we have compared the node's value with the item for which we are searching. This is inefficient in terms of disk accesses, since we are only reading in a tiny fraction of what we could read with a single disk access.

The main solution to this problem is to use a multiway search tree in which to store the data, where the maximum amount of data that can be stored at each node is close to (but does not exceed) the block size for a single disk read operation. We can then load a single node (containing many data items) into RAM and process this data entirely in RAM to determine if the item for which we are searching is present in that node, or, if not, in which direction we should branch for the next node to be searched. Although there will be some overhead in the sorting and searching operations required to insert and search for data within each node, all of these operations are done exclusively in RAM and are therefore much faster than accessing the hard disk or other external medium.

For example, if we store 127 items of data in a binary tree, we will require a tree of depth 7 (if the tree is perfectly balanced), so we may need as many as seven disk accesses to locate any given item. If we stored the same data in a balanced multiway tree which allowed up to, say, 15 items to be stored at each node, we would require a tree with a depth of only 2, requiring at most two disk accesses.

13.6.2 THE B-TREE: A BALANCED MULTIWAY SEARCH TREE

It is customary to classify a multiway tree by the maximum number of *branches* at each node, rather than the maximum number of items which may be stored at each node. If we use a multiway search tree with M possible branches at each node, then we can store up to $M - 1$ data items at each node. A binary tree is a special case of this: each node can have up to two children, and a single item is stored at each node.

Since multiway trees are primarily used in databases, the data that are stored are usually of a fairly complex type. For example, a typical database entry for personal data may contain the person's name, address, telephone number, some unique identification number and various other details. It is usual to use one or two of the fields in this data structure as *keys* for searching purposes within the tree. If a personal data record contains an identification number as one of its fields, that may be used as the key by which the record is stored in a tree.

In each node of a multiway search tree, we may have up to $M - 1$ keys labeled

k_1, k_2,..., k_{M-1}, and M branches b_1, b_2,..., b_M. If we are searching for key k_s, then at each node we compare k_s with each key in turn. If $k_s < k_1$, we follow branch b_1. If $k_s = k_1$, our search is over. If $k_1 < k_s < k_2$, we follow branch b_2, and so on.

To get the greatest efficiency gain out of a multiway search tree, we need to ensure that most of the nodes contain as much data as possible, and that the tree is as balanced as possible. There are several algorithms which approach this problem from various angles, but the most popular method is the *B-tree*. The definition of the B-tree data type is:

1   A B-tree is a multiway search tree with a maximum of M branches at each node. The number M is called the *order* of the tree.

2   There is a single root node which may have as few as two children, or none at all if the root is the only node in the tree.

3   At all nodes, except the root and leaf nodes, there must be at least half the maximum number of children.

4   All leaves are on the same level.

A B-tree is shown in Fig. 13.23. This B-tree is of order 5, which means that up to five branches (and therefore four data items) may occur in each node. Each node other than the root must contain at least 5/2 = 2 (using integer division) data items, and all leaves must occur on the same level. It can be seen that this tree satisfies these conditions.

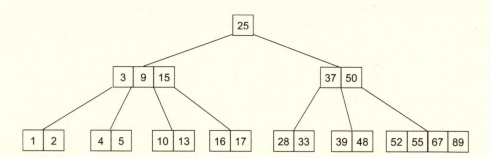

Figure 13.23.   A B-tree.

As an example of how a B-tree (or any multiway tree) is searched for an item, let us search this tree for the item 13. We begin at the root, and compare the target (13) with the root's value (25). Since 13 < 25, we branch to the left, and arrive at the node with elements 3, 9, and 15. Depending on how these items have been stored in the node, we must use an appropriate searching technique to locate the branch between 9 and 15, since our target lies between these two numbers. Having found this branch, we follow it to the node containing values 10 and 13, where another search locates the target.

Had we searched for a key that was not present in the tree, for example the key 12, we would follow the same steps as above until we reached a leaf. A search in this leaf would not locate the target, but would find the branch between the two data values where the target would lie. This branch would be represented by a `null` pointer, indicating that the key is not in the tree.

For the purposes of calculating the efficiency of a B-tree, we usually count only the number of nodes visited in a search, and not the number of individual comparisons within each node. This is because B-trees are primarily used in those situations where reading a node requires a disk access, which is much slower than the in-RAM calculations that are required to locate a particular branch or data item within a node.

We can divide up the efficiency calculations into the number of node accesses required for successful and unsuccessful searches, just as we did with the searching algorithms in Chapter 10. For the B-tree shown above, the average number of node accesses required for a successful outcome is $(1 \times 1 + 5 \times 2 + 16 \times 3) / 22$ = 2.68, since there is one data item on level 1, five items on level 2 and 16 on level 3. Since all leaves in a B-tree are on the same level, the number of node accesses required for any unsuccessful search is always just the depth of the tree, in this case, three.

13.6.3 CONSTRUCTING A B-TREE

The insertion method for a B-tree is somewhat different to that for the other trees we have studied, since the condition that all leaves be on the same level forces insertion into the upper part of the tree. It is easiest to learn the insertion procedure by example, so we will construct an order-5 B-tree from the list of integers:

    1 7 6 2 11 4 8 13 10 5 19 9 18 24 3 12 14 20 21 16

Since each node can have up to five branches, each node can store up to four keys. Therefore, the first four keys can be placed in the root, in sorted order, as shown:

$$\boxed{1}\ \boxed{2}\ \boxed{6}\ \boxed{7}$$

The fifth key, 11, will require the creation of a new node, since the root is full. From your experience with binary trees, you might think that the procedure would be to compare the new key with those already present in the root, discover that $11 > 7 = k_4$, so we should insert a new node as branch b_5 from the root. However, we cannot do this, since it violates one of the conditions on a B-tree: the root is not allowed to have only a single child.

Instead, we split the root at its midpoint and create *two* new nodes, leaving only the middle key in the root. This gives the tree shown:

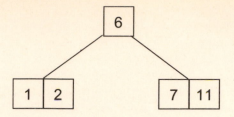

We can now add the next three keys without having to create any more nodes:

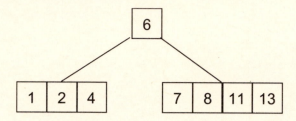

When we wish to add key 10, though, it would fit into the right child of the root, but this node is full. Therefore, we split this node, putting the middle key into the node's parent (which happens to be the root), giving the tree shown:

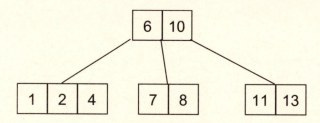

We can now insert the next four keys without any problems:

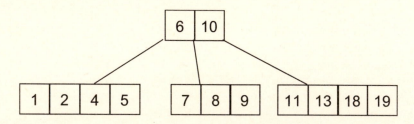

Inserting the key 24 causes another split and increases the number of keys in the root to three:

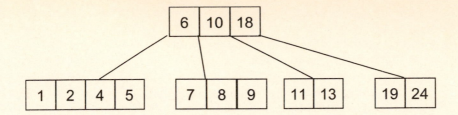

We can insert the next five keys with another split, resulting in the root being full:

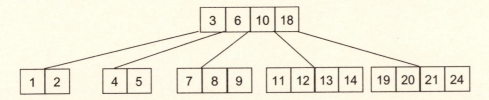

Insertion of the final key, 16, causes the fourth leaf from the left to split, and pushes its middle key, 13, upwards. However, the parent node is also full, so it must split as well, following the same rules. This results in a new root node, and increases the height of the tree to three levels. The completed B-tree is shown in Fig. 13.24.

The algorithm for insertion into a B-tree can be summarized as follows:

1   Find the node into which the new key should be inserted by searching the tree.

2   If the node is not full, insert the key into the node, using an appropriate sorting algorithm.

3   If the node is full, split the node into two and push the middle key upwards into the parent. If the parent is also full, follow the same procedure (splitting and pushing upwards) until either some space is found in a previously existing node, or a new root node is created.

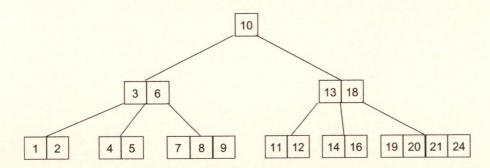

Figure 13.24.   The completed B-tree.

Although the algorithm for insertion may look straightforward on paper, it contains quite a few subtleties which only come out when you try to program it. A program implementing this insertion routine is a non-trivial affair, and could be used as the basis for a programming project. Because B-trees are used primarily when writing databases for handling very large amounts of data, we will not present any stand-alone Java code for implementing them. For most smaller-scale applications where all the data fits into RAM when the program is running, some form of binary tree is usually adequate from the point of view of efficiency.

As with the AVL tree, the algorithm for deleting a node from a B-tree while preserving the B-tree properties is fairly complex. If deletions are expected to be infrequent, lazy deletion is probably the best option.

13.7 Summary

We have introduced the *tree* data structure in this chapter. A tree has a single *root* node. Each node may have one or more branches to other nodes in the tree. A node at the end of a branch is called a *child* of the node at the beginning of the branch. A node with no children is called a *leaf.* The maximum number of branches emanating from any one node is called the *order* of the tree. The most common form of tree is the *binary tree* (a tree of order 2).

We considered algorithms for inserting nodes into a binary tree in such a way that when the nodes of the tree are *traversed* in *inorder* fashion (the left subtree is traversed, followed by the root node, and then the right subtree, and so on recursively), the nodes will be listed in sorted order. These routines were then coded in Java. A routine for deleting items from a binary tree was considered.

Since the efficiency of a binary tree improves if the tree is *balanced* (the left and right subtrees of any node are roughly the same height), we studied the AVL algorithm for constructing a binary tree by balancing the tree, if necessary, after each node is added. The AVL algorithm requires that a few nodes in the tree are rearranged using either a single or double rotation, if the tree loses its balance after an insertion. Java code was given for inserting nodes into a tree using the AVL algorithm.

We then considered the *heap.* A heap is a binary tree which is stored as an array, rather than as a linked structure. The nodes in a heap are arranged so that the largest element is always at the root. The main use of a heap is as a *priority queue,* that is, a queue in which items are processed in order of priority rather than strictly in the order in which they were added to the queue. Algorithms for constructing a heap from randomly ordered data and for extracting the root element and rearranging the remaining nodes to retain the heap property are given and coded in Java.

Finally, we considered the B-tree, which is a *multiway* search tree. Each node in a B-tree of order N may have up to N branches and store up to $N - 1$ data items. Although the depth of a B-tree is much less than that of a binary tree storing the same data, the fact that several data items are stored at each node means that extra work is required to store and find a data item at each node. However, the main use of B-trees is in large database systems where the entire data set is too large to store in RAM. Blocks of data are read from the hard disk and then searched in RAM. Since a disk access is much slower than processing in RAM, a B-tree is used to minimize the number of disk accesses. The algorithm for constructing a B-tree is given but no Java code is given since B-trees are not often used in small or medium sized programs.

Exercises   13.8

1   (a) Insert the following numbers, in the order given, into an ordinary binary search tree:

    342 206 444 523 607 301 142 183 102 157 149

    (b) For the tree constructed in part (a), calculate the average number of nodes visited for (i) a successful search; (ii) an unsuccessful search of this tree.

2   (a) Design a computer experiment to calculate the average number of comparisons required for successful and unsuccessful searches of a binary search tree for tree sizes from 50 to 1000 nodes, in steps of 50. Generate the binary search trees by using a pseudo-random number generator.
    (b) Extend your experiment to calculate the average number of comparisons and assignments to sort a list of data by inserting them into a binary search tree and then traversing the tree.
    (c) Compare the results from parts (a) and (b) with those for other sorting and searching methods.

3   Write a *non-recursive* Java method which inserts a new node into an ordinary binary search tree. Use this method in place of the recursive version, and repeat the experiments in question 2. Is recursive insertion more or less efficient than non-recursive insertion?

4   (a) Insert the following numbers, in the order given, into an AVL tree:

    342   206   444   523   607   301   142   183   102   157   149

    (b) For the tree constructed in part (a), calculate the average number of nodes visited for (i) a successful search; (ii) an unsuccessful search of this tree. Compare your answers with those for the ordinary binary tree in question 1.

5   Repeat question 2 for AVL trees. Compare the results of questions 2 and 5.

6   Write a `DeleteNode()` method for an AVL tree using the lazy deletion method suggested in the text. That is, use the special `RefValue` to label a node as a deleted node without actually removing it from the tree. Alter the other AVL tree functions, as necessary, to deal with deleted nodes.

7 (a) Insert the following numbers into an array:

342 206 444 523 607 301 142 183 102 157 149

Apply the algorithm in the text (by hand) to convert this array into a heap.

(b) Use the heapsort algorithm to sort this array. Count the number of comparisons and assignments required by the algorithm for this list of numbers.

8 Design a computer experiment to measure the efficiency of heapsort. Generate pseudo-random lists of integers of lengths from 50 to 1000, in steps of 50, and calculate the numbers of assignments and comparisons required to sort them. Compare your results with other sorting methods.

9 Write a Java method which may be used as a `RemoveItem()` function in a priority queue. The function should extract and return the root node from a heap and rearrange the remaining nodes so that the heap structure is restored.

10 Write a Java method which adds a single node to an already-constructed heap, provided that there is enough space in the array.

11 (a) Insert the following numbers into a B-tree of (i) order 3; (ii) order 5:

659 767 702 157 728 102 461 899 920 44 774 264 384
344 973 905 999

(b) Calculate the average number of (i) node accesses; (ii) comparisons within nodes for a successful and unsuccessful search of these B-trees.

(c) Insert the same list of numbers into an ordinary binary tree, calculate the quantities in part (b) for this tree, and compare the results with the values for the two B-trees.

CHAPTER 14

GRAPHS

14.1 Definitions

The graphs we shall study in this chapter are not the type where a curve is drawn on a pair of axes. The term *graph* as used here has an entirely different meaning, though these kinds of graphs also comprise a branch of mathematics.

A graph is a generalization of a tree, in the sense that it consists of nodes connected together by line segments, but many of the restrictions imposed on the construction of a tree are removed when building a graph. To talk clearly about graphs, we need to introduce a bit of notation.

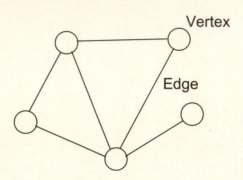

Figure 14.1.   Connected, undirected graph.

A graph (see Fig. 14.1) is a collection of nodes, each of which is called a *vertex* (plural: *vertices*), which may be connected in pairs by line segments called *edges*. The edges in a graph may be of two types, though usually the edges in any one graph will be all of one type. Graphs in which the edges have no specific direction are called *undirected* (Fig. 14.1), while graphs in which each edge has a direction are called *directed* (Fig. 14.2). Directed graphs are sometimes called *digraphs* for short.

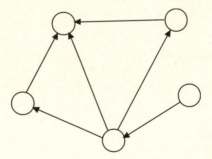

Figure 14.2.   A connected, directed graph.

A graph where there is a path along the edges between any two vertices is said to be *connected* (Figs 14.1 and 14.2). A graph where this is not true is *unconnected* (Fig. 14.3).

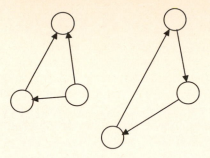

Figure 14.3.   An unconnected digraph.

Like trees, graphs may be used as diagrams that illustrate the relationship between pairs of elements in a set of objects. You may have seen maps of a country in which airline routes are shown as lines connecting pairs of cities, for example. If each line indicates that scheduled flights connect the two cities at either end in both directions, such a map may be represented as an undirected graph, with the cities as the vertices and the lines connecting them as the edges.

A street map of a city may also be represented as a graph, with the road junctions as vertices and the roads themselves as the edges. If the city contains one-way streets, the graph needs to be a digraph, since some edges permit traffic flow in only one direction. A two-way street connecting two junctions A and B would be represented on a digraph by two edges: one from A to B and one from B to A.

Typical problems which graphs can help us solve are those concerned with finding the shortest or most economical route between two vertices, or the smallest set of edges which connect all the vertices in a graph.

There are a great many graph algorithms: far too many for us to study them all in this book. Therefore, we shall restrict ourselves to describing how graphs can be implemented in a computer and describing a few of the more common graph algorithms.

Implementing graphs on a computer   14.2

In order to define a graph, we need a list of its vertices and another list of its edges. In computer languages such as Pascal, in which an explicit representation of sets is supported, a graph may be represented as two sets: one of vertices and one of edges. Most languages do not support sets directly, however, so we must consider how to implement graphs in such languages.

In Java, we have two options. First, we could use the `set` class that we defined in Chapter 8 (but we will see that we do not need it to implement graphs).

The other option is to use more conventional data structures such as arrays and linked lists to implement graphs, which is what we will do here. There are various ways this might be done.

The first possibility is to use a two-dimensional square array. The dimension of the array is the largest number of vertices we allow our graph to have. We shall number the vertices from 0 upwards, to be consistent with the array indexing convention in Java. In the simplest implementation of a graph, the array contains `boolean` elements. In a graph represented by an array named `graph`, the element `graph[i][j]` is then `true` if vertex *i* is connected to vertex *j* by an edge and `false` if it is not. An undirected graph is represented by a symmetric array, meaning that the values of `graph[i][j]` and `graph[j][i]` are always equal, since in an undirected graph, two vertices are either connected or they are not, regardless of the order in which they are listed. A digraph need not be symmetric, since it is possible for vertex *i* to be connected to *j* without *j* being connected to *i*.

A purely array-based representation of a graph is called an *adjacency table*. It is a list of which vertices are connected to which other vertices. The number of vertices in the graph is given by the dimensions of the array. An adjacency table is a clear representation that allows random access to the information for any vertex. However, for *sparse* graphs, that is, graphs where there may be many vertices but few edges connecting them, it can be wasteful of space, since most of the entries in the table will be `false`. In such cases, it may be useful to bring in a representation based either wholly or partially on linked lists.

A representation based entirely on linked lists is called an *adjacency list*. First, a linked list of all the vertices is constructed (Fig. 14.4). Each of these vertices has a pointer which points to a list of edges originating at that vertex. Since each edge connects a vertex with another vertex, each node in the list also points back to a node in the vertex list corresponding to the other end of the edge. Such a linked representation of a graph is efficient from a space-saving point of view, but as you can see from Fig. 14.4, the representation can produce a complex tangle of pointers. All of this is not really a problem provided that the graph has been constructed properly, but debugging such a tangle of links can be extremely difficult. In addition, many graph algorithms require random access to the set of vertices, and this purely linked version requires a traversal of the vertex list to find any single vertex and its associated edges.

Another solution to the implementation problem is to combine arrays and linked lists, in a fashion similar to that used in the chaining method of resolving collisions in a hash table (see Chapter 12). Here, we define a one-dimensional array in which each element corresponds to a vertex (Fig. 14.5). Each of these elements contains a pointer to a list of edges which originate at that vertex. Such an arrangement still allows us to trace a path through the graph since each entry in the list of edges contains the index number of the vertex which corresponds to the other end of the edge. We can then jump to the corresponding array element and search the list of edges originating from there to continue our traversal of that path.

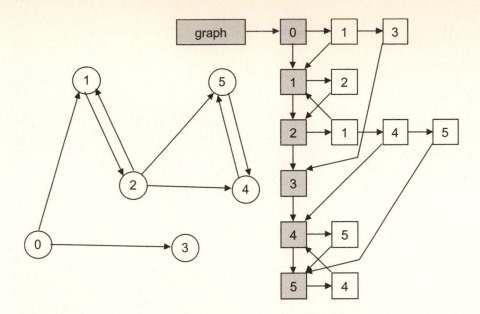

Figure 14.4. A digraph represented as an adjacency list. The main list of vertices is shaded.

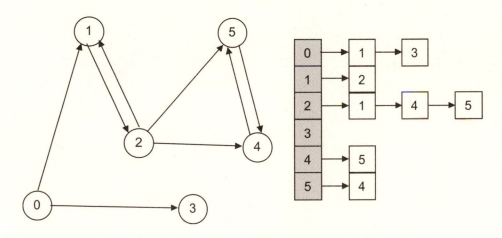

Figure 14.5. A combined array-linked list representation of a graph. An array of pointers (shaded) represents the vertices in the graph.

Graph traversal   14.3

Just as with trees, many graph algorithms require us to visit all the vertices in the graph. With a tree, however, there is one special root node from which our algorithms start. In most graph algorithms, the nodes are all 'created equal', so the starting point is left up to us. There are two commonly used methods of traversing a graph: *depth-first traversal* or DFT, and *breadth-first traversal* or BFT.

14.3.1 DEPTH-FIRST TRAVERSAL

The traversal algorithms in this chapter arc easier to understand (and to work through on paper) if we first construct an *edge table* for the graph. An edge table is built by listing all the vertices of the graph in a vertical column. Next to each entry in the column we list all vertices to which that entry is connected directly (that is, by a single edge). For example, consider the undirected graph in Fig. 14.6.

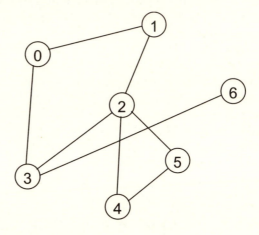

Figure 14.6. An undirected graph.

The edge table for this graph is shown in Fig. 14.7.

The order in which the connections are listed in the edge table isn't really important, but it is conventional to list them in ascending order for each vertex.

0	1	3		
1	0	2		
2	1	3	4	5
3	0	2	6	
4	2	5		
5	2	4		
6	3			

Figure 14.7. The edge table for the graph shown in Fig. 14.6.

Since graph vertices need not be labeled with numbers, however, the meaning of 'ascending order' may have to be redefined for other graphs.

The graph in the figure is an undirected graph, so we list all vertices that are connected to each vertex by any edge. In a directed graph, we would list only those vertices that have a directed edge from the starting vertex pointing to them.

To do a depth-first traversal of this graph, we first choose a starting vertex. Again, the choice of vertex may depend on the context of the problem. We start with vertex 0 here.

The idea of a depth-first traversal is to follow the chain of edges as far as we can into the graph before we backtrack to pick up other vertices. As we visit each vertex, we cross it off everywhere it appears in the edge table. Since we are starting with vertex 0, we cross it off everywhere it appears (which is in the rows corresponding to vertices 1 and 3). We now begin the traversal. For this graph, starting at vertex 0, we move to vertex 1 since it is the first vertex listed as one of those to which vertex 0 is connected. We cross off vertex 1 everywhere it appears in the table. We now look at the row in the edge table corresponding to vertex 1, ignoring for the moment the fact that vertex 0 is also connected to vertex 3. We see that vertex 1 is connected to vertices 0 and 2. However, vertex 0 has already been visited and is crossed off, so we move along to vertex 2. The depth-first traversal has so far visited vertices in the order $0 \rightarrow 1 \rightarrow 2$ (it is important to keep track of the order in which the vertices are visited, since we may need to backtrack later on), and the edge table is as shown in Fig. 14.8.

0	*1*	3		
1	*0*	*2*		
2	*1*	3	4	5
3	*0*	*2*	6	
4	*2*	5		
5	*2*	4		
6	3			

Figure 14.8. The edge table after vertices 0, 1, and 2 have been visited. Visited vertices are shown in ***bold italic***.

To continue, we examine the row corresponding to vertex 2. The first unvisited vertex in this row is vertex 3, so we add that to our traversal, cross it off everywhere it appears in the table, and go to the row corresponding to vertex 3. This leads us to vertex 6. We have visited vertices $0 \rightarrow 1 \rightarrow 2 \rightarrow 3 \rightarrow 6$, the traversal so far is 0 1 2 3 6, and the state of the edge table is as shown in Fig. 14.9.

If we visit the row corresponding to vertex 6, we see that there are no unvisited vertices listed. Therefore, we must backtrack until we find the last row already examined that has an unvisited vertex listed on it. Recall that the order in which we have traversed the table so far is: $0 \rightarrow 1 \rightarrow 2 \rightarrow 3 \rightarrow 6$. We backtrack by

```
0 | 1  3
1 | 0  2
2 | 1  3  4  5
3 | 0  2  6
4 | 2  5
5 | 2  4
6 | 3
```

Figure 14.9.   The edge table after vertices 0, 1, 2, 3, and 6 have been visited.

going backwards one vertex at a time in this list until we come to a vertex that has some untraversed edges arising from it. Backing up from vertex 6 to vertex 3, we see from the edge table that all its vertices have been visited, so we back up one more step to vertex 2. Here the first unvisited vertex is 4, so we add that to our traversal, and visit row 4, where we find that the only remaining unvisited vertex, 5, is listed. We add that to our traversal, which completes the exercise. The final traversal is then 0 1 2 3 6 4 5. Had we encountered a dead end again, we would have repeated the backtracking procedure.

Note that depth-first traversals of a graph are not unique. If we had listed the vertices in each row of the edge table in a different order, we would get a different traversal. You should try this yourself: change the order of the rows in the table, or use a different starting vertex, or change the orders of the vertices within each row.

This algorithm (using an edge table) also takes account of disconnected graphs. If at any point we run out of vertices to add to the traversal, and there are still rows in the edge table that have not yet been visited, we move to the next unvisited row in the table and start again. For example, suppose we add some rows to the edge table above to get the result shown in Fig. 14.10. (You should draw the graph corresponding to this edge table.)

```
0 | 1  3
1 | 0  2
2 | 1  3  4  5
3 | 0  2  6
4 | 2  5
5 | 2  4
6 | 3
7 | 9
8 | 9
9 | 7  8
```

Figure 14.10.   The edge table for the graph in Fig. 14.6 with added vertices.

After starting at vertex 0 and applying the above algorithm for a depth-first traversal, we obtain the same sequence (0 1 2 3 6 4 5) as before, and the edge table looks like Fig. 14.11.

0	*1*	*3*		
1	*0*	*2*		
2	*1*	*3*	*4*	*5*
3	*0*	*2*	*6*	
4	*2*	*5*		
5	*2*	*4*		
6	*3*			
7	9			
8	9			
9	7	8		

Figure 14.11.   The edge table after traversing vertices 0 through 6.

The three extra vertices (7, 8, 9) form a disconnected subgraph. Therefore, we continue our traversal by moving down to row 7 and applying the algorithm again to yield the final traversal 0 1 2 3 6 4 5 7 9 8.

Looking forward to our Java implementation of DFT, we note that the algorithm is recursive. As each node is visited, it is recorded in the traversal, and the same algorithm is called for the first unvisited vertex arising from that point. If a dead end is reached, backtracking is done automatically as the recursive calls return in the reverse order to that in which they were invoked, until a vertex with an unvisited edge is found.

14.3.2 BREADTH-FIRST TRAVERSAL

Breadth-first traversal, or BFT, can be implemented on paper using an edge table in a similar way to depth-first traversal. The idea here is to list *all* vertices connected to each vertex before moving on in the edge table. Consider the same edge table as before (Fig. 14.7).

We begin, as before, with vertex 0. Also, as before, we cross off each vertex as it is added to the traversal. However, this time we add *all* the vertices in each row visited to the traversal. The easiest way to handle this is to use a queue. Each time we add a vertex to the traversal, we add to the queue all unvisited vertices listed in the row corresponding to the added vertex. We then add the vertex at the head of the queue to the traversal, and add any unvisited vertices in *its* row to the tail of the queue. We continue until all vertices in the graph have been added to the traversal, at which point the queue should be empty.

Adding vertex 0 to the traversal, we add vertices 1 and 3 to the queue. Vertex

1 is at the head of the queue, so it is the next vertex to be added to the traversal. Looking at row 1 in the edge table, we see that the only unvisited vertex in that row is vertex 2, so it is added to the queue. The vertex at the head of the queue is now vertex 3, so it is added to the traversal, and the only unvisited vertex in row 3 of the table is added to the queue. At this point, the traversal contains vertices 0 1 3, and the queue contains the vertices 2 and 6. The edge table is now as shown in Fig. 14.12.

$$
\begin{array}{c|cccc}
\mathbf{0} & \mathbf{1} & \mathbf{3} & & \\
\mathbf{1} & \mathbf{0} & \mathbf{2} & & \\
\mathbf{2} & \mathbf{1} & \mathbf{3} & 4 & 5 \\
\mathbf{3} & \mathbf{0} & \mathbf{2} & \mathbf{6} & \\
\mathbf{4} & \mathbf{2} & 5 & & \\
\mathbf{5} & \mathbf{2} & 4 & & \\
\mathbf{6} & \mathbf{3} & & &
\end{array}
$$

Figure 14.12.

Note that vertices are crossed off when they are added to the queue *or* to the traversal. We now continue by removing vertex 2 from the queue and adding it to the traversal, which now contains 0 1 3 2. The vertices 4 and 5 which are present in row 2 of the edge table are added to the queue, so that the queue now contains the vertices 6 4 5. All vertices have now been crossed off in the edge table, so the remainder of the traversal simply removes the items from the queue in order, and adds them to the traversal, giving the final traversal 0 1 3 2 6 4 5.

As with the depth-first traversal, disconnected portions of the graph are handled by starting the algorithm again at the first untouched row in the edge table. With the same extension to the graph as given above, the extra three vertices would be added in the order 7 9 8 to the traversal.

14.4 Topological sorting

As an example of the two forms of graph traversal, we shall consider a *topological sorting* or *topological ordering* of the vertices in a digraph. In any digraph without cycles (a *cycle* is a path in the graph where you may start at one vertex and return to that vertex by following the edges in the graph), it is possible to list the vertices so that, as we progress from left to right through the list, we travel only in the direction of the edges connecting the vertices, never against the direction. For example, for the digraph shown in Fig. 14.13, one possible topological ordering is 9 6 3 4 8 2 0 5 1 7. For most digraphs, several different orderings are possible.

Various applications of topological orderings exist. For example, the courses in a university degree programme must usually be taken in some definite order,

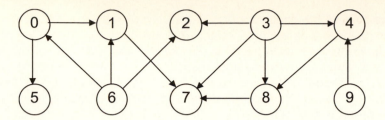

Figure 14.13.

with some courses requiring other courses as prerequisites. We could draw a graph in which each vertex is a course and each directed edge indicates that the course at the starting end of the edge is a prerequisite for the course at the finishing end. A topological ordering of this graph would show a possible order in which the courses could be taken.

A computer program can also be represented as a directed graph, in which each vertex is a function call. If the program contains no recursive or mutually recursive calls (cases where function A calls function B which in turn calls function A, creating a cycle), we can connect the vertices by directed edges showing which functions are called by which other functions. A topological ordering of this graph would then show one possible order in which the functions could be declared in a program so that each function is declared before it is called by another function.

The algorithms for topological sorting can be worked out on paper using edge tables, just as depth- and breadth-first traversals.

14.4.1 DEPTH-FIRST TOPOLOGICAL SORT

Consider the directed graph shown above. Its edge table is shown in Fig. 14.14. The depth-first topological sort is a recursive procedure, similar to the depth-first traversal described earlier. The procedure here, however, works in the opposite direction to the DFT we studied earlier. The idea behind a depth-first topological

```
0 │ 1   5
1 │ 7
2 │
3 │ 2   4   7   8
4 │ 8
5 │
6 │ 0   1   2
7 │
8 │ 7
9 │ 4
```

Figure 14.14.

ordering is to find those vertices that have no successors *first*, so that we build up the traversal from right to left, rather than the more usual left to right. We can use the same recursive procedure, except that we record a vertex in the topological ordering when the recursive call *returns*, and not when it is first called.

We begin with vertex 0, and using the depth-first algorithm, locate a vertex that has no successors. Following the chain of directed edges, we go from 0 to 1 to 7. Vertex 7 has no successors, since there are no vertices listed in row 7 of the edge table. Therefore, we write vertex 7 down at the *right* side of the topological sort. Note that we cross off vertices *when they are visited*, and *not* when they are added to the traversal, in order to avoid visiting a vertex more than once. As with the DFT, it is important to remember the order in which the vertices have been visited: so far we have $0 \rightarrow 1 \rightarrow 7$. The edge table at this point is shown in Fig. 14.15.

$$
\begin{array}{c|cccc}
0 & \mathbf{1} & 5 & & \\
1 & \mathbf{7} & & & \\
2 & & & & \\
3 & 2 & 4 & \mathbf{7} & 8 \\
4 & 8 & & & \\
5 & & & & \\
6 & \mathbf{0} & \mathbf{1} & 2 & \\
7 & & & & \\
8 & \mathbf{7} & & & \\
9 & 4 & & &
\end{array}
$$

Figure 14.15.

We now back up one stage to vertex 1. Vertex 1 now has no unvisited successors, since vertex 7 is crossed off. Therefore, we may write down vertex 1 to the left of 7. Backing up one more step, we encounter vertex 0 again. It has one other unvisited successor, namely vertex 5, so we must trace this path until we encounter a vertex with no successor. Vertex 5 itself is an endpoint in the traversal, so we can write it down to the left of vertex 1 in the traversal. Since vertex 0 now has no unvisited successors, we write it down next. At this point, the topological sort contains the vertices 0 5 1 7, and the edge table looks like Fig. 14.16.

Since we have returned to the top level in the recursion, and there are no more vertices left to process in row 0 of the edge table, we proceed to the next unvisited row, which is row 2. Vertex 2 is itself an endpoint without successors, so we can add it directly to the traversal and cross it off. The next unvisited row is row 3. We do a depth-first trace starting from vertex 3, which leads us through vertices 4 and 8. Vertex 8 is now a dead end, since vertex 7 has already been included in the traversal. We may therefore add vertex 8 to the left of vertex 2. Backing up to vertex 4, we see it has no further successors, so we can add vertex 4 to the left of 8. Backing up one more stage we arrive back at vertex 3 again,

```
0 | 1  5
1 | 7
2 |
3 | 2  4  7  8
4 | 8
5 |
6 | 0  1  2
7 |
8 | 7
9 | 4
```

Figure 14.16.

which now has no further successors, since vertex 8 has been used. We now add vertex 3 to the left of vertex 4. The topological sort at this stage looks like this: 3 4 8 2 0 5 1 7. There are still two unvisited rows in the edge table: rows 6 and 9. Neither row has any successors remaining, so we may add these two rows in either order to complete the topological sort: 9 6 3 4 8 2 0 5 1 7.

14.4.2 BREADTH-FIRST TOPOLOGICAL SORT

The breadth-first topological sort is similar to the breadth-first traversal discussed earlier, but we must include an additional check to ensure that topological order is preserved. Rather than search for vertices without successors, as in the depth-first sort, we search for vertices without predecessors.

When we construct the edge table, we add an extra column to the left in which we note down the number of immediate predecessors each vertex has (that is, the number of incoming edges). For the same graph as before, we obtain the table shown in Fig. 14.17.

```
1 | 0 | 1  5
2 | 1 | 7
2 | 2 |
0 | 3 | 2  4  7  8
2 | 4 | 8
1 | 5 |
0 | 6 | 0  1  2
3 | 7 |
2 | 8 | 7
0 | 9 | 4
```

Figure 14.17.   An edge table with an added column on the left showing the number of predecessors for each vertex.

We search for all rows in which the corresponding vertex has no predecessors, and begin a queue by adding these vertices to the queue. In this case, the queue begins with vertices 3 6 9.

The main part of the algorithm now begins. We remove the vertex at the head of the queue, add it to the topological sort, and adjust the predecessor count of all vertices of which this vertex was a predecessor. When vertex 3 is removed from the queue and added to the topological sort, we observe from row 3 in the edge table that vertex 3 is a predecessor of vertices 2, 4, 7, and 8, so we decrement the predecessor counts of these four vertices. Any vertices whose predecessor count is reduced to zero by this decrement are added to the queue. In the case of vertex 3, all its successor vertices had two or more predecessors, so no new vertices are added to the queue at this stage.

We now remove the next vertex from the queue and repeat the procedure. Removing 6 and adding it to the traversal requires us to decrement the predecessor counts of vertices 0, 1 and 2. This reduces the predecessor counts of vertices 0 and 2 to zero, so they are added to the queue. The traversal at this point contains the vertices 3 6, and the queue contains vertices 9 0 2. Removing 9 from the queue and adding it to the traversal reduces the predecessor count of vertex 4 to 0, so it is added to the queue. The process continues until the queue is empty. In this case, the topological ordering produces the list 3 6 9 0 2 4 1 5 8 7.

Note that it is not necessary to cross off any vertices in the edge table since the sole determining factor as to when a vertex is added to the queue is when its predecessor count is reduced to zero. This algorithm works equally well for connected or disconnected graphs.

14.5   Java code for graph traversal

14.5.1 REPRESENTATION OF A GRAPH IN JAVA

Of the various methods described above for representing a graph on a computer, we will adopt the two-dimensional array, since it is conceptually simpler for most people, and allows all the algorithms in this chapter to be implemented fairly easily.

You should keep in mind, however, that the two-dimensional array representation of a graph can be very wasteful of space if the graph contains many vertices but few edges. In such a case it is worth considering a representation that relies partly or entirely on linked lists. Such an implementation is left to the exercises at the end of the chapter.

The beginning of the definition of the `Graph` class and its constructor are as follows:

```java
public class Graph
{
    static final int MAXVERTEX = 10;
    static final int DIRECTED = 0;
    static final int UNDIRECTED = 1;
```

```
private int NumVertex;
private int Edge[][] = new int[MAXVERTEX][MAXVERTEX];
private boolean Visited[] = new boolean[MAXVERTEX];
private int depthFirstList[] = new int[MAXVERTEX];
private int breadthFirstList[] = new int[MAXVERTEX];
private int depthFirstTopList[] = new int[MAXVERTEX];
private int breadthFirstTopList[] =
   new int[MAXVERTEX];
private int travIndex;
private int Directed;

Graph()
{
   NumVertex = 0;
   travIndex = 0;
   for (int row = 0; row < MAXVERTEX; ++row)
   {
      Visited[row] = false;
      for (int col = 0; col < MAXVERTEX; ++col)
         Edge[row][col] = 0;
   }
}

...
}
```

The class data field `MAXVERTEX` defines the maximum number of vertices that this graph can contain. The other two class fields `DIRECTED` and `UNDIRECTED` are flags indicating whether the graph is directed or undirected.

The variables that we will introduce at this stage are:

- `NumVertex` – the number of vertices in the current graph. Must be less than or equal to `MAXVERTEX`.
- `Edge[][]` – the two-dimensional array containing the edges. At the moment, the elements of this array can take on only the values 0 or 1, indicating the absence or presence of an edge, respectively. Later in this chapter we will see that an edge can have an associated *cost* or *weight*. The `Edge` array will then be allowed to take on other values as well.
- `Visited[]` – a working array which records which vertices have alredy been visited during a traversal.
- `depthFirstList[]` – an array that contains the depth-first traversal.
- `breadthFirstList[]` – an array that contains the breadth-first traversal.
- `depthFirstTopList` – an array that contains the depth-first topological ordering.
- `breadthFirstTopList` – an array that contains the breadth-first topological ordering.
- `travIndex` – a marker that keeps track of the current index in either

`depthFirstList` or `breadthFirstList` during a traversal.

- `Directed` – a flag indicating whether the graph is directed or undirected.

Other fields may be added later (either directly into this class, or using inheritance) to implement the other algorithms in this chapter.

The constructor initializes the graph to be empty: `NumVertex` is zero, no vertex has been visited (`Visited[row]` = `false`), and there are no edges (`Edge[row][col]` = 0). As usual in Java, none of these initializations is strictly necessary, since all data fields are initialized to 0, `null`, or `false`, depending on their type, but it is reassuring to state this explicitly.

We now consider the methods used to add vertices and edges to the graph.

```
public void AddVertex() throws GraphException
{
   if (NumVertex == MAXVERTEX)
      throw new GraphException("Cannot add vertex:
         graph is full.");
   ++NumVertex;
}
```

The method `AddVertex()` checks that there is room for another vertex and then just increments `NumVertex`. No edges are associated with this new vertex yet. To do that, we need a method for adding an edge between two vertices:

```
public void AddEdge(int startVertex, int endVertex,
   int weight, int graphMode) throws GraphException
{
   if (startVertex >= 0 && startVertex < NumVertex &&
      endVertex >= 0 && endVertex < NumVertex)
      Edge[startVertex][endVertex] = weight;
   else
      throw new GraphException("One or both vertices
         not in graph.");

   if (graphMode == UNDIRECTED)
      Edge[endVertex][startVertex] = weight;
}
```

The `AddEdge()` method requires four arguments:

- `startVertex`, `endVertex` – the source and destination of the new edge. The distinction between source and destination is only important, of course, for a directed graph.
- `weight` – the weight or cost associated with the edge. For now, only two values are acceptable: 0 (indicating no edge is present) or 1 (indicating an edge is present).
- `graphMode` – whether the graph is directed or undirected.

A check is made that both vertices are members of the graph. If so, the `Edge` array is modified to record the new edge. If the graph is `UNDIRECTED`, the edge pointing in the opposite direction between the same two vertices is also added.

14.5.2 DEPTH-FIRST TRAVERSAL IN JAVA

As usual with recursive algorithms, the depth-first traversal code in Java consists of a public interface method and an internal, recursive method:

```java
private void recursiveDFT(int vertex)
{
   if (!Visited[vertex])
   {
      depthFirstList[++travIndex] = vertex;
      Visited[vertex] = true;
      for (int nextVertex = 0; nextVertex < NumVertex;
         ++nextVertex)
         if (Edge[vertex][nextVertex] != 0)
            recursiveDFT(nextVertex);
   }
}

public void depthFirstTraversal()
{
   int vertex;
   travIndex = -1;
   for (vertex = 0; vertex < NumVertex; ++vertex)
      Visited[vertex] = false;
   for (vertex = 0; vertex < NumVertex; ++vertex)
      recursiveDFT(vertex);
}
```

The public `depthFirstTraversal()` method initializes `travIndex` to –1, and clears the `Visited` array. It then calls `recursiveDFT()` for *all* vertices in the graph.

This may seem unnecessary – after all, the whole point of a traversal is that it starts with a specific vertex and finds a path from that vertex to all other vertices in the graph on its own. However, in some graphs, there is no path from the starting vertex to every other vertex in the graph. An unconnected graph is one example, but even in connected (directed) graphs, it is possible for this to happen. Therefore, this loop over all vertices ensures that if the first vertex for which `recursiveDFT()` is called does not pick up all the vertices in the graph, we will try with another starting point to get those vertices that have not yet been visited.

The `recursiveDFT()` method accepts a vertex as its starting point. If that vertex has not been visited, the traversal index parameter `travIndex` is incremented, and the current vertex is added to the traversal. The vertex is then flagged as `Visited`. Then a loop over all the vertices in the graph is started. This loop first checks to see if an edge exists from the current vertex to this other vertex. If so, `recursiveDFT()` is called to continue the DFT from that point. The loop takes care of the backtracking, since if the DFT hits a dead end and the recursion backs up to this point, the loop checks to see if there are any further paths starting with the current vertex. If there are, the recursive method is called again to explore them. If not, then this level in the recursion finishes and control passes one level up where the process continues.

14.5.3 BREADTH-FIRST TRAVERSAL IN JAVA

Since the BFT is a non-recursive algorithm, it can be coded in a single method:

```java
public void breadthFirstTraversal()
{
    int vertex, nextVertex, addVertex;
    Queue vertexQueue = new Queue();

    travIndex = -1;
    for (vertex = 0; vertex < NumVertex; ++vertex)
        Visited[vertex] = false;
    for (vertex = 0; vertex < NumVertex; ++vertex)
    {
        try {
            if (!Visited[vertex])
            {
                vertexQueue.Add(vertex);
                Visited[vertex] = true;
            }
            while (!vertexQueue.Empty())
            {
                addVertex = vertexQueue.Remove();
                breadthFirstList[++travIndex] = addVertex;
                for (nextVertex = 0; nextVertex < NumVertex;
                    ++nextVertex)
                    if (Edge[addVertex][nextVertex] != 0 &&
                        !Visited[nextVertex])
                    {
                        vertexQueue.Add(nextVertex);
                        Visited[nextVertex] = true;
                    }
            }
        } catch (QueueException e);
    }
}
```

The `travIndex` parameter is used here as well to keep track of the index in the `breadthFirstList` array where the next element in the traversal is to be added. The `Visited` array is initialized to `false`. The second (and main) for loop in the method implements the algorithm described above for the BFT. The entire list of vertices is included in the loop for the same reason as with the DFT: there may not be a path from the starting vertex to all the other vertices.

The `for` loop begins by testing the starting vertex to see if it has been visited. If not, it is added to a queue, and the vertex is flagged as having been visited. The `while` loop inside the `for` loop then implements the breadth-first traversal starting from the vertex that was just added to the queue. The `while` loop continues until the queue is empty. The next vertex to be added to the traversal is extracted from the queue as variable `addVertex`, and then added to the traversal at the location indicated by `travIndex`. Then, a nested `for` loop finds all the unvisited vertices to which `addVertex` is connected and adds them to the queue. Once this internal `for` loop has finished, the `while` loop continues the BFT by extracting the next element from the queue, and finding all unvisited vertices to which *it* is connected, and so on. When the queue becomes empty, the outer `for` loop then checks to make sure that all vertices have been visited. If the first try at a BFT has missed any, this outer `for` loop will pick them and apply the BFT algorithm to these leftover vertices.

Topological ordering in Java   14.6

14.6.1 DEPTH-FIRST TOPOLOGICAL ORDERING

The depth-first topological ordering of a graph is a variant on the DFT considered above. The algorithm is the same as for the DFT except that we don't actually add any of the vertices to the ordering until we reach the end of the recursive descent into the graph. We add the vertices on the way back up in the recursion, rather than on the way down.

As before, the recursive procedure takes the form of a public interface method and an internal recursive method, as shown:

```java
public void depthFirstTopSort()
{
    int vertex, place;

    for (vertex = 0; vertex < NumVertex; ++vertex)
        Visited[vertex] = false;
    place = NumVertex;
    for (vertex = 0; vertex < NumVertex; ++vertex)
        if (!Visited[vertex])
            place = DFRecursiveSort(vertex, place);
}

private int DFRecursiveSort(int vertex, int place)
{
    int nextVertex;
```

```
            Visited[vertex] = true;
            for (nextVertex = 0; nextVertex < NumVertex;
               ++nextVertex)
            {
               if (Edge[vertex][nextVertex] > 0 &&
                  !Visited[nextVertex])
                  place = DFRecursiveSort(nextVertex, place);
            }
            depthFirstTopList[--place] = vertex;
            return place;
         }
```

The public method, depthFirstTopSort(), after initializing the Visited array and the parameter place, which will be used to keep track of the next location in the array where a vertex is to be added, loops over all the vertices in the graph and calls DFRecursiveSort() for any unvisited vertices. Note that the place parameter is kept up to date between recursive calls by having its value returned by the recursive function.

The DFRecursiveSort() method expects two arguments: vertex; which is the vertex at which the recursive traversal will start, and place; which is one location *above* that at which the next vertex in the topological ordering is to be placed.

The first action of DFRecursiveSort() is to mark the current vertex as Visited. Then it follows almost the same algorithm as for the DFT: all unvisited vertices to which vertex is connected are looped over by the for loop, and DFRecursiveSort() is called for each of these vertices to perform a DFT on them. However, note that vertex is not added to depthFirstTopList until *after* all these recursive calls have completed. This ensures that all the vertices to which vertex is connected will be added to the ordering at positions further along in the array than vertex itself, which is the required condition for a topological ordering of the graph.

14.6.2 BREADTH-FIRST TOPOLOGICAL ORDERING

The Java method that implements the breadth-first topological ordering algorithm again follows the steps above very closely. The algorithm can be coded in a single method:

```
public void breadthFirstTopSort()
{
   int predecessorCount[] = new int[MAXVERTEX];
   Queue vertexQueue = new Queue();
   int vertex, nextVertex, place, tempVertex;

   for (vertex = 0; vertex < NumVertex; ++vertex)
      predecessorCount[vertex] = 0;
   for (vertex = 0; vertex < NumVertex; ++vertex) {
      for (tempVertex = 0; tempVertex < NumVertex;
```

```
                ++tempVertex)
        {
            if (Edge[vertex][tempVertex] > 0)
                predecessorCount[tempVertex]++;
        }
    }
    for (vertex = 0; vertex < NumVertex; ++vertex)
    {
        try
            if (predecessorCount[vertex] == 0)
                vertexQueue.Add(vertex);
        catch (QueueException e);
    }
    place = 0;
    while (!vertexQueue.Empty()) {
        try {
            vertex = vertexQueue.Remove();
            breadthFirstTopList[place++] = vertex;
            for (nextVertex = 0; nextVertex < NumVertex;
                ++nextVertex)
            {
                if (Edge[vertex][nextVertex] > 0)
                    predecessorCount[nextVertex]--;
                if (Edge[vertex][nextVertex] > 0 &&
                    predecessorCount[nextVertex] == 0)
                    vertexQueue.Add(nextVertex);
            }
        } catch (QueueException e);
    }
}
```

A local array `predecessorCount` is declared to hold the number of predecessors of each vertex, and local queue is declared. After initialization of
`predecessorCount`, the doubly-nested `for` loops calculate the number of predecessors for each vertex. Following this, the next `for` loop adds all vertices with
no predecessors to the queue.

The main part of the method is the `while` loop. This loop continues until the
queue is empty. The first `vertex` is removed from the queue and added to
`breadthFirstTopList`. The internal `for` loop then subtracts 1 from the predecessor count of all vertices to which `vertex` is connected. Any vertex whose
predecessor count is reduced to zero by this subtraction is then added to the queue.

Note that no auxiliary `for` loop over all the vertices of the graph is required
here to pick up those vertices not included in the first application of the `while`
loop. This is because any section of the graph that is not accessible from any chosen vertex must have at least one vertex with no predecessors (draw out a few
graphs to convince yourself). Therefore, each section of the graph will have at least
one vertex added to the initial queue.

14.7 Minimum cost spanning trees

14.7.1 KRUSKAL'S ALGORITHM

The graphs we have studied so far have vertices that are connected by simple edges, where an edge serves only to indicate that there is a path from one vertex to another. We can generalize the concept of a graph a bit so that each edge includes a *weight* or *cost* as well. For example, if we represent airline routes as a graph with the cities as the vertices, the weight associated with each edge could be the distance between the two cities, or the cost of a flight between the cities. In such cases, we may need to know the shortest or cheapest route between two cities. The algorithm we consider in this section deals with finding such paths in a graph.

For an undirected, connected graph with N vertices, we can find a set of $N -$ 1 edges which connect all the vertices. Such a set of edges is guaranteed not to have any cycles, and is therefore referred to as a *spanning tree*. For a graph where each edge has an associated cost, we define the *minimum cost spanning tree* as the spanning tree where the sum of all the weights on the edges is a minimum.

There are several algorithms for finding minimum cost spanning trees, but we will consider just one representative of them: Kruskal's algorithm. Kruskal's algorithm is an example of a *greedy algorithm*, that is, one which seeks maximum gain at each step. The algorithm, on paper at least, is very simple. Given a connected, undirected graph, we wish to select those edges, one at a time, that comprise the minimum cost spanning tree. We begin by choosing the edge with the minimum cost (if there are several edges with the same minimum cost, we select any one of them) and add it to the spanning tree. In the next step, we select the edge with the next lowest cost, and so on, until we have selected $N - 1$ edges to form the complete spanning tree.

The only thing of which we must beware is that we don't form any cycles as we add edges to the spanning tree. This is fairly easy to ensure for small graphs which we draw on paper, since we can see just by looking at the diagram we are drawing if adding an edge would create a cycle. However, we must find some way of coding this in Java, so we can't rely on pictures.

At each stage in the algorithm, the partially formed spanning tree will consist of several sets of vertices which form connected subgraphs. If we keep a list of these sets, we can use them to determine if a new edge will form a cycle. Suppose that, at some point in the algorithm, vertices 1 and 2 have been connected in the spanning tree, as have vertices 3, 4, and 5, but vertex 0 has not yet been connected to any other vertex. We may write this state of affairs in set notation by saying that the list of sets of connected vertices in the spanning tree is {0}, {1,2}, {3,4,5}. Now suppose that the edge with the next lowest cost is that connecting vertices 2 and 3, which we write as (2,3). Adding the edge (2,3) would connect the second and third of these sets because each end of the edge lies in a different set. Therefore, the edge (2,3) will not form a cycle, so it is safe to add. After its addition, the sets of vertices in the spanning tree are {0}, {1,2,3,4,5}. If the next edge up for consideration is (3,4), this would connect two vertices that are already inside the same set, so this would provide an alternative path between vertices 3 and 4, thus creating a cycle. Therefore, we should *not* include the edge (3,4).

Kruskal's algorithm, with the addition of this check for avoiding cycles, is therefore:

1   Initialize the spanning tree *T* to contain all the vertices in the graph *G* but no edges.

2   At the start of the algorithm, each vertex will be in its own set, since no edges have yet been added to the tree, so create sets of the tree *T* with one vertex per set.

3   Choose the edge *e* with lowest weight from graph *G*.

4   Check if both vertices from *e* are within the same set in the tree *T*, for all such sets of *T*. If not, add the edge *e* to the tree *T*, and replace the two sets that this edge connects with their union.

5   Delete the edge *e* from the graph *G* and repeat from step 3 until there are no more edges to add or until the spanning tree *T* contains *N* – 1 vertices.

As an example of Kruskal's algorithm, consider the graph shown in Fig. 14.18. We begin our spanning tree by filling it with the vertices, but none of the edges, in the original graph (Fig. 14.19).

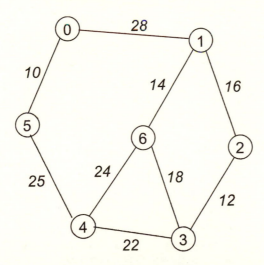

Figure 14.18.   An undirected, weighted graph.

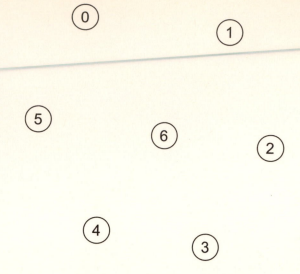

Figure 14.19.   The beginning state for Kruskal's algorithm.

We select the edge with the lowest cost (the edge (0,5)) and add it to the tree (Fig. 14.20). The sets of vertices in the spanning tree are now {0,5}, {1}, {2}, {3}, {4}, {6}. We continue by adding the edges (2,3), (1,6), and (1,2). At this point, the tree looks like Fig. 14.21.

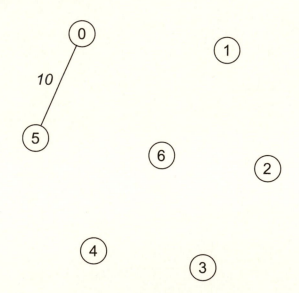

Figure 14.20.   Adding the edge with the lowest cost.

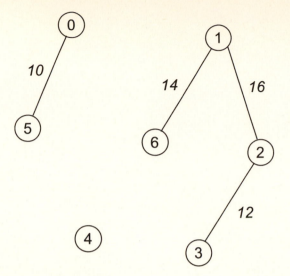

Figure 14.21.

The sets of vertices now consist of {0,5}, {1,2,3,6}, {4}. Looking at the original graph, the next edge that must be considered is (3,6). We can see from the diagram that adding this edge would create a cycle. We can also see this from the list of sets of vertices, since vertices 3 and 6 are both in the same set. We therefore pass over this edge and add edge (3,4). The next edge that would be considered is (4,6), but this would also create a cycle. Finally, the edge (4,5) is added to complete the tree (Fig. 14.22).

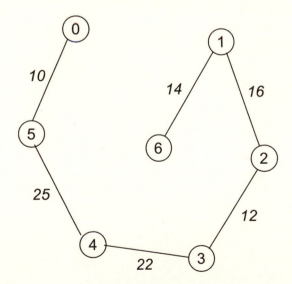

Figure 14.22.   The completed spanning tree.

14.7.2 JAVA CODE FOR KRUSKAL'S ALGORITHM

Although the code for Kruskal's algorithm follows the algorithm as we have described it in the last section, there are a few subtleties that must be considered. We present the method first and discuss its function afterwards.

The spanning tree will be stored in additional two-dimensional array:

```java
private boolean SpanningTree[][] =
    new boolean[MAXVERTEX][MAXVERTEX];
```

which can either be added to the Graph class above, or included in a new class derived from the Graph class. The array is boolean – an element is true if the corresponding edge is part of the spanning tree, false if not:

```java
public void Kruskal()
{
    private boolean VisitedEdge[][] =
        new boolean[NumVertex][NumVertex];
    private Set Cycles[] = new Set[NumVertex];
    private int index, row, col;

    for (index = 0; index < NumVertex; ++index)
    {
        try {
            Cycles[index] = new Set(NumVertex);
            Cycles[index].Insert(index);
        } catch (SetException e);
    }

    for (row = 0; row < NumVertex; ++row)
        for (col = 0; col < NumVertex; ++col)
        {
            VisitedEdge[row][col] = false;
            SpanningTree[row][col] = false;
        }

    boolean MoreEdges = true, SameSet = false;
    int minEdge, minRow = 0, minCol = 0;
    int SetIndex1 = 0, SetIndex2 = 0;
    int UnionSetIndex = 0, OtherSetIndex = 0;
    while (MoreEdges)
    {
        MoreEdges = false;
        minEdge = Integer.MAX_VALUE;
        for (row = 0; row < NumVertex; ++row)
        {
            for (col = 0; col < NumVertex; ++col)
            {
```

```
           if (Edge[row][col] > 0 &&
              !VisitedEdge[row][col] &&
              Edge[row][col] < minEdge)
           {
              minEdge = Edge[row][col];
              minRow = row; minCol = col;
              MoreEdges = true;
           }
        }
     }
     if (MoreEdges)
     {
        SameSet = false;
        VisitedEdge[minRow][minCol] = true;
        if (Directed == UNDIRECTED)
           VisitedEdge[minCol][minRow] = true;
        for (index = 0; index < NumVertex; ++index)
        {
           if (Cycles[index].Contains(minRow))
              SetIndex1 = index;
           if (Cycles[index].Contains(minCol))
              SetIndex2 = index;
        }
        if (SetIndex1 == SetIndex2)
           SameSet = true;
        if (!SameSet)
        {
           try {
              UnionSetIndex = SetIndex1 < SetIndex2 ?
                 SetIndex1 : SetIndex2;
              OtherSetIndex = SetIndex1 < SetIndex2 ?
                 SetIndex2 : SetIndex1;
              Cycles[UnionSetIndex] = Cycles[SetIndex1].
                 Union(Cycles[SetIndex2]);
              Cycles[OtherSetIndex].Clear();
              SpanningTree[minRow][minCol] = true;
              if (Directed == UNDIRECTED)
                 SpanningTree[minCol][minRow] = true;
           } catch (SetException e);
        }
     }
  }
}
```

The general plan of this method is as follows. We are provided with the graph in the form of a two-dimensional array Edge, which contains the weights on the edges. This array is constructed using the AddEdge() method described in Section 14.5. While proceeding through Kruskal's algorithm, we need to keep track of which edges have been either added to the spanning tree, or excluded because they would form a cycle. Therefore, we declare a local `boolean` array `VisitedEdge` whose elements are `true` if the edge has been considered and `false` otherwise.

We also declare an array of `Set`s (using the `Set` class from Chapter 8). These sets will be used to store the subsets of connected vertices as the algorithm progresses.

Kruskal's algorithm begins with a `for` loop in which each `Set` is initialized to contain a single vertex, followed by another `for` loop which initializes the two `boolean` arrays `VisitedEdge` and `SpanningTree`. Following this several local variables are declared which are used as parameters in the main part of the method.

The parameter `MoreEdges` is `true` as long as there are unvisited edges in the graph. The `while` loop continues until `MoreEdges` is `false`. The first thing we must do on each iteration of the loop is determine the unvisited edge with the smallest cost. A parameter `minEdge` is used to find this. We initialize `minEdge` to the largest `int` possible in Java by using `Integer` class variable `MAX_VALUE`. Then the doubly-nested `for` loop finds the edge with the smallest cost and saves its location in the two parameters `minRow` and `minCol`. Note that `MoreEdges` is only set to `true` if such an edge is found.

If an edge is found, it must now be determined if the endpoints of this edge lie within the same set. If they do, adding the edge to the spanning tree would cause a cycle, so it must be rejected. The `if` statement following the `while` loop does this check.

The parameter `SameSet` will be set to `true` if the two endpoints lie within the same set. The `for` loop finds in which set each endpoint lies in (each vertex can lie in only one set), storing the set numbers in `SetIndex1` and `SetIndex2`.

If the two endpoints are found to be in the same set, the iteration of the `while` loop finishes for that edge (in effect rejecting it, since it is not added to the spanning tree). Otherwise, the final `if` statement takes the union of the two sets containing the two endpoints. The parameter `UnionSetIndex` finds the smaller of `SetIndex1` and `SetIndex2`, while `OtherSetIndex` finds the larger of the two. The union of the two sets is stored in the set with index `UnionSetIndex` and the other set is cleared (set to the empty set). This ensures that each vertex is found in only one set. Finally, the edge is added to the spanning tree.

14.8 Shortest paths in a directed graph

14.8.1 DIJKSTRA'S ALGORITHM

We turn now to the problem of finding the shortest or least costly path between two vertices in a graph. It turns out that it is easiest to do this by finding the shortest path from one vertex, called the *source*, to all other vertices in the graph. The algorithm for doing this is also a greedy algorithm, and is generally known as *Dijkstra's algorithm* (pronounced 'Dike-stra').

Dijkstra's algorithm is usually used with directed graphs, though it works equally well with undirected graphs if each edge is considered as two directed edges, one in each direction.

The algorithm is as follows:

1   Choose the source vertex.

2   Define a set S of vertices and initialize it to contain only the source vertex. The set S will store those vertices to which a shortest path has been found as the algorithm progresses.

3   Label each vertex *not* in the set S (at this stage, this simply means 'any vertex other than the source') with the minimum distance from the source vertex, but only if this vertex can be connected *by a single edge* with the source. If there is no single edge connection between the source and the vertex not in S, label the vertex not in S with a distance of infinity.

4   Add to S that vertex with the smallest distance as determined in step 3 (or step 5 on subsequent iterations of the algorithm).

5   Check the distances to all vertices not in S. If the latest addition to S in step 4 provides a *single edge connection* between a vertex in S and the vertex not in S, or a shorter path now exists, then adjust the distance to that vertex. Otherwise, do not change the distance.

6   Repeat the algorithm from step 4 until either all vertices are in the set S or all vertices not in S have an infinite distance to them. In the latter case, these vertices are not reachable from the source vertex at any cost.

Let us follow the algorithm for the graph shown below, and find the shortest paths from vertex 6 to the other vertices. Fig. 14.23 shows the graph after steps 1, 2, and 3 in the algorithm above have been executed.

The first time step 4 is executed, vertex 4 is added to S, since its distance of 4 is currently the smallest to a vertex not already in S. Adding vertex 4 to S opens a path to vertex 5, since vertex 5 has a one-edge link from vertex 4. Therefore, we adjust the distance to vertex 5 to 14 (4 from vertex 6 to 4, plus 10 from vertex 4 to 5). Vertex 4 also offers an alternative path to vertex 3. The total distance to vertex 3 via vertex 4 is 16, which is less than the direct link from vertex 6 to 3, with a cost of 22. Therefore, we adjust the distance to vertex 3. The graph now looks like Fig. 14.24.

The shortest distance to a vertex not in S is now 14, which occurs for both vertices 1 and 5. It doesn't matter which vertex we choose to add at this stage, so we take vertex 1. This opens up a path to vertex 0, with a distance of 17.

We continue by adding the vertices 5, 3, and 0, in that order. There is no path from vertex 6 to vertex 2 so the distance to vertex remains infinite after the algorithm finishes. The final state of the graph is shown in Fig. 14.25.

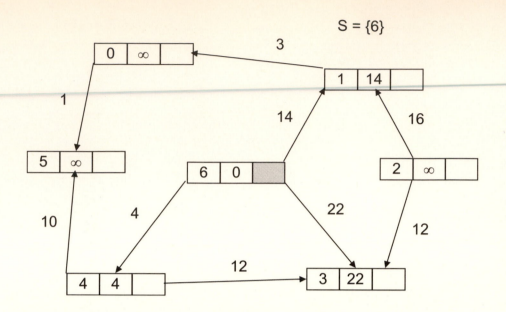

Figure 14.23. A graph at the beginning of Dijkstra's algorithm. Each vertex is represented by a box with three entries. The first entry is the vertex label, the second entry is the current minimum distance from a vertex in the set S to that vertex (or the minimum distance from the source vertex (6) to that vertex if the vertex is in the set S), and the last box is shaded if the vertex is in the set S.

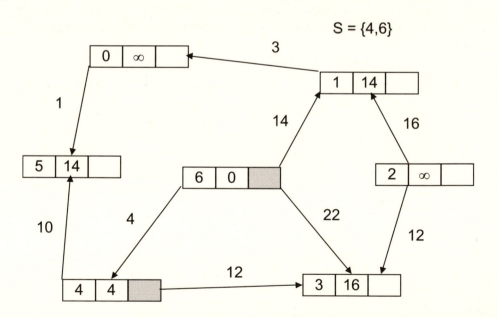

Figure 14.24.

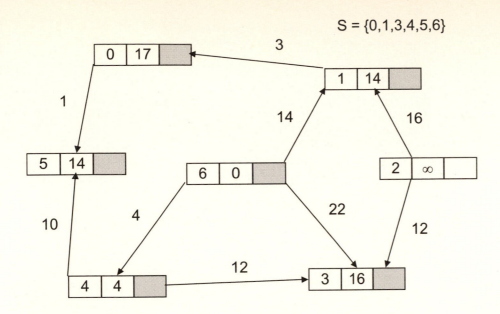

$S = \{0,1,3,4,5,6\}$

Figure 14.25.   The final state obtained from Dijkstra's algorithm.

Java code for Dijkstra's algorithm   14.9

The code for Dijkstra's algorithm stores the list of shortest distances in an array which can be added to the Graph class, or in a class derived from Graph:

```
private int MinDistance[] = new int[MAXVERTEX];
```

The actual code for Dijkstra's algorithm is contained in the main method Dijkstra() and a short auxiliary method getWeight():

```
private int getWeight(int begin, int end)
{
   return Edge[begin][end] > 0 ?
      Edge[begin][end] : Integer.MAX_VALUE;
}

public void Dijkstra(int start)
{
   Set pathFound = new Set(NumVertex);
   int tempmin = start, end, cost, vertex, mindist;

   try
      pathFound.Insert(start);
   catch (SetException e);
```

```
        MinDistance[start] = 0;
        for (vertex = 0; vertex < NumVertex; ++vertex)
          if (vertex != start)
            MinDistance[vertex] = getWeight(start, vertex);

        for (vertex = 0; vertex < NumVertex; ++vertex)
        {
          mindist = Integer.MAX_VALUE;
          if (vertex != start)
          {
            for (end = 0; end < NumVertex; ++end)
            {
              if (!pathFound.Contains(end))
              {
                if (MinDistance[end] < mindist)
                {
                  tempmin = end;
                  mindist = MinDistance[end];
                }
              }
            }
            if (mindist < Integer.MAX_VALUE)
            {
              try
                pathFound.Insert(tempmin);
              catch (SetException e);
              for (end = 0; end < NumVertex; ++end)
                if (!pathFound.Contains(end))
                {
                  cost = getWeight(tempmin, end);
                  if (cost < Integer.MAX_VALUE &&
                    mindist + cost < MinDistance[end])
                    MinDistance[end] = mindist + cost;
                }
            }
          }
        }
      }
```

The getWeight() method returns the weight of the edge connecting its two arguments begin and end if an edge exists between these two vertices; otherwise it returns Integer.MAX_VALUE, the largest int in Java. This is the equivalent of infinity, and indicates that no direct connection exists between these two vertices.

The Dijkstra() method begins by declaring a Set pathFound in which vertices can be stored as they are added to the set of vertices to which a path has been found. This set is equivalent to the set S used in the discussion of Dijkstra's algorithm above.

The starting vertex `start` is inserted into the set and the distance from the `start` vertex to itself is set to zero before anything else is done. Then the remainder of the `MinDistance` array is initialized, using the `getWeight()` method, to the costs from the `start` vertex to any other vertices to which it is directly connected, or to 'infinity' if no such direct connection exists.

The `for` loop now calculates the minimum distance between elements within the set `pathFound` and a vertex not in this set. It uses the parameter `mindist` to keep track of the distances as the comparisons proceed. If an external vertex (represented by `end`) has a `MinDistance` that is less than the current value of `mindist`, its location is recorded in the parameter `tempmin`, and `mindist` is reassigned to `MinDistance[end]`. After the `for` loop, a test is made (if (`mindist < Integer.MAX_VALUE`)) that a connection has actually been found (that is, the minimum distance from within the set `pathFound` to a vertex outside the set is not infinite). If so, the vertex with the smallest distance is added to the `pathFound` set.

The final `for` loop adjusts the costs for direct connections between vertices within the set `pathFound` and vertices outside the set. Since the only way any of these costs can change is if there is a direct connection between the vertex `tempmin` that was just added to the set and a vertex that is still outside the set, we examine these costs (using the statement `cost = getWeight (tempmin, end)`). If the cost is finite, and if the sum of `mindist` (the cost from the set `pathFound` to the vertex `tempmin` *before* the vertex `tempmin` was added to it) and `cost` (the cost of the edge from `tempmin` to `end`) is *less* than the previously recorded minimum cost to this vertex (`MinDistance[end]`), then `MinDistance[end]` is updated to this new, smaller, cost. The main loop then continues by choosing the next edge between `pathFound` and a vertex outside the set. The process ends when no such edge with a finite cost exists.

Summary   14.10

This chapter introduced the *graph* data structure. A graph is a generalization of a tree, consisting of *vertices* connected with *directed* or *undirected edges*. The vertices of a graph can be traversed in several ways, including *depth-first traversal*, *breadth-first traversal*, and for a directed graph, *topological ordering*. Algorithms for performing these traversals are given.

Graphs can be represented in Java using arrays (the *adjacency table*), linked lists (the *adjacency list*) or a combination of the two. A Java class using an adjacency table is defined and used to implement code for depth-first and breadth-first traversals and depth-first and breadth-first topological orderings.

Graphs can have *weights* or *costs* associated with their edges. A weight represents the cost of traveling from one vertex to another. A *minimal cost spanning tree* is a selection of edges from a weighted graph that spans all vertices in the graph and gives the smallest sum of weights for such a tree. Kruskal's algorithm may be used to find a minimal cost spanning tree. Dijkstra's algorithm may be used to find the shortest or least expensive path from one source vertex to all other vertices in a weighted graph. Java code is given for implementing both these algorithms.

14.11 Exercises

1   Consider the directed graph shown:

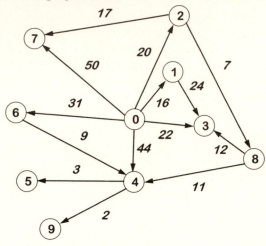

(a) Write out an edge table for this graph.
(b) Find depth-first and breadth-first traversals of this graph, starting at vertex 0.
(c) Find depth-first and breadth-first topological orderings for this graph.
(d) Use Dijkstra's algorithm to find the minimum cost paths from vertex 0 to all other vertices in the graph.

2   Consider the undirected graph shown:

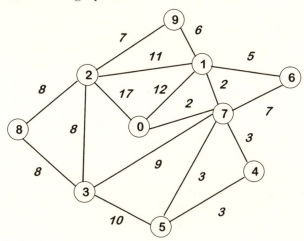

(a) Write out an edge table for this graph.

(b) Find depth-first and breadth-first traversals of this graph, starting at vertex 0.

(c) Use Kruskal's algorithm to find a minimal spanning tree for this graph.

3   Write an alternative to the `Graph` class in which the edge table is represented as an array of linked lists, as shown in Fig. 14.5. Each edge must contain the identity of the vertex to which it leads, and its weight or cost.

Rewrite the methods for traversal and topological ordering using this new representation.

4   Measuring the efficiency of a graph algorithm can be done by running computer experiments as we have done for other data structures and algorithms in this book. The situation for graphs is complicated slightly in that the efficiency of traversal algorithms depends not only on the number of vertices in the graph, but also on the number of edges.

To get a feel for the efficiency, we can count the number of steps required in two extreme cases: a fully connected graph (where all possible pairs of vertices are connected by edges), and a graph consisting of a spanning tree (that is, a graph with the minimum number of edges needed to be connected). A fully connected graph with n vertices will have n^2 edges (since every vertex will be connected to every other vertex, including itself); a spanning tree with n vertices will have $n - 1$ edges.

Measure the efficiency of the depth first traversal algorithm by counting the number of times the `recursiveDFT()` method is called, for both a fully connected graph and a spanning tree. Repeat the experiment for graphs ranging in size from 5 vertices up to as large a graph as your computer will handle. The maximum size of graph will be determined by the number of edges: a fully connected graph with 1000 vertices will have 1,000,000 edges. Draw graphs similar to those in Chapter 11 in an attempt to determine the order of the algorithm.

5   Measure the efficiency of the breadth first traversal algorithm using a similar method to that in question 4. In this case, count the number of times the `Visited[]` array is examined in the `breadthFirstTraversal()` method.

6   Measure the efficiency of the two topological ordering algorithms.

7   An alternative to Kruskal's algorithm for finding the minimum cost spanning tree in an undirected graph is *Prim's algorithm* (which was also discovered independently by Dijkstra):

Choose a starting vertex (any vertex will do). At the first step, choose the vertex that is connected to the starting vertex by the edge of least cost, and add that vertex to the spanning tree. For the remaining steps, choose that vertex that is not yet part of the spanning tree, but is connected to the partially formed tree by the edge of least cost, and add that vertex to the tree. Continue until all vertices are part of the spanning tree.

(a) Use Prim's algorithm on the graph in question 2.

(b) Write a Java method to implement Prim's algorithm which may be added to the `Graph` class in the text.

CHAPTER 15

JAVA CASE STUDY:
AN ADVENTURE GAME

15.1   Introduction

In this book, we have covered many features of the Java language, and many data structures and algorithms. In most cases, relatively small example programs have been given to illustrate the concepts involved. However, the true value of many of the features in this book can only be realized when they are used in a larger program.

An 'industrial-strength' program would be far too large for a book of this size and scope, but in this chapter we will present a Java program that contains more than just a few classes, and illustrates how many of the data structures and algorithms may be used together.

Most readers will probably have played a computer adventure game at some point. The idea behind an adventure game is that player takes on the role of a fictional character who explores a series of rooms or locations on a map. Within each room may be found various items such as food, weapons, or treasure, which the player may pick up and carry. The character may also encounter other creatures which are usually unfriendly, and will attack the character.

The objective of an adventure game is to explore the various locations, killing monsters and collecting treasure, and ultimately overcome some 'final obstacle' or solve some puzzle. An adventure game is the computer version of the popular role-playing game, in which one person plays the role of gamesmaster (he or she designs the adventure by drawing the map and populating the locations with monsters and collectible objects). The other players each take the role of a fictional character, and together these characters explore the map created by the gamesmaster.

In a computer version of a role-playing game, the computer takes on the job of gamesmaster, and the user guides the character through the map contained within the computer program. Therefore, it is up to the computer to respond to commands entered by the user.

Early adventure games were entirely text-based. The user would type in some simple command such as 'go east' or 'attack dragon'. If the command was understandable to the computer, it would process the command and print a reply. More modern adventure games (many are available for almost any make of computer) contain exotic graphical interfaces, usually involving animation and sound. Since our main goal in this chapter is to produce a Java program that illustrates the use of the various data structures we have studied, we won't be quite that ambitious, but with a bit of imagination, you should be able to extend the program in this chapter in many ways.

For any program larger that a page or two, it is always a good idea to do some advance planning and design before plunging into the coding. In fact, the field of software engineering is largely devoted to the design of the overall structure of a software project, and there are many formal methods that may be used. We are not assuming the reader to be familiar with any formal method, so the design for the adventure game presented in this chapter will be a bit more relaxed.

There are four main stages to the development of large object-oriented software package. They are:

1   Requirements specification. This is primarily a textual description of what the software is to do. The description should be given in detail, so that the program's behavior in all cases is spelt out.

2   Object-oriented design. At this stage, the structure and relationship of the various classes to be used are decided.

3   Coding. The code for the classes and definitions for all the methods are written.

4   Testing. Sufficient input data to test all the different paths through the program should be given. Testing should proceed in parallel with coding – after each method or logical block of code is written, it should be tested as far as possible.

Requirements specification   15.2

The general idea behind an adventure game was sketched out in the last section, but here we need to give a more detailed description of the game to be written in this chapter.

A good adventure game is based on a motivating story, and will require that the player collects items, solves puzzles, and defeats opponents in some connected fashion in order to reach the ultimate goal. Putting this amount of detail in the program, however, would detract from our main goal of illustrating how the various data structures and algorithms we have discussed in this book may be used together in a larger program. Therefore, we will develop the game to the point where it contains the functionality required for the basic operations of an adventure game, such as drawing and populating the map, moving from one location to another, picking up and dropping objects, fighting opponents, and so on. The requirements specification follows.

The map   The floor plan of the game will consist of a set of rooms. The rooms will be laid out on a rectangular grid, and each room may connect to any number of its four neighbors by means of a door in the corresponding wall. Each room will have a description which is printed each time the player enters, and may contain any number of items (see the description of items below) with which the player may interact.

Creatures   There must be a provision to include 'creatures' or 'monsters' in one or more rooms. A creature cannot move out of the room in which it is placed. Each creature has a number of 'hit points', which are reduced whenever the creature is successfully attacked. When the the number of hit points is reduced to (or below) zero, the creature is dead. When a creature successfully attacks the player's character, it causes an amount of damage (measured in hit points) which is chosen randomly from a range between a given minimum and maximum. A particular creature is allowed a certain number of attacks for each 'round' in a combat. Each creature also has an 'armour rating' which is a measure of how hard it is to hit, and is used in determining whether or not an attack on the creature is successful.

The player's character   The player will control a character which is guided around the map. The player's character has all the properties of a creature, but in addition, it can move between rooms, can wield a weapon, and can carry a pack in which items found in rooms can be placed. There is a maximum weight which the character can carry. The character attacks creatures in the same way as a creature attacks the character, except that the amount of damage done depends on the weapon being wielded by the character.

Items   An 'item' is something which is either found in a room, or is initially in the player's pack. Items can be picked up by the character (if doing so does not exceed the character's weight limit), carried to different locations, and dropped. Some items are specialized types (for example, weapons) which can be used for specific purposes once the character has picked them up. A basic item, which is not of any specialized type, has only a description and a weight. Other specialized types can add other properties. For example, a weapon has minimum and maximum damage values in addition to its description and weight.

For the purposes of this chapter, we will include only the weapon as a specialized item type, and leave the addition of other types as exercises for the reader.

Game play and interface   The Java interface should consist of a single-line text area into which the user types commands, a multiline text area in which the computer prints responses to commands, and a canvas area in which a map of the floor plan is drawn as the character explores the rooms. Commands will be simple phrases consisting of only one or two words.

In addition, there should be an 'undo' feature which allows the user to back up, undoing the effects of all commands that actually caused any change in the game's configuration. There should be an 'Undo' button in the applet.

Commands   The general format of a command is [verb] or [verb] [noun], where [verb] means that some action verb (such as 'take', 'attack', etc.) is entered, and [noun] is the name of some object. A complete command may be something like 'take sword'. Certain special words may be entered as commands. For example, the four cardinal directions (north, east, west, south) should be interpreted as commands to move in that direction, and the word 'inventory' should bring up a list of items being carried by the character.

In order to provide intelligent error messages when the user types an incorrect or meaningless command, we will classify the verbs into two types: transitive and intransitive. For those readers whose English grammar may not be fresh in their minds, we remind you that a *transitive verb* is a verb that requires an object on which to act, while an *intransitive verb* may stand on its own, without an associated object. For example, 'take' is a transitive verb in this game, since the object which is to be taken must also be specified. The command 'look' is treated as an

Object-oriented design 373

intransitive verb, since it always provides a description of the current room. We will stretch the meaning of the term 'verb' somewhat here by classifying any one-word command as an intransitive verb. Such words as 'inventory' and the four cardinal directions are, therefore, taken as intransitive verbs, since they are valid commands when given on their own.

Given this classification, we can then incorporate some error checking when we read the command from the user. For example, we can check for an unaccompanied transitive verb and ask for an associated object. The command 'take', on its own, would then produce the response: 'What do you want to take?'. Similarly, an intransitive verb followed by another word could produce an error message that is tailored to the type of grammatical error the user has made, rather than producing a generic error message such as 'I don't understand.'.

Combat   The combat system used in the game is borrowed from that used in several popular role-playing games. In a non-computer version of a role-playing game, the player wishing to make an attack specifies which weapon is being used, and then rolls some dice. The score obtained on the dice is compared with a table which indicates whether or not the attack succeeded in hitting the opponent. This success may depend on many factors, such as the armour being worn by the opponent, the dexterity of the attacker and the opponent (that is, how likely it is that the opponent will be able to dodge the attack), and so on. If the attack hits the opponent, more dice are rolled to determine the amount of damage done. The opponent subtracts the damage from its hit point total, and then attacks back in the same fashion.

To keep things simple, we will consider only the armour worn by the opponent in working out the success of an attack. It is fairly easy to work in other modifiers if so desired. The 'dice' rolled by the computer will give an integer in the range 0 through 100 (inclusive). This number is then compared with a 'base chance' of hitting the opponent, modified by adding on the armour rating of the opponent. For example, if the base chance of hitting is set at 25% (meaning that any attack has at least a 25% chance of hitting), and the opponent's armour rating is 15, the attacker must generate a value that is greater than $25 + 15 = 40$ in order to score a hit. Obviously, the higher the opponent's armour rating, the harder it is for the attacker to score a hit.

If a hit is scored, the amount of damage done is determined by 'rolling' another random number, this time determined by the type of weapon being used. This number is then deducted from the opponent's hit point total.

Object-oriented design   15.3

15.3.1 PRODUCING A DESIGN

As we mentioned in Chapter 1, object-oriented design is an important stage in the development of any programming project, particularly a larger one. There are many professional packages called CASE (for Computer-Assisted Software Engineering) tools which help the programmer design projects on-screen, but these methods require an understanding of one or more underlying object-oriented design methods. These methods are typically not studied until the later years of a university computing degree, usually in a course on software engineering, so we will not assume that the user has any knowledge of them here.

Many books on software engineering (or at least the honest ones) will admit that, no matter how sophisticated your design method or how user-friendly your CASE tool, the actual process of design ultimately comes down to listing all the things you want your program to contain, and all the actions the program is to perform, and then trying to organize these lists into a logically consistent set of classes. This invariably involves some (usually a lot of) trial and error. The design methods and CASE tools are helpful primarily in checking a design for inconsistencies after the basic design has taken shape on paper or in the programmer's head.

Since the study of object-oriented design is a book-length topic in itself, we will not attempt to produce a rigorously tested and professionally designed structure for the adventure game. Even without these techniques, however, it is still possible to produce a design that is logically consistent and easy to use, which is hopefully what we have managed to do. The reader is urged to think carefully about how we have organized the data fields and methods into the various classes. Ask yourself if you would have done it the same way, or if you can find a more efficient way of defining the class structure.

15.3.2 DESIGN DIAGRAMS

There are two main types of relationships that exist in our design for the adventure game. The first is a 'contains' relationship, in which a class contains one or more instances of other classes. For example, the `Dungeon` class contains a `Player` object representing the adventurer, a `Map` object representing the floor plan of the dungeon, and so on.

The second relationship is the 'type of' relationship that is implemented by inheritance. For example, the `Weapon` class inherits the `Item` class because a weapon is a 'type of' item – it shares all the properties of an item, but requires some new properties of its own.

Professional object-oriented design methods have specialized types of notation to indicate these types of relationships (and many other types as well). To keep things simple here, we will use two different diagrams to show the two types of relationships used in this program.

We will consider first a diagram showing which classes contain instances of other classes. The top layer of this diagram is shown in Fig. 15.1. The purpose of each of these classes is as follows:

- `Dungeon` – The `Dungeon` class is the main class of the game. It extends the `Applet` class from `java.awt`, and so contains initialization routines that are called when the applet is loaded into a browser. The class also serves as a

Figure 15.1.

central communication point through which other classes pass each other messages. We will see more of this when we consider the code below. For now, it will suffice to say that the `DisplayPanel`, `Map`, and `Player` classes are able to access the public methods of the `Dungeon` class in order to pass messages between themselves.

- `DisplayPanel` – The `DisplayPanel` class extends the `Panel` class from `java.awt`. It provides a base on which all the graphical components are laid out.
- `Map` – The `Map` class contains a description of the floor plan in the dungeon. The rooms and their interconnections are defined here.
- `Player` – The `Player` class defines the adventurer controlled by the user.
- `StringStack` – The `StringStack` class contains a stack in which each element is a Java `String`. The stack is used to store each command entered by the user so that the user can undo commands, thus allowing the game to backup and restart from an earlier point.
- `WordList` – A `WordList` is a hash table in which a set of `String`s is stored. Each `String` represents a word that is recognized by the game as part of a command. The `Dungeon` class contains three `WordList`s: one for transitive verbs, one for intransitive verbs, and one for nouns. The type of each word in a command is checked in the `WordList`s to determine if the command is a valid command.

We now consider the second layer in Fig. 15.1 and expand each class to show what classes it uses. The `DisplayPanel` class is shown in Fig. 15.2.

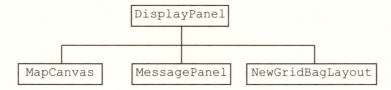

Figure 15.2.

- `MapCanvas` – The `MapCanvas` class extends the `Canvas` class of `java.awt`. It is used to draw a map of the floor plan as the adventurer explores the dungeon. `MapCanvas` makes use of an auxiliary class called `Arrow` which defines a straight line with an arrowhead on one end. `Arrow` objects are used to indicate passageways between rooms on the map.

- MessagePanel – The MessagePanel class extends the Panel class of java.awt. It is used to display components such as text areas and push buttons by which the user inputs commands and reads the responses from the program. A MessagePanel receives an image of the Dungeon object so that it has access to the public methods in Dungeon, and can use these methods to communicate the effects of commands to the other classes.

- NewGridBagLayout – This class provides a simplified interface to the GridBagLayout class in java.awt. NewGridBagLayout contains an instance of GridBagConstraints, and manages this object internally, rather than requiring the programmer to specify constraints separately from the layout manager.

The Map class expands as shown in Fig. 15.3.

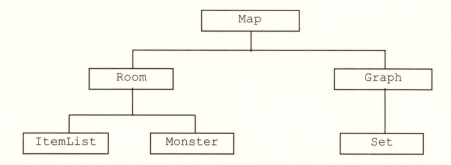

Figure 15.3.

- Room – Describes one of the rooms in the dungeon. The description includes a list of Items contained in the room (held in a linked list, defined in the ItemList class), and possibly a Monster, which is a creature that will attack the adventurer.

- Graph – This Graph class is a modification of the Graph class developed in Chapter 14, which allows Dijkstra's algorithm to be used to find the shortest path between two rooms. As in Chapter 14, Dijkstra's algorithm uses a Set in its calculations.

The Player class expands as shown in Fig. 15.4.

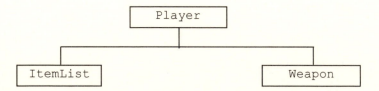

Figure 15.4.

- `ItemList` – The `Player` is carrying some items which are held in a linked list of `Items`, represented by the `ItemList` class. This is the same class as that used to hold the contents of a `Room`.
- `Weapon` – A `Weapon` is a special type of `Item` with added data fields representing such things as the amount of damage caused.

The `StringStack` and `WordList` classes are slightly modified forms of the stack and hash table data structures treated earlier in the book. They do not contain instances of any other user-defined classes.

As implied by the discussion of the diagrams above, some of the classes are related through inheritance. Some classes extend classes defined in `java.awt`, such as `Canvas` and `Panel`. However, there are two cases where inheritance has been used to define special cases of user-defined classes. These are shown in Fig. 15.5.

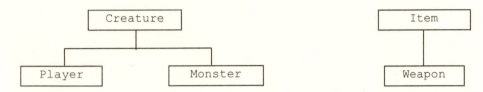

Figure 15.5.

The `Player` and `Monster` classes are 'types-of' `Creature`, in that they share many attributes, so an inheritance relationship is appropriate here. In the game itself, there are no instances of the base `Creature` class.

In the case of the `Item` class, most of the items found in rooms or carried by the adventurer are instances of the base class. Only the `Weapon` carried by the `Player` is an instance of the derived class. In an expanded game, there could be many other specialized item types, such as magic items, food, poison, and so on.

A full design specification would now expand each class and define the data fields and methods within it. We will, however, proceed directly to the coding.

Coding   15.4

15.4.1 INTRODUCTION

We will present and discuss the code for the adventure game in a top-down fashion, presenting the classes in the same order as that in which they were discussed in the previous section.

15.4.2 THE Dungeon CLASS

The `Dungeon` class is the central class of the entire application, and serves as a nerve center which controls and coordinates all the other objects in the game. As such, many of the data fields and methods in Dungeon cannot be fully understood without reference to the other classes which follow.

The declarations in Dungeon are as shown:

```
import java.applet.Applet;
import java.awt.*;

public class Dungeon extends Applet {
   static final int ROOMS = 4;
   static final int MAXROOMITEMS = 50;
   static final int MAXBACKUPSTEPS = 100;
   static final int PANELWIDTH = 500;
   static final int PANELHEIGHT = 500;
   private DisplayPanel mainPanel =
      new DisplayPanel(this, PANELWIDTH, PANELHEIGHT);
   private Map dungeonPlan = new Map(this, ROOMS);
   private Player character = new Player(this, "Frodo",
      10, 0, 1, 4, 10, 100);
   private StringStack backupStack =
      new StringStack(MAXBACKUPSTEPS);
   private WordList TransVerbs = new WordList(100);
   private WordList IntransVerbs = new WordList(100);
   private WordList Nouns = new WordList(100);
   private String[] TransVerbWords = {"take", "drop",
      "wield", "unwield"};
   private String[] IntransVerbWords = {"attack",
      "inventory", "look", "north", "east", "west",
      "south"};
   private String[] NounWords = {"scroll", "bottle",
      "sword", "book", "chair", "lamp", "bed",
      "clock", "bedpan", "stove", "knife", "dragon"};
```

The class constants are used to define the number of rooms to be created (ROOMS), the maximum number of items that can be stored in each room (MAX-ROOMITEMS), the maximum number of actions that can be stored on the stack used to 'undo' user commands (MAXBACKUPSTEPS), and the dimensions of the panel used to display the map (PANELWIDTH and PANELHEIGHT).

Following this, the main objects of the game are declared and initialized by calling the corresponding constructors. We will examine the code for each of these classes in detail below.

The three String arrays are used to hold the lists of recognized words; lists of intransitive verbs, transitive verbs, and nouns are defined.

Since the Dungeon class defines the applet which is loaded and run by the browser, the init() method initializes the game:

```
public void init()
{
```

```
    int word;

    try {
      for (word = 0; word < TransVerbWords.length;
        ++word)
        TransVerbs.Store(TransVerbWords[word]);
      for (word = 0; word < IntransVerbWords.length;
        ++word)
        IntransVerbs.Store(IntransVerbWords[word]);
      for (word = 0; word < NounWords.length; ++word)
        Nouns.Store(NounWords[word]);
    } catch (WordListException e);
    add(mainPanel);
    addRoomsToMap();
    drawMap();
  }
```

The three word lists are loaded into their hash tables (see the description of the `WordList` class below). Then the `mainPanel` is added to the layout of the `Dungeon` applet – since it is the only graphical object to be added, we do not specify any fancy layout manager; we just use the default `FlowLayout`.

Then the class methods `addRoomsToMap()` and `drawMap()` are called to construct the floor plan and draw the initial room in the display panel. The `addRoomsToMap()` method is as follows:

```
private void addRoomsToMap()
{
    // Main hall - starting point
  Room mainHall = new Room("Main hall.", 36,
    PANELHEIGHT-116);
  mainHall.addItem(new Item("scroll", 1));
  mainHall.addItem(new Item("bottle", 5));
  mainHall.addItem(new Weapon("sword", 10, 1, 8));
  mainHall.setDoors(2, 1, -1, -1);
  mainHall.setVisited(true);

    // Library
  Room library = new Room("Library.", 152,
    PANELHEIGHT-116);
  library.addItem(new Item("book", 5));
  library.addItem(new Item("chair", 50));
  library.addItem(new Item("lamp", 20));
  library.setDoors(3, -1, 0, -1);

    // Bedroom
  Monster dragon = new Monster(this, "dragon",
    10, 25, 1, 5, 1, "Big, red, and scaly.");
  Room bedroom = new Room("Bedroom.", 36,
```

```
          PANELHEIGHT-232, dragon);
    bedroom.addItem(new Item("bed", 100));
    bedroom.addItem(new Item("clock", 34));
    bedroom.addItem(new Item("bedpan", 4));
    bedroom.setDoors(-1, 3, -1, 0);

        // Kitchen
    Room kitchen = new Room("Kitchen.", 152,
        PANELHEIGHT-232);
    kitchen.addItem(new Item("stove", 200));
    kitchen.addItem(new Item("knife", 2));
    kitchen.setDoors(-1, -1, 2, 1);

    // Add rooms to map
    try {
        dungeonPlan.addRoom(mainHall, 0);
        dungeonPlan.addRoom(library, 1);
        dungeonPlan.addRoom(bedroom, 2);
        dungeonPlan.addRoom(kitchen, 3);

          // Add corridors
        dungeonPlan.addCorridor(0, 1, 10);
        dungeonPlan.addCorridor(1, 0, 5);
        dungeonPlan.addCorridor(2, 0, 5);
        dungeonPlan.addCorridor(0, 2, 1);
        dungeonPlan.addCorridor(2, 3, 1);
        dungeonPlan.addCorridor(3, 2, 5);
        dungeonPlan.addCorridor(1, 3, 5);
        dungeonPlan.addCorridor(3, 1, 5);
    } catch (MapException e);
}
```

Each of the four rooms is created, some `Items` are added to it, and its doors are defined. The map size defined here allows up to 16 rooms to be drawn, but in the interest of clarity, we have only included 4 rooms in the present game. In the case of the main hall, we also set its 'visited' attribute to `true`. Only those rooms that have been visited by the player are drawn on the map. Consult the descriptions of the `Room` and `Item` classes below for details of how their attributes are used.

After the `Rooms` have been defined and stocked with `Items`, we add them, and the corridors connecting them, to `dungeonPlan`, which is the master map of the dungeon. Consult the `Map` class for details.

Once `dungeonPlan` has been fully specified, we draw it into the applet using the `drawMap()` method:

```
private void drawMap()
{
    Room mapRoom = new Room();
```

```
    for (int roomNum = 0; roomNum < ROOMS; ++roomNum) {
      if ((mapRoom =
        dungeonPlan.getRoom(roomNum)).getVisited())
        mainPanel.drawRoom(mapRoom);
    }
  }
```

We loop through all the Rooms and for each, if it has been visited, we call the drawRoom() method of the DisplayPanel class (of which mainPanel is an instance) to draw the room onto the map. Note that we make use of public interface functions for all operations – in no case do we access any data fields of other classes directly.

Apart from setting up the main objects in the game and initializing the floor plan and map, the main function of the Dungeon class is to interpret commands entered by the user, and call appropriate methods to process these commands. Since most commands require reading and/or changing data in one or more of the objects in the game, the methods that process commands necessarily rely on the structures of these other objects. We will describe the other classes in full below; for now the reader should be able to see how the lines of control are handled inside the Dungeon class.

The user will type a command into a text area inside a MessagePanel object, which is contained with the mainPanel object within Dungeon. When the user presses the 'enter' key after typing a command, the text is read by methods within MessagePanel, and the resulting String is passed to the doCommand() method within the Dungeon class. The doCommand() method calls checkCommand() to see if the command is a valid command (that is, that it satisfies the conditions of being grammatically correct, and contains only words contained in the word lists defined earlier). If the command is valid, a specialized method which deals with that particular command is called to process the command. Once the command is processed, the applet waits for more input from the user.

The doCommand() method is as follows:

```
public void doCommand(String[] command,
  boolean backup)
{
  String message = new String();
  Monster monster = null;
  boolean monsterFirst = false;

  if (character.getDead()) {
    if (command[0].equals("yes")) {
      message = doResurrect();
      setMessage(message);
      return;
    } else {
      setMessage("You are dead.\nDo you want another
        game?\n");
```

```
            return;
        }
    }

    if (!backup) {
        monster = dungeonPlan.getRoom(character.
            getLocation()).getMonster();
        if (monster != null && !monster.getDead()) {
            int monsterInitiative =
                (int)(Math.random() * 100);
            int playerInitiative =
                (int)(Math.random() * 100);
            monsterFirst =
                (playerInitiative < monsterInitiative);
            if (monsterFirst) {
                message += doMonsterAttack(monster);
                if (character.getDead()) {
                    message += "You are dead.\nPlay again?";
                    setMessage(message);
                    return;
                }
            }
        }
    }

    if (!backup && !checkCommand(command))
        return;
    if (command[0].equals("inventory"))
        setMessage(message += character.inventory() +
            "\n");
    else if (command[0].equals("look"))
        setMessage(message += dungeonPlan.getRoom(
            character.getLocation()).getDescription());
    else if (command[0].equals("take"))
        setMessage(message += doTake(command, backup));
    else if (command[0].equals("drop"))
        setMessage(message += doDrop(command, backup));
    else if (command[0].equals("north") ||
        command[0].equals("east") ||
        command[0].equals("west") ||
        command[0].equals("south"))
        setMessage(message += doMove(command, backup));
    else if (command[0].equals("path"))
        setMessage(message += doPath(command));
    else if (command[0].equals("wield"))
        setMessage(message += doWield(command, backup));
    else if (command[0].equals("unwield"))
        setMessage(message += doUnwield(backup));
    else if (command[0].equals("attack"))
```

```
        setMessage(message += doAttack(command));
    else if (command[0].equals("restore") && backup)
        setMessage(doRestore(command));
    else if (command[0].equals("heal") && backup)
        setMessage(doHeal(command));
    else if (command[0].equals("status"))
        setMessage(doStatus());
    else
        setMessage("Unrecognized command.");

    if (!backup) {
        if (!monsterFirst) {
            setMessage(message + doMonsterAttack(monster));
            if (character.getDead()) {
                message += "You are dead.\nPlay again?";
                setMessage(message);
                return;
            }
        }
    }
}
```

The doCommand() method accepts as arguments an array of Strings called command, and a boolean parameter called backup. The command array contains the command typed by the user, with each element of the array comprising one word from the command. The backup parameter is true if the doCommand() method is being called as a result of the user pushing the 'Back up' button, which means that the last move is to be undone.

Apart from processing the user's command, the doCommand() method must also handle death of the adventurer and involuntary combat, if appropriate. If the adventurer is in a room containing a monster, the monster will attack the player no matter what the player does, so the first section of doCommand() handles this situation.

The first if block calls the getDead() method of the Player class (inherited from the Creature class). If the character is currently dead, and the user has typed the command 'yes' in response to being asked if they wish another game, the doResurrect() method is called to bring the player back to full health and start a new adventure. The doResurrect() method, like most methods in the Dungeon class, returns a String which is a message that is to be displayed in the descriptionArea of the MessagePanel. The setMessage() method sets the text in descriptionArea. Any other command entered when the adventurer is dead will simply result in the 'You are dead. Do you want another game?' reply.

If the character is still alive, the next thing that is checked is the backup flag. Monster attacks are only done if the user is not undoing a previous move. The monster in the current room is retrieved by using a combination of 'get' type methods: the getLocation() method of the Player class is used to find the current location of the character, then the getRoom( ) method of the Map class finds the corresponding Room object. The getMonster( ) method of the Room class returns the Monster object in that room, or null if there is no monster in the room.

If the monster exists and is still alive, a round of combat is performed. First, the *initiatives* of the monster and player must be found. A random integer between 0 and 100 is generated for the player, and another for the monster. Whichever has the smaller number gets the chance to attack first. (Of course, if the user's command is not 'attack', the character doesn't get to attack at all, but the initiative determines whether the monster's attack comes before or after the user's command is processed.)

If the monster wins the initiative, the doMonsterAttack( ) method does the attack and returns a message saying what the result was. The attack may have killed the player, so a check for this is made, and if the player has died, the turn ends before the user's command is processed.

If the character survives the combat, the user's command can be processed. If this isn't a 'back up' command, and the checkCommand( ) method verifies the command as legal, a lengthy set of if..else statements processes all legal commands. These statements should be fairly obvious – we will consider the methods for processing each command separately later.

Finally, if the monster did not win initiative for combat, it now gets its chance to attack after the user's command has been processed.

We now consider the checkCommand( ) method. The code is as follows:

```
private boolean checkCommand(String[] command)
{
    String message = new String();

    if (IntransVerbs.Retrieve(command[0]) != null)
    {
        if (command[1] != null)
        {
            message = "The " + command[0] +
                " command should be a single word.";
            setMessage(message);
            return false;
        } else {
            return true;
        }
    } else if (TransVerbs.Retrieve(command[0]) != null)
    {
        if (command[1] == null)
        {
            message = "What do you want to " +
                command[0] + "?";
            setMessage(message);
            return false;
```

```
        } else if (command[2] != null) {
          message = "Too many words for a " + command[0]
            + " command.";
          setMessage(message);
          return false;
        } else if (Nouns.Retrieve(command[1]) == null) {
          message = "You can't " + command[0] + " that!";
          setMessage(message);
          return false;
        } else {
          return true;
        }
      } else if (Nouns.Retrieve(command[0]) != null)
      {
        message = "What about the " + command[0] + "?";
        setMessage(message);
        return false;
      } else {
        setMessage("I don't understand what you mean.");
        return false;
      }
    }
```

Recall that we have sorted the acceptable commands into two groups: a command of a single word from the intransitive verb list, and a command of two words, the first being from the transitive verb list and the second from the noun list. This method checks that the command is of one of these two types. (Clearly, if the reader wished to expand the number of command types that are accepted it would be fairly easy to do at this point. For example, a command of the type 'give food to dragon' would be of the type <transitive verb> <noun> 'to' <noun>.)

The IntransVerbs word list is checked first. If the first word in the command array (command[0]) is in that list, then the second word in the command array must be null, since intransitive verb commands must consist of a single word.

Otherwise, we test the first word to see if it is a transitive verb. If it is, but there is no second word, we print the message 'What do you want to ...' followed by the verb. If there are more than two words in the command, we print another error message. Finally, if the second word isn't in the Nouns word list, we print the message 'You can't <verb> that!'

If the first word is a noun, we print the message 'What about the <noun>?' Finally, if the user has entered a word that is not in any of the word lists, we print 'I don't understand what you mean.'

We now consider the individual methods for handling specific commands. The 'take' command is handled by doTake():

```
private String doTake(String[] takeCommand,
    boolean backup)
```

```
{
    String message = new String();
    Item takeItem = dungeonPlan.getRoom(character.
        getLocation()).contains(takeCommand[1]);
    if (takeItem != null) {
        if (character.addItem(takeItem)) {
            dungeonPlan.getRoom(character.getLocation()).
                removeItem(takeItem);
            message = "You take the " + takeCommand[1]
                + ".";
            if (!backup)
                try
                    backupStack.Push("drop " + takeCommand[1]);
                catch (StackException e);
        } else
            message = "You cannot carry the " +
                takeCommand[1] + ".";
    } else
        message = "There is no " + takeCommand[1] +
            " here.";
    return message + "\n";
}
```

The `doTake()` method begins by declaring an `Item` and then accessing the current `Room` object to see if the room contains the requested object. If `takeItem` isn't `null`, the `addItem()` method of the `Player` class is called in an attempt to add the item to the character's inventory. This method may return `false` if the character cannot carry the item (due to weight restrictions, for example). If the character can carry it, the item is removed from the current `Room` and the message 'You take the <noun>.' is printed. If this 'take' command is *not* being processed as a result of a 'back up' request, the opposite command must be pushed onto the `backupStack`. The opposite of a 'take' is a 'drop', so the corresponding 'drop' command is pushed onto the stack.

If the requested item is not present in the room, the message 'There is no <noun> here.' is printed. Note that we need not check if the second word exists, nor if it is a recognized noun, since the `doTake()` method would never have been called if the `checkCommand()` method hadn't approved the command.

The `doDrop()` method processes the 'drop' command:

```
private String doDrop(String[] dropCommand,
    boolean backup)
{
    String message = new String();
    Item dropItem =
        character.isCarrying(dropCommand[1]);
    if (dropItem != null) {
        character.removeItem(dropItem);
```

```
            dungeonPlan.getRoom(character.getLocation()).
              addItem(dropItem);
          message = "You drop the " + dropCommand[1] + ".";
          if (character.getWielded() != null &&
             character.getWielded().getDescription().
                equals(dropItem.getDescription())) {
             character.unwieldWeapon();
             message += " You are now empty-handed.";
             if (!backup)
               try
                 backupStack.Push("wield " +
                   dropCommand[1]);
               catch (StackException e);
          }
          if (!backup)
             try
               backupStack.Push("take " + dropCommand[1]);
             catch (StackException e);
       } else
          message = "You are not carrying a " +
             dropCommand[1] + ".";
       return message + "\n";
   }
```

This method is more or less the reverse of the doTake() method, so most of its statements should be fairly obvious. The character's inventory is checked to see if the character is carrying the item. If so, it is removed from the character's inventory and added to the inventory of the current Room. A check must also be made to see if the dropped item was a wielded weapon, in which case the attack status of the character must be changed. If the command is not a 'back up' command, appropriate commands are pushed onto the stack.

Wielding and unwielding a weapon are handled by the doWield() and doUnwield() methods:

```
   private String doWield(String[] command,
     boolean backup)
   {
     if (character.wieldWeapon(command[1])) {
       try
         backupStack.Push("unwield");
       catch (StackException e);
       return "You are now wielding the " +
         command[1] + ".\n";
     }
     else
       return "You are not carrying a " +
         command[1] + ".\n";
   }
```

```
private String doUnwield(boolean backup)
{
   if (character.unwieldWeapon()) {
      try
         backupStack.Push("wield " +
            character.getWielded().getDescription());
      catch (StackException e);
      return "You are now empty-handed.\n";
   } else
      return "You are not wielding a weapon.\n";
}
```

In doWield(), the wieldWeapon() method of the Player class is called to attempt to wield the object specified by the second command word. Similarly, the doUnwield() method calls the unwieldWeapon() method of the Player class.

Combat is handled by two methods: one for attacks by monsters and one for attacks by the character. The character's attacks are implemented using the doAttack() method:

```
private String doAttack(String[] command)
{
   Monster monster = dungeonPlan.getRoom(
      character.getLocation()).getMonster();
   if (monster == null || monster.getDead())
      return "There is nothing here to attack.\n";

   int attackRoll = (int)(Math.random() * 100);
   if (!Attack.doHit(attackRoll, monster.getArmour()))
      return "You missed.\n";
   int damageRoll = (int)(Math.random() *
      (character.getMaxDamage() -
      character.getMinDamage() + 1) +
      character.getMinDamage());
   String message = "You do " + damageRoll +
      (damageRoll == 1 ? " point" : " points") +
      " of damage.\n";
   monster.adjustHitpoints(-damageRoll);
   String pushCommand = new String("restore " +
      Integer.toString(character.getLocation()) + " "
      + Integer.toString(damageRoll));
   try
      backupStack.Push(pushCommand);
   catch (StackException e);
   if (monster.getDead())
      message += "The " + monster.getName() +
         " is dead.\n";
   return message;
}
```

First, the current `Room` is checked to see if there is a monster present and, if so, if it is still alive. If so, a random `int` between 0 and 100 is generated. The `doHit()` method of the `Attack` class (considered below) is called, being passed the `attackRoll` and the monster's armour rating. The `doHit()` method returns `true` if a hit was scored; otherwise it returns `false` and the `doAttack()` method returns.

If a hit was scored by the character, a random amount of damage, constrained by the minimum and maximum damage values of which the character is capable, is determined. The damage is subtracted from the monster's hit point total by calling the `adjustHitPoints()` method.

To permit backing up over an attack, a 'restore' command is constructed and pushed onto the stack. The present version of the game allows only a single monster in each room, so the restore command specifies the room number and the number of hit points to restore. More involved versions of the game may allow more than one monster per room; in such a case, a different method for restoring hit points would need to be specified.

Finally, a check is made to see if the monster has been killed by the character's attack.

The `Attack` class is a special class which contains the `static  doHit()` method:

```
class Attack
{
    static final int BASEHITCHANCE = 25;

    static public boolean doHit(int attackRoll,
        int armour)
    {
        return (attackRoll > BASEHITCHANCE + armour);
    }
}
```

The BASEHITCHANCE value is the base percentage chance that any attack will hit. The `doHit()` method determines whether a specific attack hits by comparing the `attackRoll` with the base chance, adjusted for the effect of armour worn by the defender. In more complex combat systems, other effects may be taken into account by overloaded versions of the `doHit()` method, allowing for such things as magical weapons and/or armour, effects of injuries or enhanced abilities, and so on.

The methods for handling attacks could have been included in the `Creature` class or its descendents, but combat is, in many ways, an independent concept, so it makes some sense to create a separate class for handling it. The idea here is similar to that of the `Math` class in `java.lang`, which consists primarily of `static` methods for calculating the common mathematical functions such as exponentials, logarithms, and trigonometric functions. The `Attack` class can be generalized to handle 'combat' between the character and inanimate objects. For example, the character may attempt to break down a door: the door may be given an 'armour' value and a fixed number of hit points, and the character can then attempt to break the door by 'attacking' it. The door breaks when its hit point total is reduced to zero.

The monster's attack is handled by `doMonsterAttack()`:

```
private String doMonsterAttack(Monster monster)
{
    String monsterName = monster.getName();
    int attackRoll = (int)(Math.random() * 100);
    if (!Attack.doHit(attackRoll,
        character.getArmour()))
    {
        return "The " + monsterName +
            " attacks you, but misses.\n";
    }
    int damageRoll = (int)(Math.random() *
        (monster.getMaxDamage() - monster.getMinDamage()
        + 1) + monster.getMinDamage());
    String message = "The " + monsterName +
        " attacks you, and does " + damageRoll +
        (damageRoll == 1 ? " point" : " points") +
        " of damage.\n";
    character.adjustHitpoints(-damageRoll);
    String pushCommand = new String("heal " +
        Integer.toString(damageRoll));
    try
        backupStack.Push(pushCommand);
    catch (StackException e);
    return message;
}
```

The method works very similarly to `doAttack()`: an `attackRoll` is determined randomly, the `doHit()` method is used to see if a hit is scored, the amount of damage done is determined, and the character's hit points are adjusted. To reverse damage done to a character, the 'heal' command is used, so a 'heal' command is pushed onto the stack to be used if the player backs up through this attack.

The methods for restoring hit points to monsters and characters are as follows:

```
private String doRestore(String[] command)
{
    dungeonPlan.getRoom(Integer.parseInt(command[1])).
        getMonster().adjustHitpoints(Integer.parseInt
        (command[2]));
    return "The " + dungeonPlan.getRoom(
        Integer.parseInt(command[1])).
```

```
        getMonster().getName() +
        " retrieves " + command[2] + " hit " +
        (command[2].equals("1") ? "point.\n" :
        "points.\n");
    }

    private String doHeal(String[] command)
    {
        character.adjustHitpoints(
            Integer.parseInt(command[1]));
        return "You retrieve " + command[1] + " hit " +
            (command[1].equals("1") ? "point.\n" :
            "points.\n");
    }
```

Since `doRestore()` and `doHeal()` are meant to be called only as part of a back up command, and never in response to a command typed by the user, their command lines are not restricted to containing words from the lists of acceptable command words. In the case of `doRestore()`, the command must consist of the word 'restore', followed by the room number and the number of hit points to restore to the monster in that room. After this is done, a message stating how many hit points were to restored, and to which monster, is constructed and returned.

In the case of `doHeal()`, the character's hit points are adjusted, and a message is constructed and returned.

Note that, although at the moment these two methods are used only in response to a 'back up' command, they could easily be used to restore hit points for other reasons. For example, if a monster or characters eats food or drinks a healing potion, the number of hit points restored could be calculated and then one of these methods called to adjust the hit point value.

The ultimate restoration method is `doResurrect()`, which brings the character back from the dead:

```
    private String doResurrect()
    {
        if (!character.getDead())
            return "";
        character = new Player(this, "Wibble the Wizard",
            10, 0, 1, 4, 10, 100);
        backupStack = new StringStack(MAXBACKUPSTEPS);
        drawMap();
        return "Welcome back, " + character.getName() +
        ".\nYou have " + character.getHitpoints() +
        " hitpoints.\n";
    }
```

Note that the character is simply re-initialized, as is the backup stack. This means that anything the character was carrying is permanently lost, and all previous moves are erased from memory. If you feel this is a bit brutal, you could take steps to save the character's inventory before the resurrection.

In response to a 'status' command, the `doStatus()` method prints out the current state of the character:

```java
private String doStatus()
{
   String message = "Your name is ";
   message += character.getName();
   message += "\nYou currently have " +
      character.getHitpoints() + " hit points.";
   if (character.getWielded() == null)
      message += "\nYou are empty handed.";
   else
      message += "\nYou are wielding a " +
         character.getWielded().getDescription();
   return message;
}
```

The character's name, current hit point total, and wielded weapon (if any) are printed.

The `doMove()` method implements the directional commands 'north', 'east', 'west', and 'south':

```java
private String doMove(String[] moveCommand,
   boolean backup)
{
   int toRoom;

   String message = new String("You move ");
   if (moveCommand[0].equals("north") &&
      (toRoom = dungeonPlan.getRoom(character.
      getLocation()).getDoor(Room.NORTH)) != -1)
   {
      character.setLocation(toRoom);
      dungeonPlan.getRoom(toRoom).setVisited(true);
      drawMap();
      message += "north. " +
         dungeonPlan.getRoom(toRoom).getDescription();
      if (!backup)
         try
            backupStack.Push("south");
         catch (StackException e);
   }
   else if (moveCommand[0].equals("east") &&
      (toRoom = dungeonPlan.getRoom(character.
      getLocation()).getDoor(Room.EAST)) != -1)
   {
```

```
        character.setLocation(toRoom);
        dungeonPlan.getRoom(toRoom).setVisited(true);
        drawMap();
        message += "east. " +
            dungeonPlan.getRoom(toRoom).getDescription();
        if (!backup)
            try
                backupStack.Push("west");
            catch (StackException e);
    }
    else if (moveCommand[0].equals("west") &&
        (toRoom = dungeonPlan.getRoom(character.
        getLocation()).getDoor(Room.WEST)) != -1)
    {
        character.setLocation(toRoom);
        dungeonPlan.getRoom(toRoom).setVisited(true);
        drawMap();
        message += "west. " +
            dungeonPlan.getRoom(toRoom).getDescription();
        if (!backup)
            try
                backupStack.Push("east");
            catch (StackException e);
    }
    else if (moveCommand[0].equals("south") &&
        (toRoom = dungeonPlan.getRoom(character.
        getLocation()).getDoor(Room.SOUTH)) != -1)
    {
        character.setLocation(toRoom);
        dungeonPlan.getRoom(toRoom).setVisited(true);
        drawMap();
        message += "south. " +
            dungeonPlan.getRoom(toRoom).getDescription();
        if (!backup)
            try
                backupStack.Push("north");
            catch (StackException e);
    } else
        message = "You cannot move in that direction.";
    return message + "\n";
}
```

The four sections of this method all operate in the same way, so we will consider the command for moving north.

The `getDoor()` method of the Room class will return the number of the Room
to which a door in the specified direction leads, if such a door exists. If the door
does not exist, −1 is returned. Therefore, the first step is to determine if it is possible to move in the requested direction and, if so, to which room the move will

take the character. The room number is stored in the variable `toRoom`. If this value is not −1, the location of the character is set to the new room. The new room is also marked as 'visited' so that it will be shown when the map is redrawn by the `drawMap()` method. The new room's description is appended to the message to be displayed, and, if the command is not a 'back up' command, a move in the opposite direction is pushed onto the stack.

Finally, there are a few brief methods that are called by methods from other classes:

```
public boolean characterInRoom(Room currentRoom)
{
    return dungeonPlan.getRoom(character.getLocation())
        == currentRoom;
}

public String popBackupStack() throws StackException
{
    return backupStack.Pop();
}

public void setMessage(String message)
{
    mainPanel.setMessage(message);
}
```

As their names imply, these three methods respectively check if the character is in the room specified, pop an action off the backup stack, and set the message in the `MessagePanel`'s main display to the given message.

15.4.3 THE `DisplayPanel` CLASS

We now consider the class used as the base for displaying the applet in a browser. The applet appears as shown in Fig. 15.6.

The top portion of the applet shows a map of the floor plan, where each room is drawn only after the character has moved into it for the first time. The bottom section consists of two text areas and a push button. The top text area displays the computer's reply to commands entered by the user. The lower text area is where the user types in commands, and the push-button allows users to 'back up' or 'undo' previous moves.

The code for the `DisplayPanel` class is fairly brief:

```
class DisplayPanel extends Panel {
    private MapCanvas mapCanvas = new MapCanvas();
    private MessagePanel textPanel;

    private NewGridBagLayout layout =
        new NewGridBagLayout();
```

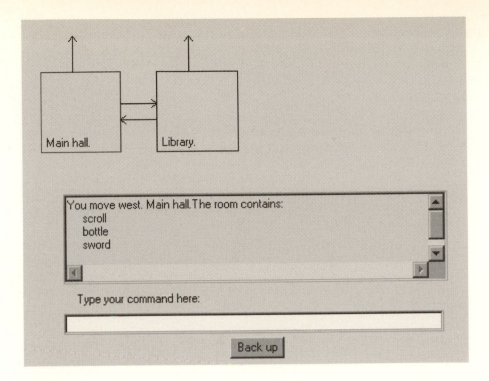

Figure 15.6.

```
private Dungeon parent;

DisplayPanel(Dungeon owner, int mapCanvasWidth,
   int mapCanvasHeight)
{
   parent = owner;
   textPanel = new MessagePanel(parent);
   mapCanvas.resize(mapCanvasWidth, mapCanvasHeight);
   mapCanvas.setBackground(Color.orange);
   setLayout(layout);
   layout.setRareConstraints(
      GridBagConstraints.CENTER,
      GridBagConstraints.NONE,
      new Insets(2,2,2,2), 0, 0, 1, 1);
   layout.setPositionSizeAdd(mapCanvas, this,
      0, 0, 1, 1);
   layout.setPositionSizeAdd(textPanel, this,
      0, 1, 1, 1);
}

public void setMessage(String message)
{
```

```
          textPanel.setDescriptionArea(message);
      }

      public void drawRoom(Room mapRoom)
      {
          boolean currentLocation =
             parent.characterInRoom(mapRoom);
          mapCanvas.setRoom(mapRoom, currentLocation);
          mapCanvas.paint(mapCanvas.getGraphics());
      }
  }
```

A `MapCanvas` and a `MessagePanel` object (each class will be considered below) are declared in which to hold the map and the text boxes for user input and computer response. The layout manager for the `DisplayPanel` is a `NewGridBagLayout`, considered in Chapter 3. A pointer to the `Dungeon` object that owns the `DisplayPanel` is provided, so that methods within a `DisplayPanel` can communicate with `Dungeon` methods and, in turn, with methods from other classes owned by `Dungeon`.

The constructor for `DisplayPanel` initializes the variables, sets the size and color of the `mapCanvas`, and defines the parameters for the layout manager. The `mapCanvas` and `textPanel` are then added to the layout.

The `setMessage()` method displays a message in the 'computer reply' text area in the `textPanel`, and the `drawRoom()` method redraws the specified room, taking account of a recent move of the character. The room currently occupied by the character is drawn in red, with all other rooms in black, so every time a character moves from one room to another, the two rooms concerned must be redrawn.

15.4.4 THE `MapCanvas` CLASS

The `MapCanvas` class is the canvas on which the map of the dungeon floor plan is drawn as the character explores the various rooms.

```
  class MapCanvas extends Canvas {
      static final int ROOMEDGE = 80;
      static final int ROOMGAP = 36;
      private int roomX, roomY;
      private String roomDescr;
      private Arrow[] door = new Arrow[4];
      private boolean characterHere;

      public void paint(Graphics canvasG)
      {
          if (characterHere)
              canvasG.setColor(Color.red);
          else
              canvasG.setColor(Color.black);
```

```
canvasG.drawRect(roomX, roomY, ROOMEDGE, ROOMEDGE);
canvasG.setColor(Color.black);
canvasG.drawString(roomDescr, roomX + 5, roomY +
    ROOMEDGE - 5);
for (int doorNum = 0; doorNum < 4; ++doorNum)
    if (door[doorNum] != null) {
        canvasG.drawLine(door[doorNum].Tail.x,
            door[doorNum].Tail.y,
            door[doorNum].Head.x, door[doorNum].Head.y);
        canvasG.drawLine(door[doorNum].Head.x,
            door[doorNum].Head.y,
            door[doorNum].Pointer1.x,
            door[doorNum].Pointer1.y);
        canvasG.drawLine(door[doorNum].Head.x,
            door[doorNum].Head.y,
            door[doorNum].Pointer2.x,
            door[doorNum].Pointer2.y);
    }
}

public void setRoom(Room mapRoom,
    boolean characterInRoom)
{
    roomX = mapRoom.getMapLocation().x;
    roomY = mapRoom.getMapLocation().y;
    roomDescr = mapRoom.getShortDescription();
    for (int doorNum = 0; doorNum < 4; ++doorNum)
        door[doorNum] = null;
    if (mapRoom.getDoor(Room.NORTH) != -1)
        door[Room.NORTH] =
            new Arrow(roomX + ROOMEDGE/2 - ROOMEDGE/10,
                roomY, roomX + ROOMEDGE/2 - ROOMEDGE/10,
                roomY - ROOMGAP);
    if (mapRoom.getDoor(Room.SOUTH) != -1)
        door[Room.SOUTH] =
            new Arrow(roomX + ROOMEDGE/2 + ROOMEDGE/10,
                roomY + ROOMEDGE,
                roomX + ROOMEDGE/2 + ROOMEDGE/10,
                roomY + ROOMEDGE + ROOMGAP);
    if (mapRoom.getDoor(Room.WEST) != -1)
        door[Room.WEST] =
            new Arrow(roomX, roomY + ROOMEDGE/2 +
                ROOMEDGE/10,
                roomX - ROOMGAP,
                roomY + ROOMEDGE/2 + ROOMEDGE/10);
    if (mapRoom.getDoor(Room.EAST) != -1)
        door[Room.EAST] =
            new Arrow(roomX + ROOMEDGE, roomY + ROOMEDGE/2
                - ROOMEDGE/10,
```

```
                                    roomX + ROOMEDGE + ROOMGAP,
                                    roomY + ROOMEDGE/2 - ROOMEDGE/10);

                    characterHere = characterInRoom;
            }
    }
```

The parameters ROOMEDGE and ROOMGAP specify the length of the sides within each room (rooms are squares), and the gap between adjacent rooms, both in pixels. A room is drawn with its upper-left corner at roomX, roomY, and contains a description given by the String roomDescr. If a room has a door in a particular direction, an arrow is drawn pointing away from the room in that direction. A special Arrow class (considered below) is used to construct these arrows. Finally, characterHere is a boolean flag that specifies if the character is currently in the room.

The MapCanvas class extends the Canvas class of the java.awt and, therefore, must provide its own version of the paint() method if anything is to be drawn within it. In practice, the setRoom() method is called first to define which room is being drawn, then the paint() method is called to draw (or redraw) that room. Therefore, we consider the setRoom() method first.

The setRoom() method accepts a Room and a boolean as arguments. The Room specifies which room is to be drawn, and the boolean flag is true if the character is currently in the room.

The location and description of the room on the map are retrieved from the Room object. Then an Arrow object (see below) is constructed for each door leading out of the room, and the value of the characterHere variable is set. The room is now ready to be drawn in the paint() method.

Within paint(), the drawing color is set to red if the character is in the room, and black otherwise. The square outline of the room is then drawn, and the color returned to black for the other drawing operations. The description of the room is drawn in the lower left corner of the square. Then, for each door leading out of the room, the arrow is drawn.

The Arrow class is used to define an arrow pointing in one of the four cardinal directions. Its code is:

```
class Arrow {
    static final int HEADWIDTH = 4;
    static final int HEADHEIGHT = 5;
    public Point Tail, Head, Pointer1, Pointer2;

    Arrow(int TailX, int TailY, int HeadX, int HeadY)
    {
        Tail = new Point(TailX, TailY);
        Head = new Point(HeadX, HeadY);
        Pointer1 = new Point(0,0);
        Pointer2 = new Point(0,0);
```

```
            if (Tail.x == Head.x) {              // Vertical arrow
               Pointer1.x = Head.x - HEADWIDTH;
               Pointer2.x = Head.x + HEADWIDTH;
               if (Head.y > Tail.y) {            // South pointing
                  Pointer1.y = Head.y - HEADHEIGHT;
                  Pointer2.y = Head.y - HEADHEIGHT;
               } else {                           // North pointing
                  Pointer1.y = Head.y + HEADHEIGHT;
                  Pointer2.y = Head.y + HEADHEIGHT;
               }
            } else {                              // Horizontal arrow
               Pointer1.y = Head.y - HEADWIDTH;
               Pointer2.y = Head.y + HEADWIDTH;
               if (Head.x < Tail.x) {             // West pointing
                  Pointer1.x = Head.x + HEADHEIGHT;
                  Pointer2.x = Head.x + HEADHEIGHT;
               } else {                           // East pointing
                  Pointer1.x = Head.x - HEADHEIGHT;
                  Pointer2.x = Head.x - HEADHEIGHT;
               }
            }
         }
      }
   }
```

The parameters HEADWIDTH and HEADHEIGHT define the shape of the arrowhead in pixels. The Point class is provided in java.awt and is used for defining a geometric point in two-dimensional space. Two Points are used to define the ends (the head and tail) of the main shaft of the arrow. Then two other Points, Pointer1 and Pointer2, are used to define the endpoints of the two line segments in the arrowhead. Only one endpoint for each line segment need be defined, of course, since the other end is the same as the Head point.

The type of arrow desired is worked out from the relative values of the coordinates in the head and tail. The code should be self-explanatory.

15.4.5 THE MessagePanel CLASS

The MessagePanel class is used to define the input/output section of the applet, comprising the lower section in Fig. 15.6. The code is as follows:

```
import java.awt.*;
import java.util.StringTokenizer;

class MessagePanel extends Panel {
   static final int MAXTOKENS = 2;
   private TextArea descriptionArea =
      new TextArea(5,60);
   private TextField entryField = new TextField(60);
   private Button backupButton = new Button("Back up");
```

```java
    private Dungeon parent;

    private NewGridBagLayout layout =
        new NewGridBagLayout();

    MessagePanel(Dungeon owner)
    {
        parent = owner;
        setLayout(layout);
        layout.setRareConstraints(GridBagConstraints.WEST,
            GridBagConstraints.NONE,
            new Insets(2,2,2,2), 0, 0, 1, 1);
        layout.setPositionSizeAdd(descriptionArea, this, 0,
            0, 1, 1);
        layout.setPositionSizeAdd(new
            Label("Type your command here:"), this,
            0, 1, 1, 1);
        layout.setPositionSizeAdd(entryField, this,
            0, 2, 1, 1);
        layout.setRareConstraints(
            GridBagConstraints.CENTER,
            GridBagConstraints.NONE,
            new Insets(2,2,2,2), 0, 0, 1, 1);
        layout.setPositionSizeAdd(backupButton, this,
            0, 3, 1, 1);
        descriptionArea.setEditable(false);
        entryField.setEditable(true);
        descriptionArea.setBackground(Color.cyan);
        entryField.setBackground(Color.yellow);
    }

    private String[] parseInput(String input)
    {
        StringTokenizer inputTokens =
            new StringTokenizer(input.toLowerCase(), " ,.;");
        String[] returnString = new String[MAXTOKENS];

        int tokenIndex = 0;
        while (inputTokens.hasMoreTokens() &&
            tokenIndex < MAXTOKENS)
            returnString[tokenIndex++] =
                inputTokens.nextToken();
        return returnString;
    }

    public void setDescriptionArea(String message)
    {
        descriptionArea.setText(message);
        entryField.setText("");
```

```
        }

        public boolean action(Event event, Object object)
        {
            if (event.target == entryField) {
                parent.doCommand(parseInput
                    (entryField.getText()), false);
                entryField.setText("");
            } else if (event.target == backupButton) {
                try
                    parent.doCommand(parseInput(
                        parent.popBackupStack()), true);
                catch (StackException e)
                    parent.setMessage(
                        "There are no more events to retrieve.\n");
            }
            return true;
        }
    }
```

Note that we must import the `StringTokenizer` class from the `java.util` package, since we use a `StringTokenizer` to parse the input command.

We define `MAXTOKENS` to represent the maximum number of words we will accept in a command. At the moment, we consider only commands of up to two words, but the code here is easy to generalize to any number of words simply by changing this parameter.

The `TextArea` named `descriptionArea` is used for messages generated in response to user commands. The `entryField` is a single-line `TextField` which is where the user types in commands. The `Button` is used to back up or undo commands. Again, the `Dungeon` pointer called `parent` is used for direct communication with the master `Dungeon` object, allowing `MessagePanel` to access directly the methods in `Dungeon` and hence communicate with other classes. The layout manager of the `MessagePanel` is the `NewGridBagLayout`, described in Chapter 3.

The constructor sets up the layout manager and adds all the components. The `descriptionArea` is made read-only by calling the `setEditable()` method with an argument of `false`. The background colors are set for the two text boxes.

In the `parseInput()` method, we use a `StringTokenizer` object to parse (split) a `String` at one or more separator characters. Here, the `input` string is parsed at any of the characters listed in the second argument to the `StringTokenizer` constructor – a blank, comma, full stop, or semi-colon. Note that `input` is converted to lower-case before the parsing is done.

An array of `Strings`, `returnString`, is created, and a separate word is parsed out of `inputTokens` on each iteration in the `while` loop. The completed array of words is then returned. Note that since Java automatically initializes all array elements to `null`, any unused elements in the `returnString` array will be null, which may be used elsewhere to identify how many words were actually typed in by the user. We used this technique in the Dungeon method checkCommand().

The setDescriptionArea() message sets the text displayed in the descriptionArea, and clears the entryField to make it ready for the next command.

The action() method deals with events in either the entryField (generated when the user presses the 'enter' key after typing a command) or the backupButton, when the user wishes to undo a previous command.

If the event's target is the entryField, the parseInput() method is called to parse the command, and then the doCommand() method of the Dungeon class is called (via the parent pointer) to process the command. The boolean second argument to doCommand() is set to false to indicate that the call is a new command, and not a back up request.

If the backupButton is pressed, an attempt is made to pop the backupStack in the Dungeon object to retrieve the first command to be undone. If this attempt is successful (meaning that the stack isn't empty), the command is parsed and sent to the doCommand() method in the Dungeon class, but with a boolean parameter of true, indicating that this *is* a back up request. If the pop attempt throws a StackException indicating an empty stack, the catch clause prints an error message in the descriptionArea and no further action is taken.

15.4.6 THE Map CLASS

The floor plan of the adventure, including the rooms and their interconnections, is stored in the Map class. Its code is:

```
class Map
{
   Room[] rooms;
   int numRooms, maxRooms;
   Graph roomGraph;
   Dungeon parent;

   Map(Dungeon owner, int arrayRooms)
   {
      parent = owner;
      maxRooms = arrayRooms;
      rooms = new Room[maxRooms];
      roomGraph = new Graph(maxRooms);
   }

   public void addRoom(Room newRoom, int roomNumber)
      throws MapException
   {
      if (roomNumber >= 0 && roomNumber < maxRooms) {
         rooms[roomNumber] = newRoom;
```

```
         try
             roomGraph.AddVertex();
         catch (GraphException e);
     } else
         throw new MapException(
             "Can't add room - invalid room number.");
}

public void addCorridor(int fromRoom, int toRoom,
    int weight) throws MapException
{
    if (fromRoom >= 0 && fromRoom < maxRooms &&
        rooms[fromRoom] != null && toRoom >= 0 &&
        toRoom < maxRooms && rooms[toRoom] != null)
        try
            roomGraph.AddEdge(fromRoom, toRoom, weight,
                Graph.DIRECTED);
        catch (GraphException e);
    else
        throw new MapException(
            "Can't add corridor - invalid room number.");
}

public String shortestPath(int fromRoom, int toRoom)
{
    String path = new String();
    try
        path = roomGraph.depthFirstShortestPath(
            fromRoom, toRoom);
    catch (GraphException e);
    return path;
}

public Room getRoom(int roomNumber)
{
    return rooms[roomNumber];
}
}
```

The Map class contains an array of Rooms (the Room class is considered below), and a pointer to the master Dungeon object. It also contains a Graph object, in which each vertex represents a Room, and each edge a corridor connecting two Rooms. The Graph will be used to find the shortest path between two Rooms.

The Map constructor initializes the Dungeon object, and specifies the maximum number of Rooms the Map can contain. The rooms array and the Graph are created.

The addRoom() method adds newRoom, with the specified roomNumber, to the Map. The roomNumber is tested to see if it is in the correct range and, if so, the corresponding array element is initialized to the `newRoom`. A vertex representing the `newRoom` is added to the `roomGraph`.

The `addCorridor()` method adds an edge to the `roomGraph`, provided that both rooms at the ends of the corridor exist.

The `shortestPath()` method calls a new routine (based on Dijkstra's algorithm) that we have added to the `Graph` class to calculate the shortest path between two rooms. We will consider this in more detail when we discuss the modifications made to the `Graph` class below.

Finally, the `getRoom()` method simply returns the `Room` object corresponding to a given `roomNumber`.

15.4.7 THE Room CLASS

The `Room` class stores the properties and contents of rooms in the adventure. The declarations and constructors are as follows:

```java
class Room
{
   static final int NORTH = 0;
   static final int EAST = 1;
   static final int WEST = 2;
   static final int SOUTH = 3;

   private String description;
   private ItemList contents;
   private int[] doors = new int[4];
   private Monster monster;
   private Point mapLocation;
   private boolean visited;

   Room()
   { }

   Room(String newDescription, int mapX, int mapY)
   {
      description = new String(newDescription);
      contents = new ItemList();
      monster = null;
      setDoors(-1, -1, -1, -1);
      mapLocation = new Point(mapX, mapY);
      visited = false;
   }

   Room(String newDescription, int mapX, int mapY,
      Monster newMonster)
   {
      description = new String(newDescription);
      contents = new ItemList();
```

```
        monster = newMonster;
        setDoors(-1, -1, -1, -1);
        mapLocation = new Point(mapX, mapY);
        visited = false;
    }

    public void setDoors(int north, int east, int west,
        int south)
    {
        doors[NORTH] = north;
        doors[EAST] = east;
        doors[WEST] = west;
        doors[SOUTH] = south;
    }
    // other methods
}
```

The class contains a `description` of the room, an `ItemList` that contains a linked list of items currently in the room, an array of `int`s storing the locations of the doors leading out of the room, a `Monster` object (which will be `null` if the room contains no monster), a `Point` containing the coordinates of the upper-left corner of the room on the map, and a `boolean` parameter that is `true` if the character has visited the room.

There is an argumentless constructor, a constructor for creating a `Room` containing only a description and a location on the map, and a third constructor which initializes a `Monster` as well.

The `setDoors()` method sets values for the `doors` array. If a door in a certain direction does not exist, the value is set to –1; otherwise the the value is set to the number of the `Room` to which the door leads.

The next three methods adjust or check the contents of the `ItemList`:

```
    public void addItem(Item newItem)
    {
        contents.InsertEnd(newItem);
    }

    public void removeItem(Item killItem)
    {
        try
            contents.Delete(killItem);
        catch (ListException e);
    }

    public Item contains(String itemDescription)
    {
        return contents.Contains(itemDescription);
    }
```

All three of these methods merely call the corresponding method in the `ItemList` class.

The remaining methods in the `Room` class are interface methods that set or get one of the data fields:

```
public int getDoor(int direction)
{
   return doors[direction];
}

public ItemList getContents()
{
   return contents;
}

public String getShortDescription()
{
   return description;
}

public String getDescription()
{
   String descAndContents = new String(description);
   Item roomItem;
   ItemListIterator Source =
      new ItemListIterator(contents);

   if (monster != null)
      descAndContents += "There is a " +
         (monster.getDead() ? "dead " : "") +
         monster.getName() + " here.\n";

   try
      roomItem = Source.Next();
   catch (ListException e)
      return descAndContents + " The room is empty.\n";

   descAndContents   += "The room contains:\n";
   try
      while (!Source.End())
      {
         descAndContents += "         " +
         roomItem.getDescription() + "\n";
         roomItem = Source.Next();
      }
   catch (ListException e);
   return descAndContents;
}
```

```
   public Monster getMonster()
   {
      return monster;
   }

   public void setMonster(Monster newMonster)
   {
      monster = newMonster;
   }

   public void setDescription(String newDescription)
   {
      description = newDescription;
   }

   public boolean getVisited()
   {
      return visited;
   }

   public void setVisited(boolean newVisited)
   {
      visited = newVisited;
   }

   public Point getMapLocation()
   {
      return mapLocation;
   }
```

All these methods are straightforward. Note that the getDescription() method makes use of an ItemListIterator object to traverse the list of items. List iterators were discussed in Chapter 9.

15.4.8 THE ItemList CLASS

The linked list of Items is essentially just a linked list as described in Chapter 9, except that each data node is an Item rather than a primitive data type. For completeness, we reproduce the code here.

The Item class defines items that may be found in rooms or carried by the player:

```
class Item
{
   protected String description;
   protected int weight;

   Item()
```

```
    {
        description = new String();
        weight = 0;
    }

    Item(String newDescription, int newWeight)
    {
        description = newDescription;
        weight = newWeight;
    }

    public boolean equals(Item compareItem)
    {
        if (!description.equals(compareItem.description))
            return false;
        if (weight != compareItem.weight)
            return false;
        return true;
    }

    public String getDescription()
    {
        return description;
    }

    public void setDescription(String newDescription)
    {
        description = newDescription;
    }

    public int getWeight()
    {
        return weight;
    }

    public void setWeight(int newWeight)
    {
        weight = newWeight;
    }
}
```

An `Item` contains only two properties: a `description` and a `weight`. The constructors are straightforward. We have provided an overridden version of the `equals()` method (defined originally in the `Object` class of `java.lang`) which returns `true` only if both fields in both `Item`s contain the same values. The remaining methods are 'set' and 'get' interface methods.

In order to store an `Item` in a linked list, it must be encapsulated in an `ItemListNode`, which we now examine:

```
class ItemListNode
{
   Item Element;
   ItemListNode Next;

   ItemListNode(Item NewElement, ItemListNode Node)
   {
      Element = NewElement;
      Next = Node;
   }

   public String getDescription()
   {
      return Element.getDescription();
   }

   public void setDescription(String newDescription)
   {
      Element.setDescription(newDescription);
   }

   public int getWeight()
   {
      return Element.getWeight();
   }

   public void setWeight(int newWeight)
   {
      Element.setWeight(newWeight);
   }
}
```

The class is identical to the `ListNode` class defined in Chapter 9, with the addition of several interface methods for accessing fields of individual data fields in the node.

The `ItemList` class itself is also modelled on the `IntList` class from Chapter 7:

```
class ItemList
{
   protected ItemListNode Head;

   ItemList()
   {
      Head = new ItemListNode(new Item(), null);
   }

   public Item Contains(String FindElement)
```

```
    {
        ItemListNode Marker;
        for (Marker = Head.Next; Marker != null;
           Marker = Marker.Next)
           if (Marker.Element.getDescription().
              equals(FindElement))
              return Marker.Element;
        return null;
    }

    public void InsertEnd(Item NewElement)
    {
        ItemListNode Marker;
        for (Marker = Head; Marker.Next != null;
           Marker = Marker.Next);
        Marker.Next = new ItemListNode(NewElement,
           Marker.Next);
    }

    public void Delete(Item DelElement)
        throws ListException
    {
        ItemListNode Marker;
        for (Marker = Head;
           Marker.Next != null &&
               !Marker.Next.Element.equals(DelElement);
           Marker = Marker.Next);

        if (Marker.Next != null &&
           Marker.Next.Element.equals(DelElement))
           Marker.Next = Marker.Next.Next;
        else
           throw new ListException(
              "Cannot delete: element not in list.");
    }
}
```

The function of each of these methods should be obvious after comparison with the code and discussion in Chapter 9.

Finally, we consider the `ItemListIterator` class:

```
class ItemListIterator extends ItemList
{
    ItemListNode CurrentNode;

    ItemListIterator(ItemList List)
    {
        CurrentNode = List.Head;
    }
```

```
Item Next() throws ListException
{
    if (!End())
        CurrentNode = CurrentNode.Next;
    else
        throw new ListException(
            "Attempt to access beyond end of list.");

    if (!End())
        return CurrentNode.Element;
    else
        throw new ListException(
            "Attempt to access beyond end of list.");
}

boolean End()
{
    return CurrentNode == null;
}
}
```

This class parallels the `IntListIterator` class described in section 9.3.

15.4.9 **THE REVISED** Graph **CLASS**

To illustrate one use of a graph in the adventure game, we have modified the `Graph` class originally presented in Chapter 14 so that it will calculate and display the shortest path between two vertices. As we saw in Chapter 14, Dijkstra's algorithm will find the shortest *distance* between one source vertex and all other vertices, but the way the algorithm is programmed, it does not provide the actual path that will produce this shortest distance. However, because of the way Dijkstra's algorithm works, the path is actually found during the calculation – it is just not saved for later use.

Therefore, we provide a modified form of Dijkstra's algorithm that saves the shortest path information in a second `Graph` object, and then traverses this second graph using a depth-first traversal to find the shortest path between the two specified vertices.

Recall that in each iteration of Dijkstra's algorithm, one vertex is added to the set *S* of vertices to which the minimum distance has been found. In the previous version of the algorithm, we simply identified this vertex and added it to the set *S*, but we did not bother to identify or save the *edge* by which this vertex was reached. In the new version of the algorithm, we identify this edge and then add it to the second graph. When Dijkstra's algorithm is complete, the second graph will be a spanning tree of the original graph, and the path from the source vertex to any other vertex within this spanning tree will be the shortest path between those two vertices.

To incorporate this feature into the `Dijkstra()` method in the new `Graph` object, we declare an array of ints called `sourceVertex`. In the first round of

Dijkstra's algorithm, the minimum distance from the starting vertex to another vertex is defined to be the weight on the edge connecting the two vertices, if such an edge exists, or else infinity if the edge does not exist. During this initial round, we also initialize the sourceVertex array to contain the source or starting vertex for any edge that leads directly to one of the other vertices.

For example, in Fig 14.23 in the previous chapter, the value of the sourceVertex element would be 6 (the starting vertex for that example) for vertices 1, 3, and 4, since those vertices have a direct connection from the starting vertex 6. All other elements of sourceVertex are set to –1 at this stage.

In the main section of the algorithm, one vertex is added to the set S in each iteration. The spanning tree is also updated in each iteration. When a vertex is added to the set S, the sourceVertex element for that vertex contains the index of the vertex at the other end of the edge by which that vertex was reached. Therefore, we can identify the vertices at both ends of the edge, and can add this edge to the spanning tree.

The next stage in Dijkstra's algorithm involves updating the distances from those vertices now within the set S to those vertices remaining outside S. This is done by examining the vertex that was just added to S to see if it has a direct connection to any of these exterior vertices and, if so, whether this connection provides a smaller distance to that vertex than the currently known distance. If it does, the distance is updated. We can update sourceVertex at the same time by noting that, if a direct edge between the last vertex added to S and an exterior vertex exists which gives a new smaller distance to that exterior vertex, then the source vertex for the edge reaching that exterior vertex must be the vertex that was just added to S.

For example, the first vertex to be added to S in the graph in Fig. 14.23 is vertex 4. Adding vertex 4 to S opens up a new path to vertex 3 that proves to be shorter than the old path (the new distance is $4 + 12 = 16$; the old distance was 22). Therefore, the sourceVertex value for vertex 3 is changed from 6 to 4, since if vertex 3 is added to the set S during the next iteration, it will be via the edge from vertex 4, and not via the edge from vertex 6.

Continuing in this way – updating the sourceVertex array and then using this array to add the correct edge to the spanning tree in each iteration – allows us to build up the spanning tree at the same time as we determine the shortest distances between the specified starting vertex and all other vertices.

To make use of the spanning tree to produce the shortest path between the starting vertex and some other vertex, we must have a way of traversing the tree to find the desired path. We can do this by means of a modified depth-first topological sort.

Recall from Chapter 14 that the depth-first topological sort used the depth-first graph traversal algorithm to locate a vertex that had no successors, placed this vertex at the top end of an array, and then filled the array from top to bottom (or right to left, depending on your point of view) in such a way that any vertex lay to the right of any other vertex with an edge leading from the other vertex to the first vertex.

We can apply the topological sort to the spanning tree produced during the modified version of Dijkstra's algorithm. However, rather than producing a topological ordering of the entire spanning tree, we only want that portion of the tree containing the path between the two specified vertices. Therefore, we can start at the source vertex and use the depth-first traversal algorithm until we find the destination vertex. Once we find the destination, we stop the recursion and record, in an array, what vertices were visited on the way to the destination. These vertices will be already stored for us in the stack of recursive method calls that were made to find the destination in the first place, so all we need to do is record the vertex in each method as the recursion backtracks.

Since a depth-first traversal might have to explore several branches of the tree without finding the destination before success occurs, the recursive calls will have to partially backtrack and then restart several times before the desired path is found. Therefore, we define a `boolean` flag which is set to `true` when the destination is located, and only record the vertices during the backtracking of the recursion when this flag is `true`.

With this description of the modifications to the algorithms, we can now present our modified `Graph` class. Since most of the methods are the same as in the original `Graph` class in Chapter 14, we will only present the new ones here.

The declarations and constructor are now as follows:

```
class Graph
{
    int MAXVERTEX;
    static final int DIRECTED = 0;
    static final int UNDIRECTED = 1;

    private int NumVertex;
    private int Edge[][];
    private boolean Visited[];
    private int depthFirstList[];
    private int breadthFirstList[];
    private int depthFirstTopList[];
    private int breadthFirstTopList[];
    private boolean SpanningTree[][];
    private int ShortestPathTree[][];
    private int ShortestPath[];
    private int MinDistance[];
    private int travIndex;
    private int Directed;

    public Graph(int maxvertex)
    {
        MAXVERTEX = maxvertex;
        Edge = new int[MAXVERTEX][MAXVERTEX];
        Visited = new boolean[MAXVERTEX];
        depthFirstList = new int[MAXVERTEX];
```

```
breadthFirstList = new int[MAXVERTEX];
depthFirstTopList = new int[MAXVERTEX];
breadthFirstTopList = new int[MAXVERTEX];
SpanningTree = new boolean[MAXVERTEX][MAXVERTEX];
ShortestPathTree = new int[MAXVERTEX][MAXVERTEX];
ShortestPath = new int[MAXVERTEX];
MinDistance = new int[MAXVERTEX];
NumVertex = 0;
travIndex = 0;
for (int row = 0; row < MAXVERTEX; ++row)
{
    Visited[row] = false;
    for (int col = 0; col < MAXVERTEX; ++col)
        Edge[row][col] = 0;
}
}
// other methods
}
```

In order to allow the number of vertices to be specified when the `Graph` object is declared, we have made `MAXVERTEX` a variable and initialized it in the constructor. The creation of all the arrays is therefore deferred to the constructor as well.

The new data fields are `ShortestPathTree`, used to store the spanning tree created in the modified Dijkstra's algorithm, and `ShortestPath`, used to construct the shortest path between two vertices in the modified topological sort.

The modified version of the `Dijkstra()` method is as follows:

```
public void Dijkstra(int start)
{
    Set pathFound = new Set(NumVertex);
    int tempmin = start, end, cost, vertex, mindist;
    int[] sourceVertex = new int[NumVertex];

    try
        pathFound.Insert(start);
    catch (SetException e);
    MinDistance[start] = 0;
    sourceVertex[start] = start;

    for (vertex = 0; vertex < NumVertex; ++vertex) {
        for (end = 0; end < NumVertex; ++end)
            ShortestPathTree[vertex][end] = 0;
        if (vertex != start) {
            MinDistance[vertex] = getWeight(start, vertex);
            sourceVertex[vertex] = (MinDistance[vertex] <
                Integer.MAX_VALUE) ? start : -1;
        }
```

```
    }

    for (vertex = 0; vertex < NumVertex; ++vertex)
    {
       mindist = Integer.MAX_VALUE;
       if (vertex != start)
       {
          for (end = 0; end < NumVertex; ++end)
          {
             if (!pathFound.Contains(end))
             {
                if (MinDistance[end] < mindist)
                {
                   tempmin = end;
                   mindist = MinDistance[end];
                }
             }
          }
          if (mindist < Integer.MAX_VALUE)
          {
             try
                pathFound.Insert(tempmin);
             catch (SetException e);
             ShortestPathTree[sourceVertex[tempmin]]
                [tempmin] = getWeight(
                sourceVertex[tempmin],tempmin);
             for (end = 0; end < NumVertex; ++end)
                if (!pathFound.Contains(end))
                {
                   cost = getWeight(tempmin, end);
                   if (cost < Integer.MAX_VALUE &&
                      mindist + cost < MinDistance[end]) {
                      MinDistance[end] = mindist + cost;
                      sourceVertex[end] = tempmin;
                   }
                }
          }
       }
    }
}
```

This method follows the modifications described above exactly, so it should be easy to follow once these modifications are understood.

Finally, the modified topological sort that finds the shortest path is implemented in two methods. The first is non-recursive and starts off the second, recursive method.

```
public String depthFirstShortestPath(
```

```
      int sourceVertex, int endVertex)
      throws GraphException
{
   int vertex, place;
   MyBoolean savePath = new MyBoolean(false);

   Dijkstra(sourceVertex);
   if (MinDistance[endVertex] == Integer.MAX_VALUE)
      throw new GraphException("No path from " +
         sourceVertex  + " to " + endVertex);
   for (vertex = 0; vertex < NumVertex; ++vertex) {
      ShortestPath[vertex] = -1;
      Visited[vertex] = false;
   }
   place = DFRecursiveShortestPath(sourceVertex,
      endVertex, NumVertex, savePath);
   String pathString = new
      String(Integer.toString(ShortestPath[0]));
   for (vertex = 1; vertex < NumVertex; ++vertex)
      pathString += " " +
         Integer.toString(ShortestPath[vertex]);
   return pathString;
}

private int DFRecursiveShortestPath(int vertex,
   int end, int place, MyBoolean savePath)
{
   int nextVertex;

   Visited[vertex] = true;
   if (vertex == end)
      savePath.setValue(true);
   else if (!savePath.getValue())
      for (nextVertex = 0; nextVertex < NumVertex;
         ++nextVertex)
      {
         if (ShortestPathTree[vertex][nextVertex] > 0 &&
            !Visited[nextVertex] && !savePath.getValue())
            place = DFRecursiveShortestPath(nextVertex,
               end, place, savePath);
      }
   if (savePath.getValue())
      ShortestPath[—place] = vertex;
   return place;
}
```

The calculation of the shortest path between two vertices actually begins with a call to depthFirstShortestPath(), specifying the sourceVertex and the endVertex. This method calls the modified Dijkstra() method to find the spanning tree beginning at `sourceVertex`. Then the `MinDistance` array is checked to make sure that a path between the two vertices actually exists. If it does, the `ShortestPath` and `Visited` arrays are initialized, and a call to `DFRecursiveShortestPath()` is made to start the recursion off.

The arguments to the recursive method specify the `sourceVertex` and `endVertex` of the requested path, the `place` where the next vertex number should be stored in the `ShortestPath` array (the first entry in this array must be stored at the extreme right-hand end, so `NumVertex` is passed as the initial value), and the boolean flag `savePath` which is set to `true` when the `endVertex` is first found.

Note that `savePath` is actually declared as a `MyBoolean` variable. This is because it must be passed by reference in order that its value can change and be passed back and forth in a chain of recursive calls. Ordinarily, a primitive data type such as `boolean` can be converted into a reference data type by using Java's built-in wrapper classes, such as `Boolean`. However, there does not seem to be any way to change the value of the actual `boolean` data stored within a `Boolean` object (someone must have been asleep the day this wrapper was defined), so the author created his own `MyBoolean` class that allows this:

```
class MyBoolean
{
   private boolean toggle;

   MyBoolean(boolean initial) { toggle = initial; }

   public boolean getValue() { return toggle; }

   public void setValue(boolean newValue) { toggle =
      newValue; }
}
```

Once the recursive method has finished, the actual path is converted into a printable `String` by looping through the `ShortestPath` array and constructing `pathString`, which is returned.

The `DFRecursiveShortestPath()` method is similar to the original `DFRecursiveSort()` method used in Chapter 14 for performing a depth-first topological ordering. The only differences involve checking the value of the boolean flag `savePath`. If this flag is `true`, we have located the end vertex, and no further recursive calls should be made. Therefore, the `vertex` value stored within each recursive version of this method is stored in the next available location in `ShortestPath`, and that location is then returned to the next higher level in the recursion.

If the `savePath` flag is still `false`, we check to see if we have found the end vertex on the latest recursive call. If not, we scan all other vertices in the spanning tree in the `for` loop. If an edge from the current `vertex` to the `nextVertex` exists (as determined by checking the `ShortestPathTree` array), and the nextVertex hasn't yet been visited, *and* we haven't found the end vertex yet (checked by examining savePath), we make another recursive call to explore the tree starting at nextVertex.

At present, this path-finding feature is only used to print out the list of vertices (which are actually Room numbers in the adventure game) corresponding to the shortest path between two rooms. It would be fairly easy to incorporate this feature more realistically into the game. For example, a shortcut command taking a character from one room to another room in the dungeon by the shortest route could be included, perhaps with a bit of animation on the map showing each room in the path highlighted in red as the character passed through it. The main purpose of including the command here was to show that 'advanced' data structures such as graphs can be used to good effect in many situations.

15.4.10 THE Creature, Player, Weapon, AND Monster CLASSES

The remaining classes are fairly straightforward. The classes used to represent the 'hero' and the monsters in the adventure are derived from a common Creature base class:

```java
class Creature
{
    protected String name;
    protected boolean dead;
    protected int hitpoints, maxHitpoints;
    protected int armour;
    protected int minDamage, maxDamage, numberOfHits;
    protected Dungeon parent;

    Creature(Dungeon owner, String newCreature,
        int newMaxHitpoints, int newArmour,
        int newMinDamage, int newMaxDamage,
        int newNumberOfHits)
    {
        parent = owner;
        dead = false;
        name = newCreature;
        hitpoints = maxHitpoints = newMaxHitpoints;
        armour = newArmour;
        minDamage = newMinDamage;
        maxDamage = newMaxDamage;
        numberOfHits = newNumberOfHits;
    }

    public String getName()
    {
        return name;
    }
}
```

```
      public boolean getDead()
      {
         return dead;
      }

      public void setDead(boolean newDead)
      {
         dead = newDead;
      }

      public int getMinDamage()
      {
         return minDamage;
      }

      public int getMaxDamage()
      {
         return maxDamage;
      }

      public int getArmour()
      {
         return armour;
      }

      public int getHitpoints()
      {
         return hitpoints;
      }

      public void adjustHitpoints(int changeHitpoints)
      {
         hitpoints += changeHitpoints;
         if (hitpoints <= 0)
            setDead(true);
         else
            setDead(false);
      }
   }
```

This class contains the features and methods that are common to the `Player` and `Monster` classes, and everything here should be fairly obvious.

The `Player` class extends the `Creature` class to allow for special features of adventurers:

```
class Player extends Creature
{
   static final int FISTMINDAMAGE = 1;
```

```java
    static final int FISTMAXDAMAGE = 3;

    private int maxWeight, carryingWeight;
    private ItemList carrying;
    private int location;
    private Weapon wielded;

    Player(Dungeon owner, String newName,
        int newHitpoints, int newArmour,
        int newMinDamage, int newMaxDamage,
        int newNumberOfHits, int newMaxWeight)
    {
        super(owner, newName, newHitpoints, newArmour,
            newMinDamage, newMaxDamage, newNumberOfHits);
        maxWeight = newMaxWeight;
        carryingWeight = 0;
        carrying = new ItemList();
        location = 0;
        wielded = null;
    }

    public int getLocation()
    {
        return location;
    }

    public void setLocation(int roomNumber)
    {
        location = roomNumber;
    }

    public Weapon getWielded()
    {
        return wielded;
    }

    public boolean addItem(Item newItem)
    {
        int itemWeight = newItem.getWeight();
        if (carryingWeight + itemWeight <= maxWeight) {
            carrying.InsertEnd(newItem);
            carryingWeight += itemWeight;
            return true;
        }
        return false;
    }

    public void removeItem(Item killItem)
    {
```

```
      try
         carrying.Delete(killItem);
      catch (ListException e);
      carryingWeight -= killItem.getWeight();
   }

   public Item isCarrying(String itemDescription)
   {
      return carrying.Contains(itemDescription);
   }

   public String inventory()
   {
      ItemListIterator Source =
         new ItemListIterator(carrying);
      String packList = new String("You are carrying:");
      Item packItem;

      try
         packItem = Source.Next();
      catch (ListException e)
         return packList + " nothing.";

      try
         while (!Source.End())
         {
            packList += " " + packItem.getDescription();
            packItem = Source.Next();
         }
      catch (ListException e);
      return packList;
   }

   public boolean wieldWeapon(String weaponDesc)
   {
      Weapon weapon;

      if ((weapon =
         (Weapon)isCarrying(weaponDesc)) != null) {
         wielded = weapon;
         minDamage = weapon.getMinDamage();
         maxDamage = weapon.getMaxDamage();
         return true;
      }
      return false;
   }

   public boolean unwieldWeapon()
   {
```

```
          if (wielded == null)
             return false;
          wielded = null;
          minDamage = FISTMINDAMAGE;
          maxDamage = FISTMAXDAMAGE;
          return true;
      }
   }
```

The two `static` fields specify the maximum and minimum damage that the `Player` can do bare-fisted (that is, when not wielding a weapon). The `maxWeight` and `carryingWeight` specify the maximum and current weight that may be carried by a `Player`, respectively. The list of `Items` carried by the `Player` is stored in an `ItemList`, just as are the contents of a `Room`.

The constructor calls the `Creature` constructor using the `super()` method. Note that this must be the *first* statement in a constructor, if it is used at all.

Most of the other methods are 'set' and 'get' interface methods, and should be fairly obvious. The `wieldWeapon()` and `unwieldWeapon()` methods adjust the damage range possible when the `Player` attacks something.

The `Weapon` class is an extension of the `Item` class, and adds maximum and minimum damage properties, and associated methods:

```java
class Weapon extends Item
{
   private int minDamage, maxDamage;

   Weapon(String newDescription, int newWeight,
      int newMinDamage, int newMaxDamage)
   {
      super(newDescription, newWeight);
      minDamage = newMinDamage;
      maxDamage = newMaxDamage;
   }

   public int getMinDamage()
   {
      return minDamage;
   }

   public int getMaxDamage()
   {
      return maxDamage;
   }
}
```

The `Monster` class also extends `Creature`, and contains nothing noteworthy:

```
class Monster extends Creature
{
  private String description;

  Monster(Dungeon owner, String newName,
      int newHitpoints, int newArmour,
      int newMinDamage, int newMaxDamage,
      int newNumberOfHits, String newDescription)
  {
    super(owner, newName, newHitpoints, newArmour,
      newMinDamage, newMaxDamage, newNumberOfHits);
    description = newDescription;
  }

  public String getDescription()
  {
    return description;
  }

  public void setDescription(String newDescription)
  {
    description = newDescription;
  }
}
```

15.4.11 THE `StringStack` AND `WordList` CLASSES

The last two classes required for the adventure game are variants of standard data structures treated earlier in the text.

The `StringStack` is just a stack storing `String`s instead of primitive data types. The code is identical to that given in Chapter 7 for the `IntStack` with the `Element` array declared as an array of `String` instead of `int`.

The `WordList` class is essentially the same as the hash table implemented in the `OpenAddress` class in Chapter 12. Java has a built-in hash function method for the `String` class, called `hashCode()`. Keep in mind, though, that this method can return negative `int`s, so if the value of this function is to be used as an array index, it must be converted to a positive integer first.

A suitable use of the `hashCode()` method for a `String` is:

```
private int HashFunc(String newElement)
{
  int hashValue = newElement.hashCode();
  if (hashValue < 0)
    hashValue = -hashValue;
  return hashValue % TableSize;
}
```

15.5 Summary

The adventure game presented in this chapter is a fairly extended example of Java code. If you actually play the game, you won't find it terribly interesting in its current form, since it contains only four rooms, and only one monster. However, the design and code given here provide a solid foundation for building a fairly sophisticated game, once the number of rooms is expanded, and some more specialized types of items, rooms, and creatures are introduced.

Besides giving an extended example of a Java program, this chapter has also illustrated how many of the data structures introduced in this book may be used in 'real-life' situations. In many cases, intelligent use of data structures will provide a program design that is more logical, and easier to understand, extend, and maintain.

A P P E N D I X

JAVA SYNTAX

This appendix serves as a review and summary of Java syntax. It is not intended to be complete, but will cover all Java syntax used in this book.

A.1 Data types

In Java, data types are divided into two main groups: *primitive* data types and *reference* data types. The main difference between the two groups is that primitive data types are handled by value, and reference data types are handled by reference.

What this means is that a primitive data object is passed to a method by value (a copy of the object is made locally within the method, and any changes to that copy do not affect the original object). A reference object is passed to a method by reference (only the *pointer* to the object is copied to the method, so any changes to the object pointed to by this pointer *will* affect the original object). Unlike many other languages, such as C and C++, Java does not contain a mechanism for passing any one object to a method by value or by reference – the data type fixes the method by which it is passed to a method.

There are eight primitive data types in Java, as shown in the table.

Data type	Contents	Size	Range
boolean	true/false	1 bit	true or false
char	character	16 bits	Unicode character set
byte	signed integer	8 bits	-128 to $+127$
short	signed integer	16 bits	-32768 to $+32767$
int	signed integer	32 bits	-2147483648 to $+2147483647$
long	signed integer	64 bits	-9223372036854775808 to $+9223372036854775807$
float	floating point	32 bits	$\pm 3.40282347 \times 10^{38}$ to $\pm 1.40239846 \times 10^{-45}$
double	floating point	64 bits	$\pm 1.79769313486231570 \times 10^{308}$ to $\pm 4.9406564581246544 \times 10^{-324}$

Java provides default values for all primitive data types when they are declared. The default value for all numerical types is 0 (for integers) or 0.0 (for floating point numbers). A boolean object is initialized to false, and a char is initialized to the null character. Most computers do not support the full Unicode character set at the time of writing, but ASCII codes may be used for the standard keyboard characters in Java.

All other data types in Java are reference data types. This includes all data types that are defined by the programmer. It is important to understand the implications of using a reference data object, beyond the fact that it is passed by reference to a method. Probably the most important consequence is that the assignment (=) operator works differently for primitive and reference data types. For example, consider the following fragment of Java code.

```
MyObject obj1, obj2;
obj1 = new MyObject();
obj2 = obj1;
obj1.ChangeData();
```

What you might expect to happen with this code is that `obj2` makes a copy of `obj1`, then some data field in `obj1` is changed by the `ChangeData()` method, resulting in that data field being different in `obj1` and `obj2`. However, it turns out that the data stored in `obj1` and `obj2` are *both* changed by the last line.

The reason for this odd behavior is that `obj1` and `obj2` are really *pointers* to objects of type `MyObject`, and the assignment statement `obj2 = obj1` sets the `obj2` pointer to point to the same location in memory as the `obj1` pointer. Therefore, when the `ChangeData()` method is called to change the data at the location pointed to by `obj1`, the same change is made to the object to which `obj2` points, since it points to the same place as `obj1`.

If you really do need a copy of a reference data type, you may be able to use the `clone()` method (if the class implements the `Cloneable` interface and therefore contains a `clone()` method). In that case, you could replace the assignment `obj2 = obj1` with the statement:

```
obj2 = obj1.clone();
```

which effectively uses the `new` operator to allocate space for `obj2` to point to, and then copies `obj1` into that space. However, not all classes contain a `clone()` method, so you may need to write your own.*

Another important implication of the reference data type is that the equality operator `==` will, when applied to two reference data objects, only test whether their pointers are equal, and *not* whether their contents are equal. In other words, the `==` operator will return `true` only when the two objects are physically in the same location in memory (and are therefore the same object). In order to test whether two reference objects that are in physically different locations contain the same values, a separate method (such as the `equals()` method that is defined for some classes) must be used.

Pointers in Java   A.2

We have made frequent use of the word 'pointer' in the previous section, which will no doubt cause Java purists to throw up their hands in horror. It is often said that 'Java has no pointers'. Although it *is* true that Java greatly restricts the

---

* Early beta versions of Java contained a `copy()` method that would copy one reference object into another, but this was removed in the first official version of Java.

programmer's access to pointers compared to a language such as C++, it is the author's view that treating 'pointer' as a taboo word when talking about Java greatly inhibits a clear understanding of things like the difference between primitive and reference variables. It is quite comical to see how some authors attempt to find synonyms for 'pointer' just to avoid using the 'p-word'.

Let's come clean: Java makes as much use of pointers as any other language, and we are all adult enough to talk about it openly. What Java does prohibit the programmer from doing is to access pointers directly, so that you cannot, for example, 'cast' one data type into another, or compute the actual size in bytes of any object.

Therefore, we will use the term 'pointer' throughout this book.

A.3 Classes and objects

All reference data types in Java must be defined as *classes*. An instance of a class is an *object* (with a small 'o'). Creating an object is a two stage process: first the object must be *declared* and then it must be *initialized*. Declaring an object tells the compiler to allocate space for a single pointer to an object whose data type is specified by the object's class. Initializing the object assigns some memory location to the pointer, either by dynamically allocating some new area of memory (using the `new` operator), or by assigning the pointer to some previously allocated memory (using the = operator).

For example, if a `class MyObject` has been defined previously, we can create an object of type `MyObject` as follows:

```
MyObject obj1;            // declaration
obj1 = new MyObject();  // initialization
```

An object that has been declared but not initialized has its pointer set to the keyword `null`, and attempting to access any fields of a `null` object generates a `NullPointerException` (which does make it pretty obvious that the designers of Java knew they were dealing with pointers!).

Java has *automatic garbage collection*, which means that any dynamically allocated memory that is no longer being used by the program is automatically freed up for use by other processes.

All data fields within a `class` must be either of a primitive data type or of another, previously defined, reference type.

A class may also contain any number of methods. A method's *prototype* specifies the method's name, its return type, and its argument list. For example, the method prototype:

```
int FindNumber(int number, float score)
```

declares a method whose name is `FindNumber`, returns an `int` and requires an `int` and a `float` as arguments.

Within a single class, it is permissible to *overload* a method, which means that two or more methods with the same name may be defined. However, the argument lists must be different for all methods with the same name. (The return type may be the same or different for overloaded methods.)

A class may have a special method called a *constructor*. A constructor for a class has no return type (not even `void`), and is usually used for initializing values of the data fields. The name of a constructor is always the same as the name of its class. Constructors may be overloaded in the same way as other methods.

Java has a bewildering collection of keywords which may be used to restrict access to data fields and methods within a class. The main keywords are:

- `public` – field is accessible to all methods in all packages.*
- `private` – field is accessible only to methods within the same class.
- `protected` – field is accessible only to methods within the same package.†
- `static` – field (can be either a data field or a method) is a property of the class, and not of any particular instance of the class. For example, the `random()` method is a member of the `Math` class, but can be called without any reference to a `Math` object by using the syntax `Math.random()`.
- `final` – applied to a data field, it means that the field is constant; applied to a method, it means that the method cannot be overridden in a class that inherits the current class (see inheritance below and in Chapter 1); applied to a class, it means that the class cannot be inherited.

Inheritance A.4

As described in Chapter 1, one of the main features of object-oriented programming is the ability of a class to *inherit* the fields of another class. Java allows single inheritance but not multiple inheritance (that is, a class may inherit at most one other class). Inheritance is achieved using the Java keyword `extends`, as in `class MyApplet extends Applet`, indicating that `MyApplet` inherits `Applet`.

The Java keyword `super()` is a special method name that calls the superclass (the class from which the current class is derived) constructor for a given class from within the derived class's constructor. If `super()` is used in a constructor, it must be the *first* statement in the constructor. If no call to `super()` is made in a derived class constructor, Java will automatically insert such a call,

---

* A *package* in Java is a collection of classes that are grouped together and stored in a particular location in the directory structure. For example, the package `java.awt` contains all the classes used for constructing the graphical user interface. We do not study user-created packages in this book.

† C++ programmers should note the difference between the use of the `protected` keyword in Java and C++. In C++, a `protected` field is accessible to its own class and to any class derived from that class, but nowhere else. This is *not* true in Java. Early versions of Java defined a `private protected` data field that would do this, but this is no longer supported.

and attempt to call an argumentless constructor from the superclass. If no argumentless constructor exists, a compilation error occurs.

Note that it is possible to create a chain of inherited classes, so initializing an object of the last class in the chain will result in a chain of constructor calls extending back to the first class in the chain. Since the call (explicit or implicit) to `super()` must be the first statement in a constructor, the constructors are called in order from the earliest base class down to the last derived class.

In addition to extending a single class, a class can also implement any number of *interfaces*. An interface in Java is essentially a class without any method definitions. That is, the data fields and method prototypes are defined in the interface, but each class that implements an interface must provide its own definitions for all the methods in the interface. Interfaces provide a sort of poor man's multiple inheritance. They are described in more detail in Chapters 6 and 8.

The main concepts related to inheritance, and their implementation in Java, as discussed in more detail in Chapter 1.

A.5   Java statements

A single-line *statement* in Java consists of a single Java construct (assignment, conditional operation, loop, etc.) terminated by a semi-colon. For example:

```
x = y + z;
for (i = 0; i < 10; i++) x[i] += y;
if (x > y) x += 2 * y;
```

are all valid single-line Java statements.

A *compound statement* is a set of single-line statements (or other compound statements enclosed in braces. For example:

```
for (i = 0; i < 10; i++)
{
  x[i] += y[i];
  y[i] = 2 * z[i];
}
```

contains a two-line compound statement as the body of the `for` loop.

A.6   Operators

The most common Java operators are shown in the table, in order of *precedence*. The precedence of an operator determines the order in which an operator is executed within a compound expression. For example, in the expression `x + y * z`, the precedence of the `*` operator is higher than the `+` operator, so the multiplication is done first.

Operator	Precedence	Effect	Return value
++	1	increment by 1	Before operand: returns operand after increment; After operand: returns operand before increment
−−	1	decrement by 1	As ++
!	1	Logical NOT	Opposite of boolean operand
*,/,%	2	multiplication, division, remainder	product, quotient or remainder of operands
+,−	3	addition & subtraction	sum or difference of two operands
+	3	`String` concatenation	Joined `String` operands
<,<=, >,>=	4	Comparison	`boolean` result of comparison
instanceof	4	Comparison of `event` types	`boolean` result of comparison
==, !=	5	Equals, not equals	`boolean` result of comparison: compares data values for primitive types, compares identity of objects for reference types
&&	6	Logical AND	`boolean` result of combining operands
||	7	Logical OR	`boolean` result of combining operands
?:	8	Convenience operator for `if else`	First operand is `boolean`, returns second operand is first is `true`, third operand if first is `false`
=	9	Assignment	Returns value or object assigned
+=, −=, *=, /=	9	Operation with assignment	Returns value or object assigned

There are several other Java operators, but they are used primarily for bitwise operations that are not used in this book.

Conditional statements and loops   A.7

Java supports two conditional statements: the `if...else  if...else` statement, and the `switch` statement. The syntax for the two types is as follows.

The `if` statement has one of the forms shown:

```
if (<boolean expression>)
  <single or compound statement>

if (<boolean expression>)
  <single or compound statement>
else
  <single or compound statement>

if (<boolean expression>)
  <single or compound statement>
else if (<boolean expression>)
  <single or compound statement>
else
  <single or compound statement>
```

In the first form, the statement is executed if the boolean expression is `true`. If the expression is `false` control passes to the first statement following the `if` statement. In the second form, the first statement is executed if the boolean expression is `true`, and the second statement (following the `else`) if the expression is `false`.

In the the final form, a chain of `else if` clauses may be inserted between the initial `if` and the final `else` to test any number of boolean expressions. The final `else` clause is optional in this last form.

The `switch` statement is a more convenient way of writing a series of `else if` statements. Its syntax is:

```
switch (<integer valued expression>) {
case <option 1>:
  <statement(s)>
  break;
case <option 2>:
  <statement(s)>
case <option 3>:
  <statement(s)>:
  break;
default:
  <statement(s)>
}
```

The first argument of a `switch` statement *must* be an integer valued expression. Each `case` statement selects one possible value of this expression, and provides some statements to be executed if the expression evaluates to that value. Inserting a `break` statement at the end of a set of statements within a `case` block causes control to pass to the first statement after the `switch` statement. Omitting the `break`, as with *option 2* above allows control to 'fall through' to the next `case` block after the first one is finished. For example, if *option 2* is selected above, the statements for both *option 2* and *option 3* would be executed.

The `default` statement is executed if no match occurs with any of the `case` statements. It is optional.

Loops   A.8

Java offers the same looping features as C and C++: the `while`, `for`, and `do...while` loops.

The `while` loop has the syntax:

```
while (<boolean expression>)
    <single or compound statement>
```

The statement comprising the body of the `while` loop is executed repeatedly until the boolean expression is `false`. If the expression is `false` when the loop is first encountered, the body of the loop is never executed.

If you want the body of a loop to be executed *before* the termination condition is tested for the first time, use the `do...while` loop:

```
do
    <single or compound statement>
while (<boolean expression>);
```

The `for` loop has the form:

```
for (<initial statement(s)>; <boolean expression>;
        <loop expression(s)>)
    <single or compound statement>
```

The initial statement(s) can be any valid Java statement or comma-separated list of statements. This section of the `for` statement is executed once only, the first time the loop is encountered, and is usually used to initialize the loop counter.

The body of the loop is executed repeatedly as long as the boolean expression is `true`. If the expression is `false` the first time the loop is encountered, the body of the loop is never executed.

The loop expression(s) is executed *after* each iteration of the loop. As with the initialization statement(s), the loop expression(s) can be a comma-separated list of Java statements. It is usually used to increment the loop counter.

Arrays   A.9

An array in Java can be treated as a reference object, in that it can be passed to methods as a whole. It is important to realize that creating an array of reference objects is a two stage process. However, first the array must be declared, and then the individual elements of the array must be created, either by using the new operator to allocate memory for each element, or by assigning each array element to an already existing object of the same data type.

The syntax for creating an array is as follows:

```
    // Array of primitive type
int intArray[];
intArray = new int[100];
    // ..or..
int[] intArray = new int[100];

    //----------------------------//
    // Array of reference type
MyObject objArray[];

    // Create pointers to array elements
objArray = new MyObject[50];

    // Create array elements themselves
for (int i = 0; i < 50; i++)
    objArray[i] = new MyObject();
```

Creating an array of a primitive type (such as int) is a two-step process, as shown. The new operator is used to dynamically allocate the required memory. It is permissible to place the empty brackets [ ] either after the data type or after the variable name when declaring an array.

The array of the reference type MyObject is created by first allocating the memory for the array, but all this does is allocate space for an array of *pointers* to objects of type MyObject. The for loop allocates space for each of these pointers to point to, thus completing the creation of the array. (It is a common error for C and C++ programmers to forget the second step! If you do, you will get a NullPointerException the first time you try to use the array.)

For the most part, an array behaves just like any other reference data type. All methods of the Object class may be used with arrays (recall that the Object class is the class that is at the root of all reference classes in Java). The number of elements in an array named intArray can be accessed with the notation intArray.length.

An array may be passed to a method using the following syntax:

```
int[] intArray = new int[100];

// intArray elements now initialized to various values

arrayMethod(intArray);

// ... other code ...

void arrayMethod(int[] intArray)
```

```
{
   // code for arrayMethod
}
```

Java allows multidimensional arrays as well. The syntax for creating a two-dimensional array of floats is:

```
float twoDimFloatArray[][];
twoDimFloatArray = new float[10][20];
```

Creating a multidimensional array of reference data types is similar, except that you must initialize each element, just as with the one-dimensional array above.

Strings   A.10

Unlike languages such as C, a character string is not represented as an array of type `char`. Rather, Java provides, as part of the `java.lang` package, a `String` class which makes life much easier when handling text.

The `String` class has a rich menagerie of methods (some 40 or 50 methods are built in). You are advised to consult the Java documentation to see a complete list, but some of the more basic `String` operations are shown here.

A `String` may use several constructors, but one of the more common initializes a `String` to a constant text:

```
String testString("A test string.");
```
The + operator may be used with `Strings` to concatenate them:

```
String anotherString("A second test string.");

String joinStrings = testString + anotherString;
```

The number of characters in a `String` may be found with the `length()` method:

```
int stringLength = joinStrings.length();
```

Two `Strings` may be compared using the `equals()` method. The following code compares the contents of `testString` and `equalsString` and assigns `anotherString` to `equalsString` if they contain the same text:

```
String equalsString("A test string.");
if (testString.equals(equalsString))
   anotherString = equalsString;
```

Note that the `equals()` method and the `==` operator do *not* do the same thing when used with `Strings` (or any reference type). The `boolean` expression testString == equalsString is true only if the two Strings are identical, in the sense that they occupy the same memory location. After the code fragment above, it is true that anotherString == equalsString but it is false that equalsString == testString.

There are many other String methods that allow the programmer to do most of the common tasks with text strings.

A.11   Files

For security reasons, Java does not allow file input or output in an applet – you must run your program as an application to be able to access the disk.

To write data to a disk file, you have several choices of format in which the data may be written. To write data to a text file, so that all the output appears in ASCII characters, you would use the PrintStream class from the java.io package. To write data in a format that is more easily read into another program, the DataOutputStream is probably more useful.

To produce ASCII output, you must associate a FileOutputStream with a file name, then connect a PrintStream to the FileOutputStream. The PrintStream class contains many methods which allow data of various types to be printed as ASCII text to a file. A simple example is as follows.

```java
import java.io.*;

public class testFile
{
   public static void main(String args[])
   {
      try {
         PrintStream outStream = new PrintStream(
            new FileOutputStream("testfile.dat"));
         outStream.println("This is a test line.");
         outStream.close();
      } catch (IOException e)
      { System.out.println("Error:
         File could not be opened."); }
   }
}
```

Note that we must import the java.io package to have access to input and output features. The main() method creates a FileOutputStream connected to the disk file named testfile.dat. Then a PrintStream is connected to this FileOutputStream. The println() method then prints a String to this file. There are overloaded versions of the println() and print() methods (the print() method prints its argument but does not append a 'return' character onto the end) for all the primitive data types, and also for the Object and String classes. The PrintStream is explicitly closed with the close() method after use.

If you are a C or C++ programmer, you should note that there are no analogous Java methods to the `printf()` or `cout` functions. In other words, there is no Java method that takes a variable number of arguments, so if you want to print out a list of variables, you must either make a separate `print()` call for each variable, or else construct a `String` by concatenating the variables, and then print the `String`.

As mentioned earlier, there is a second alternative which allows primitive data types and `Strings` to be written to files in a format which is more easily read into other Java programs. The `DataOutputStream` class contains separate methods for writing each of the primitive data types. To use a `DataOutputStream`, it must be initialized in a manner similar to the `PrintStream` above:

```
DataOutputStream outStream = new DataOutputStream(
    new FileOutputStream("testfile.dat"));
```

Now the various methods, such as `writeInt()`, `writeFloat()`, and so on, may be used to write the appropriate data types to the stream, and hence to the the file to which it is connected. Data written this way may be read directly back into variables of the correct type using methods from the `DataInputStream` class.

For example, two `ints` may be written to a file in the following way:

```
try {
   DataOutputStream   outStream =
      new DataOutputStream (new
      FileOutputStream("testint.dat"));
   int a = 42, b = 57;
   outStream.writeInt(a);
   outStream.writeInt(b);
   outStream.close();
} catch (IOException e)
{ System.out.println("Error:
      File could not be opened."); }
```

The file `testint.dat` produced by this bit of code is a binary file and will not be readable in a text editor. It can be understood, however, by a `DataInputStream` object in another Java program:

```
try {
   DataInputStream inStream = new DataInputStream
      (new FileInputStream("testint.dat"));
   int a = inStream.readInt();
   int b = inStream.readInt();
   System.out.println("a = " + a + "; b = " + b);
   inStream.close();
} catch (IOException e)
{ System.out.println("Error:
```

```
                    File could not be opened."); }
```

This code fragment creates a `DataInputStream` object called `inStream` and associates it with the file `testint.dat`. The `readInt()` method is used twice to read in the `int`s written to this file by the previous code fragment. The results are then printed to the screen.

Note that files created with a `PrintStream` instead of a `DataOutput-Stream` will not be readable by a `DataInputStream` object in the same format. However, the `readLine()` method of the `DataInputStream` class *will* read in a line of text from an ASCII file, and return the result as a `String`. This `String` can then be parsed in the usual way (perhaps using methods from the `StringTokenizer` class, or methods from the various wrapper classes, such as `Integer.parseInt()`) to extract any information it contains.

INDEX